Taking It to the Bridge

Taking It to the Bridge

Music as Performance

NICHOLAS COOK *and*
RICHARD PETTENGILL,
Editors

The University of Michigan Press · *Ann Arbor*

Published in the United States of America by
The University of Michigan Press
Manufactured in the United States of America
⊗ Printed on acid-free paper

2016   2015   2014   2013   4   3   2   1

A CIP catalog record for this book is available from the British Library.

Library of Congress Cataloging-in-Publication Data

Taking it to the bridge : music as performance / Nicholas Cook and Richard
    Pettengill, editors.
     pages   cm
     Includes index.
       ISBN 978-0-472-07177-7 (cloth : alk. paper) — ISBN 978-0-472-05177-9
     (pbk. : alk. paper) — ISBN 978-0-472-02930-3 (e-book)
       1. Music—Performance.   I. Cook, Nicholas, 1950–, editor.   II. Pettengill,
     Richard, editor.
     ML457.T35   2013
     781.4'3—dc23   2013006635

Contents

Editors' Preface

JAMES BROWN, the "Godfather of Soul," was famously adept at "taking it to the bridge." The term *bridge*, of course, has various meanings in addition to "a structure carrying a pathway or roadway over a depression or obstacle." In musical terms, a bridge is "a musical passage linking two sections of a composition" or "a short section which links together—perhaps by a key change—two important sections of a large-scale symphony or similar work."[1] James Brown took it to the bridge every time he performed "Sex Machine," a funk groove in a single key with a few lyrics that he repeated again and again with spectacularly energetic and inventive variation:

> Get on up, get on up
> Stay on the scene
> Like a sex machine

Brown would perform his trademark high-energy dance moves and emit steady streams of sweat until he was ready to pop the question: "Hey, can I take it to the bridge? Should I take it to the bridge?" He would ask several times, at first seemingly not satisfied or convinced by the overwhelmingly positive response from the ensemble players that he held in a legendarily authoritative iron grip. Ready at last, he would turn to signal the band, kicking them into the bridge section. After a few bars, Brown would signal a return to the lead groove, continuing his improvisatory gyrations all the while.

Taking a cue from James Brown, the fields of musicology and performance studies have lately been "taking it to the bridge" in a different sense: moving into a new key with the benefit of an alternative perspective, thereby building bridges between the disciplines. Performance studies is a relatively new academic field that trains an analytical eye on staged performances as well as those that occur in everyday life, while musicology has traditionally focused on musical texts rather their performance. But for some years now, scholars in both fields, which previously have had little or no contact, have been examining the performance behavior of musicians. They have also begun to take note of and pay attention to one another's work, and to incorporate each other's views.

An example of such bridging that helped to spur the present volume is the opening paragraphs of the essay "Musical Personae" by performance studies scholar Philip Auslander, in which he engages with the performance-oriented work of musicologist Nicholas Cook. Auslander writes:

> Traditional musicology, often characterized as worshipful of the musical work and disdainful of performance, has been undergoing a "performative turn" in recent years, a development well-documented by Nicholas Cook in "Between Process and Product: Music and/ as Performance" (2001). As someone committed to finding ways of discussing musicians as performers, whose primary discipline is performance studies, I am cheered by this development and grateful to Cook both for his careful mapping of disputed territory and his advocacy for the "music as performance" approach.[2]

Our purpose in this volume is to further such interdisciplinary collaboration and engagement by presenting current "music as performance" work by scholars in both fields.

The idea for this volume came about through a meeting of the Association for Theatre in Higher Education in 2008, at which Philip Auslander convened a panel of papers devoted to the various ways musicians behave on stage, the personae they construct for the purpose of stage performance, and the song characters they take on when they enact lyrics. The panel featured speakers from both performance studies and musicology, and the suggestion arose that it might be developed into a book of essays sampling this new, cross-disciplinary field. The coeditors (one from musicology and one from theater and performance studies) have aimed at a balanced representation of both fields, in the hope that this will stimulate further productive interaction between them.

The book begins at the musicological end of the spectrum, with Elisabeth Le Guin's Foreword and Susan Fast's essay on *U2 3D*, the 3D film of a 2008 concert by the Irish band, in which she explores the difference between mediatized and live performance. The opera historian Philip Gossett offers an essay on vocal ornamentation in Rossini's *Il barbiere di Siviglia*, while Dana Gooley writes about the political significance of a piano recital in nineteenth-century Vienna. Ingrid Monson explores the social and visual elements of a performance by Neba Solo, a musician from Mali, while Roger Moseley writes about ways in which, during their brief heyday, the games *Guitar Hero* and *Rock Band* represented and reconfigured aspects of real-world performance within the domain of the virtual. David Borgo develops Christopher Small's idea of "musicking" into the virtual realm, while Nicholas Cook subjects performance data captured from recordings to computational analysis and relates this work to the field of performance studies.

On the performance studies side, Joseph Roach investigates the idea of "cutting the body loose" in the traditional jazz funerals of New Orleans, while Daphne Brooks shows how Lauryn Hill's 2005 performance of Roberta Flack's "Killing Me Softly (With His Song)" encapsulates and affirms her pivotal role as the iconic voice of post–Civil Rights cultural insurgency. Margaret Savilonis shows how two 1960s-era African-American bands, Labelle and Parliament, moved from the traditional, restricting dress and choreography of the 1950s toward the more liberating style of 1970s glam rock. Richard Pettengill offers a close reading of a few minutes of the Grateful Dead transitioning from an extended improvisation into a song: a moment of seeming confusion resolving in collective concord exemplifies the band's improvisational aesthetic, philosophy, and practices. Aida Mbowa argues that jazz singer Abbey Lincoln uses such techniques as screaming to inspire her audience into a listening that is "bone deep," bringing to life specters from the collective unconscious of the African-American past, while Jason King show how the film *This Is It* evidences Michael Jackson's extraordinary skill as a performer and so calls into question widespread misconceptions about Jackson as an artist. Maria Delgado describes the avant-garde performance techniques of opera company director/composer/performer Carles Santos, while Philip Auslander views improvisation as a social contract between musicians and listeners; Auslander has also provided an Afterword for the volume.

We wish to thank Philip Auslander, Elizabeth Patterson, and LeAnn Fields for their encouragement and collaboration throughout the process of assembling this volume.

NICHOLAS COOK

RICHARD PETTENGILL

NOTES

1. The first two of these definitions come from *Miriam Webster Online*, and the third from the *Oxford Dictionary of Music*.

2. Philip Auslander, "Musical Personae," *TDR: The Drama Review* 50, no. 1 (2006): 100.

ELISABETH LE GUIN

A Backward-Looking Foreword

Jeu

IT IS A WELL-KNOWN FEATURE of the composition of books that the material that ends up positioned at the beginning is usually the last thing written. I write this Foreword from the happy but not unusual vantage point of having been able to read the entire book which it precedes. But this position feels funny, because the book in question is about performance. The atemporal freedom we enjoy as writers—scooting around silently within the text, writing the first part last and the last part first, re-arranging sentences and whole paragraphs with the click of a few keys, thinking and composing non-linearly—enacts the fundamental tension between textuality and performance.

Edited collections are a perfect example of the way reading, as well, has a sharply oblique relation to textuality. Think about it: when was the last time you "obeyed the text" of an edited collection and read it through from beginning to end? I honestly can't say I have ever done so except when explicitly engaged to do a pre- or post-publication review—or, as in this case, to write a Foreword. In general, I do with edited collections what I assume most of us do: I "mine" them for that one essay by that one scholar whose work really interests me just now. I read, digest, and cite it, and ignore the rest. (Even less often do I bother with reading Forewords to edited collections!) Readerly involvement with this book likely embodies some degree of divergent or resistant performance. There are nearly infinite possibilities: atemporal (re-reading or skipping about), incomplete (skimming, multi-tasking), or deconstructive engagements, as well as plain old misconstrual.

Performance is everywhere; we can scarcely avoid it in any medium. Nevertheless it has too often dropped out of sight in the academic study of music, where an insistence on musical texts as ends in themselves has led to a corresponding neglect of the study of how those texts were and are enunciated in real time. A woefully divided disciplinary terrain has resulted. As a performer and scholar of music, I heartily share in the Editors' determination to address this divide and reach across it to create some sort of new union. But I wonder whether our determination shouldn't involve, to some degree, remembering and recreating an old union. For I am also a historian; and history offers some fine examples of how we might re-think, re-experience, or deconstruct entirely the division of performance from text.[1]

Histoire

The dividedness against which this book labors is in many ways a relatively recent phenomenon. There has long been tension between text and act (to borrow Richard Taruskin's succinct phrase), but it was less than it now is, and it was somewhat differently located. Most strikingly: in Western cultures, the act of reading a text used to mean reading aloud. Only gradually, through a long process of internalization that seems to have begun around the eleventh century and continued into the eighteenth, did it became the solitary and silent activity that we now chiefly attribute to the verb.[2] Until very recently in its history, reading *was* performance.

Writing, by the same token, was the preparation of a score for that performance. Quintilian's rhetoric treatise *Institutio oratoria*, written in the first century CE, became the foundational guide to mastering verbal persuasion and expression for the next eighteen hundred years of Western history—and all of it is geared toward spoken delivery. It was not until very late indeed—basically, within the last hundred and fifty years—that we began routinely lopping off the last two of the five phases, *inventio—dispositio—ornamentatio* (*elocutio*)—*memoria—actio*, that together comprise a splendidly integrated process of composition. It is a structure of how to think and how to communicate thought, learned by countless generations of writers, humanists, poets, and lawyers, and very deeply woven into Western culture.

In St. Augustine's *Confessions* (386 CE) we see one of the first definite recorded instances of silent reading. Augustine marvels at the great scholar Ambrose of Milan.

> But while reading, his eyes glanced over the pages, and his heart searched out the sense, but his voice and tongue were silent. Oft-

times, when we had come (for no one was forbidden to enter, nor was it his custom that the arrival of those who came should be announced to him), we saw him thus reading to himself, and never otherwise . . .[3]

It is clear that Augustine considered this kind of readerly engagement to be extraordinary. The norm at this time, and for long after, was to utter the written word; it had no power, it was "dead," until given life (performative force) by the human voice. Alberto Manguel has suggested that the old phrase *scripta manent, verba volant* (written words remain, spoken ones fly), now generally understood as a lament upon the ephemerality of speech, was in fact praise: like the Holy Spirit itself, the spoken word has wings, it reaches human souls.[4] Letters silent upon the page remain inanimate clay. This metaphorical conceit of the written word as "dead" and the utterance as "alive" has a long history. A culmination of sorts might be said to reside in Rousseau's famous repudiation of writing in the *Essay on the Origin of Languages:*

Writing, which would seem to crystallize language, is precisely what alters it. It changes not the words but the spirit, substituting exactitude for expressiveness. Feelings are expressed in speaking, ideas in writing.[5]

Early libraries and scriptoria, and later salons, coffeehouses, and schoolrooms, were lively places. So too, it seems, the study or office of the writer. Juan Díaz Rengifo, a poet and philologue who lived from 1553 to 1615, left us a fascinating glimpse into a writerly process that incorporates performance—including singing!—as a matter of course:

Let him who wishes to know how to make verses without it being too much work and study, seek out one, two or three couplets in every type of verse, that are, in the estimation of some good Poet, elegant, well-constructed, and show the perfection of everything we have been talking about . . . then recite them by memory, say them as an actor would say them, or sing them. Then try to make others that have that sound, and don't worry if at first they don't make much sense, or aren't as good as you'd like, for it is first necessary that the ear get used to the sound and flow of the verse; with this accomplished, the polishing and writing down . . . is a business for your whole life long.[6]

Composing a verbal text for performance has equally lively implications for style. As Margit Frenk puts it:

> Whoever writes to be heard will impress upon his discourse a dynamism attentive to a reception that flows forward, without the possibility of return. Privileging variety in form and content . . . he will seek effects capable of keeping the listeners in a constant state of alertness . . . attention to rhythm and sonorities, repetitions and parallelisms, episodic structure and division of the discourse into brief units, apostrophes to the listener, etc.[7]

These techniques, common to poets, essayists, politicians, and preachers— and yes, great academic writers too—bring writing and reading/listening far into the sonorous realm of music-making. And in the process, just like the techniques and practices described in the essays in this volume, they trouble any too-simple division between text and act.

What we know of early music-making suggests a similar degree of elision, intrication, and cross-fertilization. Some of the musicologists concerned with these early repertories never did really participate in the disciplinary divisions that were opening up during the course of the twentieth century; their work confounds disciplinary "nationalism" and text-bound myopia to grapple with the larger implications of historical performance practice. This resistant kind of musical-historical scholarship seems, at long last, to be developing some momentum.[8]

Envoi

This book takes its place in the silenced latter day of a splendidly vociferous history; but its subject matter makes it do so uneasily, for performance swarms out past efforts at discursive containment, implicating not only the themes and subjects of the discourse, but also those participating in it. The Editors have voiced the hope that, as a result of reading this book, "the wide variety of scholars who study musical performance will get more into the habit of reading one another's work, resulting in better informed and more productive communication across the disciplines." I hope this too. But I would close with a somewhat less sober exhortation.

You, dear reader, cannot remain tidily exempt from what your eye surveys in these pages. Your voice—not the metaphorical construct, but your real, live, sounding voice, primary instrument of reading (in the old sense) and musicking, and (if we are to follow Rousseau) the one, definitive proof of your feeling existence—your voice is implied by the history of what you are doing with your eyes right now, and that history is challenging you, playfully but also urgently. Take this book across the hall and read some of it aloud to your colleague skeptical of performance studies. Take it across campus to that other department, and do the same. Make your students re-cite the good bits from memory, perhaps with suitable oratorical gestures. Have a public debate about it. Start a study group, or a book group, that heartening contemporary resuscitation of the early modern salon. Start a pamphlet war, complete with satirical songs. Onward and upward, then; but hearkening also to the past.

NOTES

1. Here I want to push back gently against the idea of "the old performance practice paradigm" offered by Philip Auslander (quoting Alejandro Madrid) in this volume's Afterword. While I know perfectly well what sort of scholarship Madrid is lamenting, I would rather rehabilitate the study of historical performance practice than reject it.

2. Of course the English verb "to read" can still mean "to say written words or sentences aloud," depending on context. The OED gives its most ancient roots as the Sanskrit *rādh-* "to succeed, accomplish," and it (possibly) shares the same Indo-European base as Old Irish *rádim* "to say, speak." The action/reflection divide is even more stark, and more recent, in derivatives of the Latinate verb *leggere*. The first dictionary of the Spanish language (Covarrubias, 1611) is unambiguous: *leer* meant "to pronounce with words that which is written in letters." The *Diccionario de Autoridades* (1732) defines it as "To pronounce that which is written, or review it with the eyes." And the present-day Larousse Spanish dictionary is just as unam-biguous as Covarrubias, but in the opposite direction: *leer* is "To visually go over what is seen or printed in order to understand it."

3. Augustine of Hippo, *Confessions* (397–98 CE), trans. J. G. Pilkington (New York: Liveright, 1943), Book VI, Chapter 3.

4. This is pointed out by Alberto Manguel, *A History of Reading* (New York: Viking, 1996), 45.

5. Jean-Jacques Rousseau, *Essai sur l'origine des langues* (1751/1781). Chapter V, "Sur L'Écriture," trans. John H. Moran in *On the Origin of Language: Jean-Jacques Rousseau, Essay on the Origin of Languages; Johann Gottfried Herder, Essay on the Origin of Language* (New York: F. Ungar, 1967), 21.

6. Juan Díaz Rengifo, *Arte poética española, con una fertilissima Sylua de conso-nantes, propios, esdruxulos, y reflexos...* (Salamanca, 1592). Facsimile edition, with an Epilog by Antonio Martí Alanis (Madrid: Ministerio de educación y ciencia, 1977), "Metodo breue para hazer versos. Cap. XX," 22.

7. Margit Frenk, *Entre la voz y el silencio* (Alcalá de Henares: Centro de estudios cervantinos, 1997), 15–16.

8. Without attempting in the least to be exhaustive or exclusive, in this august company I place the medievalists Richard Crocker and Ismael Fernández de la

Cuesta, and my own adviser, the scholar of Renaissance and Enlightenment rep-
ertories Daniel Heartz. Among the next generation of scholars, I would give pride
of place to two fine monographs on eighteenth-century opera: Mary Hunter's *The
Culture of Opera Buffa in Mozart's Vienna: A Poetics of Entertainment* (Princeton:
Princeton University Press, 1999), and Martha Feldman's *Opera and Sovereignty:
Transforming Myths in Eighteenth-Century Italy* (Chicago: University of Chicago
Press, 2007). The generation following theirs is already legion.

NICHOLAS COOK *and*
RICHARD PETTENGILL

Introduction

THE WONDER IS NOT THAT music and performance studies come together in this book, but that they ever needed to be brought together. After all, what is music if not performance, real-time collective practice that brings people together as players and listeners, choreographs social relationships, and expresses or constructs individual or group identities? There are answers to this question, of course: music can also take the form of recordings, and in the case of some traditions, scores. But recordings and scores are meaningful insofar as they represent actual or possible (or sometimes impossible) performances, and insofar as they are given meaning through being heard, read, and acted upon—and these are themselves performative acts. Take away the act, take away the performance, and you take away the music.

There are many academic disciplines that bear in one way or another on music, including psychology, sociology, anthropology, cultural studies, media and communication studies, acoustics, mathematics, and computer science. The encounters staged in this book, however, are mainly between musicology—which comes in various shapes and sizes but generally works from music to an understanding of its cultural contexts—and performance studies, a broader field of which music is just one, relatively minor part. With just a few exceptions, there has been startlingly little contact between these fields, and the reasons for this are largely historical. The sources of musicology as a discrete discipline lie in the nineteenth-century European quest for national origins, a major aspect of which was the recovery (or, depending on your viewpoint, invention) of national literatures: this was the age of monumental editions that aimed to present historic texts in as authentic a manner as possible, purged of later accretions and bowdlerizations. It was, so to speak, the age of the original.

Musicology came into being as the application to musical texts of the approaches that philologists applied to literary texts, and so its disciplinary identity was built around the idea that music is something written down, a kind of text, an obscure branch of literature. Of course, many of the musical editors who applied philological methods were performers, or worked with performers, but performance itself was generally seen as lying outside the disciplinary purview of musicology (in much the way that Eduard Hanslick recognized the emotive powers of music but saw them as lying outside the purview of aesthetics). Only in the twentieth century did the study of performance come to be seen as falling within the bounds of musicology, and even then it was approached in a manner that prioritized the text. The basic question was how historical knowledge—of notational conventions, period instruments, and performing practices—could be brought to bear on performance in order to ensure the most adequate realization of composers' intentions. This set up a hierarchical relationship between the musicological purveyors of knowledge and performers, as well as making performance seem more a matter of correctness than of artistry or creativity.

The genealogy of performance studies could hardly be more different, and as an academic field it is far more recent. One of its sources is theater studies, itself the product of a reaction against the textualist orientation that defined philology and literary studies more generally. Whereas the traditional literary approach to Shakespeare's plays is to conceive them as texts, to be read in the same way that novels and poems are read, the theater studies approach is to see them as prescriptions for or traces of dramatic productions, stressing the multiple meanings that arise in the act of performing them: the focus is on the act of performance as well as the text that prompts the act. Performance studies retains that focus but extends it far more broadly. According to one origin narrative (there are several), the field emerged from a conversation between theater director/performance theorist Richard Schechner and anthropologist Victor Turner. The two realized that their respective interests in performance—Schechner's in theater and performance art, Turner's in the study of rituals and rites of passage in global societies—could be integrated into a field of inquiry that would embrace what Schechner called the "broad spectrum approach" to performance: this meant seeing "performative behavior, not just the performing arts, as a subject for serious scholarly study."[1] The essential insights behind this approach are that meaning is created in the act of performance, and that (again in Schechner's words) "anything and everything can be studied as performance."

Other important factors in the formation of performance studies included the growth of communication studies as an academic discipline, and work in folklore and oral culture by anthropologist Richard Bauman; Bauman's work at Indiana University forged connections between performance studies and ethnomusicology (the study of world music). But there was a further crucial ingredient in the mix: J. L. Austin's idea of the performative.[2] According to this, utterances such as curses, bets, and christenings are not just representations or descriptions of actions, but actions in their own right: when the bride and bridegroom say, "I do," they are indeed doing something. The coolly philosophical tone of Austin's writing belies its explosive implications. Judith Butler called widespread attention to Austin's ideas in her writing on gender construction. One of her central claims is that "gender is real only to the extent to which it is performed." The traditional approach to gender is that it is grounded in sexual difference: the biological distinction of male and female identity is expressed by gendered behaviors that vary from one culture to another. Butler turns this upside down: in her much quoted phrase, gendered behaviors "effectively constitute the identity they are said to express or reveal."[3] To see gender this way, as a social performance, throws a completely new light on issues of sexuality, choice, and freedom.

Landmarks in the development of performance studies included Schechner's establishment of the Department of Performance Studies at New York University in 1980 and the creation of a similar department at Northwestern University where performance ethnographer Dwight Conquergood served as chair during the 1990s. Since then, other programs and courses have proliferated worldwide. Indeed, performance studies has become such a broad, rich, and multifaceted field that the Association for Theatre in Higher Education (ATHE) has established a series of working groups that take the performance studies approach into new areas and forge relationships with neighboring disciplines: there have been working groups in Neuroscience, Cognitive Science, and Performance; Performance and Ecology; Mixed Media; Philosophy and Performance; Site-Specific Performance; Performance and Ethnography; and Dance Studies. The ATHE working group that relates most directly to this volume, however, is Music as Performance (or MAP, as it is known among those who work in this area).

The neighboring disciplinary field most relevant to MAP is musicology, but only if that term is understood in a broad sense to cover a constellation of approaches to the study of music. We have seen that there is a gulf—it would not be going too far to call it an ontological standoff—between the approach of performance studies and that around which musicology originally came into being. And textualist approaches remain in evidence within core areas of music history and theory, which largely retain the traditional focus on musical scores and works, understood as repositories of meaning placed there by their authors. But without going through the kind of disciplinary convulsion that gave rise to performance studies, musicology—especially when considered in the broader sense—has been undergoing its own processes of transformation. Historical work oriented toward the Western "art" tradition jostles for space alongside such areas as popular music studies and ethnomusicology. These fields were from the start disciplinary hybrids. As the career of Simon Frith illustrates, serious study of popular music began in academic departments of sociology, English, and media studies, in fact almost anywhere except in music departments—a situation that has altered radically in the last decade or two, under the impact of both changing academic attitudes toward popular culture and developing student demand. (Frith is now Tovey Professor of Music at the University of Edinburgh.) From the start, scholars of popular music were interested in it as a cultural phenomenon, embracing its different contexts of production and reception, and often with a focus on ethnographic approaches; performance was in this way an integral element of the field of study.

As for ethnomusicology, it is in essence anthropology applied to music, and is traditionally distinguished by its close attention to individual cultural contexts. Ethnomusicologists have traditionally been area specialists, with deep knowledge of the musical practices and concepts of specific geographical, national, or ethnic groups, and like popular culture scholars they see performance as an integral dimension of their subject matter. But it goes further than that, because performance is also a particularly accessible way for researchers to engage with a culture that is not their own, and accordingly the classic ethnomusicological method is participant observation: the researcher takes lessons with musicians from the culture under investigation, or plays alongside other performers, and in this way attempts to gain an understanding of that culture's discourses and practices from the inside. That also means that performance is understood in terms not just of the final artistic product (such as a ritual, concert, or recording) but of the broader spectrum of activities which together make up a performance culture. Increasingly common in work on Western "art" and popular musics as well, this orientation is also shared with performance studies.

For a long time there was a general assumption that musicologists studied Western "art" music while ethnomusicologists studied music from the rest of the world, but this is no longer realistic. Ethnomusicologists have increasingly worked on aspects of Western "art" music (examples include ethnographies of conservatories by Henry Kingsbury and Bruno Nettl, of the Boston early music scene by Kay Shelemay, and of the Buxton Gilbert and Sullivan Festival by Stephanie Pitts).[4] But equally, musicologists are refocusing their attention from scores and works toward practices of music-making and consumption. The result is a general realization of the potential of ethnographic approaches for the study of any and all of the musics that populate today's world. In this way, thinking about the Western "art" tradition, now seen as just one component of a more broadly conceived musicology, has come to draw increasingly on thinking about other musical traditions, encouraging a still-ongoing process of disciplinary renewal.

This volume has its origins in the wish of the MAP group to reach out toward musicologists, which is why it has one editor based in theater/performance studies and another in musicology. But what made it viable is the way in which this initiative on the MAP group's part coincided with the extension of a performative focus from popular music studies and ethnomusicology to musicology as a whole. In terms of Western "art" traditions, opera was a vanguard case where the influence of performance studies was felt (for instance in Philip Gossett's editorial approach to nineteenth-century Italian opera, based on the paradigm of the dramatic production rather than the literary work). But musicology's performative turn has affected the study of the "art" traditions more generally and has taken such drastically different forms as document-based historical research and computational analysis of sound recordings, as well as ethnographical investigation of present-day performance practices.

In the United Kingdom, the Arts and Humanities Research Council has funded two high-profile research centers in this area (the AHRC Research Centres for the History and Analysis of Recorded Music, and for Musical Performance as Creative Practice), while conservatories have been at the forefront of projects bringing together academic researchers and performers. A notable aspect of such work is the collaborative relationship between these parties, by contrast to the older, hierarchical model: in projects involving the reconstruction of historical styles, for example, performers help scholars make sense of period treatises by trying to put their prescriptions into effect, just as scholars help performers to open up previously unsuspected interpretive pathways. Or performers may work with composers and technologists to develop new playing techniques or modes of interaction. At its best such work is a marriage of knowledge and creativity. And while some of it gives rise to academic publications, outcomes also take the form of performances informed by research. This has a parallel in the movement within performance studies to present research outcomes not only in academic prose but also through the medium of performance.[5]

If musicology generally involves working from scores and sounds toward an understanding of cultural contexts, then the MAP approach can be seen as extending the musicological purview: it adds a more comprehensive understanding of the meaning-producing potential of performances that includes the effects of musicians' stage interactions and demeanor, or of gestures and modes of (un)dress, as well as of audience behavior, critical interpretation, and historical representation. In this way, musicology and performance studies can be seen as highly complementary. Western "art" musicologists have developed sophisticated techniques of close reading and listening, but have traditionally shied away from the issues of personal, social, and cultural meaning that emerge from the act of performance. Performance theorists address the latter, but as both editors complain in their contributions to this book, the specific ways in which these meanings are conditioned by sounds and their representations within specific musical cultures sometimes seem to slip through the net. We see forging a closer relationship between musicology and performance studies as a project that has equal benefits for both parties, promising the dovetailing of approaches with very different intellectual histories.

Those contributors to this volume whose background is more musicological, then, draw on the performance studies approach to expand the traditional musicological focus on works, pieces, or songs in order to encompass a variety of larger contexts of meaning production. Dana Gooley discusses the nineteenth-century pianist Sigismond Thalberg's program planning, while Susan Fast discusses how U2 structured their shows. Similar issues arise in the contributions coming from performance studies: Jason King's investigation of the posthumous Michael Jackson film *This Is It* throws light onto the planning of a mega-series of concerts, while Richard Pettengill explains how the Grateful Dead thought in terms of not just songs and shows, but entire tours. Philip Auslander emphasizes the importance of the personae or stage presences that performers construct and maintain over extended periods of time. Other contributors are concerned with the wide range of social, cultural, political, and ideological contexts within which performances reflect, project, or generate meaning: they offer case studies of how such meaning is articulated by voice, instrument, or gesture, drawing on classical, popular, and non-Western repertories. As Auslander has said (in an article cited by Nicholas Cook), when musicologists take it for granted that performances are performances "of" works, they are ignoring other dimensions of performative representation, of which the performance of identity is perhaps the most important. Seen this way, what a musicologist might think of as "the music" serves as just one component of the "expressive equipment," to borrow Erving Goffman's term, that musicians deploy in identity construction.

Cook observes that these different dimensions of performative meaning production are by no means mutually exclusive, and their relative importance is in part a function of historical contingency: Gooley claims that, in the special circumstances of revolutionary Vienna, "Theater events and concerts temporarily ceased to be mainly about 'works' and became performed experiments, embodied ones, for the new kinds of social and political conditions they expected to bring into being." Doing justice to performance, then, requires input from a variety of disciplinary perspectives, even if they at times involve opposed premises. For Aida Mbowa, speaking of Abbey Lincoln's performance of the "Protest" segment from *We Insist! Max Roach's Freedom Now Suite*, "to attempt to put into language precisely what one hears . . . would be a self-defeating enterprise," since it is the role of music to signify what words cannot—and yet it is precisely that attempt that defines musicology. (Etymologically, "musicology" denotes the conjunction of music and words.) In bringing together work from varied disciplinary backgrounds, then, the editors of this book do not aspire to a wholly unified approach to the study of musical performance. Our goal is not the establishment of an autonomous sub-discipline with its own standardized discourse, conferences, journals, and celebrities. We have a more modest hope: that the wide variety of scholars who study musical performance will get more into the habit of reading one another's work, resulting in better informed and more productive communication across the disciplines.

Of course, productive communication across disciplines puts cherished disciplinary premises on the line, some of which we have already mentioned. Musicology's traditional starting point is "the music itself," essentially pitches, rhythms, and dynamics, with everything else being seen as less important, or at least as not relevant to musicology: from this perspective, issues such as what performers wear lie beyond the pale. This collides with Baz Kershaw's claim, as cited by Cook, that "it is a fundamental tenet of performance theory . . . that no item in the environment of performance can be discounted as irrelevant to its impact." And even when our contributors talk about musicologically familiar topics, they often view them in a musicologically unfamiliar light. As an example of the latter, musicologists have traditionally viewed instruments as, in essence, vehicles for the communication of abstract musical contents. By contrast, Maria Delgado describes how in his staged performances Carles Santos treats pianos as quasi-theatrical protagonists or even adversaries (Auslander has explored the same phenomenon in other contexts, such as Lucille, B. B. King's guitar—or rather succession of guitars, as they were all called Lucille).[6] And Daphne A. Brooks, who observes that African American contralto vocalists "compress and translate suffering into acousmatic dreamscapes of black historical memory remixed and resounded."

More often, however, what is at issue is dimensions of performance traditionally written out of musicology: Pettengill, Auslander, and Cook treat stage presence and gesture as integral dimensions of rock, jazz, and classical performance respectively, while Margaret Savilonis and Ingrid Monson, along with Delgado, Mbowa, and King, treat music as an inherently multimedia phenomenon, in which relationships between different media and their connotations are integral to the meanings that emerge in the course of performance. This holistic approach to music as performance takes us deep into issues of cultural meaning and the politics of identity. For Mbowa, understanding the racial signification of Abbey Lincoln's "screaming singing" entails "theorization of the liberatory potential at the convergence of blackness and audiovisual performance," while Daphne Brooks suggests that "unquantifiable, 'ghostly' racial pain is itself perhaps the recurring theme and the core subtext of late twentieth-century black popular culture." At the same time King, who sees Jackson as exercising a spectral presence in *This Is It*, deploys techniques of close reading in order to locate and deconstruct the essentializing ideologies that so easily become attached to black performance: "While the racist and primitivist imaginary assumes that performers of color are intrinsically more energetic and spontaneous than their white counterparts—which is another way of saying performers of color don't have to work hard to get good results—watching Jackson painstakingly shape his concert in collaboration with fellow musicians and a superbly talented band and crew is a telling reminder of the incredible labor that undergirds the best of black performance."

To understand music's meaning as emerging from the relationships between all dimensions of the performance event is of course to problematize the fact that we habitually consume it through audio and video recordings—media that represent only a few dimensions of live performance, and give rise to quite different ways of consuming music. Recordings can, of course, be analyzed by researchers as more or less reliable traces of live performances (this is how Pettengill, Cook, and Monson respectively treat recordings by the Grateful Dead, Grigory Sokolov, and Neba Solo). And even though most commercial recordings are not in any simple sense the traces of live performances, that is how people generally hear them: recordings are experienced as representing performances that never in fact took place. But this is representation in a complex, semiotic sense: hearing recordings this way involves a form of diegesis comparable to that involved in making sense of narrative film. Just as nobody thinks of conflating theater and cinema, so Fast claims "that live and recorded performances are fundamentally different, that *both are indispensable*, and that the distinctions between them need to be preserved." Mbowa, too, emphasizes the differences between live performances and recordings, showing how in her recordings Lincoln achieved solely by means of her voice the same emotional characterization she achieved in live performance through facial expression and physical gesture; for her, "sonic liberatory potential is confounded by, but also enabled through, the fact that the sound is a deliberate reproduction of imagined sounds produced in vastly different circumstances."

It might seem to follow from this that rather than treating recordings as copies of live performances—or for that matter vice versa—we should see them as something other than performances, the proper focus of "recording studies" rather than "performance studies." That, however, would probably be a mistake. Auslander, for whom improvisation is less something that musicians do than an assumption or contract shared by musicians and listeners, argues that when we hear recorded improvisations, we hear them *as* improvisations just to the extent that, in listening, we "restage the performance where we are, so to speak, rather than . . . travel imaginatively back to its original circumstances." The implication is that technology has broadened and redefined the scope of performance, rather than simply providing a surrogate for it: this is the conclusion that David Borgo draws from his investigation of recent and developing convergences in the technologies of live and recorded performance. Or to look at it from another perspective, sound reproduction and manipulation technologies have become embraced within the liveness of human real-time action: King concludes from his study of what would have been an unprecedentedly extravagant series of multimedia events that "for all the modern talk of 3D and 4D technology as immersion and intimacy, Jackson cultivates intimacy first with his body and soul. Sharing good feeling produces a proximity and depth and scale of immersion that no 3D glasses could ever provide." It is this integrated and expanded notion of performance that is addressed in the present book.

The study of performance entails the deconstruction of other widely accepted binaries, too. Two linked binaries are composer versus performer, and performer versus listener. The book is framed by Fast's essay, which sees the limitation of three-dimensional concert movies in their lack of interaction, and Borgo's, which sees the interactivity supported by Web 2.0 as essential to the development of what he calls "transmusicking" (an adaptation of Christopher Small's "musicking"). The essays between them span the range from relatively passive concert-hall listening at one extreme to the fully participatory musicking represented in different ways by the jazz funerals described by Joseph Roach, the "highly evolved collaborative listening and feedback" of Michael Jackson's rehearsals, and the digital games described by Roger Moseley. Between them, Fast, Auslander, and Monson show how performances of rock, jazz, and African music are co-creations between performers and listeners.

To some extent this applies even to classical music, where the virtual immobility of concert audiences may be deceptive, since listening is the work of the imagined as well as the physical body—and in any case, most classical music is heard not in the concert hall but on personal stereo or at home, where very different behaviors may prevail. And classical performers, like others, talk about their interaction with listeners—how they play an audience, and how an audience may play them. But because scores are radically selective representations of music, co-creation is more obvious in the relationship between composers and performers: this point is made by Borgo and Delgado, but perhaps with the greatest force by Gossett, whose scholarly research both draws on and feeds into his consultancy work for numerous operatic productions. He shows on the basis of documentary evidence how nineteenth-century Italian operatic composers relied extensively on performance elaboration by singers, so that performing the music as written—in the service of a literalist "authenticity"—is in fact the most inauthentic way in which it could possibly be performed. As he observes, modern performers have the right to perform music anachronistically, but they should do so by choice rather than through ignorance.

Another binary that comes under attack is between performance and improvisation. Auslander points out that there is an improvisatory dimension to all performance, even the most regulated. Conversely, even the freest improvisations operate within certain frameworks of convention: in this sense all performance can also be said to involve dimensions of re-production or repetition (terms which, like representation, carry multiple connotations that vary between performance studies and musicology). But whether we are talking about a musical work or a religious ritual, meaning may be said to inhere in the excess of performance over repetition: as Joseph Roach puts it, performances are always "repetitions with revisions. . . . there is always a space, larger or smaller, within the act of re-doing into which invention enters." (Roach is here troping on Henry Louis Gates Jr.'s definition of "Signifyin(g)" as "repetition and revision, or repetition with a signal difference";[7] the specifically black genres of performance which several of our contributors address might be seen as presenting in an explicit form aspects of performative meaning that are implicit, and hence harder to discern, in other traditions.) Indeed, Savilonis quotes Marvin Carlson's injunction that we recognize how repetition "attempts to establish and control the 'other' as 'same,'" and instead conceive of performance as—in Peggy Phelan's famous phrase—"representation without reproduction":[8] in this way performance becomes an act of resistance that "can disrupt the attempted totalizing gaze and thus open a more diverse and inclusive representational landscape." This is illustrated by Savilonis's argument that through their collective and individual onstage personas—through their defiance of the forces of reproduction—the 1970s girl group Labelle deconstructed restrictive stereotypes of African-American women.

Seen in this light, performative value lies far from academic or conservatory criteria for the correct or incorrect reproduction of notational prescriptions. Pettengill briefly grapples with a related issue in his close reading of a moment of seeming confusion in a 1972 set by the Grateful Dead, when Jerry Garcia strums a D chord as a signal for the band to segue from a group improvisation into a song, but Bob Weir reads (or chooses to read) the cue as signaling a different song; Garcia continues with his intended song for a few moments before realizing that the rest of the band has gone along with Weir, and then aligns himself with the direction the band has collectively chosen. As Pettengill comments, moments like Weir's response to Garcia's cue "should not be seen as errors or missteps. They are, rather, the way the band operates, the way they fulfill their audience's expectations. Such practices are the direct outcome of their apparent aesthetic and philosophy." It is in this aesthetic and philosophy that the most significant value and meaning of the Dead's music is to be found, in the "cooperative and egalitarian spirit" that they enacted on stage as much as at their communal homes in Novato and later San Francisco.

This is the same kind of musically facilitated community that Auslander describes in relation to jazz improvisation, with its negotiation of musical roles between players as well as its contract between players and listeners, and that Monson identifies in the deftly coordinated interweaving of musical elements both within and between individual musicians' playing that she terms "Senufo counterpoint." Brooks similarly suggests that Lauryn Hill's "brand of musical aesthetics draw[s] on the critical memory of soul music culture to do a specific kind of interventionist socio-political work in her performative repertoire," while also characterizing the concert film *Dave Chappelle's Block Party* as "an effort to revitalize communal solidarity, quotidian collective joy and celebration." Perhaps the clearest illustration of the musical mediation of social dynamics, however, is provided by Moseley's discussion of games like *Rock Band* and *Guitar Hero*, where the technology gives direct expression to the collaborative and competitive behaviors that are ubiquitous, but less explicit, under other conditions of performance.

The efficacy of music in the generation and negotiation of social meaning lies in its ability to embrace both sameness and difference. It can consolidate totalizing group identities, as illustrated by Gooley's discussion of national anthems, but also by the same token it can articulate constructions of local identity through differentiation from a larger group (as Dick Hebdige argued of the punk movement).[9] National anthems are intended to impose the same meaning on everyone (a tendency that is of course capable of subversion, for example, by Jimi Hendrix), but most music is semantically more fluid: it means different things to different individuals or groups, yet unites them in a shared experience of meaningfulness and purpose. Hence the way in which, as Monson tells us, Neba Solo's music creates cultural collectivity in the ethnically and linguistically diverse context of Mali.

There is, of course, nothing new in the idea that music can symbolize community, nationality, and other expressions of shared identity. But the point is that, as performance, music not only symbolizes but also enacts cultural identities, especially when they are contested or repressed. When Mbowa says it is self-defeating to put what one hears into words, her argument is that the history of racial suffering we hear in Lincoln's musicalized screaming is literally unspeakable: its meaning can emerge only through what (following Fred Moten) Mbowa calls "bone-deep listening." Again, Roach's study of jazz funerals shows how performances induce change in those liminal areas of culture that lie beyond rational expression: "Bereavement is a kind of madness," he says, "on which unempathetic passersby might look with embarrassment or even disgust, but which will force its way out somehow through crevices and fissures that performance opens up in tradition."

Performance, then, realizes a variety of critical socio-cultural roles. As Brooks shows in the context of neo-soul and Monson in the context of Mali, performance is a means by which traditions are perhaps unconsciously refashioned or modernized; with over a hundred years of recorded music now accessible, we can hear how the accumulation of imperceptible changes in performance style leads to wholesale transformations in what is ostensibly the same music. And if, as Mbowa argues, music embodies long-term cultural and racial memories, then equally it illustrates how change can take place through the intervention of individual agents, rather than as a function of impersonal historical or ideological forces: in an increasingly administered world, performance remains one of the ways in which individuals can make a difference. In short, performance emerges from the many case studies that comprise this book as a form of social and cultural critique.

The present volume, in summary, seeks to build an interdisciplinary bridge between different approaches to music as performance. Though we have aimed to embrace a wide variety of styles and traditions, with representation of "art," popular and world musics, our overriding aim has not been balanced or comprehensive coverage but rather to present a wide variety of distinctive takes on the subject, strong voices with a contribution to make to this developing area. Our contributors include both scholars whose background is in music studies, but whose work converges to a greater or lesser degree with the interdisciplinary performance studies perspective, and scholars in interdisciplinary performance studies, for whom music is a major research interest. The resulting collection is cross-disciplinary in two senses. First, a number of the authors explicitly combine distinct disciplinary approaches, sometimes attempting to assess their relative contributions to the understanding of particular performances. Second, the juxtaposition of different approaches illustrates not only the variety of emerging ways to understand music as performance but also the ways in which they can cross-fertilize. We hope the book makes a compelling case both for the potential of MAP approaches in rethinking musicological practice and for the potential of musicological approaches to inform broader, culturally oriented studies of performance across the entire musical spectrum. In short, we hope the book amounts to more than the sum of its parts.

The fifteen essays that make up this book represent a wide range of contrasted, complementary, and at times contradictory studies of music as performance. We have organized them into an initial group of essays with a primarily theoretical or methodological focus, another group that focuses on the meanings generated by performance, and two final essays that focus on ways in which performance is being reshaped by new technologies. But these categorizations are loose, and each essay stands, and may be read, on its own. To provide orientation for readers who wish to create their own pathways through the book, therefore, we close with individual descriptions of each essay.

Susan Fast investigates the relationship between live performance and its recorded representation through a study of *U2 3D*, an IMAX film based on the Irish band's *Vertigo* tour of 2005–6. Despite the three-dimensional effects, which are used to engage the audience in ways not possible in conventional film, the experience of watching *U2 3D* in a cinema is not at all the same as that of being at a concert: unlike watching a film, live music is a co-creation of musicians and audiences, a social interaction that takes place in the real time of performance. The publicity for *U2 3D* claimed that it offered a better experience than live performance, while some commentators have argued that the distinction between live and recorded performances has become increasingly blurred: rather than seeing them as converging or seeing one as subordinate to the other, however, Fast follows Peggy Phelan in arguing that they should be seen as fundamentally different— and complementary—modes of musical experience.

Until recently, scholarship on the Grateful Dead has focused primarily on the band as a counter-cultural phenomenon; **Richard Pettengill**'s essay, by contrast, is part of a growing movement to elucidate the band's singular approach to free-form group improvisation. Pettengill examines the band's performance of authenticity along with the role of non-verbal communication as the band collectively improvises its music and makes decisions in the moment as to which song to play next. He offers a close reading of the transition between "Dark Star" and "El Paso" in a videotaped performance from 1972, giving special attention to an aural cue delivered by lead guitarist Jerry Garcia, and an unexpected response on the part of rhythm guitarist Bob Weir. A moment of seeming confusion resolving in collective concord exemplifies the band's improvisational aesthetic, philosophy, and practices.

Philip Auslander takes issue with philosopher Lee Brown's arguments that recordings are the "enemy" of improvised music because of their lack of surprise and spontaneity, and that audience members can always tell when live music is improvised. Using Ella Fitzgerald's performance of "The Cricket Song" as an example, Auslander argues that the audience often has no idea whether a performer is in fact improvising or not. Improvisation, he argues, is better understood in terms of a social contract between musicians and listeners: musicians act "as if" they are improvising, and audience members act "as if" they are viewing an improvised performance—even if no improvisation is in fact taking place. Auslander illustrates how this works through a close reading of interactions between Miles Davis and John Coltrane in a 1959 performance of "So What."

Nicholas Cook's contribution relates to a developing strand of musicological research into performance that is not otherwise represented in this volume, in which performance data is captured from recordings and subjected to computational analysis. Such work runs the risk of perpetuating the atemporal, reified approaches of traditional score-based analysis, but Cook claims that it can be reconciled with the principles and concerns of interdisciplinary performance studies. He illustrates his argument by reference to video recordings of Chopin's Mazurka op. 63, no. 3 by Grigory Sokolov and others, concluding that while the interdisciplinary performance studies approach helps to clarify *what* performances mean, more empirical approaches help to clarify *how* performances mean what they mean.

Philip Gossett's essay on vocal ornamentation in nineteenth-century opera is in essence a study in the relationship between musical scores and their performances. Traditionally, musicologists have seen scores as texts to be reproduced in performance, but performing a Rossini or Verdi opera as written is an act of historical misunderstanding. Gossett sees scores as less like texts than like recipes, providing key directions for performances but at the same time relying on performers' knowledge of relevant conventions and ability to make aesthetically viable judgments: he illustrates his argument by reference to a range of alternative performance notations for Rossini's *Il barbiere di Siviglia*. It follows that musical works, which are an amalgam of notated and oral traditions, should be seen as collaborations between composers and interpreters: performance is not a supplement to a musical tradition that is essentially literary, but rather an integral element of it.

Aestheticians of Western "art" music have traditionally seen it as transcending its social and political contexts. Opposing this viewpoint, **Dana Gooley** argues that music is capable not just of symbolizing social and political change but of enacting it. An obvious example is national anthems, but Gooley shows how, in the revolutionary circumstances of 1848, even instrumental music came to acquire political significance. His specific focus is a concert given in Vienna by Sigismond Thalberg, the official court pianist and a virtuoso frequently compared to Liszt, just twelve days before the Emperor Ferdinand and his family fled for their lives. Making use of Joseph Roach's concept of "surrogation," Gooley shows how Thalberg's concert was interpreted as in effect a performance of imperial authority: the negative response to it was a judgment on the Habsburg monarchy.

Joseph Roach offers a tandem study of the cultural performance of "cutting the body loose" in the traditional jazz funerals of New Orleans (where singing, dancing, and drinking are embraced as a part of the bereavement process), and of famed cornettist Buddy Bolden, the subject of Michael Ondaatje's novel *Coming Through Slaughter*. At one level the link between these two strands is the belated jazz funeral held for Bolden in 1995 (sixty-four years after his death), but underlying this are questions of the performative meaning of jazz funerals: Roach charts how issues of the sacred and the profane are negotiated in "cutting loose" and how the tradition of jazz funerals was transformed in the context of the crack wars of the 1990s.

Aida Mbowa argues that jazz singer Abbey Lincoln uses such techniques as screaming to inspire her audience into a listening that is "bone deep," in order to bring to life specters from the collective unconscious of the African-American past. Since the justice system has failed overall to redress slavery, she argues, performers such as Lincoln turn to their medium to express their feelings and psychological agony. Through this project, the artist can begin to address his or her pain. By opening herself up in this way, Lincoln uses her voice as a vessel through which her enslaved ancestors can speak, so activating a "sonic liberatory potential." Mbowa also discusses the potential that recorded performances open up through affording unlimited new hearings: quoting Weheliye, she calls this the "ephemoromateriality of recorded sound."

Margaret Savilonis charts how two 1960s-era African-American bands, Labelle and Parliament, moved from the traditional, restricting dress and choreography of the 1950s toward the more liberating style of 1970s glam rock. This enabled them to expand their expressive range, to the point of conveying overt political messages through their lyrics and performance styles. Labelle, a girl group famous for "Lady Marmalade," deployed various aspects of performance to define their own sexuality and to celebrate their status as black women, while Parliament challenged stereotypical views of race by dressing as spacemen and promoting the funk style. Both groups defied sexual norms of the day, refusing to allow society to define their sexualities and genders while using their music to demonstrate their power as African-American men and women.

Daphne Brooks's essay examines Lauryn Hill's "comeback" performance in the concert film *Dave Chappelle's Block Party*, using it as a window on the politics of post-soul cultural memory. Her reading of "Killing Me Softly (With His Song)" shows how Hill's performance encapsulates and affirms her pivotal role as the iconic voice of post-civil rights cultural insurgency. Brooks also assesses the lasting impact on popular music culture of *The Miseducation of Lauryn Hill*, the artist's one full-length studio album, arguing that both the album and Hill's distinctive aesthetic of live performance expressed a re-imagining of the gendered politics of soulfulness within the black public sphere.

Jason King investigates Columbia Pictures' 2009 film posthumously assembled from raw video footage of Michael Jackson during his final rehearsals in Los Angeles. Directed by Kenny Ortega, this commercially successful film was marketed to the public as a must-see revelation of the "authentic" Michael Jackson in the throes of pure creativity. That "authentic" portrait is only made possible because the filmmakers de-contextualize the rehearsal footage on which the film relies. But despite its mythologizing quality, *This Is It* is a revelation in a way the filmmakers did not intend: it foregrounds Jackson's inestimable performance skills and so controverts widespread misconceptions about Jackson as an artist and auteur. Through scenes of joyous soul and funk performances, *This Is It* affirms the recalcitrant power of spirit: energetic good feeling between artists bent on getting together and sharing together.

Maria Delgado's contribution describes the avant-garde performance techniques of opera company director/composer/performer Carles Santos, a Catalan composer and pianist who employs what might seem very peculiar directorial choices to present his messages in the theater. Delgado first provides background on Santos and on the opera scene in Barcelona, and then goes on to describe in detail some of these choices, which include having his singers perform acrobatic tricks such as walking a tightrope, wrestling with each other, speeding around on a motorcycle, and being submerged in water—all while continuing to sing. Delgado also analyzes how each of these choices might contribute to the overall meaning of Santos's productions.

Neba Solo is a virtuoso of the *bala* (xylophone) and perhaps the most famous musician in Mali. **Ingrid Monson** sketches the cultural and historical circumstances that underlie the special role he occupies within the political establishment of Mali, showing how his music articulates problematic relationships between tradition and modernization. At the same time she focuses closely on performance of one of his own compositions, *Tchekisse*, coining the term "Senufo counterpoint" to describe the interweaving of parts that shapes the social dimension of the performance. Monson's essay is a reflection on several methodological aspects of the study of performance: the need to consider its social, visual, and kinesthetic as well as aural dimensions, the value of studying multiple performances of the same music (including those that are in some way problematic), and the relationship between the performer's and the scholar's knowledge and interpretation.

Recently developed PlayStation games based on rock music, such as

Rock Band and *Guitar Hero*, create new ways to interact with music and in this way represent a further stage in the evolution of technologically mediated modes of musical consumption: they add another dimension to the concept of performance. **Roger Moseley** contextualizes these games both historically, in terms of their development from Japanese arcade games, and theoretically: for example, he draws on Roger Caillois's taxonomy of games to bring into focus the kinesthetic, collaborative, and competitive dimensions of the games. He shows how they represent and reconfigure aspects of real-world performance within the domain of the virtual. At the same time, he argues that study of games can act as a valuable heuristic tool, bringing to light dimensions of play in real-world performance that musicologists have found all too easy to overlook.

Taking as his starting point Christopher Small's idea of "musicking"—in essence, music understood as process rather than product—**David Borgo** develops the idea of "transmusicking": musicking reconfigured by digital technology to challenge conventional constructions of artwork, artist, and audience. He complements a historical outline of the development of successive musicking paradigms—in effect, different musical ontologies—with three case studies: of telemusicking, where geographically remote musicians collaborate in real time through the Internet; the RjDj app for the iPhone, which enables users to program their own sonic experiences based on environmental sounds; and Sensuous Geographies, a responsive sound and video environment created by Sarah Ribudge and Alistair MacDonald. While there is a utopian dimension to Borgo's prognosis for the future of performance in cyberspace, he is careful to balance this against real-world issues of access and intellectual property: the performance of music, it appears, will for the foreseeable future remain an arena for contestation and negotiation between opposed hegemonies, interests, and values. That is a way of saying that it is a vital dimension of what it means to be human.

NOTES

1. Richard Schechner, "Performance Studies: The Broad Spectrum Approach." In *The Performance Studies Reader*, ed. Henry Bial (London: Routledge, 2004), 7–9.

2. J. L. Austin, *How to Do Things with Words* (Cambridge: Harvard University Press, 1962).

3. Judith Butler, "Performative Acts and Gender Constitution: An Essay in Phenomenology and Feminist Criticism," *Theater Journal* 40, no. 4 (1988): 519–31.

4. Henry Kingsbury, *Music, Talent, and Performance: A Conservatory Cultural System* (Philadelphia: Temple University Press, 1988); Bruno Nettl, *Heartland Excursions: Reflections on Schools of Music* (Urbana: University of Illinois Press, 1995); Kay Shelemay, "Toward an Ethnomusicology of the Early Music Movement: Thoughts

on Bridging Disciplines and Musical Worlds," *Ethnomusicology* 45, no. 1 (2001): 1–29; Stephanie Pitts, "'Everybody Wants to be Pavarotti': The Experience of Music for Performers and Audience at a Gilbert and Sullivan Festival," *Journal of the Royal Musical Association* 129 (2004): 143–60.

5. See Michal M. McCall and Howard S. Becker, "Performance Science," *Social Problems* 37, no. 1 (1990): 117–32.

6. Philip Auslander, "Lucille Meets GuitarBot: Instrumentality, Agency, and Technology in Musical Performance," *Theatre Journal* 61, no. 4 (2009): 603–16.

7. Henry Louis Gates Jr., *The Signifying Monkey* (New York: Oxford University Press, 1988), xxiv.

8. Peggy Phelan, "The Ontology of Performance: Representation without Reproduction," Phelan, *Unmarked: The Politics of Performance* (London: Routledge, 1993), 146–66.

9. Dick Hebdige, *Subculture: The Meaning of Style* (London: Methuen, 1979).

SUSAN FAST

U2 3D

Concert Films and/as Live Performance

CONCERTGOERS HAVE FINALLY MADE IT into the stadium, and they run, barreling through turnstiles and into the vast expanse of the arena, vying for a place near the stage—up against it, if at all possible. The journey to their destination is frantic, chaotic, fast; bodies move at full speed, exerting maximum effort for what they hope will be a big payoff: closest possible proximity to the musicians. Finally, they arrive, the band erupts into the first song, and the sea that is the audience roars and pumps its fist, "swinging to the music," as the singer puts it; "Vertigo" is an apt title for an opening song at a stadium concert, when 20,000 fans or more burst to life in a way that can make one's head spin.

Yet I am silent, my body sitting motionless next to other motionless and silent bodies. I am not at the stadium in Buenos Aires depicted in this scene, but rather in the Scotiabank IMAX theater in Toronto, watching U2's concert film, *U2 3D*. Released early in 2008, it was the first live-action 3D film of any kind.[1] It was directed by Irish filmmaker Catherine Owens, who has been responsible for many of the innovative uses of technology U2 have made, including the video installations on their last four tours. Utilizing the very latest in high-definition 3D film technology—a far cry from earlier forays in B-rated action and horror movies—it captured the band toward the end of its 2005–2006 *Vertigo* tour. There were claims in the popular press that 3D concert films like this could serve as a replacement for seeing live concerts ("If you can't be front and center at the concert, then you see it in 3-D," declared a promoter),[2] or might even surpass them ("In many ways *U2 3D* is superior to a real concert," wrote *Toronto Star* critic Peter Howell).[3] The band's front man, Bono, suggested the film may act as a substitute for those (apparently younger) fans who can't afford concert tickets: "I'm hoping that all the people in high school or who are college-age and don't have the cash to go see us can go see us for a low price with this film."[4] But as my silent body (and silly glasses) at the screening of the U2 film attest, this is not the same as being at the concert. The film follows cinematic conventions, not the conventions of live popular music performance, so why would the discourse around the film suggest that one can stand in for the other?

Theatrical release of concert films has not been a customary way for fans to see popular musicians in concert; indeed, one commentator calls this genre of film "an afterthought" in the movie industry, although this may be changing.[5] Such films have tended to mix musical performance with an over-arching, albeit sometimes loose, narrative constructed outside of the concert performance which can include interviews and offstage action, turning the film into a full-fledged documentary: in Jack Ellis and Betsy McLane's words, "Notable music documentaries are not fiction films that use rock and roll, or straight-ahead filmed concerts, nor are they simply records of performances. These are fully realized creative efforts."[6] Among the most well-known of such films are Martin Scorsese's of The Band, *The Last Waltz* (1978), Madonna's *Truth or Dare* (1991), until recently the highest-grossing concert film, and U2's own *Rattle and Hum* (1988).[7]

It is the novelty of seeing the artist both in and out of the live concert setting that makes these films special and appealing. One feels as though one has a different kind of access to the artist than at a live show: this is especially the case when there are scenes backstage before, during, or after the concert, scenes that capture the band in rehearsal, or, as in Led Zeppelin's concert film *The Song Remains the Same*, that show the musicians in their "everyday" settings (at home, with family) before the tour begins, however fictitious these scenes might actually be. Along with audio recordings, live concerts, interviews with and articles and books about the artist, the music documentary/concert film has become *one more* way to consume popular music, but certainly not a substitute for one of the other media. Further, the vast majority of pop music concert films are released as DVDs for home use, not for theatrical release; indeed, it has become standard practice for artists to release a version of every concert tour they do in DVD form, as U2 did with the *Vertigo* tour in 2005.

U2 3D does not follow the usual contours of the concert film genre. Aside from the opening shots of audience members running toward the stage, the film presents *only* the concert: no interviews, no backstage shots, no shots taken before or after the concert, in fact even very little of Bono talking to the live audience. According to Bono, the decision was made to "focus only on the music, not the personalities," eliminating everything deemed "extraneous."[8] In director Catherine Owens's words:

> I wanted to document the pure performance. It's tempting to do a lot of B-roll [backstage footage, etc.], because a lot of people do, but I think there's too many films about how many trucks it takes to load in the gear. And even though I know the fans really want to know that, I just wanted to give the band what it is that they had invested in. The band were very happy just to focus on that.[9]

This is one reason why the commentary has suggested it might serve as a substitute for a live show, although the notion of "purity" here is suspect: as if at a live show there is not action that happens outside of the presentation of a number of songs. It is also, of course, the use of 3D, high definition, and IMAX theater technologies that has led to speculation about whether this is the wave of the future for concertgoers. But do the film's form and the technology work to replicate the concert experience (could it, indeed, ever work as a substitute for going to a concert?), or do they ultimately serve to distance the audience from the performance? Or are such totalizing, either/or questions the wrong ones to be asking? In what follows, I will examine the U2 film from two perspectives: Erving Goffman's concepts of frame and event, and the use of 3D technology. In the process, I will take up issues of liveness, the ontology of performance, and the nature of performance events. These issues have received considerable attention from theater and performance studies scholars, who have, necessarily, given their disciplinary orientation, focused much more on theater than on music; music scholars have given them little attention. Yet the study of popular music performance has some unique aspects to contribute to this discussion, including the role of an audience in creating a live performance, the question of effort expended by an audience at a live event, and the ways in which performers and audiences interact.

Frame/Event

In one of the few sustained accounts of the subject, Philip Auslander discusses live popular music as a form of authentication for audio and video recordings. Live performances prove that the musicians who made the recording not only were one and the same, but have the musical ability to reproduce the record live; after the advent of music video in the 1980s, Auslander argues, live performance served to authenticate the video.[10] He also argues that the distinction between live and what he calls "mediatized" performance, the latter defined as "performance that is circulated on television, as audio or video recordings, and in other forms based in technologies of reproduction," is increasingly blurred and probably insignificant:[11] "The progressive diminution of previous distinctions between the live and the mediatized," he writes, "in which live events are becoming ever more like mediatized ones, raises for me the question of whether there really are clear-cut ontological distinctions between live forms and mediatized ones."[12] Live and mediatized performance are, for Auslander, "parallel forms that participate in the same cultural economy."[13] With respect to stadium or arena concerts of popular music, he writes that "the spectator sitting in the back rows of a Rolling Stones or Bruce Springsteen concert . . . hardly participates in it as such since his/her main experience of the performance is to read it off a video monitor."[14] While it is beyond the scope of this essay to interrogate Auslander's ideas in full, I raise them because the discourse surrounding the U2 film would seem to prove his points: the film can be viewed in lieu of seeing the live show, or, the film is actually *better* than the live show because anyone watching gets the "best" seat in the house.

While to some extent fans do go to live concerts to authenticate what they have heard and seen in recordings—and this is more true for some genres (heavy metal, for one)[15] than for others—the question of authenticity is only one of many reasons fans go to concerts. Absent from Auslander's discussion is the idea of live performance as event,[16] of the constitutive formal elements of such an event, of space,[17] of its social dimensions, or of the body—both the individual and the collective body of fans at a show (bit by bit I am returning to my still body in the movie theater). If one is sitting at the back of a stadium, one may watch a live rock performance largely on a video screen, but it is still fundamentally different to *be there*, in that stadium, than to be listening to a recording, watching a video, or watching a concert film. And what about those who are *not* at the back of the stadium, but up front, a concertgoing population that Auslander never addresses? As Paul Woodruff notes, "film resembles theater in several ways, but it does not serve the same need as theater. . . . In the theater you are part of a community of watchers, while in the cinema you are alone. . . . We become close to each other when we watch the same things."[18] While it can obviously be argued that those in a cinema audience watch a film together, Woodruff is right to see this kind of watching as a predominantly solitary experience (even if one is with friends), compared to the kind of watching that occurs at a live show (my silent body, despite the presence of enthusiastic friends, at the U2 screening, makes the point again). So rather than arguing for live and mediatized performance as "parallel" forms that are increasingly undifferentiated, I would argue, with Peggy Phelan, that live and recorded performances are fundamentally different, that *both are indispensible*,[19] and that the distinctions between them need to be preserved (indeed, I believe the distinctions are intact in fans' minds). The persistence of rock music tours, the incredible speed with which they sell out, and the profound excitement of fans at the announcement of a tour, all suggest that people want the experience of going to a live show and view it as special: it does not replace audio and video recordings, with which fans also have important encounters, but offers something fundamentally different. Whether or not there are elements of the mediatized in a live concert, *being present* creates the conditions for a particular kind of event.

Our understanding of an event, according to Goffman, comes through the principles of organization which govern it: "It has been argued that a strip of activity will be perceived by its participants in terms of the rules or premises of a primary framework, whether social or natural."[20] A movie event and a live concert event have two distinctly different frames. My still body at the screening of *U2 3D* constitutes part of the frame of this event. I am at a movie theater, not a live concert, and those of us in the audience understand what we are witnessing as a movie, not a concert. (I saw the film four times and the audience response was the same on every occasion, although I concede that in other theaters it could have been different.) More than one reviewer I read suggested that the film gives you all of the benefits of a live concert experience with none of the headaches: you not only get a great view, but you are not stuck in traffic for hours while trying to leave the stadium after a show, or faced with the considerable ordeal—indeed, near impossibility—of obtaining tickets, given that tickets for arena and stadium concerts sell out so quickly.[21]

But, in fact, these elements, along with entering the stadium with thousands of other people, enduring (or even occasionally enjoying) opening acts, watching the stage being set up, instrument technicians tuning instruments, lighting checks, the crowd growing louder as the recorded music played before the entrance of the band increases in volume, the lights dimming as the band takes the stage, the exit from the building at the end of the show, when one might encounter street vendors selling posters of the band—all of these serve as part of the frame of the live stadium concert experience. Indeed, Richard Schechner argues that these "before and after elements" are not just a frame but as much a part of the performance as the "during" elements.[22]

And the same applies to the rituals that take place while the band is on stage. Whether one is in a "good" seat or watching the action on video monitors, when a performer asks you to sing along, you sing, when you are asked to clap, to raise your fist, to stand up, or sit down, you generally participate, you become part of the collective audience/fan body. When a member of the audience close to the stage has an encounter with the performers, the rest of the crowd responds to that encounter, feels a part of it through their presence in the same space, with events unfolding in the present.[23] In theatrical events, as Willmar Sauter writes, creation and the experience of the creation are simultaneous processes.[24] This is why Peggy Phelan argues that "performance's only life is in the present."[25] Further, there is the question of effort expended before, during, and after a live show. It requires effort to obtain tickets, effort to get to a venue and to negotiate crowds. Effort is required to participate during a show (both physical and sometimes emotional effort). In general, it requires much more effort to take in a live show than it does a film; live shows are expensive, not only monetarily, but in terms of energy expended. This lends to their specialness (there are very few artists for whom I will expend this kind of effort).

Aside from the audience stillness at the *U2 3D* screening, the frame of this event differed from the live concert in several other significant ways. The film is eighty-five minutes long—a little more than half the length of the live show. It is unclear why the decision was made to keep it so brief (many feature-length films run over two hours), but because of its brevity many songs that were performed at the live shows on this tour were omitted in the film; the decision was made to cut, for example, a foray into the band's very early, less known material, in effect turning the film into a "greatest hits" compilation—something U2 shy away from in their live concerts, where they always play a substantial amount of new, and/or much older, obscure material. Of course this leads to a different kind of overall flow. Concerts are not just reproductions of individual recordings, as is sometimes suggested, but are rather based on a precisely worked-out running order for the songs, which are accordingly recontextualized and understood in relation to their position within the concert as a whole.[26] *U2 3D*, then, creates quite a different flow, based on a different running order, than the live shows from which the footage for the film was assembled (five shows performed in Latin America in 2006, as well as a performance for the cameras only, with no live audience present),[27] even though it has been edited to create the illusion that one is watching a seamless, single live performance at a single venue. Because of the "greatest hits" running order, this is not a show that one would ever get if one went to a live show.

Other framing elements derive from the fact that *U2 3D* was made for viewing in IMAX theaters, which means that it had a limited release:

there were at that time only 320 IMAX theaters, spread across forty-two countries (it was also shown in a few non-IMAX theaters).[28] Films made for IMAX theaters are shot with special cameras and are shown on enormous projection screens, more than twenty feet high. As the company explains, the theaters are built using a particular "theater geometry," which "maximizes the field of view" through the shape and positioning of the screen. They include sound systems that deliver remarkably clear and well-mixed audio. All of this is intended to create "the most immersive ways to enjoy Hollywood's biggest event movies and ground-breaking documentaries," with the audio designed to "deliver laser-aligned digital sound that envelops each audience member"; in particular, the company suggests that IMAX movies "mak[e] the viewer feel as if they are *in* the movie," because the 3D technology "enabl[es] images to leap off the screen and into the laps of the audience, further enhancing the immersive experience." Certainly the high-definition images and the particular kind of access the viewer gets to the stage in *U2 3D* are noteworthy. The camera often moves across the audience in the film, swooping in very low to the stage, close enough to see the grain of the wooden floor—the floor on which the action takes place, on which the performers stand. There are also a number of overhead shots of the band; most notable among these are when the camera moves over Larry Mullen Jr., the drummer, giving the viewer full access to the drum kit, even from the back, which video screens at concerts rarely capture. We see not only the way Mullen's feet work the bass drum, but also the pink-colored drink sitting next to him. It is interesting how often the camera exposes Mullen's (private) performance space, perhaps precisely because drummers are generally the band members least exposed to an audience in live performance, shielded from view by their instruments and position at the back of the stage.

Not only is this film shorter than a live concert, and dominated by a particular technology different from that of live concerts, but it is a historical document. The performers are unable to respond to the theater audience; conversely, moviegoing conventions dictate that the audience sit still, rather than participate (we were, after all, not encouraged to participate by the immediate presence of the performer asking us to do so). And because the band decided to focus on "the songs" rather than framing them with pre- or post-concert activities, or backstage shots, the film has a particularly artificial quality: it could easily have begun with several minutes of the crowd anticipating the band's arrival on stage, or watching them filter out of the stadium after the show, but other than the brief opening shots of the fans running in, there are no such scenes. The concert exists in a kind of cinematic vacuum. In pointing this out, I do not mean to suggest that the film is without its merits, but rather to pinpoint its particular nature. U2's foray into this genre is in keeping with their long history of innovative concert presentation, both live and on film, in which they have pushed—again, with Catherine Owens's guiding hand—the boundaries of new technology.[29] In particular, the use of 3D technology in this film opens up a new level of signification: it is used not merely to shock or titillate, but to focus attention in particular ways. 3D effects are turned on and off, so that this "mediating technolog[y] . . . openly construct[s] a performative frame" and thereby creates what Jem Kelly calls "an oscillation between 'immediacy' and 'hypermediacy' in which . . . artifice is acknowledged as constructive of a performance system."[30]

Yet even so, the use of this technology seems always compensatory, as if to point to a lack—an ontological lack, a lack of presence. I will turn now to a more detailed examination of these effects and explain why I believe this to be so.

3D

The concertgoers running toward the stage at the opening of the film hold general admission floor tickets, which means no reserved seats. The stage design for this show featured two curved ramps stretching out from either side of the main stage, on which the performers walked, creating a nearly enclosed inner circle. The quicker you got in, the closer to this "heated center" you would be.[31] The shots of the crowd arriving at the stadium are establishing shots, but the decision to begin with these locates the spectator as central; we are, presumably, to understand the show from the fan's perspective. Privileging the die-hard fans running to get the best seats suggests a theater audience identification with this particular kind of fan—the one presumably most committed, excited, and engaged (although in reality such fans often end up sitting further away from the stage)—or at least an identification with this kind of fan's experience. Although there are some very wide shots of the audience during the film, it is mostly those closest to the stage and the rest of the "inner circle" who are shown, thereby giving the theatergoer the illusion that he or she is close to the action. Of course this is a feature of most concert films, 3D or not, and it is this feature that makes them appear to give those viewing a "better" and "more real" experience than actually going to the live show and sitting in the nosebleed seats of the arena or stadium (a concert film shot from this perspective would be interesting indeed).

The scene of running fans is overlaid with the first 3D images, of confetti sprinkles and block-letter titles that stand out from the concertgoers, hovering in front of the theater audience. The 3D technology is used in the first instance to offer information *about* the concert, external to it, information that frames the film as film, where opening titles and credits are a commonplace feature of the medium. (I have only once encountered credits at a rock concert—they rolled on the video screens on Tina Turner's 2008 tour—and found them incongruous with the concert setting; such information normally appears in the printed program of a live event.) Once the show begins, the next 3D effect comes into view: a point-of-view shot of the stage taken from some way back in the "inner circle." The audience members closest to the camera, backs facing those in the theater audience, are projected in 3D, so that they appear to be at the front of the movie theater, blending in with the theater audience. Before we see any of the band members in 3D, then, we see the audience in 3D, and it is used to create the illusion that concert and theater audiences are somehow merged. But how, exactly? Is this effect intended to make us, the theater audience, feel as though we are at this show? Is the intention to remind us that we are part of the larger fan community? Or is it to invite the theater audience to replicate the behavior of the "live" audience—should it spur us on to action of some kind, get us out of our seats, make us move to the music? (As I have already indicated, it certainly did not have this effect on the Toronto audiences.)

Like all of the other 3D effects in this film, this one appears sporadically. Because the effect is momentary and unstable, it does not "immerse" the theater audience in the show (as the IMAX propaganda suggests) but points, bluntly, to the technology and its effect, and to the director's hand. The repetition of this effect throughout the show serves as a reminder that the theater audience is, indeed, *not* at the concert, their bodies are *not* "swinging to the music" like those in the projection. What the 3D projection of the audience does accomplish, however, is to reinforce the initial importance of the audience in this film: every time the projection occurs, one's focus is drawn away from the stage and toward the crowd.

The other 3D image that is often repeated throughout the film is that of a microphone on its stand, with no one singing behind it. The image floats across the field of vision and then disappears. In live shows singers often turn the microphone out toward the crowd inviting it to sing along, or even to sing instead of the singer (the live *Vertigo* show ended, for example, with only drummer Larry Mullen on stage, keeping time as the audience repeatedly sang the refrain of the song "40"). In the same way, the empty microphone stand in *U2 3D* is offered up to the audience as an enabling technology, its 3D projection making it clear that the invitation is to the theater audience and not the crowd in the stadium, its emptiness calling out for a taker.[32] The decision not to project Bono in 3D along with the microphone, asking the crowd to sing, takes the emphasis away from the performer and his celebrity: the technology makes the singer superfluous in extending the invitation to participate (this is also consistent with the decision that the film should focus on "the music itself" and not "personalities"). At the same time, it is also the microphone that enables a singer to perform to a large crowd, and so is among the technologies that signify "authentic" live performance. The repetition of this 3D image, therefore, also impresses the more general idea of "liveness" upon the theater audience.[33]

Both of these repeated 3D "gestures" are more about the artful use of 3D technology than they are about realism, or even the hyperreal; in both cases, the technology is used to add a layer (literally as well as figuratively) of meaning that is only possible through its use. 3D images of band members, however, bring questions about the real and hyperreal into play. Like all 3D images in this film, those of band members come and go throughout. They appear at various distances from the viewer; some are almost uncomfortably close, intruding on one's personal space and creating a sense of intimacy that on the one hand is thrilling (up close and personal with rock star celebrity) and on the other disquieting (should one be privy to this much information about a stranger?). One is almost never this intimate with a performer at a live show, which suggests that, while the concert operates in the public sphere, the use of 3D aims to create much more of a sense of the private sphere, that is, of a personal and private encounter between performer and audience member.[34] One especially effective use of the 3D close-up occurs midway through the film, during the song "Sunday Bloody Sunday." For years, this song has served in the band's live performances as a springboard for Bono to address the crowd about various political issues, usually in the form of a spoken monologue (one instance can be seen in the film *Rattle and Hum*, where he talks about "The Troubles" in Ireland). In *U2 3D*, rather than the usual speech, Bono's image appears in 3D, so close in front of the viewer that it feels possible to reach out and touch it. In fact, Bono encourages the viewer to do so by stretching out his own hand, looking directly, it appears, into each individual audience member's eyes. The audio production on his voice loses all traces of echo, an effect that most often serves to distance the singer from the listener: the dry sound brings his voice close, making it intimate, a private communication, as he sings "wipe your tears away." While it often seems as though 3D images of band members appear at random, this one is deliberately placed at what, I would argue, is the emotional center of the film. But it is crucial to take the sound of this moment—the dry production value—into account as well as the 3D image: it is the combination that creates the intimacy of the moment. In addition, all live audience noise is filtered out (something that can never be done at a live show), placing singular focus on the singer, the lyrical message, and the one-on-one relationship that image and sound produce with each member of the theater audience.

Jem Kelly defines "inter-medial" pop music performances as those "in which mediated images modulate a sense of presence," and suggests that such images can serve to enhance the presence of a performer in live concerts:

> Inter-medial pop performance can . . . provide an experience in which the physical presence of the performers and their music is framed by technologies of the spectacular. This visual dimension appears to enhance the aura of presence . . . rather than attenuating it, which offers a paradox in that the cinematic referent is always absent, in contrast to the performer's body, which is right there, on stage in front of the spectator.[35]

Arguing against Walter Benjamin's notion that technological reproduction will "devalue the here and now of the artwork," Kelly speaks of a "doubling of presence" through the use of "real time" video at concerts.[36] He also argues that "performance registers," that is, "relationships of presence between performer and spectator during the live event," are modulated by the technology used at these events; registers change throughout the concert. Kelly's way of theorizing the use of real-time video at live pop music concerts brings us closer to an understanding of how, even if one is watching some of the concert on the video monitor, this is decidedly not the same thing as watching a video recording; the *real-time* video serves to enhance the presence of the body on stage, not to substitute for it. Further, Kelly's registers account for the spectator's ability to move his or her gaze from the performer's body to video monitor and back, from the action on the stage or in the audience that is not displayed on the video monitor back to the action that is. The technology also gives those presenting the show the ability to modulate registers: to display real-time video images, or not (I have been at some arena concerts where the video monitors are dark for some of the show, so that one *must* look at the live action on the stage), to display pre-recorded images (for example, from the artist's music videos) alongside real-time images, to display audience activity, and so on.

But how is this significant for *U2 3D*? In a concert film there are neither live performers nor spectators, and so Kelly's registers do not literally apply; but I would argue that the use of 3D images in U2's film is an attempt to reinstate them, only in virtual form. The repetition of the 3D images causes the spectator constantly to refocus attention, from virtual image, to stage, to video monitor at the live concert, and so on, in effect to shift registers. While those of us in the theater may not get the material body, as the concertgoers in Buenos Aires did, we do get the virtual 3D body, though only at the discretion of the film's director. (At a live concert the viewer always has the option of looking at the material body on the stage, no matter how small it may appear, which gives one a sense of control.) The 3D technology is used, in effect, to occasionally and temporarily break the fourth wall between theater and concert audiences. But while it may break the boundary between performer and theater audience, between live and filmed event, the technology also serves as a constant reminder that such a boundary exists and, for most of the time, is intact. And while the intent may have been to permeate the fourth wall, its use did not lead to changed behavior by the theater audience. No one took up the offer to stand up and move, to shout, or to sing, all of which a gesture from Bono to a live concert audience achieves instantaneously and effortlessly.

Perhaps it is the use of 3D technology to permeate the boundary between performers on film and theater audience that led the filmmakers (and the band?) to omit one of the most persistent rituals at a U2 concert: Bono bringing an audience member up on stage to dance with him.[37] Most often this occurs near the end of a show, and it is almost always a woman, with whom Bono dances. This woman represents the audience—she stands in for the collective fan community. Bringing her on stage and dancing with her, sharing a moment of "keeping bodies together in time,"[38] represents the final collapse of the boundary between audience and performer (already breached by the performers reaching out to touch audience members, or the audience singing along). In the DVD concert video of the *Vertigo* tour, Bono twice brings audience members onto the stage with him: a young boy, perhaps seven or eight years old, near the beginning of the show, as the band plays "Into the Heart" from U2's first album, *Boy*, and a woman during the performance of the song "Mysterious Ways," near the end of the show. In the *U2 3D* film, however, no one is brought up on stage: instead the band's virtual bodies are projected out into the audience. While interesting, this is not nearly as special, in part because the bodies are virtual, so that there is no real interaction, but largely because the audience member who goes up on stage must be invited to do so and intrudes on an otherwise forbidden space.

In fact, as the film nears its end, the live audience fades in importance. The end credits are preceded and interspersed with 3D animations (of a city being built) that take the viewer away from the concert altogether, and although the band returns—the credits are broken up by a final performance—the film ends without the theater audience seeing the crowd at the end of the show. Unlike, for example, the Iron Maiden documentary film, *Flight 666*, which shows fans leaving several of the live shows featured in the concert (including one fan in tears, some screaming, and others filtering out of the arena singing along to the recorded music), the theater audience at *U2 3D* never shares in what effect this concert had on the people who were there. Perhaps this is because of the film's aim to "focus only on the music": those who have watched the film are expected to have their own reactions.

THE RELEASE OF 3D concert films from Miley Cyrus/Hannah Montana and The Jonas Brothers followed quickly on the heels of *U2 3D* in 2008; the Hannah Montana film grossed $53.4 million in the first two weeks of its release.[39] The worldwide gross for *U2 3D* as of April 2009 was a little more than $21 million.[40] Martin Scorsese's concert film of the Rolling Stones, *Shine a Light*, was also released in theaters in 2008 (not a 3D film, but shown in IMAX theaters). And as I walked into a theater in Toronto to see the Iron Maiden documentary mentioned previously, I noticed a poster advertising an upcoming Diana Krall concert film. Suddenly, concert films seem to be everywhere, coming from every kind of artist. There is certainly a commercial element to this surge: "By targeting a vociferous fan base and utilizing new technology that makes the experience more like a live concert and less like a cheesy monster movie," Ann Donahue observes, "the concert film is on the cusp of becoming a viable—and very profitable—means to reach fans."[41] While artists routinely release a DVD after every concert tour, these are intended for home use—they are not screened in theaters. By contrast, 3D, high-definition, and theater technologies used by a company such as IMAX are not currently reproducible at home (although during the lapse of time between writing this essay and its publication, 3D televisions for use at home have come on the market), so this new technology is a way to get fans into the theater, a way in which the music industry can regain some of the control over the distribution of music-related products that it has lost since the advent of file sharing. As reported in *Billboard* magazine, "[record] labels and [music] publishers may benefit from concert films on several levels, ranging from negotiated licenses upfront for use of the music, to reaching new potential fans, to residual catalog sales."[42]

Still, it is unlikely that such films will eliminate fans' desire to go to live shows. As I argued earlier, live concerts and films of live concerts are two different media, each with its own conventions. Even some of the journalists who reviewed *U2 3D* conceded that there was a "disconnect" in the film, resulting from "the irresistible urge to stand, cheer and sing along, actions that might irk [theater] patrons less inclined to shake their jujubes."[43] As is clear from some of the literature I have relied upon, debate about the superiority of live performances over video and film recordings of such performances has been ongoing for some time by performance studies theorists, with little reference to popular music; it is also, of course, an unquestioned aesthetic dogma in critical writing about jazz and classical music. As I hope to have shown, live performance in popular music offers perhaps one of the best instances of the idea that audience and artist co-create live performance, and in the end 3D technology cannot overcome the loss of this significant element in the medium of the concert film. My silent body at the screening of *U2 3D*, in contrast with my standing, dancing, singing, producing, *creative* body at the *Vertigo* shows I attended, points to a critical experiential difference, one that includes, among other things, effort. Watching the film required none, while being at the concert required a considerable amount.

I am aware that in my arguments I have tended to privilege live performance and to question the claims of "realism" arising from new 3D concert films; I have a certain soft spot for the very powerful experience of seeing live musical performance. Nonetheless, recordings of live musical performances, whether audio or video, 3D or not, can be phenomenally impressive documents, in some cases, such as James Brown's *Live at the Apollo*, or Peter Frampton's *Frampton Comes Alive!*, career making or changing. Some of the bias toward live performance that I have expressed in this article comes from arguments that want to equate live with mediatized performance, as Auslander does, and to suggest that experiences with one are the same as with the other. This just does not ring true for me. For most rock musicians, live performances of songs do not simply replicate studio recordings, and in many cases, live versions are deemed superior. This is why bootleg recordings of live shows have, in the case of many rock musicians, been so highly prized. Live and recorded popular music performances, then, are both invaluable in the production and consumption of popular music. Live *simulcast* theatrical broadcasts of pop music concerts, in 3D or not, may be another story altogether, if and when this should happen. Live radio and television broadcasts of music have happened for many years, of course, and movie theaters have been broadcasting opera live for some time now, a practice that has revivified the genre and introduced it to new audiences.[44] But simulcast broadcasts of live popular music events in theaters is almost non-existent. David Bowie experimented with a live simulcast when he launched his album *Reality* in 2003, beaming his show, performed live for only three hundred members of his fan club in London, to cinemas in the United Kingdom and eight other European countries.[45] Those developing the new 3D technology have already commented that "live 3D broadcasts of sports is the killer application, we believe, whether that's soccer or the Superbowl."[46] But perhaps simulcast popular music concerts will also prove to be a "killer application," especially if the technology allows theater audiences to co-create their experience with the "live" audience and the performers.

NOTES

1. Live action refers to film not produced using animation. The trailer for the film, as well as other information related to it, can be found at http://www.u23d movie.com/.

2. Jeff Boch, a box-office analyst at Exhibitor Relations, quoted in Ann Donahue, "Screen Sirens: Hannah Montana and U2 Use New Generation of Concert Film to Lure Audience," *Billboard*, February 2008, 14.

3. Peter Howell, "U2 3D: Best Concert Seats Ever," *Toronto Star*, January 25, 2008, http://www.thestar.com/entertainment/article/297267.

4. Anthony Breznican, "U2 Writes Sundance Soundtrack with New Film '3D,'" *USA Today*, January 21, 2008, http://www.usatoday.com/life/movies/mov ieawards/ sundance/2008-01-21-u2-sundance_N.htm?loc=interstitialskip/.

5. Donahue, "Screen Sirens," 14.

6. Jack C. Ellis and Betsy A. McLane, *A New History of Documentary Film* (New York: Continuum, 2005), 287.

7. Information on concert films since 1980, including box office gross numbers, can be found at www.the-numbers.com.

8. Reported in Breznican, "U2 Writes Sundance Soundtrack with New Film '3D.'"

9. "The Director Interviews: Catherine Owens," *Filmmaker: The Magazine of Independent Film* (Winter 2009), accessed June 26, 2009, http://filmmakermagazine .com/directorinterviews/2008/01/catherine-owens-u2-3d.php.

10. Philip Auslander, *Liveness: Performance in a Mediatized Culture*, 2nd ed. (London: Routledge, 2008), 105.

11. Ibid., 4.

12. Ibid., 7.

13. Ibid., 5.

14. Ibid., 25.

15. See Robert Walser, *Running With the Devil: Power, Gender and Madness in Heavy Metal Music* (Hannover, NH: Wesleyan University Press, 1993), for a full account of the importance of live performance in heavy metal. Briefly, the prominent place of instrumental and vocal virtuosity in metal make seeing it live a crucial aspect of fandom.

16. Simon Frith takes popular music performances as events, although he does not explain how, nor does he explain his use of the term "frame." Simon Frith, *Performing Rites: On the Value of Popular Music* (Cambridge: Harvard University Press, 1996), 203–26.

17. Paul Woodruff writes of the "sacred space" of theater (theater here defined as a range of activities that include watching and being watched). Sacred space is marked off by time (the time of the performance) and space, which may be temporarily or permanently marked as sacred. Paul Woodruff, *The Necessity of Theater: The Art of Watching and Being Watched* (New York: Oxford University Press, 2008), 108–13.

18. Ibid., 17.

19. Peggy Phelan, *Unmarked: The Politics of Performance* (New York: Routledge, 1993). Phelan argues that recordings are not performances at all; I differ with her on this count. I have oversimplified a complex issue here, which deserves more attention in and of itself, but for which there is no space here. In some genres such as disco, where recordings clearly predominate, live performances are of less importance, unless one considers dancing to these recordings in a club a live performance, which is certainly plausible. In the context of this essay, I am dealing specifically with rock music.

20. Erving Goffman, *Frame Analysis* (Boston: Northeastern University Press, 1986), 158.

21. Bob Mondello, "U2–3D—Better Than the Real Thing?," *NPR Online*, accessed June 25, 2012, http://www.npr.org/templates/story/story.php?storyId=18345673, writes, "There's no three-hour parking mess at the end of the show." Howell, "U2 3D: Best Concert Seats Ever," writes, "This time I don't have to put up with the rowdy drunks who blocked my view at the Air Canada Centre."

22. Richard Schechner elaborates his model in "Towards a Poetics of Performance," *Performance Theory*, rev. ed. (New York: Routledge, 2005), 170–210. Particularly relevant here is the following statement: "Surrounding a show are special observances, practices, and rituals that lead into the performance and away from it. Not only getting to the theater district, but entering the building itself involves ceremony: ticket-taking, passing through gates, performing rituals, a place from which to watch: all this—and the procedures vary from culture to culture, event to event—frames and defines the performance. Ending the show and going away also involves ceremony: applause or some formal way to conclude the performance and wipe away the reality of the show re-establishing in its place the reality of everyday life" (189–90).

23. Thanks to Kip Pegley for the term "collective body" as I use it in this context.

24. Wilmar Sauter, *The Theatrical Event: Dynamics of Performance and Perception* (Iowa City: University of Iowa Press, 2000), 5.

25. Phelan, *Unmarked: The Politics of Performance*, 146.

26. In an otherwise excellent article, Jem Kelly makes this assumption, writing, "Pop-music performance is a re-enactment in which the recorded musical corpse is revived and re-presented through physical action." "PopMusic, Multimedia and Live Performance," *Music, Sound and Multimedia: From the Live to the Virtual*, ed. Jamie Sexton (Edinburgh: Edinburgh University Press, 2007), 106. Auslander's entire argument about live performances authenticating recordings is based on the idea of individual songs, not songs as they are contextualized within live performance.

27. Edna Gunderson, "U2 3D: Lifelike Rattle and Hum," *USA Today*, January 22, 2008, http://www.usatoday.com/life/movies/reviews/2008-01-22-U2-3D_N.htm.

28. See the company's website, www.imax.com, for all quotes. Last accessed April 2009.

29. For a historical overview of U2's technologically innovative stage shows, see Diana Scrimgeour, *U2 Show* (London: Orion Books, 2004).

30. Kelly, "PopMusic, Multimedia and Live Performance," 109.

31. Schechner speaks of "heated centers" and "cool rims" at performance events. Richard Schechner, "Towards a Poetics of Performance," 176.

32. My thanks to Liss Platt for suggesting this interpretation.

33. My thanks to Kip Pegley for this idea.

34. My thanks to Catherine Graham for suggesting this perspective.

35. Kelly, "PopMusic, Multimedia and Live Performance," 109–10.

36. Ibid., 110.

37. Interestingly, this ritual was also suspended in the tour that followed *Vertigo* and the release of *U2 3D*, which was called *U2 360*. It is not clear why.

38. This is a paraphrase of the title of William McNeil's important book *Keeping Together in Time: Dance and Drill in Human History* (New Haven: Harvard University Press, 1995), which lays out the importance of what he calls "muscular bonding," that is, people's bodies moving in time together, as a way to generate "euphoria" and a more general sense of well-being.

39. Statistic from Donahue, "Screen Sirens: Hannah Montana and U2 Use New Generation of Concert Film to Lure Audience," 14.

40. Statistic from http://www.the-numbers.com/movies/2008/U2N3D.php, accessed October 24, 2010.

41. Donahue, "Screen Sirens," 14.

42. Ibid., 14.

43. Gunderson, "U2 3D: Lifelike Rattle and Hum."

44. A 2007 article in *Variety* reported that the simulcast of the Metropolitan Opera's production of Rossini's *Barber of Seville* in 275 U.S. movie theaters in March 2007 grossed $853,600, selling almost 58,000 tickets. The Met's general manager commented, "The future of the institution . . . was in peril. We needed a resuscitation program" (Elizabeth Guider and Ian Mohr, "Pop Goes the Opera: Met Brings Classics to the Masses at the Plexes," *Variety*, April 2007, 5).

45. Paul Sexton, "Bowie Simulcasts 'Reality': Singer Bows New CD with Live Gig Beamed to Theaters," *Billboard*, September 2003, 6.

46. Gordon Smith, "Even Better Than the Real Thing?," *Independent.ie*, accessed June 19, 2012, http://www.independent.ie/business/technology/even-bet ter-than-the-real-thing-1297453.html.

RICHARD PETTENGILL

Performing Collective Improvisation
The Grateful Dead's "Dark Star"

JOURNALISTIC WRITING ON THE GRATEFUL DEAD, the San Francisco–based band that was active from 1965 until the death of lead guitarist Jerry Garcia in 1995, tends to focus more on the band's countercultural fan base—the hordes of devoted followers that followed the band from city to city—than the actual music they played. When the music is mentioned, the references are usually to the best-known songs on The Dead's two iconic 1970 studio albums, *Workingman's Dead* and *American Beauty* ("Uncle John's Band," "Casey Jones," "Truckin'"), and their one Top 40 hit from 1987, "Touch of Grey." Although journalists occasionally pay lip service to the band's penchant for improvisation,[1] such accounts, until recently, seldom have displayed understanding and appreciation for the most distinctive aspect of the band's musical achievement, which I believe is the art of collective free-form improvisation: the ability to improvise in a collective mode in which all musicians contribute to various extents and in various ways to a performed group exploration.

Much of the scholarly work to date has focused more on The Dead as a cultural phenomenon rather than as a group of skilled improvisational musicians or as performers.[2] Nancy Reist, for example, has written about the legions of Deadheads who claimed that the concerts were "magical, transforming experiences" that helped them "make decisions, solve problems and cope with the stresses of life."[3] Reist argues that fans became Deadheads for the same reasons that humans throughout history have turned to myth: because their participation in that community helped them to "make sense of the world, particularly by acting as links between one's direct material experience and one's concept of the unseen forces that are believed to shape or at least influence that experience."[4] But Reist makes little substantive reference to the band as a musical ensemble. Nadya Zimmerman takes a step in a more substantive direction by exploring the irony of the band's non-commercial ideology (they allowed and even encouraged fans to record their concerts) alongside their Fortune 500 status, but also pays refreshing musicological attention to the structure of two of their more rhythmically adventurous songs, "The Eleven" and "Sugar Magnolia."[5] Zimmerman does not, however, touch upon the band's improvisational ability, or on the individual band members as performers.

Thankfully, this neglect has been rectified by a recent volume of essays entitled *The Grateful Dead in Concert: Essays on Live Improvisation.*[6] This volume, containing such essays as "Pouring Its Light Into Ashes: Exploring the Multiplicity of Becoming in Grateful Dead Improvisation" by Jim Tuedio and "'Searching for the Sound': Grateful Dead Music and Interpretive Transformation" by Jason Kemp Winfree, complements without supplanting my work in this essay, which ultimately focuses on about fifteen seconds of improvised interaction between members of the band.

I suggest that the mythology that has so dominated discourse on this band could not have emerged without the foundation of their musicianship along with the personae they projected in performance. The music they created onstage was facilitated, I believe, by the relationship between both of these elements: by performing "authentic" personae, part and parcel of which were the subtle gestures, movements, and facial expressions that facilitated their onstage musical communication, this group of musicians was able to excel as an organic, interdependent improvisational juggernaut. Accordingly, my focus in this essay will be on the Grateful Dead's onstage performance behavior as a way to enhance our understanding of their distinctive approach to improvisation and, I hope, the field of improvisational performance studies as a whole. In order to articulate the nature of this approach, I want to pay attention to two videotaped performances of their improvisational magnum opus, "Dark Star."

One significant strain of the jazz/rock music of the late 1960s was what many scholars refer to as "psychedelic rock," the suggestion being that the music was either fueled by or was both lyrically and musically reflective of the experience of hallucinogenic drugs. Within this genre lies a sub-genre of predominantly instrumental music that I call extended, collective improvisation, a form more commonly heard in jazz than in rock. Examples that in my view warrant close attention (and are available on video) are Cream's live 1967–68 performances of "Spoonful" and "I'm So Glad," and Miles Davis's "Call It Anything," the forty-five-minute "jazz rock" group improvisation he performed at the 1970 Isle of Wight Festival.[7] In the case of Cream, the launching pad for improvisation is a clearly defined song structure, and Cream's collective explorations always came back around to the original song structure to complete each unit of performance. Davis's Isle of Wight performance was free-form from the start, although careful listeners will pick up recurring themes that originated in the earlier *Bitches Brew* sessions and that Davis revisited in this subsequent period. Other practitioners of collective improvisation in the rock or jazz-rock arena include early Pink Floyd, Soft Machine, Robert Fripp and his various ensembles, and Larry Coryell.

But in the annals of collectively improvised rock music, "Dark Star" holds a special place. Composed by Jerry Garcia with lyrics by Robert Hunter, "Dark Star" began its recorded life in 1967 as an odd studio single that received little attention from listeners and critics alike. But the song quickly found its niche in the band's repertoire not so much as a "concise song structure"[8] in and of itself, but rather as a launching pad for the band's trademark onstage explorations. Two years later, in 1969, the band decided to place a twenty-four-minute version as the lead track of their first live album, *Live/Dead*.[9] This pivotal decision can be seen in retrospect as a major artistic statement at a key moment in their career: that they were first and foremost a live band, that you must experience them in concert to know what they are about, and that "Dark Star" is the flagship both of this album and generally of the band in concert.

Without becoming enmeshed in definitional issues about exactly what constitutes improvisation, I first want to reiterate that what I refer to as the band's collective free-form improvisation goes beyond the more common phenomenon of soloists improvising over a more or less fixed rhythmic and chordal structure. Rather, I'm concerned with situations in which all the group members are improvising all together all at the same time, as is common among jazz artists such as Ornette Coleman, John Coltrane, Sun Ra, and the Art Ensemble of Chicago. As R. Keith Sawyer writes, "in jazz, no single musician can determine the flow of the performance: It emerges out of the musical conversation, a give-and-take as performers propose new ideas, respond to other's ideas, and elaborate or modify those ideas as the performance moves forward."[10] And Paul Berliner likens jazz improvisation to both a musical conversation and a journey. He says that players "must take in the immediate inventions around them while leading their own performances toward emerging musical images [and] constantly interpret one another's ideas, anticipating them on the basis of the music's predetermined harmonic events." Berliner could just as easily be discussing the Grateful Dead when he writes:

Without warning, however, anyone in the group can suddenly take the music in a direction that defies expectation, requiring the others to make instant decisions as to the development of their own parts. When pausing to consider an option or take a rest . . . the player must have the presence of mind to track its precise course before adding his or her powers of musical invention to the group's performance. Every maneuver or response by an improviser leaves its momentary trace in the music. By journey's end, the group has fashioned a composition anew, an original product of their interaction.[11]

While Berliner's view of the product of improvisation as "composition" is not universally agreed upon and is in fact controversial,[12] let us keep it in mind as we look at these performances of "Dark Star." While each performance of the song yielded new musical ideas, each one also returned to and recapitulated a number of recurring themes, "maneuvers," and "momentary traces." This unpredictable distinctiveness, coupled with a degree of familiarity, I would argue, was one of the major factors leading to fervent devotion on the part of their fans throughout the thirty years leading up to the death of lead guitarist Jerry Garcia in 1995. Although there were multiple reasons for fan devotion, one of the reasons was because, as Greg Kot has written, they knew that every concert "would be one-of-a-kind."[13] As Doug Collette writes about a nine-CD set of a 1973 run of performances at San Francisco's Winterland Ballroom:

Invigorated by the songs they are playing, the band generate then ride one rush after another, the apogee of which waxing and waning may in fact materialize on the final night in the form of over a half-hour of "Dark Star"; here the band utilizes the theme of the tune only as a touchpoint for free exploration, thereby consummating the run [of concerts] as other performers, thinking in much more narrow terms, devise their individual concerts.[14]

Collette is correct to point out that the band conceived of their overall achievement in much broader terms than just individual concerts; it would seem that they viewed their artistic objectives and achievements in terms, say, of an entire tour of shows rather than by individual shows. Just as each individual concert provided the band with an opportunity to explore uncharted territory, so each concert tour also provided a canvas for developing the band's larger artistic mission and goals. The sheer volume of the band's song repertoire (over a thousand songs), coupled with the infinite possibilities of improvisation, allowed them to conceive their artistic agenda in gargantuan strokes. The numerous iterations of "Dark Star" endure as an intertextual mass, and the endless variations exponentially increased the number of texts and the possibilities of cross-referencing them.[15]

This "touchpoint for free exploration" called "Dark Star," then, provides rich material for the analysis of the performance of collective improvisation. In order to achieve such richly nuanced and varied improvisational "compositions," the band not only practiced the art of onstage non-verbal communication, both aural and gestural, but they also upheld the egalitarian ideals that they lived by early on at their Novato ranch and later at their communal home at 710 Ashbury St. in San Francisco's Haight-Ashbury district. While bassist Phil Lesh has written that Garcia early on emerged as the "undeclared leader" of the band,[16] my performance analysis will show that each of the other core band members also exercised leadership when the band entered what Lesh calls "the zone," the realm of collective musical creation.[17] What emerges from a close reading of this footage, and what I suggest is essential to the success of collective improvisation, is that each core band member (lead guitarist Garcia, rhythm guitarist Weir, bassist Lesh, and drummer Kreutzmann)[18] at different moments can be seen enacting personae that signal, push, and indicate a new direction in the movement of the composition. Each of them also appears willing at various times to cede control and go along with a bandmate's suggested new direction. My interest here extends beyond the band's collective musical creation toward, if you will, an improvised set list. That is, I will not only point out examples of non-verbal communication during the playing of both improvisational music and pre-determined song structures, but will also highlight an instance of the band members non-verbally deciding in the musical moment which song to play next.

Musicologist Rob Bowman has commented on this band's penchant for deciding in the moment the direction that each song sequence will take: "Although the Dead had long been extending individual songs via extensive and wide ranging collective improvisation, 'Dark Star' was one of the first, if not the first, songs that the Dead deliberately left open-ended, each night attempting to ferret out a new avenue via which to eventually segue into another piece."[19] He also points out that the band segued *into* "Dark Star" during this period from a number of songs: "Getting into 'Dark Star' was much less predictable, changing virtually nightly, although some of the nicest versions [including the one on *Live/Dead*] grew out of 'Mountains of the Moon.'" Accordingly, then, since the band's improvisation of the music itself and also the next song to play were both integral aspects of their free-form agenda, my analysis will examine their choices in both of these areas.

Before I begin to discuss the various personae that the core band members enacted in performance onstage and the way they facilitated their collective musical decisions, it will be useful to review Philip Auslander's systematization of Simon Frith's tripartite scheme for the enactment of persona in musical performance. In his essay "Performance Analysis and Popular Music: A Manifesto," Auslander encourages the use of Frith's scheme in the analysis of the performance behavior of popular musicians. He refers to Frith's three layers as: (1) "the real person (the performer as human being)," (2) "the performance persona (which corresponds to Frith's star personality or image)," and (3) "the character (Frith's song personality)."[20] Although Auslander suggests that "sound recordings of musical performances [along with videos] should . . . be considered legitimate objects for performance analysis,"[21] and while contributors to this volume such as Susan Fast and Aida Mbowa have convincingly utilized recorded music for this purpose,[22] I will take advantage of the visual perspective offered by these two performance documents because of the nuances of movement and gesture that they reveal.

Let us begin with some highlights of a live outdoor performance in Veneta, Oregon, from August 27, 1972.[23] As lead guitarist Garcia and bassist Lesh play the unison opening riff of "Dark Star" (1/4: 00:04–00:25) and head into the song's theme (a syncopated A–G progression), we see Garcia attentively facing Lesh and making rhythmic leg movements as the rhythm and tempo of the song's introductory elements stabilize. His repetitive movements establish a short-lived ambience of calm, stability, and consistency. But within seconds, as Garcia begins his improvised lead work (1/4: 00:25), he assumes his default physical position onstage: his body faces toward the audience but his attention is focused almost entirely on the fretboard on the neck of his guitar. The persona he is enacting here, indeed that of everyone in the band, is one of seriousness, of interiority, with a focus on their instruments not unlike Auslander's description of guitarist Jorma Kaukonen, in which he notes that the Jefferson Airplane guitarist "looked only at his left hand on the fretboard while playing his solo."[24]

In case we are tempted to believe that Garcia relies on his ocular focus on the fretboard as a necessary condition for the playing of his melodic lead lines, we then see him turning his gaze "out into space" as he continues to play just as intricately. Clearly, then, Garcia is not dependent on it constantly being within his view. And yet his focus, while physically directed toward the audience, appears to be more inward than outward (1/4: 01:00 ff.). Just a minute later, in fact, he actually turns his back on the audience and begins to walk upstage toward his amplifier (02:00). This action may bring to mind Miles Davis's notorious reputation for turning his back on the audience and the implied scorn or lack of regard that the stance implied.[25] But it is immediately clear that Garcia has done so not to reject the crowd but rather to adjust the knobs on his amplifier. Although his onstage persona does not seem to show great regard for or attentiveness to his audience, it is unlikely that his fans would even begin to take offense at this momentary turning away, especially when it is so apparent that it was to make a technical adjustment. And I would further suggest that Garcia's concern goes beyond the technical; that it is evidence of his seriousness as a musician, and that it conveys his own kind of concern for the audience: he is ensuring that his playing sounds precisely a certain way in terms of volume and/or tone. Although we have no way of knowing what he was thinking as he made these adjustments, one way of reading his actions is to say that he honors his audience's musical discretion by fine-tuning the sound that comes from his amp; he wants to produce the best possible sound for them, and may believe that they can hear the difference.

Soon after, and in a similar spirit, Garcia seems again to shift his focus across the stage toward Lesh, as if to signal a coming change of musical direction. But once again it seems that his concern is for the sound of his guitar: he is turning toward the headstock of his Stratocaster in order to tune the strings. Whereas more theatrical performers seem at times oblivious to technical considerations onstage,[26] Garcia's onstage persona is clearly comfortable and not at all self-conscious when it is necessary to attend to technical matters, especially when the outcome is likely to be the enhancement of his sound. Almost never (with the exception of some slightly out-of-tune notes) does the music suffer as a result of his relaxed and efficient adjustments. Indeed, the slightly out-of-tune notes would hardly be noticeable were it not for our ability to see Garcia attending to the strings.

How then shall we account for the persona being enacted in this close-up of Garcia gazing seemingly into space (1/4: 04:07)? Garcia himself has said on the question of their onstage identities, "We're not performers strictly speaking . . . we're musicians more than anything else."[27] Indeed, he and his mates have not dressed up for the occasion or painted their faces: they're wearing casual jeans and T-shirts; they're dressed as they might be on an average day at home when they are enacting Frith's first level, just being themselves. They play sensible guitars that are not covered in psychedelic paint or glitter. Their enactment of Frith's second-level performance persona has them standing on stage mostly looking down, occasionally at each other, almost never at the audience, and occasionally off into space. They attend to technical adjustments when necessary. It would appear that that they are being themselves onstage, that they are being authentic.

And yet, these musicians are onstage and are unquestionably perform-ing. The fact that they appear as though they are being themselves does not negate or deny their performative state. They are "performing authen-ticity"; they are doing their best to appear like themselves, even though they are actually performing a version of authentic behavior. Although the experience of playing music onstage to thousands of people is undoubtedly different than playing, say, alone in one's living room, the band members (to invoke Richard Schechner for a moment) are not actually being them-selves, and yet they are not *not* being themselves, either. And even alone in one's living room, an implied audience may be present.

A bit further on (1/4: 06:35), we encounter an intriguing frontal per-spective on the entire band: they are facing toward the audience but, again, not visibly interacting with or acknowledging them. The music grows in intensity and fervor, anchored by Kreutzmann's driving beat, and Garcia begins to improvise increasingly aggressive bent two-string chords as he looks intently across the stage (1/4: 07:30). Garcia then initiates the first of two sets of arpeggios that signal coming transitions or changes of direc-tion as the band members make their way toward the non-improvised part of the song: the theme and verse. His visual focus on the other musicians signals the imminent arrival of what Sawyer calls the "group riff" or what I am calling the "Dark Star theme": the syncopated A–G pattern and ac-companying lead melody (2/4: 01:20).

As Garcia settles into the theme and begins to sing the lyrics, he begins to enact Frith's third layer, the enactment of the song personality or char-acter (2/4: 01:40).

> Dark star crashes, pouring its light into ashes.
> Reason tatters, the forces tear loose from the axis.
> Searchlight casting for faults in the clouds of delusion.
> Shall we go, you and I while we can
> Through the transitive nightfall of diamonds?
>
> Mirror shatters in formless reflections of matter.
> Glass hand dissolving to ice petal flowers revolving.
> Lady in velvet recedes in the nights of good-bye.
> Shall we go, you and I while we can
> Through the transitive nightfall of diamonds?[28]

One way to characterize the third-level persona that Garcia is enacting here is to analyze the song's lyrics. Lyricist Robert Hunter employs oxy-moronic imagery in both the song's title and its opening lines. This star is dark, whereas a star by definition gives off light. Or, as David Dodd has written, a dark star is "the brightest of objects, seen as the absence of brightness."[29] Yet this dark star pours "its light into ashes," which presumably extinguishes any of the light it previously possessed. The star is not placed immovable in the firmament but is moving toward an unspecified collision point that obliterates its light. While the imagery of Hunter's first line is a melding of the cosmic ("star") and the earthly ("ashes"), his subsequent focus on "reason" moves the song firmly in the direction of human concerns: "Reason tatters; the forces tear loose from the axis." The dissolution or tattering of human rationality results in a chaotic decentering reminiscent of Yeats's "The Second Coming": "Things fall apart; the centre cannot hold."[30] Human and earthly concerns also dominate the next image of a "searchlight casting for faults in the clouds of delusion." Note here that a searchlight casting about for faults is examining the "clouds of delusion," which inherently contain "fault" since they contain delusion. Once again, Hunter's imagery melds the earthly ("searchlight"), the cosmic ("clouds"), and the human ("faults" and "delusion"). Hunter has said that he was influenced by T. S. Eliot's "The Love Song of J. Alfred Prufrock," which he was reading at the time that he wrote the lyrics,[31] and to his consciously derivative homage he appends a characteristic image that has been embraced as the title for one of the band's live releases ("Through the transitive nightfall of diamonds?").[32] These lines have also been read as an invitation to the listener to engage in the musical journey that the band is about to undergo.[33]

The lyrics do not engage in literal narrative as do song characters like the rogue cowboy of "Me and My Uncle" or the touring musicians of "Truckin'." I would suggest that Garcia's third-level persona in "Dark Star" is that of a beckoning Hunter-esque poet: he is not telling a story, but rather is painting provocative, complex, and multi-faceted images that are entirely consonant with the nature of the instrumental explorations that are integral to the song. In the second verse, as with "reason" and "searchlight," earthly phenomena such as "mirror," "glass hand," and "lady in velvet" give way in each line to abstractions that transcend the earthly or corporeal. Hunter recapitulates his Eliot-inspired line in the refrain, which typifies the song's melding of concrete and earthly with the abstract and imagistic. In enacting these lyrics, Garcia's poet persona delivers perplexing imagery without engaging in eye contact or performative gestures that would explicitly acknowledge the audience's presence. His persona is highly appropriate to the song's lyrical content, as this imagery is challenging to absorb in the moment, and encourages on the audience's part an abstract or, if you will, a "psychedelic" frame of mind that is receptive to the challenging musical ideas that are to ensue.

Moving back to a consideration of performance choices, the band evolves toward an even more intense level of energy and aggressiveness, although continually anchored by drummer Kreutzmann's steady, driving tempo (2/4: 07:00). Suddenly, Garcia makes a decisive move: he walks forward in front of rhythm guitarist Weir, increasing his physical proximity with Kreutzmann and Lesh (2/4: 07:20). Some change appears imminent. Weir himself, momentarily out of the circle of communication, stops for a few moments, takes a deep breath, and looks around, as if to take a brief break and ready himself for a new direction (2/4: 08:05). Garcia observes Weir's pause, then moves decisively toward bassist Lesh, looking intently, nodding, signaling (2/4: 08:15). Kreutzmann slows his tempo almost to a standstill (3/4: 00:18), allowing a transition into a drum solo that Lesh quickly joins in on. Kreutzmann and Lesh here exemplify Berliner's view that "the drummer and bass player must be married," or completely in sync, because they are the "anchor . . . for the more adventurous performances of the rest of the band."[34] Taking full advantage of this "anchor," the rest of the band members insinuate themselves back into the fray to the point where Garcia is once again playing lightning-fast atonal leads that again evolve into frenetic wah-wah leads, then again into shift-signaling arpeggios (3/4: 09:10). Lesh picks up the cue and advances toward a new direction with heavy bass lines that soon evolve into a series of crashing two-string bass chords or "bombs" (4/4: 00:25).

Now an illuminating interaction takes place over the span of about fifteen seconds. Lesh's bombs provide an intersection between improvised music and improvised segue, leading to a momentary misunderstanding on Garcia's part of the direction that Weir has decided to take the band. Weir wants to lead them toward a seamless segue or transition into another song, but he hasn't yet revealed which song he has in mind. He signals his intention to take the lead by facing Lesh and Kreutzmann (4/4: 00:38), then offers a clue by chiming, with characteristic understatement, a soft D chord (4/4: 01:28). His strum is almost inaudible, but it's there. There are a number of Dead songs that begin with a strummed D chord on Weir's part, so things could go in a number of directions at this moment. Perhaps because Lesh is still immersed in his bombs when Weir sounds the D, he does not immediately register the cue and follow up on it. Also, Weir has his back to Garcia, so Garcia is out of the visual loop and has only aural cues to go by. Attempting to rectify his momentary marginalization, Garcia walks over to join the circle of communication, and interprets Weir's strum juxtaposed with Lesh's chords as the introduction to "Morning Dew" and jumps in with his own complementary riff for the "Morning Dew" introduction. Based on what he has seen and heard, Garcia's interpretation is a perfectly reasonable one. In fact, as musicologist Rob Bowman has written, "In 1972, as often as not, 'Dark Star' would give way to 'Sugar Magnolia,' 'Drums,' or 'Morning Dew.'"[35] So a segue into "Morning Dew" is a fair assumption and is entirely consistent with what the band has been doing in that phase of their historical trajectory.

But Weir is not, it turns out, cueing "Morning Dew": he is indicating "El Paso," Marty Robbins's early '60s country-and-western hit that The Dead played 365 times between 1969 and 1995.[36] "El Paso" also begins with a D chord but also incorporates alternating D and A bass notes along with an ascending line from the lower A back up to the D (4/4: 01:38). Kreutzmann immediately picks up on the "El Paso" elements of Weir's cue and kicks in with his distinctive introductory "El Paso" bass drum beat (4/4: 01:40). On hearing Kreutzmann, Garcia immediately realizes he had gotten onto a different track, then jumps right in with his own melodious "El Paso" lead lines on top of Weir, Kreutzmann, and now Lesh too. Garcia shows himself to be more than ready, despite being the "undeclared leader" of the band, to follow what he thought was Weir's suggestion to play and sing "Morning Dew," and is happy to turn on a dime and play "El Paso" as well, once he realizes his bandmate's true intent. Weir threw Garcia a bit of a curveball when he made a surprising choice, but Garcia got on board in no time.

This fifteen seconds demonstrates the extraordinary non-verbal and aural communication—not to mention the cooperative and egalitarian spirit—that the Grateful Dead at their best manifested in the thick of performance. Garcia's alternate interpretation of aural cues and quick realization of and self-alignment with the band's collective direction exemplifies the essential nature of the band's practices. It makes no difference whether they went into "Morning Dew" or "El Paso"—there are no wrong answers. The Grateful Dead embodied a Zen-like sense that there are no mistakes, there are numerous roads to take, and that all roads lead to places worth inhabiting. In the context of the procedures that the band established for itself, the audience may actually expect Weir to forget a lyric (as he frequently did) or the band to need to find its way into a new tune. Moments where band members seem to be going astray should not be seen as errors or missteps. They are, rather, the way the band operates, the way they fulfill their audience's expectations. Such practices are the direct outcome of their apparent aesthetic and philosophy.

In one additional performance example of "Dark Star" six years later, the band demonstrates an entirely different set of moves and reactions.[37] The overall mood of this one is considerably more upbeat. Garcia and Lesh are bobbing animatedly as they move from the opening riff toward the verse. Lesh in particular is smiling, having fun, and moving rhythmically as the initial song structure progresses. Their onstage personae here are far more outwardly performative than in the previous more subdued example of performed authenticity. For one thing, this was the first time in four years that the band had played the song,[38] which might account both for the visible excitement of both Garcia and Lesh and also for what appears to be an actual error on Lesh's part; it's been a while since he's played this song. After Garcia sings the final line of the second verse ("Through the transitive nightfall of diamonds"), Lesh is supposed to play a melodic and transitional bass line that is part of the composed fabric of the song, but he fails to do so. His sheepish facial expression and gesture suggest an immediate realization of his omission, but he quickly jumps to attention, employing physical proximity, eye contact, and bended knees to restore his connection with both Garcia and with the song overall. He smiles broadly at Garcia as if to say, "Whoops, I slipped up, but I'm back in the pocket now," and "Dark Star" proceeds with new assurance.

Despite the prevailing perception of the Grateful Dead as pied pipers of a social phenomenon, I am convinced that the improvisational work done around "Dark Star" exemplifies the abilities that make this band a singular phenomenon in the history of American rock music. While they early on established their ability to create concise song structures, a number of their songs ("Dark Star" being foremost among them) are primarily and essentially vehicles for their singular ability to engage in collective group improvisation, to create nuanced and compelling compositions entirely in the moment through a singular ability to engage in non-verbal, aural, and gestural communication.

NOTES

1. Peter Watrous, for example, writes about a 1992 performance in "Pop and Jazz in Review," *New York Times*, June 18, 1992, 16, that "those moments came where improvisation, the group's distinct sound and the audience all melded." Greg Kot probes more deeply when he writes in "Grateful Dead: Ahead of Its Time," *Chicago Tribune*, August 26, 2009, 6-1, 6-4, that "Fans paid to see multiple shows on the same tour, knowing that each would be one-of-a-kind. . . . The band improvised its way through thousands of shows, and suggested that songs were not immutable

artifacts, but organic entities that could be bent, folded, and occasionally mutilated to suit the needs of the moment."

2. One exception I have found is Steven Skaggs's "'Dark Star' as an Example of Transcendental Aesthetics," which is posted on "The Annotated Grateful Dead Lyrics," accessed June 26, 2012, http://artsites.ucsc.edu/GDead/agdl/ds.html, rather than an academic journal. Skaggs analyzes the experience of "Dark Star" in terms of Eco's *Theory of Semiotics* (by way of Schopenhauer, Croce, Collingwood, and Jakobson), arguing that "the crux of Eco's semiotics of aesthetic experience . . . is exemplified beautifully by . . . 'Dark Star.'" Taking off from Eco's view that ambiguity, rather than "producing pure disorder . . . focuses my attention and urges me to an interpretive effort," Skaggs goes on to discuss a performance of "Dark Star" (February 27, 1969) in some detail in light of the "surprise" that he sees as inherent in Eco's aesthetics as well as the experience of the band's improvisation with each "Dark Star."

3. Nancy Reist, "Counting Stars by Candlelight: An Analysis of the Mythic Appeal of the Grateful Dead," *Journal of Popular Culture* 30, no. 4 (1997): 183–209.

4. Ibid., 183–209.

5. Nadya Zimmerman, "Consuming Nature: The Grateful Dead's Performance of an Anti-Commercial Counterculture," *American Music* 24, no. 2 (2005): 194–216.

6. Jim Tuedio, "Pouring Its Light into Ashes: Exploring the Multiplicity of Becoming in Grateful Dead Improvisation," *The Grateful Dead in Concert: Essays on Live Improvisation*, ed. James A. Tuedio and Stan Spector (Jefferson: McFarland, 2010), 133–51; Jason Kemp Winfree, "'Searching for the Sound': Grateful Dead Music and Interpretive Transformation," *The Grateful Dead in Concert: Essays on Live Improvisation*, ed. James A. Tuedio and Stan Spector (Jefferson: McFarland, 2010), 152–63.

7. Cream performances from 1968 can be viewed on *Cream: Fresh Live Cream*, directed by Martin G. Baker (1968; Image Entertainment, 1993), DVD, and on *Cream—Farewell Concert*, directed by Tony Palmer (1968; Image Entertainment, 1977), DVD. Davis's Isle of Wight concert is available on DVD as well: *Miles Electric—A Different Kind of Blue*, directed by Murray Lerner (1970; Eagle Rock Entertainment, 2004), DVD.

8. Phil Lesh coins this phrase in an interview in the DVD *Classic Albums—The Grateful Dead: Anthem to Beauty*, directed by Jeremy Marre (1967–71; Eagle Rock Entertainment, 1998), DVD.

9. Although this version is just one of 232 that the band performed during its thirty-year career, it is this version that (by virtue of repeated listenings) has become seared in the consciousness of their fans.

10. R. Keith Sawyer, *Group Creativity: Music, Theater, Collaboration* (Mahwah, NJ: Lawrence Erlbaum Associates, 2003), 4.

11. Paul Berliner, *Thinking in Jazz: The Infinite Art of Improvisation* (Chicago: University of Chicago Press, 1994), 348–49. The Dead have at times been compared to jazz musicians. Bill Graham, the rock promoter, often placed them on the same bill as jazz artists such as Miles Davis, and critic Ralph Gleason has referred to them as "really a jazz band" (see Zimmerman, "Consuming Nature," 208).

12. Philip Auslander, in the essay included in this volume, offers a good summary of the various and at times conflicting musicological viewpoints regarding improvisation as a form of composition.

13. Greg Kot, "Grateful Dead: Ahead of Its Time," *Chicago Tribune*, April 26, 2009, 6:1.

14. Doug Collette, *Grateful Dead: Winterland 1973—The Complete Recordings*, posted June 29, 2008, http://www.allaboutjazz.com /php/article.php?id=29832.

15. In the two-CD set *Grayfolded* (1995; Recall Records UK, 1999), John Oswald explored the intertextual possibilities of numerous "Dark Star" performances by "folding" them together into an extraordinary aural mélange.

16. Phil Lesh, *Searching for the Sound: My Life with the Grateful Dead* (New York: Little, Brown, 2005), 135.

17. As Lesh has said in an interview, "We were manifesting this togetherness or this unity or this single organism. And we just grew and grew in that direction. In fact, I still feel that I'm a finger on a hand. We used to [say that] if we could be the finger on a guitarist['s hand], each of us could be one finger playing one rhythm, [and] that would be ideal." *Classic Albums—The Grateful Dead: Anthem to Beauty* (1998).

18. I have not included keyboardist Keith Godchaux as a "core member" in this formulation for two reasons: (1) he was a temporary member of the band throughout the '70s prior to his death in an automobile accident, and (2) while he was a competent musician he was not a particularly assertive one. I acknowledge, however, that Godchaux may well have been influential in ways that are not readily apparent to me.

19. Liner notes to *Grayfolded*, The Grateful Dead, Recall Records UK, 1995.

20. Philip Auslander, "Performance Analysis and Popular Music: A Manifesto," *Contemporary Theatre Review* 14, no. 1 (2004): 6.

21. Ibid., 5.

22. In the book *In the Houses of the Holy: Led Zeppelin and the Power of Rock Music* (New York: Oxford University Press, 2001), Susan Fast writes that "the performer's body is very much present" in Zeppelin's recordings. And Mbowa, in her essay "Abbey Lincoln's Screaming Singing and the Sonic Liberatory Potential Thereafter" (this volume) writes, "To record, to make a record is to make something seemingly ephemeral such as sound into a material object."

23. I invite readers at this point to go onto YouTube (assuming the clips are still available) to familiarize themselves with the performance I am about to discuss. This performance was filmed with the intention of being released as the first feature-length Grateful Dead concert film called *Sunshine Daydream*, but the poor image quality led the band to decide to abandon the project. However, it has long made the rounds among aficionados of the band and is, as of March 2013, available on YouTube. The first of four clips comprising this performance of "Dark Star" can be seen at http://www.youtube.com/watch?v=YLzUme1gN8c. Alternatively, one can search "Grateful Dead Dark Star 1972" on YouTube.com to find these four clips. I will refer to these clips as 1/4, 2/4, 3/4, and 4/4.

24. In Philip Auslander's *Performing Glam Rock: Gender and Theatricality in Popular Music* (Ann Arbor: University of Michigan Press, 2006), 18, he contrasts the flamboyance and theatricality of such glam rockers as Marc Bolan and David Bowie, Ray Wood, and Suzi Quatro with what he calls the "anti-ocularity" or "anti-theatricality" of what he and other writers refer to as "psychedelic rock musicians."

25. See John Szwed, "Miles: The Voice, the Man," *So What: The Life of Miles Davis* (Simon and Schuster, 2002) for an illuminating discussion of Miles's "turning of his back" on audiences and the extensive controversy it engendered.

26. A striking example of a musician who is truly oblivious to technical matters onstage is Marc Bolan, shown in concert in the film *Born to Boogie*, directed by Ringo Starr (1972; Sanctuary Records, 2005), DVD. Bolan's Les Paul, which he wields as though he were a child with a new toy, is horrendously out of tune, but both he and his audience appear neither to notice nor to care; a splendid time is nonetheless guaranteed for all.

27. *Classic Albums—The Grateful Dead: Anthem to Beauty* (1998).

28. As was occasionally the case in certain performances of "Dark Star," Garcia in this iteration never gets around to singing the second verse. But it will be worthwhile to reproduce those lyrics here in order to draw parallels between the song's lyrical and musical content.

29. See David Dodd, "The Annotated 'Dark Star,'" accessed June 26, 2012, http://artsites.ucsc.edu/GDead/agdl/darkstar.html.

30. Willliam Butler Yeats, "The Second Coming," accessed June 26, 2012, http://www.online-literature.com/yeats/780/.

31.

> "Let us go then, you and I,
> When the evening is spread out against the sky
> Like a patient etherised upon a table."

32. *Nightfall of Diamonds: Meadowlands Sports Arena, E. Rutherford, New Jersey, October 16, 1989 [LIVE]* Performed by The Grateful Dead (1989; Arista, 2001), CD.

33. Jurgen Fauth posts in "The Annotated 'Dark Star'" (February 28, 1995) that "the song actually talks about itself; the 'transitive nightfall of diamonds' being the ensuing jam, or to put it the other way 'round, the jam does its best to define the 'transitive nightfall of diamonds' every time the song is played, differently every time. . . . This would make 'Shall we go . . . ' Jerry's (or the implied narrator's) invitation to the listener to join the band on the ensuing musical journey." http://artsites.ucsc.edu/GDead/ agdl/darkstar.html.

34. Berliner, *Thinking in Jazz*, 349, 353. I should point out here that Berliner refers to a standard drums-and-bass configuration of jazz, whereas the usual configuration in the Grateful Dead (and in other bands such as The Allman Brothers) is bassist and two drummers. This concert is unusual in that it took place during a hiatus of the band's second drummer Mickey Hart.

35. Liner notes to *Grayfolded*, 1995.

36. This segue from "Dark Star" into "El Paso" can be seen at http://www.you tube.com/watch?v=pCG-kLnsX2s. Alternatively, one can search "Grateful Dead 1972 El Paso" on YouTube.com.

37. This performance is commercially available on the DVD *The Closing of Winterland*, The Grateful Dead (1978; WEA/Rhino, 2003).

38. According to Bowman, "When they resumed regular touring [following a hiatus] in the summer of 1976, 'Dark Star' was nowhere to be found. In fact, it would not be played again until 1978." Liner notes to *Grayfolded*, 1995.

PHILIP AUSLANDER

Jazz Improvisation as a
Social Arrangement

MY STARTING POINT is an essay by the philosopher Lee B. Brown entitled "Phonography, Repetition and Spontaneity" in which he argues that the repetition of musical performances made possible by recording is "the enemy of improvised music," for which jazz is his point of reference.[1] He argues (as others also have) that recording turns improvised jazz performances into fixed compositions by "transform[ing] an improvisatory process into a depersonalized, structured musical tissue."[2] He further claims that those who listen seriously to jazz are interested not only in the music's sound and structure but also in "a performer's on-the-spot decisions and actions that generate the sonic trail. . . . But this interest is at odds with one of phonography's chief 'virtues,' namely its capacity for repetition."[3] Subjected to repeated listening, recordings of jazz improvisation become wholly predictable, rather than spontaneous, and, ultimately, boring.

Although I sympathize with Brown's desire to assert and preserve jazz improvisation's identity as performance rather than composition, I do not agree with his argument that one can experience jazz as improvisational performance exclusively in live settings because recordings reify improvisation in a way that eventually robs it of interest. Brown's general arguments are vulnerable on several grounds. For one thing, they take for granted a clear distinction between improvisation, on the one hand, and composition and playing from score, on the other, a distinction that is in fact highly problematic. Carol S. Gould and Kenneth Keaton argue, for example, that inasmuch as even the performers of scored music have to make choices not specified by the score, all performed music is improvised to some extent, and, therefore, "jazz and classical performances differ more in degree than in kind."[4] Whereas Philip Alperson argues, like Brown, that improvisation

52

is different from scored playing because it draws our aesthetic attention primarily to actions rather than works, other writers (e.g., Ed Sarath) agree with Brown for different reasons, seeing improvisation and composition as two distinct, perhaps even opposed practices.[5] Still others, by contrast, see jazz improvisations as appropriate subjects of formal analysis and, therefore, as comparable to compositions (e.g., Frank Tirro, Lewis Porter).[6] One can only agree with the ethnomusicologist Bruno Nettl when he writes, "Obviously the relationship of improvisation to composition and notation is a complex one, on which there is no general agreement."[7]

Another difficulty with Brown's argument is that the kind of listening he attributes to consumers of recorded music bears a strong resemblance to "structural listening," a concept derived from the work of Theodor Adorno and Arnold Schoenberg "intended to describe a process wherein the listener follows and comprehends the unfolding realization, with all of its detailed inner relationships, of a generating musical conception."[8] The idea that structural listening is the ideal mode of listening has been roundly criticized within musicology, particularly by Rose Subotnik, and seems out of touch with a world in which "ubiquitous listening," a mode of listening that "blends into the environment, taking place without calling conscious attention to itself as an activity in itself," seems closer to the norm.[9]

Yet another problem with Brown's account of the baleful effects of phonography is his assumption that the listener experiences the same recording so many times, and remembers it so well, that at some point it becomes predictable and dull. While this may be true in principle, Jacques Attali notes that the stockpiling of potential musical experiences made possible by recording means that most listeners own far more recordings than they have time to listen to, let alone grow overly familiar with![10] For the sake of argument, however, I will accept Brown's premises—including the clear distinction between improvised and non-improvised music, and the implicit characterization of the analytical listener who has the time and strength of memory to listen to the same recording until it becomes overly familiar—and offer a counter-argument that addresses a differently problematic dimension of Brown's position.

In another essay, Brown describes the jazz musician's activity and the listener's experience in the following terms.

> In typical jazz improvisations, players can be heard probing and testing possibilities latent in the music they are making. . . . Correlatively, we take a special kind of interest in this activity—in how a performer is faring, so to say. If things are going well, I wonder if the

player can sustain the level. If he seems to be getting into trouble, I wonder about how he will address the problem. When he pulls the fat out of the fire, I applaud—as when Louis Armstrong rushes too quickly, if thrillingly, into the first notes of the introduction in his famous Okeh recording of *West End Blues*.[11]

This account of listening to jazz exemplifies the central problem inherent in Brown's analysis. I agree with Brown's characterization of jazz improvisation as entailing musical exploration and problem solving, and I am not saying Brown has misunderstood the way listeners think about the performance of jazz. The problem, rather, is that Brown assumes that listeners respond the way they do *because they can hear that the music is improvised* (clearly one would not have the same concerns when listening to music heard as composed because one would assume that the composer took the time to solve any problems created by particular compositional choices rather than forcing the musician to solve them in performance). In reality, however, the audience cannot possibly hear improvisation: the fact that music is improvised is not accessible or verifiable through the act of listening. Sitting in a jazz club listening to a brilliant solo, there is no way for me to know whether the musician is actually improvising it on the spot or playing something from memory that was originally improvised on another occasion or composed in the hotel room the night before.

There are, of course, circumstances that arise in jazz performance in which the fact of improvisation seems self-evident and irrefutable. Every jazz fan will have a favorite example; here, I will mention Ella Fitzgerald's performance of "The Cricket Song" at the 1964 Festival Mondial du Jazz Antibes in Juan-Les-Pins, France, in response to the ubiquity of the titular insect's audible chirping during her two-night stand there. Near the end of her set on the second night, expressing something like affectionate exasperation, Fitzgerald, after calling on the band to provide her with a vamp, improvised a song about the crickets whose lyrics allude not only to their presence as uninvited musical partners but also to the fact that she was inventing the song's melody and lyrics on the spot.

I will make two points in reference to examples of this kind. First: despite all evidence to the contrary, it was not possible for Fitzgerald's audience to verify that she was improvising. Keep in mind that she performed "The Cricket Song" on the second night of the gig. Perhaps she had become aware of the crickets' presence on the first night and had cooked up an informal response with her band to be presented as a spontaneous improvisation on the second night. I am not saying this is what happened—it is no part of my purpose here to debunk the idea that jazz musicians improvise or to question Fitzgerald's integrity. All I am saying is that, in principle, there would have been no way for the audience to know the difference between the prearranged "Cricket Song" I have hypothesized and the spontaneous improvisation it undoubtedly was. Second, and more important: Incidents of this kind, while anecdotally entertaining, cannot be treated as normative cases of jazz performance. If jazz audiences had to depend on this kind of evidence to behave as if improvisation is taking place before them, there would be very few instances of improvisation in jazz!

In his discussion of the performance of classical music, Stan Godlovitch makes a useful, if ultimately troubling, distinction between agent performance (what the performer does) and phenomenal performance (what the audience hears). Improvisation is an aspect of agent performance—indeed, a very important aspect, considering how long and hard jazz musicians work both to master the vocabulary of their idiom and to develop an original voice. Improvisation is thus a defining ontological characteristic of jazz. However, Godlovitch's claim that "normally, phenomenal and agent performances are directly and uniformly linked [and, in] such a case, judgments about the phenomenal performance are acceptably transferred to claims about agent performance" does not apply to improvised music because only the musician can know for sure whether or not he is improvising.[12] Since listeners cannot deduce with certainty from the phenomenal performance that the agent is improvising, they are never in a position to forge that link.

I find Godlovitch's distinction between agent performance and phenomenal performance troubling as well as useful because he seems to suggest that performers are the only active parties in the musical process: they are the agents who make music, while the audience's job is to experience what the performer does. Erving Goffman, writing on theatre in *Frame Analysis,* offers a more balanced perception of the performer-audience relationship. Goffman's account is symmetrical: what is true for performers is also true for the audience. For example, Goffman points out that actors on stage have a dual existence: they are there as both actors (that is, real people functioning in a professional capacity) and characters (that is, fictional entities that exist in the world of the play's narrative).[13] This is a fairly unremarkable observation, of course, but things get more interesting when Goffman suggests that spectators, too, are present in a similar dual capacity: as theatregoers (that is, the people who paid for the tickets, are sitting in the seats, etc.) and onlookers (that is, people absorbed into the fictional world of the play as observers).[14] Actors and theatregoers occupy the same plane of reality, while characters and onlookers interact on a different common plane. A straightforward example, from Goffman, illustrates this distinction: if we, as audience, laugh "with" a character who has said something funny, we do so in the status of onlooker, and our laughter is contained within the world of the play. If, on the other hand, an actor makes an embarrassing error and we laugh "at" her, we do so in the status of theatregoer, and the laughter is contained within the "real" world.[15]

This schema is readily adaptable to musical performance. Although I would not argue that the modes of performance involved in playing music are precisely equivalent to acting, it is nevertheless true that musicians appear before us in a dual identity: as real people functioning (like actors) in a professional capacity, and in their personae as musicians, whether the persona requires the flamboyant theatricality of a glam rocker or the decorum of a symphony player.[16] (I shall call the first entity the *musician*, the second the *player*.) The listener, too, takes on a dual identity: first, as *concertgoer* or *clubgoer*, let us say, an entity congruent to Goffman's theatregoer. I shall use the term *listener* to denote the audience role that parallels Goffman's theatrical onlooker. The listener is the version of the audience member that is absorbed into the world of the music and its performance. Even if that world is not fictional (though it can be if we include opera, program music, and highly theatricalized rock performance) it is structured around narratives and, therefore, implicitly dramatic. Brown's description of the jazz listener points in this direction: the listener is absorbed into the player's dramatic struggle with her materials and her ability to improvise successfully. The listener worries about the player's success, cheers her on, evaluates her effort, and expresses appreciation of it. This unfolding drama, and the roles of player and listener within it, take place within a reality that is distinct from that of the professional musician who almost didn't make it to the club because of traffic, and the clubgoer who is still feeling stung by the high cover and two-drink minimum.

Goffman pushes his analysis further to suggest that, in the theatre, playing the role of either character or onlooker equally requires the active and intentional assumption of a specific information state. The character, for example, has to act as if she does not know how the play ends, even though the actor playing her does know.[17] Similarly, "being part of the audience in a theatre obliges us to act as if our own knowledge, as well as that of some of the characters, is partial. As onlookers we are good sports and act as if we are ignorant of outcomes—which we may be. But this is not ordinary ignorance, since we do not make an ordinary effort to dispel it." In fact, "we actively collaborate in sustaining this playful unknowingness."[18]

Even though these particular differential information states are specific to theatre, Goffman's basic concepts provide a workable matrix for thinking about other kinds of performance. Every kind of performance involves an act of collaboration between performers and audience the terms of which are known to all even when they are not expressed overtly. In other words, there is tacit agreement among performers and audiences, and between them, on the "as ifs" that govern behavior on each side and enable performers and audience to collaborate on maintaining the performance. One important "as if" central to jazz performance is that both players and listeners will act as if every solo was a successful improvisation even when they have reason to think otherwise. It is almost unimaginable, for example, that after completing a solo a player might address the audience to say, "Sorry, that really didn't work. Stay for the next set, on me, and I promise to do better." Similarly, it is extremely rare that jazz listeners fail to applaud at the end of a solo, and even rarer that they boo, though there surely are cases in which their opinion of a particular solo does not warrant applause. In other words, part of the social contract between jazz musicians and their audiences is that everyone will behave as if virtually every solo is a worthy achievement, thus exemplifying what Howard Becker calls the "etiquette of improvisation": "The rule in conventional [jazz] improvisation is to treat everyone's contribution as 'equally good.'"[19]

But the most important "as if" of jazz performance is the status of improvisation itself. I am suggesting that the audience experiences jazz improvisation first and foremost as a social characteristic of jazz performance rather than an ontological characteristic of the music. Since the listeners cannot ascertain that the musician is actually improvising they must act "as if" that is the case when witnessing the performance. In this respect, jazz performance is no different from any other social interaction. In *The Presentation of Self in Everyday Life*, Goffman quotes William L. Thomas to the effect that "we live by inference"—we are continually in the position of having to base our understanding of, and actions toward, others on incomplete information and are therefore inclined to take things at face value unless there is a compelling reason not to do so.[20]

The framing of a jazz performance encourages the audience to act as if improvisation is taking place: the word "jazz," associated with both the venue and the performer, suggests that conventionally designated portions of the performance are to be understood as improvisational (e.g., choruses in the case of conventionally structured jazz and almost the whole thing in free jazz). In the spirit of Goffmanian symmetry, I further suggest that the musicians, too, must act "as if" they are improvising. What I mean is that they must engage in the conventional behaviors through which players frame portions of their performances as improvisations to which listeners are to attend in a different way from those moments at which they are playing the composed portions of the music. These may include moving away from other players or a music stand, stepping up to a microphone, displaying effort and concentration through physical posture and facial expression, marking the end of the solo and acknowledging audience response, and so forth. (Improvising jazz soloists are generally aided in this framing by their fellow players, who may act differently toward their peer when she is soloing than when they are playing ensemble passages. They may act, in fact, as if they are caught up in the same dramatic perspective on the soloist that Brown attributes to the listener.)

In order to provide specific examples of the way jazz musicians frame their activity as improvisation, I will briefly analyze a portion of a specific performance of "So What" by Miles Davis, with John Coltrane in his group, joined by members of the Gil Evans Orchestra, from a CBS television program entitled *The Sound of Miles Davis* that aired in April 1959.[21] The musicians in this clip mark moments meant to be perceived as improvisational and distinguish them from moments when they are playing composed music in several ways. For example, Miles Davis underlines the transition from playing the theme to improvising a solo by lowering his trumpet, then bringing it back up to his lips, moistening them, and checking his mouthpiece. Apart from this one instance, he never moves the instrument away from his lips, even between phrases when he might have time to do so. Moving the trumpet down, then back up, clearly reads as a way of segmenting the performance, of emphasizing the transition from playing composed music to improvising.

When playing the theme, Davis looks off to his right, as if he doesn't need to give this task his full attention. When he solos, however, he gazes ahead and somewhat downward, his eyes either closed or fixed in a stare that is not focused on anything, suggesting concentration and inward attention (see figures 1 and 2). He leans backward, arching his back and bending his knees in the pose that became an iconic sign for Miles Davis as seen, for example, in the cover image for the 1970 album *A Tribute to Jack Johnson*. Both his facial expressions and physical demeanor thus differentiate playing composed passages from improvising.

When Davis is finished, he steps aside, allowing Coltrane to take his place on stage. This suggests that stage position contributes to the impression of improvisation. There are, in fact, three regions in this performance, which I will describe on the analogy of areas of a baseball diamond. There

Fig. 1.

Fig. 2.

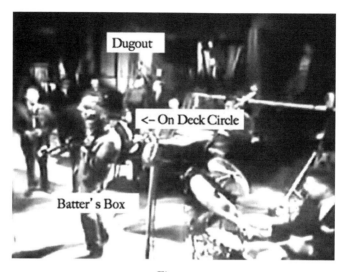

Fig. 3.

is the batter's box, the area in which the mobile soloists (i.e., the horn players, as opposed to the pianist, who also solos in this performance, though
he is positioned quite close to the batter's box) stand while improvising;
the on-deck circle, where Coltrane stands while waiting to solo; and the
dugout, where Davis retires after soloing and where other musicians stand
while waiting to play (see figure 3).[22]

The actions of other musicians also reinforce the status of the soloist
as improviser. When Coltrane is on the "on deck circle," he respectfully
focuses his attention on Davis, though not necessarily by looking at him.
Coltrane's movements of head and body, even his turning away from Davis, denote that he is giving Davis's solo his full, appreciative attention by
following its unfolding (see figures 4 and 5). (Frank Rehak, the trombone
player seen a bit later, also bobs his head to show his enjoyment and understanding of Davis's solo.) Coltrane, when soloing, behaves very similarly to Davis. Though he mostly keeps his eyes closed in an expression
of deep concentration, he too arches his back away from the microphone
as he plays. As he completes his solo, he bends forward, as if bowing, and
starts to move backward, out of the soloist's space, thus relinquishing that
status and passing it on to the pianist. It is worth mentioning that when
performing with his own groups, Coltrane would often stand completely
still when playing the theme, with only his shoulders rising and falling with
his breaths. When improvising, however, he became much more animated,

Fig. 4.

Fig. 5.

bending backward and far forward with facial expressions depicting profound effort and immersion in the moment.

The "dugout" area is a region of the kind Goffman calls "offstage," even though it's in full view. The behavior of the musicians in this area is noteworthy, since it combines the respectful attention to the soloist apparently expected of a musician in the on-deck circle with such seemingly opposite behaviors as smoking and chatting (see figure 6). This combination of engagement and detachment may be at least somewhat specific to the subgenre of jazz being played, since "cool" jazz musicians were sometimes thought to be "emotionally detached from their creation" while simultaneously recognized as virtuosic.[23] The behaviors I have described are both individuated and conventional. They signal the audience to attend to certain passages of music as if they were improvised but provide no guarantee of the actual spontaneity of the music played.

An important feature of Goffman's notion of the "as if" is that it does not depend on belief. The audience does not have to believe that the performer is improvising; it only has to agree to act as if it believes this. Likewise, the performer does not need to persuade the audience that he is improvising; rather, he must persuade the audience to enter into a social interaction in which the definition of the situation is an agreement on all sides to act as if improvisation is taking place. An example from another genre of music may further clarify this point.

> I remember an aging and justly famous star of country music sitting on the edge of the stage with his feet dangling over, thus symbolically breaking through the barrier between himself and the audience, and announcing, "We're gonna be here all night!" We all cheered, even though we knew no such thing was gonna happen; neither the theatre management nor the star's own handlers would allow the performance to run much over its allotted two hours or so.[24]

With jazz improvisation, the audience agrees to act as if something it cannot verify is taking place. In the case of the country singer, the audience agrees to alter its information state and act as if something it knows to be false is true. As an audience, we recognize the claim "we're gonna be here all night" as a convention of a certain kind of performance and realize that, as a statement, it is false on its face. Nevertheless, we maximize our pleasure in the event by agreeing to act as if it were true.

I have to insist that I am not accusing anyone of cynicism here. In no way am I suggesting that improvisation is all a matter of pretense. Presum-

Fig. 6.

ably, jazz musicians are improvising when listeners think they are the vast majority of the time. As Goffman puts it:

> When an individual . . . makes an implicit or explicit claim to be a person of a particular kind, he automatically exerts a moral demand upon the others, obliging them to value and treat him in the manner that persons of this kind have a right to expect. . . . The others find, then, that the individual has informed them as to what is and as to what they ought to see as the "is."[25]

Therefore, when a musician stakes a claim to the identity of jazz player, we, as listeners, respect the claim and treat the person as a legitimate bearer of this identity unless and until something happens to discredit the claim (for example, if I discover that a musician is actually reading notation when supposedly improvising). Improvisation is not simply something musicians do (as Godlovitch's notion of agent performance may suggest). It is, rather, a Goffmanian interactional accomplishment, a collaboration between the musicians and their audiences. It derives primarily from a social arrangement between listeners and musicians in which the appropriate response to a musician's claim to be a jazz player is to agree to act as if she is improvising when she is supposed to be even though that fact cannot readily be verified. The musician, in turn, presents a jazz player's persona that is identifiable by the audience and frames the improvisational moments of the performance differently from the non-improvisational ones.[26]

One virtue of this way of thinking about jazz improvisation is that it precludes the need for the kind of hairsplitting toward which at least some other approaches tend, particularly those emphasizing the uniqueness and spontaneity of improvisation. It is well known that "the jazz improviser reuses and reworks material from previous performances" of the same material and sometimes transfers ideas from one improvisational context to another.[27] This begs the question of spontaneity, since to reuse material developed earlier is not to act fully and exclusively in the present moment of performance. Insisting that uniqueness and spontaneity are necessary conditions for jazz improvisation leads inevitably to threshold questions: How much repetition is possible before something played ceases to qualify as improvisation? If I play essentially the same solo tonight on "I Got Rhythm" as I played last night, perhaps because I want to explore certain musical ideas, but spontaneously alter one note, is that enough to constitute my solo as a unique improvisation? Two notes? And so on. Gould and Keaton have challenged this concept of jazz by insisting that "improvisation is conceptually independent of spontaneity."[28] Whereas Brown and Alperson each emphasize the *temporality* of improvisation, its occurrence and existence only in the spontaneous present moment, Gould and Keaton define improvisation in terms of its *textuality*: "One must view improvisation not in terms of the degree of spontaneity of a performance, but rather in terms of how closely a given performance conforms to the score," understood broadly as any musical model that informs the performer.[29] My argument, by contrast, foregrounds the *social* dimensions of jazz improvisation. As long as both performers and listeners agree to act as if improvisation is taking place, this agreement obviates both the ontological question of spontaneity and the philological question of the relationship between musical text and performance. The pertinent questions are not those concerning spontaneity and uniqueness, nor those concerning the relationship between text and performance, but rather those concerning how musicians and audiences arrive at the necessary working consensus on any given occasion.

With this analysis in mind, I return now to the question of recorded jazz. In at least one respect, live and recorded jazz are identical: one can no more determine whether or not the musician is actually improvising by listening to one than the other. But Brown's concern stems specifically from the ability phonography gives us to repeat, ad infinitum, music that is, in his view, meaningful qua improvisation only in the present moment of its creation. When reduced to a repeatable form, whether a transcription or a recording, it loses its ontological specificity as performance and becomes composition.

My argument that the fact of improvisation is phenomenally inaccessible from live performance and, therefore, that the perception of improvisation arises from the social relationship between performers and audience rather than the formal or ontological characteristics of the music, invites the further supposition that our relationship as listeners to recorded performances works in a similar fashion. In other words, if live jazz performance obliges the audience to act as if the performers are improvising, perhaps recorded jazz imposes the further social obligation to act not only as if the music is the product of improvisation but also as if one is hearing it for the first time each time one plays the recording.

In fact, Goffman specifically addresses the issue of repetition in his discussion of theatre. In his comments on our willingness as theatre spectators to operate as if we were in the information state required by the event, he notes that "those who have already read or seen the play carry this cooperativeness one step further; they put themselves as much as possible back into a state of ignorance, the ultimate triumph of onlooker over theatergoer."[30] If theatre spectators who are already familiar with the material being performed can act as if they are not, for the sake of the integrity of the event, why could not listeners to jazz recordings do something similar? It is possible to view someone listening to a recording as a double entity like the theatregoer/onlooker or concertgoer/listener: in this case, the two roles might be called the *disc jockey* (the one who chooses which recording to listen to, sets up the playback, and so on) and the *listener*, which means the same thing in this context as it does in that of live performance. In parallel with Goffman's account of theatre, acting as if one is hearing an improvisation for the first time every time would represent the triumph of listener over disc jockey.

Brown entertains similar possibilities but rejects them. Discussing the work of the psychologist David Swinney, he examines aspects of memory that may enable listeners to experience afresh things they have experienced before.

> Even though we may know at a higher cognitive level what's coming in the music, at a lower cognitive level we can still experience musical options as open ones. Obviously, these options will be ruled out by the direction the music actually takes as we listen. For an instant, however, we will be kept guessing—at the lower cognitive

level, that is. We are able to savor quasi-suspense, so to say. . . . But the theory doesn't rule out the likelihood of boredom setting in for any music subjected to long-term repetition. The problem is that by the nth time around, the mechanism that kicks in to help make familiar music sound fresh would finally become stale. One would have learned the drill.[31]

Brown identifies another issue specific to recorded improvisation.

The problem is that the Swinney response only has application to our experience of preformed structures to which we have been previously exposed. But improvised music possesses no preformed structure that we could have learned and anticipated. With such music, we're not content with the quasi-suspense described earlier. Rather, we are always on the alert for real surprises. . . . With the repetition that phonography makes possible, we can clearly anticipate the choices a performer is going to make.[32]

Even though Brown provides a good description of the listener's active engagement with the unfolding drama of jazz improvisation, it is clear that he conceives the listener as a fundamentally passive entity whose experience is driven by forces over which she has no control, such as the workings of memory and the inevitability of boredom. This listener yearns for authentic experience—"real surprise" rather than "quasi-suspense"—but has no power to bring it about.[33]

Goffman, by contrast, describes the audience as an active collaborator with the performers in the construction of the event according to a mutually agreed-upon set of subjunctive behaviors—the "as ifs" embedded in their interaction. Summarizing this view, he states, "In the theater, if the cast, the critics, and the audience all play according to the rules, *real* suspense and *real* disclosure can result" even when the material performed constitutes an experience of sheer repetition for some of those involved, including members of the audience.[34] Real suspense or surprise, therefore, is not something performers create for audiences to experience; rather, it results from the collaboration between performers and audience, each of whom plays multiple roles within mutually recognized social frames. I extend this argument not only to musical performances but also to recorded music, to which we assume a listener's role that entails, in the case of jazz, acting as if we are hearing a recorded improvisation for the first time each and every time we listen to it.

This model of listening differs significantly from Alperson's account of the relationship between improvisation and recording. Alperson argues elegantly that, with improvisation, "the object of our attention is not an artifact but the creation of one" and points out that any artifact left behind by an improvisation is "a record of a (unique) action . . . from which we read off, as it were, the original action."[35] Drawing on Goffman's idea that successful participation in a performance as an audience requires acting as if we are in a specific information state even when it differs from our actual one, I am suggesting that listening to recorded jazz requires the assumption of an information state that makes it possible to hear the recording as an improvisation taking place *in the present moment of listening*, not as a document that refers us to an original (past) action. The relationship between listener and recording I have in mind is implied in Walter Benjamin's analysis of "The Work of Art in the Age of Mechanical Reproduction," where he states, "in permitting the reproduction to meet the beholder or listener in his own particular situation, [the reproduction] *reactivates* the object reproduced" (my emphasis).[36] In other words, the recording allows us to restage the performance where we are, so to speak, rather than to travel imaginatively back to its original circumstances. This reactivation results not just from the accessibility of the performance in a reproduced form but also from the audience's willingness to play a socially defined role in relation to it. From my perspective, the crucial point that Brown overlooks is that it is not just the musicians who are performing: the audience, too, performs, and its performance is crucial to the constitution of music—whether live or recorded—as improvised.

NOTES

1. Lee B. Brown, "Phonography, Repetition, and Spontaneity," *Philosophy and Literature* 24, no. 1 (2000): 119.

2. Ibid., 120.

3. Ibid., 120.

4. Carol S. Gould and Kenneth Keaton, "The Essential Role of Improvisation in Musical Performance," *Journal of Aesthetics and Art Criticism* 58, no. 2 (2000): 143.

5. Philip Alperson, "On Musical Improvisation," *Journal of Aesthetics and Art Criticism* 43, no. 1 (1984): 17–29; Ed Sarath, "A New Look at Improvisation," *Journal of Music Theory* 40, no. 1 (1996): 1–38.

6. Frank Tirro, "Constructive Elements in Jazz Improvisation," *Journal of the American Musicological Society* 27, no. 2 (1974): 285–305; Lewis Porter, "John Coltrane's 'A Love Supreme': Jazz Improvisation as Composition," *Journal of the American Musicological Society* 38, no. 3 (1985): 593–621.

7. Bruno Nettl, "Thoughts on Improvisation: A Comparative Approach," *Musical Quarterly* 60, no. 1 (1974): 3.

8. Rose Rosengarden Subotnik, *Developing Variations: Style and Ideology in Western Music* (Minneapolis: University of Minnesota Press, 1991), 150.

9. Anahid Kassabian, "Ubisub: Ubiquitous Listening and Networked Subjectivity," *Echo* 3, no. 2 (2001), http://www.echo.ucla.edu/Volume3Issue2/kassabian/Kassabian2.html.

10. Jacques Attali, *Noise: The Political Economy of Music*, trans. Brian Massumi (Minneapolis: University of Minnesota Press, 1985), 30.

11. Lee B. Brown, "Musical Works, Improvisation, and the Principle of Continuity," *Journal of Aesthetics and Art Criticism* 54, no. 4 (1996): 364–65.

12. Stan Godlovitch, "The Integrity of Musical Performance," *Journal of Aesthetics and Art Criticism* 51, no. 4 (1993): 585.

13. Erving Goffman, *Frame Analysis: An Essay on the Organization of Experience* (Cambridge: Harvard University Press, 1974), 129.

14. Ibid., 129–30.

15. Ibid., 130–31.

16. For a detailed discussion of the centrality of the performance of persona to musical performance, see Philip Auslander, "Musical Personae," *TDR: The Journal of Performance Studies* 50, no. 1 (2006): 100–119.

17. Goffman, *Frame Analysis*, 134.

18. Ibid., 135–36.

19. It is worth noting that, for Becker, respecting the "occupational myth of equality" (172) built into jazz does not yield creative music. It is only when "performers do not interact in a way that respects the conservative etiquette" of improvisation but "agree, implicitly and collectively, to give priority to what, in their collective judgment, works and to give short shrift to what doesn't, and not to be polite about it" (175) that true creativity and innovation can emerge. Howard S. Becker, "The Etiquette of Improvisation," *Mind, Culture, and Activity*, 7, no. 3 (2000): 171–76.

20. Erving Goffman, *The Presentation of Self in Everyday Life* (New York: Anchor Books, 1959), 3.

21. The full lineup for this performance: Miles Davis (trumpet); John Coltrane (tenor sax); Wynton Kelly (piano); Paul Chambers (bass); Jimmy Cobb (drums); Frank Rehak, Jimmy Cleveland, and Bill Elton (trombones). This performance is available on DVD (Miles Davis, *The Cool Jazz Sound*. MBD Video, 2005); numerous clips of it have also been posted to YouTube.com. A shorter version of the performance analysis to follow appeared originally in Philip Auslander, "Musical Persona: The Physical Performance of Popular Music," *The Ashgate Research Companion to Popular Musicology*, ed. Derek B. Scott (Aldershot: Ashgate, 2009).

22. Because it was performed for the camera in a television studio, this performance was staged in an "in-the-round" fashion not at all typical for jazz, in which musicians are usually arranged more linearly and frontally with respect to the audience.

23. Mark C. Gridley, "Cool Jazz," *Grove Music Online*, accessed March 15, 2008, http://www.grovemusic.com.

24. Christopher Small, *Musicking: The Meanings of Performing and Listening* (Middletown, CT: Wesleyan University Press, 1998), 48.

25. Goffman, *The Presentation of Self in Everyday Life*, 13.

26. My suggestion that the perception of improvisation arises from a social arrangement between jazz musicians and their audiences is compatible with other analyses of the social dimensions of jazz. Ingrid Monson, for instance, argues that "improvisational music . . . is a form of social action, as well as a symbolic system; . . . musicians articulate cultural commentary with sound itself" (313). The issue I am addressing here concerns the definition of the situation that precedes the process of communication Monson describes: performers and audience must agree as to what is fundamentally going on before such communication can take place. Ingrid Monson, "Doubleness and Jazz Improvisation: Irony, Parody, and Ethnomusicology," *Critical Inquiry* 20, no. 2 (1994): 313.

27. Tirro, "Constructive Elements in Jazz Improvisation," 286.

28. Gould and Keaton, "The Essential Role of Improvisation in Musical Performance," 145.

29. Ibid., 147.

30. Goffman, *Frame Analysis*, 136.

31. Brown, "Phonography, Repetition, and Spontaneity," 116.

32. Ibid., 117.

33. Although Brown is not alone in suggesting that surprise is an important element of improvisation (Debra Cash agrees, for instance), I am not completely persuaded of its essentiality. Tirro describes jazz solos by saying, "The series of notes may be thought of as a stochastic process, a sequence of notes that occur according to a certain probability system called a style. At any point in time, the present event can be seen to have proceeded from past events. . . . Because both the listener and the improviser are oriented to the schema which limits the probabilities allowable for a solo in a particular style, and since the initial statements in the solo carry implications for what is to follow, prediction and, hence, musical meaning are possible. Listener expectation, analysis, and criticism go hand in hand" ("Constructive Elements in Jazz Improvisation," 288–89). It is my sense as a listener that having one's expectations fulfilled can be just as satisfying as being surprised: there is something very gratifying about predicting where an improvising performer is going to go, only to have that performer go exactly where one predicted! I grant that too high a quotient of predictability in an improvisation may ultimately lead to a negative evaluation; perhaps the ideal lies in striking a balance between the predictable and the surprising. The balance may vary according to specific style: some kinds of jazz conventionally seem to entail a higher degree of improvisational predictability than others. Debra Cash, "Response to Becker's 'The Etiquette of Improvisation,'" *Mind, Culture, and Activity* 7, no. 3 (2000): 177–79.

34. Goffman, *Frame Analysis*, 136.

35. Alperson, "On Musical Improvisation," 26.

36. Walter Benjamin, "The Work of Art in the Age of Mechanical Reproduction," *Illuminations*, ed. Hannah Arendt, trans. Harry Zohn (New York: Schocken, 1968), 221.

NICHOLAS COOK

Bridging the Unbridgeable?
Empirical Musicology and Interdisciplinary Performance Studies

Performative Turns

THE TERM "MUSIC AS PERFORMANCE" has had some currency among musicologists in recent years, but it is more specifically associated with theatre studies: as mentioned in the Introduction, it is the name of a study group within ATHE, the North American Association for Theatre in Higher Education. There are two ways in which this might seem rather odd. First, why might we be talking about music as performance? As opposed to music as what? Whoever thought music might be anything else? And second, why might we find a study group on music as performance in a theatre studies association, rather than its musicological equivalent?

Actually the two questions have a common answer, and it's quite a long story. As also explained in the Introduction, theatre studies is not an old discipline but came into being through the rejection, as an unproductive way to think about theatre, of the idea that meanings are inherent in texts, placed into them by the author and (all being well) recovered by the reader or spectator. By contrast, theatre studies is defined by its focus on the meaning that is generated in the act of performance—meaning that may in some sense or to some degree be prefigured in a dramatic text (you can't make anything mean anything), but at most as a potential to be given specific realization in performance. Seen this way, musicology is like literary studies: an old, one might say unreconstructed discipline. For musicologists, as for the philologists on whom nineteenth-century musicologists modeled their emerging discipline, meaning was again inherent in the text, and the basic musicological task was seen as one of editing, of recovering and interpreting the texts of the past in order to understand the intentions of their creators. Musicology, in short, is built on the premise that music is a branch of literature: like poetry, music can be rendered in performance, but that isn't essential for critical engagement with the meanings embodied in the notated text. Small wonder then that the term "reproduction," generally used to describe the relationship between performances and recordings, has sometimes been used of the relationship between compositions and performances. The English translation of the title of T. W. Adorno's book on musical performance, *Towards a Theory of Musical Reproduction*, is a fair rendering of the German original.

All this is not to say that musicologists are uninterested in performance, and musicology did not remain untouched by the performative turn that spread through many cultural disciplines in the last decades of the twentieth century. But because of its basic identification of music with writing, musicology's performative turn took some rather strange forms. One was the authenticity or "historically informed performance" (HIP) movement that developed from around 1970, which advocated new styles of performing early music on the basis of sometimes suspect evidence of period performance practices or even more suspect evidence of composers' intentions. Since the evidence in question was produced by musicologists and based on documentary sources, the net effect was to subjugate the practice of performance to the regime of scholarship and the written word.

Much the same might be said about another of the strange forms which the performative turn took, now in the subdiscipline of music theory: what might, by analogy with the authenticity movement, be termed analytically informed performance. As illustrated by Wallace Berry's *Musical Structure and Performance* (which won the 1992 Outstanding Publication Award of The Society for Music Theory), this approach took conventional, score-based analysis as its starting point: the purpose of Berry's book was to show "how . . . a structural relation exposed in analysis can be illuminated in the inflections of edifying performance."[1] The flow of signification is in this way from analysis to performance, from text to act, from page to stage. Practice is subordinated to theory, establishing a hierarchy that is regularly enacted on North American conference platforms where a (probably tenured) theory professor explains how the music should go, and a singer or instrumentalist (probably on a fixed-term contract) demonstrates it.

Given the textualist paradigm that is deeply embedded in musicological thinking, it is not so surprising that people working in theatre studies saw the need to take matters into their own hands. Philip Auslander, who founded ATHE's "Music as Performance" group, had musicologists (including, as it happens, myself) in his sights when he argued that "it does not necessarily follow that simply because the verb *to perform* demands a direct object, that the object of performance must be a text such as choreography, a dramatic script, or a musical work."[2] He proposed a starting point for understanding performance that was diametrically opposed to Berry's: "to be a musician," he claimed, "is to perform an identity in a social realm."[3] By this Auslander does not mean the performer's everyday identity: he means what he terms the performer's "persona," an identity *as a performer* that is constructed through the act of performance, or through successive acts of performance. This approach is diametrically opposed to Berry's not only because of the focus on persona rather than work, but also because it involves a meaning that emerges from performance rather than a predefined meaning reproduced in performance. It also gets away from the abstract and metaphysical aesthetics that surrounds musicological discussions of works and reproductions: "to think of music as performance," Auslander concludes, "is to foreground performers and their concrete relationships to audiences, rather than the question of the relationship between musical works and performance."[4]

What Auslander means by "persona" is self-evident in the case of popular music: artists like Madonna and (the one previously known as) Prince have a stage identity which persists across their performances, subject to occasional or continuous reinvention, and which has no necessary relationship to their everyday identities. But in no way is persona something restricted to popular music. It applies just as readily to, for example, the legendary pianist Arturo Benedetti Michelangeli, perhaps the only artist to have advanced his career through his equally legendary concert cancellations—which only added to his romantic mystique, his quality of unattainability. One can see the construction of this persona taking place in real time in some of his filmed performances. For example, a television film of Michelangeli playing Chopin's Mazurka op. 33, no. 4, made in 1962, shows his elaborate preparations before he begins playing. He wipes the keyboard up and down with his handkerchief and then mops his cheeks. He puts his handkerchief down, and then clasps his hands together with the washing-like motion traditionally associated with clergymen and the best butlers. He rubs his right hand on his thigh, and then, with his wrist bent down, brings it smartly up to a position a few inches above his keyboard. He flicks his fingers forward and out (figure 1) before letting his hand fall in a measured descent to the keyboard to sound the first note.

Traditional musicological approaches, following the nineteenth-century

Fig. 1. Arturo Benedetti Michelangeli, about to play the first note of Chopin's Mazurka op. 33, no. 4, from a 1962 television film (RAI Turin recording, Opus Arte OA 0940 D)

aesthetics of absolute instrumental music, force a distinction between the "musical" and the "extra-musical," where the "musical" is essentially defined in terms of notation: everything that Michelangeli does before he plays the first note, then, falls into the category of the "extra-musical," from which it is but a small step (and one that musicologists and traditional aestheticians readily make) to dismiss it as self-indulgence or showmanship. Interdisciplinary performance studies acknowledges no such distinction: as the drama theorist Baz Kershaw observes, "it is a fundamental tenet of performance theory . . . that no item in the environment of performance can be discounted as irrelevant to its impact."[5] Michelangeli's performance makes Kershaw's point. His elaborate preparations heighten anticipation of the performance to follow. But they also have a ritualistic quality, aligning the playing of op. 33, no. 4 with the performance of some religious office, and presenting the pianist as the celebrant, as the representative of a higher power. Layers of meaning are unfolded in real time, and converge upon the persona that the performance sustains. In terms of the impact to which Kershaw refers, it is clear that the performance began long before Michelangeli played the first note.

Empirical Approaches: For and Against

I mentioned two of the forms which the performative turn took in musicology. A third has come increasingly into prominence since around 1990: what, by analogy with close reading in literary studies, might be termed close listening to recorded performances. At first this was generally done by ear, supplemented by the kind of simple measurement (for instance of average tempo over a given section) that could be carried out using a stopwatch, pencil, and paper: this is how Robert Philip researched his book *Early Recordings and Musical Style: Changing Tastes in Instrumental Performance, 1900–1950,* which in effect launched the musicological study of classical performance through recordings. More recently increasing use has been made of technology: spectrograms have been used to highlight details of vocal inflection, for example, while onset times and dynamic values have been extracted and graphed. In the most elaborate work, large quantities of such data, collected from many different recordings, are analyzed mathematically, in the hope of characterizing performance styles and the relationships between them. Such work builds on approaches developed within music psychology, for example by Bruno Repp, and sits across the tectonic plates of psychology, musicology, and MIR (music information retrieval). As a result it easily suffers from the problems characteristic of interdisciplinary studies: misunderstandings typically occur when scholars from different disciplines talk about the same things, but with different intellectual aims and epistemological assumptions. And when work of this kind attempts to make connections between empirical data and cultural interpretation—when it attempts to be not only empirical but also musicological—it is open to attack from both sides: from scientists for its lack of analytical rigor, and from musicologists for its naivety in matters of cultural construction and critical reflexivity. But just for that reason, it makes a revealing case study in the relationship between what might be broadly termed scientific and cultural approaches to music, and indeed to performance more generally.

As an example, a recent project at CHARM (the AHRC Research Centre for the History and Analysis of Recorded Music)[6] used empirical methods of the kind I have described to investigate phrase arching in a large corpus of recordings of Chopin's Mazurka op. 63, no. 3. *Phrase arching* refers to the tendency for performers to get louder and faster as they play into a phrase and softer and slower as they come out of it, and it has generally been seen as an essential component of musically expressive playing. The psychologist Neil Todd, for instance, not only developed a math-

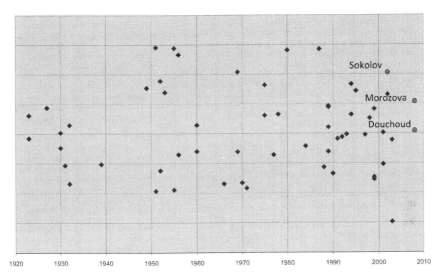

Fig. 2. Phrase arching in recordings of Chopin's Mazurka op. 63, no. 3, bars 1–16, arranged by date of recording (higher in the chart means stronger phrase arching)

ematical model of phrase arching but also suggested that it drew upon the general cognitive mechanisms underlying the sense of self-motion: that, he says, is why phrase arching sounds so "natural."[7] But does the heritage of recordings support this? The method adopted in the CHARM study was to extract tempo and dynamic information from the recording, and to analyze it for evidence of phrase arching—that is, arch-shaped profiles that appear both in tempo and in dynamics, and that are coordinated with the composed phrasing. A formula was developed that modeled the strength of phrase arching, and figure 2 shows the results set against the date of recording. As can be seen, the kind of fully coordinated phrase arching described by Todd, as represented by high values in figure 2, is by no means universal: it does not appear at all until after the Second World War, and performances involving little or no phrase arching have persisted to the present day. In short, phrase arching is a historical style, and also to some extent a geographical one, particularly associated with Russian or Russian-trained pianists.

Empirical work of this kind has obvious advantages: it makes it possible to test the often sweeping claims that are made about performance style, generally based on close listening to a small number of representative examples. (The ear is a malleable organ, so that you tend to hear what you expect to hear, and besides, you cannot know what examples are representative unless you already know all the others.) But empirical approaches are also open to some quite powerful objections. Perhaps the most fundamental is that it gives a new lease on life to musicological textualism: recordings are taken out of context and analyzed as self-sufficient objects rather than as the traces of human actions in specific social and cultural situations. Robert Philip points out how, in extracting features from recordings, empirical analysis can leave behind essential aspects of the phenomenon supposedly under investigation:

> A computer can measure accelerations and decelerations, but to the listener these have different qualities. An acceleration can seem impulsive, or uncontrolled, it can seem to be aiming precisely at a target, or to be dangerously wild. It can seem spontaneous or calculated. A deceleration can seem sluggish, calming, boring, cumulative, climactic. You can't easily measure such qualities, but they are what create the narrative of events. . . . Simply measuring tempo is only a starting point for understanding these things.[8]

Most people working in empirical musicology would probably agree with Philip's final point, and the problem with early work in this field was that it tended to extract and analyze data without going back in any useful manner to the experience of the music. With the development of more sophisticated software for working with recordings,[9] however, tempo graphs and other analytical visualizations can be incorporated into the playback environment: that makes it much easier for the analyst to link measurements with qualities, to borrow Philip's terms, so heightening perceptions, guarding against our tendency to hear what we expect to hear, and facilitating discussion of performance details.

And this suggests a response to some of the more sweeping objections that have been made against this kind of work. Richard Taruskin is targeting all musical analysis—score-based as well as performance-based—when he complains that "turning ideas into objects, and putting objects in place of people, is the essential modernist fallacy—the fallacy of reification. . . . It fosters the further fallacy of forgetting that performances, even canned performances, are not things but acts."[10] What Taruskin overlooks in saying this is that the function of musical analyses—whether Schenkerian voice-leading reductions or tempo graphs—is to prompt the kind of analytical listening I just described: in this way analyses, like performances, are themselves not things but acts. One might indeed complain that Taruskin has himself put objects in place of people, the people in this case being analysts. Yet the issue of reification is not so easily disposed of. Philip himself has related doubts:

> One of the things that recordings encourage us to do is to compare performers and performances. . . . It's a fascinating exercise, and it would be impossible without recordings. But I do begin to wonder whether this sort of comparison is wholly beneficial. Like so much to do with recordings, it diminishes the intentions, the meaning, the values, of the individual performance and performer.[11]

It is then the performer as agent who all too easily disappears from performance analysis, as illustrated by music theorists' page-to-stage approach and view of performance as reproduction, or by Todd's substitution of a mathematical model for the expressive performer. An obvious way to put performers back into the study of performance is to adopt participant-observational and other broadly ethnographic approaches, and within musicology such approaches have proliferated in just the last few years. (These approaches, of course, are also empirical, though in this essay I am applying the term to more narrowly quantitative approaches.) Much of this developing work is located in conservatories, whose research profile it helps to raise; in the United Kingdom, another institutional expression of this change is the transformation of CHARM, the bulk of whose research involved computational approaches, into its successor center, CMPCP (the AHRC Research Centre for Musical Performance as Creative Practice, based at the University of Cambridge),[12] the main focus of which is ethnographic analysis of live performance.

Another way to describe this development is in terms of a convergence between musicology and ethnomusicology, and here there is a particularly instructive precedent in the collaboration between the musicologist Peter Jeffery and the ethnomusicologist Kay Shelemay. Seeking to make sense of early chant notations, Jeffery reasoned that these represented the traces of a largely aural/oral culture, and that essential clues as to their interpretation could be gained from the study of present-day aural/oral cultures elsewhere in the world:[13] in this way ethnographic evidence could be bought to bear on the interpretation of texts. And Ingrid Monson, who studied with Shelemay, applied a similar approach to recorded music, bringing both her ethnographical training and her own experience as a trumpeter to bear upon contemporary jazz: her book *Saying Something: Jazz Improvisation and*

Interaction consists largely of close readings which focus precisely on the human actions and interactions, the real-time negotiations of agency, of which recordings of jazz form the traces. As my use of the term "reading" implies, such work might be said to constitute the recording as a kind of text, but that need not imply reification. Human agency, in short, is present in performances (even, in Taruskin's disparaging term, canned performances), if you know how to hear it.

A Marriage of Opposites

But is it possible to imagine that objective measurements and computational analysis could in any way contribute to the characterization of human agency in performance—in Philip's words, of the intentions, the meaning, the values of individual performers? I shall argue that the answer is yes, and to make my case I return to Chopin's Mazurka op. 63, no. 3, now supplementing my previous analysis with the evidence of performance context provided—in however partial or mediated a form—by video recordings. Grigory Sokolov performed this mazurka on November 4, 2002, at a packed concert held in the Théâtre des Champs-Élysées, Paris (where it was the first of five encores), and there are essential aspects of his performance that are prominent in Bruno Monsaingeon's film of the concert but would be absent from a CD. Monsaingeon writes in the liner notes that, at the start of concert, "suddenly a massive shadow appears who moves swiftly over to the keyboard, the only brightly lit surface to stand out from the large coffin-like box in the centre of the stage." This sense of the massive, almost Russian bear-like form with the fluid movements and delicate touch is part of the experience you carry away from the performance. Someone posted this track to YouTube, where many viewers addeded complimentary comments, but one of the critical postings has to do with the way Sokolov's hands fly up after he plays certain notes, almost like a marionette:

> Is a pitty a pianist who sometimes play wonderful, but sometimes his kind of "maniac" way to play the piano(Technicaly) makes hime to make some musical mistakes,specially that one of make some values shorter than they really are, owed to his "mania" of quit hands so fast from keyboard. I don't understand some very good artists who have a so big lack of self control.[14]

A more positive way to make the same point would be that Sokolov uses visible gestures to make musical points. He sways as he plays and alters his posture in a manner that is at least partly coordinated with the music, but it goes further than that. He creates accents through dynamic or agogic emphasis, or through articulation, as all pianists do, but he also does so by means of the "quit hands" gesture: his right hand flies up as soon as he has attacked the note, clipping it visually and so throwing weight onto the following note (figure 3). Again, he shapes notes after he has played them: on the first right-hand note of bar 7, for instance, he keeps his finger on the depressed key while he twists his palm to the right and back again, so lending it a visual quality of sustained shaping that is cross-domain mapped to the auditory sphere. The effect of sound and sight working together in this way is to create a lyrical effect that that is none-the-less real, none-the-less *musical*, for not being present in an audio-only recording. And within this performance Sokolov is fairly consistent in his use of these gestures. When sections repeat, he generally (though not invariably) repeats the gestures, just as he generally (but not invariably) repeats nuances of tempo, dynamics, and articulation; for instance he shapes the first note of bar 15 in very much the same way as at bar 7. Only a fetishization of what is conveyed by LPs and CDs, or the lingering effects of nineteenth-century aesthetic ideologies, could lead one into thinking that these gestures are in any meaningful sense extra-musical. On the contrary, in line with Kershaw's assertion that "no item in the environment of performance can be discounted as irrelevant to its impact," it might be said that the concept of the extra-musical is simply inapplicable to performance.

Watching Sokolov, it becomes clear how little of performance gesture is determined by the mechanics of keyboard performance, and in consequence how much is freely available for shaping and giving meaning to music in performance. It stands to reason, then, that performers in other YouTube videos of this mazurka deploy gesture to create very different effects. I shall describe just two. One is from a solo recital given at the Mannes College of Music, New York, in January 2008: the performer is Irina Morozova, who teaches in the College's Preparatory Division.[15] While Morozova has her own repertory of expressive gestures, the predominant quality of her performance is a detached, almost dream-like quality that she creates both through touch and tempo, and by the way she lifts her gaze upward at particularly expressive points (figure 4)—an established signifier of the sublime that is instantiated in any number of record sleeves.[16] Quite different again is a performance by Julien Duchoud, given in June 2007 at the Chateau de Ripaille, Haute Savoie (France). An audience member has posted a comment on the YouTube website:

Fig. 3. Grigory Sokolov performing Chopin's Mazurka op. 63, no. 3 on
4 November 2002, at the Théâtre des Champs-Elysées, Paris (Grigory
Sokolov Live in Paris, Ideale Audience International Naïve DR 2108 AV
127)

Fig. 4. Irina Morozova playing Chopin's Mazurka op. 63, no. 3 at the
Mannes School of Music, New York, on 7 January 2008 (http://www.
youtube.com/watch?v=e8BQc5ww QGU, accessed 14 February 2010)

Fig. 5. Julien Duchoud playing Chopin's Mazurka as an encore at the Chateau de Ripaille, June 2007 (http://www.youtube.com/watch?v=UflK-veX7Fk, accessed 14 February 2010)

It was a wonderful concert in the old French castle! The public was touched by emotions, no one seemed to be indifferent. Everyone could appreciate such a splendid, sensual and bright playing! Chopen's mazurka sounded very nostalgically and its polish motives were performed with the special skill by this young pianist.[17]

The intimacy of the occasion can be both heard and seen on the video. The audience sits close to the pianist, who plays from the score—something that immediately separates him from the virtuoso tradition in which memorization is *de rigueur*. The room is dimly lit, but an ordinary desk lamp, placed on the piano, throws a pool of light on the music (figure 5). And perhaps because Duchoud is playing from the score, rather than rehearsing an overlearned sequence of actions, his performance is marked by a freedom in tempo that gives it a quality of extemporization; you have the impression that he might play the music quite differently if the audience reacted differently. This further serves to bind player and listeners into the shared temporality of the occasion, so strengthening the sense of community that is reflected in the YouTube posting.

And this is where the empirical analysis of phrase arching comes into play. All these pianists may be found in figure 2, but in very different positions. Duchoud makes little use of the kind of coordinated phrase arching described by Todd: detailed analysis[18] shows that there are some elements of both tempo and dynamic phrase arching in his playing (which is why he appears around the middle of the chart), but they are not coordinated with one another. In this respect Duchoud's playing might be compared with that of early twentieth-century pianists such as Ignaz Friedmann, whose recordings convey to an even greater extent than Duchoud's a quality of gestural immediacy, a sense that the music is being unfolded unpredictably from moment to moment: it is as if the shared temporality to which I referred is being generated on the fly in the course of performance. By contrast, Morozova and Sokolov both exemplify the Russian tradition of phrase arching (both, as it happens, trained at the St. Petersburg [Leningrad] Conservatory), and this links with immediately perceptible aspects of their performance. I referred to the detached quality of Morozova's playing, relating it to the way she lifts her gaze at expressive points, but of course it is inherent in the sound too: the effect of phrase arching is to displace the locus of expression, transferring it from the evolving, moment-to-moment course of performance to the larger, more architectonic level of phrase structure. The extemporaneous effect disappears; the expressiveness remains, but it no longer seems so subjective, because it is now perceived as a dimension of the music itself, conveyed rather than created by the performer. And this gives a greater sense of formality to the occasion, creating a separation of performer and audience even within the modest dimensions of the Mannes College recital hall.

With Sokolov it goes further, much further. He is, of course, playing in a much larger space than either Duchoud or Morozova. But public performance in the virtuoso tradition is encoded into the very fabric of Sokolov's playing. The space between him and the audience has now become an unbridgeable gulf: like Michelangeli he is unattainable, mythical. One might liken the performance to a celebration of the Eucharist seen from afar in a great cathedral, or to an acrobatic display in the big top, but either way it is hard to imagine audience reaction having any impact on Sokolov's interpretation: he is giving a show, a show he has no doubt given on many previous occasions (remember this is an encore). And phrase arching, of which figure 2 shows Sokolov to be a fairly extreme exponent, lies at the heart of this. The slow, predictable oscillation of tempo and dynamics, synchronized with one another and with the formal patterning of the music, creates an immensely strong framework for the performance. It is the over-engineered scaffolding which supports the gorgeous drapery of Sokolov's extraordinarily extravagant performance—a performance that brings to the classical concert hall a choreography hardly less intricate in its conception and finely honed in its execution than one might expect to see at the ballet. Empirical analysis, in short, helps to clarify the mechanism underlying the immediately perceptible effect of Sokolov's performance, and at the same time sets it into the context of the very different performances that other performers, at different times and places, have fashioned out of "the same" music.

In Conclusion

Performance of work or performance of persona? In the passage I quoted earlier, Auslander spoke of the need to "foreground performers and their concrete relationships to audiences, *rather than* the question of the relationship between musical works and performance" (my emphases). Elsewhere in the same article he remarks, more liberally, that "in the schema I am proposing, both the musical work and its execution serve the musician's performance of a persona."[19] But I see no need for such a hierarchy between persona and work. To be sure, what happened before the Parisian audience on 4 November 2002 was a performance of Sokolov's uniquely virtuosic persona, a performance marked by the mystique, massive physique, and delicacy that are keyed in the official biography on his agent's website: "Sokolov has gained an almost mythical status amongst music-lovers and pianophiles throughout the world. . . . Sokolov has amazed everyone again and again with the enormous breadth of his repertoire and his huge, almost physical musical strength. . . . His interpretations are poetic and highly individual, and his rhythmic freedom and elasticity of phrase are perhaps unequalled among pianists today."[20] But Sokolov was performing Chopin's Mazurka op. 63, no. 3 too, which is to say not only that he was performing that particular composition but also that he was performing Chopin and playing a mazurka. And in playing a mazurka, the genre that has long been regarded as uniquely Polish, he was performing Polishness, or perhaps a Russian appropriation of the Polish. At the same time, like the celebrant of the Eucharist, he was performing his own embeddedness in tradition, perhaps even a certain confession of faith. In this way, the list of things Sokolov was performing—the list of the possible objects for the verb "to perform" in any performance—is indefinitely long. It is always possible to think of one more thing that is being performed, one more meaning that is emerging in the act of performance.

Performance, then, is an indefinitely multi-layered and complex phenomenon, the multiple aspects of which demand multiple analytical perspectives. In this essay I have focused on two approaches that come from

quite unrelated academic traditions and might be seen as diametrically opposed, but I hope to have shown how they can be productively brought
together: the approach of interdisciplinary performance studies helps to
clarify what performances mean, while more empirical approaches help
to clarify how performances mean what they mean. In the absence of
firm contextualization, the grounding of data in experience, empirical approaches all too easily lose purchase on the issues of social and cultural
meaning that form the core focus of musicology; conversely, descriptive,
experience-oriented approaches can gain definition from the incorporation of empirical data, which also helps to avoid the danger of critical cir-
cularity, whereby perception engenders expectation and expectation conditions perception. The triangulation of different disciplinary approaches, in
short, may create risks of misinterpretation, but it also creates the potential
for significant added value. And with as complex and indeed intractable a
phenomenon as performance, enacted under the exacting constraints of
real time and constantly poised on the brink of irrationality, we need every
interpretive weapon in the armory—and then some.

NOTES

1. Wallace Berry, *Musical Structure and Performance* (New Haven: Yale University Press, 1989), x.

2. Philip Auslander, "Musical Personae," *Drama Review* 50, no. 1 (2006): 101.

3. Ibid., 101.

4. Ibid., 117.

5. Baz Kershaw, *The Politics of Performance: Radical Theatre as Cultural Intervention* (London: Routledge, 1992), 22.

6. Based at Royal Holloway, University of London, from 2004 to 2009; see
www.charm.rhul.ac.uk.

7. Neil Todd, "The Dynamics of Dynamics: A Model of Musical Expression,"
Journal of the Acoustical Society of America 91, no. 6 (1992): 3549.

8. Robert Philip, "Studying Recordings: The Evolution of a Discipline,"
keynote paper at the CHARM/RMA conference "Musicology and Recordings"
(Egham, Surrey), September 2007, http://www.charm.rhul.ac.uk/content/events/r.
philip_keynote.pdf, 9.

9. Such as Sonic Visualiser (http://www.sonicvisualiser.org/).

10. Richard Taruskin, *Text and Act: Essays on Musical Performance* (New York:
Oxford University Press, 1995), 24.

11. Robert Philip, "Studying Recordings," http://www.charm.rhul.ac.uk/con
tent/events/r.philip_keynote.pdf, 7.

12. www.cmpcp.ac.uk.

13. Peter Jeffery, *Re-Envisioning Past Musical Cultures: Ethnomusicology in the
Study of Gregorian Chant* (Chicago: University of Chicago Press, 1995).

14. Posting by vtpiano7, accessed March 28, 2008, http://www.youtube.com/

watch?v= LOpW8hlvZzk. This page is no longer available owing to a copyright claim.

15. The video is at http://www.youtube.com/watch?v=e8BQc5wwQGU; Morozova's biography is at http://www.newschool.edu/mannes/facultyPreparatory Division. aspx?mid=4810, accessed January 31, 2009.

16. For an example, see the sleeve from Kathleen Ferrier's recording of *Das Lied von der Erde* (Decca LXT 5576), reproduced in Nicholas Cook, *Music: A Very Short Introduction* (Oxford: Oxford University Press, 1998), 33.

17. Posting by rozanasnegu, accessed February 1, 2009, http://www.youtube. com/comment_servlet?all_comments&v=UflK-veX7Fk&fromurl=/watch%3Fv %3DUflK-veX7Fk; the video is at http://www.youtube.com/watch?v=UflK-veX7Fk.

18. Using the methodology set out in Nicholas Cook, "Squaring the Circle: Phrase Arching in Recordings of Chopin's Mazurkas," *Musica Humana* 1, no. 1 (2009): 5–28.

19. Auslander, "Musical Personae," 102.

20. http://www.amcmusic.com/eng/bio/bio_grigory_sokolov_eng.pdf (Artists Management Company, Verona, Italy).

PHILIP GOSSETT

The Written and the Sung

Ornamenting *Il barbiere di Siviglia*

THERE IS AN EXTREME BRANCH of performance studies in which singers are believed to "subvert" the "text" of an opera, in which their participation is believed to transform a "work" in ways of which the composer might or might not have approved. (I am most emphatically not referring here to staging but to the actual music an audience is hearing.)[1] Sometimes, however, a composer's attitude might surprise us.

Although it is true that Victor Maurel, Verdi's first Iago and Falstaff, for example, was a very independent-minded singer, Verdi nonetheless wanted *Maurel* for the title role of his last opera. And when Maurel took it upon himself to introduce multiple encores of his one-minute aria (the descriptive term "aria" is of dubious value in this context), "Quando ero paggio," the last of which he tended to sing in his native French, the composer, much to the surprise of his more "faithful" interpreters, was delighted. As Verdi wrote to Arrigo Boito on 14 March 1894, "Why in a comic opera should one not write a light-hearted and brilliant passage? . . . It's written well for the voice: it's orchestrated lightly; it allows all the words to be heard without being disturbed by the usual orchestral counterpoints. . . . What is the harm if it is therefore popular?!! . . ."[2] But when Maurel went a step further and introduced cuts in his part, the irritated composer wrote to his editor, Giulio Ricordi, on 1 June 1894: "They ask me furthermore if I have authorized these cuts! Ah no! ah no! I can accept, without displeasure, that my operas aren't performed; but if they are performed I want them done as I imagined them. For this reason I turn to you, my editor, and I invoke the contract that exists between us about this relationship. Declare, then, in my name, to the directors of the Opéra Comique that they must perform *Falstaff* in its entirety, as it was the night of the first performance."[3] It was

Walt Whitman, singing of himself, who said: "Do I contradict myself? / Very well then I contradict myself, / (I am large, I contain multitudes.).["4]

Some forty years after "authors" were pronounced dead by French critics, they remain with us, a stubborn coterie of persons who refuse to be consigned to the dustbin of history. Yet we have all been sufficiently sensitized to the problems raised by Roland Barthes, Michel Foucault, and Jacques Derrida to know that simplistic views of the "text" are no longer possible. Paul Eggert has tried to cope with these problems in part by substituting the concept of "document" for that of "text," while problematizing the efforts of textual scholarship in new and original ways.[5] I tried to do similar work in *Divas and Scholars* when I substituted "Verdi's *Rigoletto*" as a descriptor of the primary source of that opera without seeking to invoke metaphysical visions of where the REAL *Rigoletto* may be located.[6]

It is clear that authors and composers took an ever greater role in trying to control their more highly defined texts during the later nineteenth and twentieth centuries. (Who can forget Stravinsky's spirited refusal on 14 October 1937 to allow Ernst Ansermet to introduce *any* cuts whatsoever into orchestral performances of his *Jeu de cartes*: "I cannot let you make cuts in *Jeu de cartes*! I think it is better not to play it at all than to do so reluctantly.")[7] Whether they were successful is a matter of continued debate in the professional literature. For earlier periods, however, it is plausible to assert for music—at the very least—that compositions were not normally conceived by their "creators" independently of other musicians who would realize these compositions (in various manners) in performance. There was no separation between a "text" and a subverting performer, because "texts" were not written as full realizations but as what my colleague Ellen Harris (working on the operas of Händel) has called "recipes."[8] It is only by using what is written together with a set of procedures developed by composers collaborating with performers, by performers themselves, or by performers working with their personal coaches or other musicians that a "recipe" can become a product presentable to the public and can even be called (however dangerous the term may be) a "work." And the "work" in this sense is not a single entity but is defined by a range of choices the performer is *expected* to make, so that each performance has a somewhat different character. *Pace* Nelson Goodman, since there is no way I can access what a composer may have had in mind when preparing the written form of a composition, even when this involved describing it in words or actually leading an orchestra in a performance, I have little interest in phantom "ideals."[9]

I do not mean to suggest that there are *no* "subversions" of compositions by performers, but rather than being subversions of a text, they are subversions of a style of performance, and they often reflect ignorance. My favorite example stems from my long acquaintance with the Italian conductor Gianluigi Gelmetti (but he is scarcely alone in his eccentricities). Gelmetti does not believe in appoggiaturas, those modifications of the first of two identical notes at the conclusion of the setting of a line of text in what the Italians refer to as a *verso piano* (we would say a feminine ending): for instance, a musical line written as "amore"—G-E-E—was usually meant to be sung as "amore"—G-F-E, with the accented syllable being altered, most typically by raising it by a step or a half step.[10] Composers during the first part of the nineteenth century depended upon singers to make these adjustments automatically: they did not write them out because, from a technical point of view, the notes are usually dissonant and hence would conventionally have been considered "errors." Only after performers began to be somewhat uncertain about how to apply appoggiaturas did composers such as Verdi write them out in full. So, in *Lucia di Lammermoor* of 1835, there are only a limited number of explicit appoggiaturas, but in *Nabucco* of 1842, every single appoggiatura is written in full.[11] As I told Gelmetti in a voice dripping with irony that he did not grasp in the slightest, he had demonstrated to me why Verdi was a great composer: he obviously *invented* the appoggiatura in 1842. To refuse on principle to introduce appoggiaturas is to "subvert" the style a composer expected his performers to understand.

There are many other types of "subversion." It is certain that Rossini expected his singers to apply a series of ornaments, variations, and cadenzas to the written score with which they were provided. In the autograph manuscript of a duet, "Lasciami, non t'ascolto," in his Venetian opera of February 1813, *Tancredi*, the composer reduced the conclusion of a melodic period for Tancredi in the *primo tempo* to the music of the following example, but anyone singing these pitches is indeed "subverting" the style:[12]

What Rossini has done is to provide an indication, a shorthand, a recipe, to indicate that at this point the singer is expected to introduce a cadenza. Which cadenza should be used is not the fundamental issue, although it might be appropriate to insist that the cadenza have something to do with the style of the music as we have come to understand it. Rossini himself, in fact, provided a realization of this cadenza for a contemporary singer, Giuditta Pasta, not in his autograph manuscript of the opera but in a separate manuscript preserved in the collection of the Pierpont Morgan Library in New York and intended to provide a suggestion for a beloved performer:[13]

The freedom, indeed the interchangeability, of such realizations is best seen in a cadenza from an opera written for and first performed at the Teatro San Carlo of Naples on 24 October 1819, *La donna del lago*: it comes at the end of the *cantabile* ("Tanti affetti") in the final rondò. The cadenza, part of what today is a *morceau favori*, is quite well known:[14]

At the time the composer wrote his *next* opera, though, *Bianca e Falliero*, to open the Carnival season of the same year at the Teatro La Scala of Milan on 26 December 1819, he was seriously pressed for time. And so, in the Cavatina for Bianca in the first act, a piece in E major rather than the E-flat major of the rondò from *La donna del lago*, this is the cadenza he wrote into his autograph manuscript:[15]

It is, of course, derived from the "Tanti affetti" cadenza. It is not identical, to be sure. The higher key, for example, is also matched by an additional group of four notes that ascends not only to the G sharp, as it would by analogy with *La donna del lago*, but further to the high B. Rossini's Neapolitan soprano, including in *La donna del lago*, was Isabella Colbran, who at that time had become his mistress and would later become his first wife. Although formally a soprano, her voice did not easily embrace the upper register, and Rossini frequently avoided high notes in her part. (Today the Colbran roles are often sung by mezzo-sopranos.) For *Bianca e Falliero*, on the other hand, he had available a full soprano, Violante Camporesi, for whom he wrote as high as C sharp and for whom the high B would have posed no problem whatsoever.

But the situation is further complicated. Rossini was short of time for his Milanese commission, and the *Donna del lago* rondò was unknown in that city, so he employed essentially the same piece to conclude *Bianca e Falliero*. He could not, of course, reuse the *same* cadenza a second time in his new opera. And so he left the end of the *cantabile* of the *Bianca e Falliero* version of the rondò without any cadenza, but merely with the suggestion that a cadenza was necessary. Consequently the "document" that is Rossini's *Bianca e Falliero* shows the following music here—music very similar to what he had written in *Tancredi* six years earlier:

[na] - sce - sti, oh Dio, per me.

It is clear that this is *not* the music anyone should ever sing. What Rossini is telling us is to insert a cadenza at this point, without which the opera is basically incomplete. Of course, it would be possible to modify the cadenza at the end of Bianca's Cavatina in order to *reintroduce* that very cadenza into its original home. It may be, however, that in the economy of *Bianca e Falliero*, and recognizing that the *Donna del lago* cadenza is well known today, a better solution would be to leave that cadenza in the Bianca Cavatina, where Rossini placed it, and to provide a new cadenza for the final rondò of *Bianca e Falliero*. None of these moves would be a "subversion" of Rossini's opera, but performing the rondò with no cadenza would be.

There is another kind of "subversion" that is perhaps more insidious: it is to introduce stylistically inappropriate music into an opera. A few years ago, Cecilia Bartoli was roundly criticized for having decided (with the approval of the conductor, James Levine) to alternate in the final scene of *Le nozze di Figaro* the two arias Mozart wrote (for two different occasions) for Susanna: one the original and justly famous "Deh vieni, non tardar," the other a later showpiece for the singer, Adriana Gabrieli del Bene (called "La Ferrarese"), "Al desio di chi t'adora."[16] Imagine how much greater would have been the uproar if instead Bartoli had introduced into "Deh vieni" a cadenza from, say, Rossini's *La Cenerentola*! Less than thirty years separate the two operas, and yet the stylistic inappropriateness of adopting a Rossini cadenza in Mozart would have been widely understood.

Now, why are we so clear about the Mozart situation, while it is common to accept without thinking the insertion of various cadenzas and variations into the music of Rossini that reflect practices developed some seventy or eighty years after the composition of, say, *Il barbiere di Siviglia*, an opera written at the beginning of 1816? Do we not know the difference? or do we not respect Rossini's style sufficiently to want to maintain it? or are we simply so used to this kind of intervention that we accept it unthinkingly? The new critical edition of Rossini's masterpiece, edited by Patricia B. Brauner and published by Bärenreiter-Verlag of Kassel, takes this question seriously for the first time.[17] To begin with, it includes in its principal volume transcriptions of the five separate manuscripts containing variants for *Il barbiere di Siviglia* that Rossini himself prepared for the opera, manuscripts currently preserved in Paris, Munich, Brussels, and Milan, only one of which (the Munich manuscript of variations for "Una voce poco fa") has ever been transcribed and published.[18] These manuscripts, which give practical solutions for certain places in the opera as realized by Rossini, are particularly precious.

It should not come as a surprise to learn that many of these variations are for Rosina's "Una voce poco fa," which Will Crutchfield has described as probably "the most-documented aria in the entire operatic repertory where ornamentation is concerned."[19] We learn from these that Rossini expected singers to intervene by adding cadenzas, by ornamenting cadential figures, and by varying exact repetitions (repetitions sometimes so exact that the composer does not bother to write them out again but indicates only a repeat "dal A al B" [from A to B]). Some of the composer's interventions have become so familiar that they seem practically untouchable. So, before the partial repetition of the cabaletta theme, "Rossini's *Barbiere*" has only this:[20]

It has become commonplace to provide a cadenza on the tonic and then to anticipate the "ma . . . ," Rossini's own approach in both the Munich and Milan manuscripts, although the rhythmic realization is a bit different in the two sources. This is the version of the Milan manuscript **A(MI)**:

From Munich and Milan, however, one would find the following music written at the opening of the partial repetition of the cabaletta theme, four bars unchanged from Rossini's original, then four varied measures. This is the passage as preserved in **A(MI)**:

What we did not know until this edition presented the evidence was that a different variation, heard regularly still today, stems directly from Rossini. This version comes from one of two manuscripts preserved in the Fonds Michotte of the Brussels Conservatory, **A(FM 331)**:

At the end of the *cantabile*, Rossini essentially repeated the final eight measures of the phrase, themselves written as four measures (leading to a deceptive cadence) plus a four-measure variation (leading to the tonic):

But the conclusion, with a big fermata over an octave leap, was certainly not intended to be sung in this way. Rossini's own cadenzas in the Milan and Munich manuscripts are similar, although with somewhat different rhythmic notation. This is the version of the last four measures from **A(MI)**:

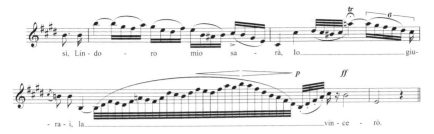

Interestingly, though, the Fonds Michotte version, **A(FM 045)**, is different: it does not ascend to the high B but contents itself with the original G sharp, ornamenting instead the lower part of the figuration, and then provides a more straightforward arpeggiation of the dominant at the end:

Particularly interesting is Rossini's approach to the final cadence of the cabaletta theme. In the original manuscript, he wrote a sequence of four descending patterns, a pattern that recurs identically in the partial repetition of the cabaletta theme:

While the "rule" derived from Rossini's own practice tends to be that no ornamentation is provided until a *repetition* of a pattern, this is an example where Rossini himself, in the two manuscripts that provide essentially the same ornamentation for this pattern, **A(MI)** and **A(Beyer)**, intervenes twice. In the first statement of the cabaletta theme, he modifies the pattern each time. The example is transcribed from **A(MI)**:

In the second statement of the theme he preserves the sequential treatment, but substitutes a much more complex figure, with rising triplets and falling sextuplets. Again, the example is transcribed from **A(MI)**:

e cen-to trap - po - le fa - rò,____ fa - rò____ gio - car,

What Rossini provides, in short, is a kind of master plan for *how* he considered singers needed to intervene in the performance of his music. It is possible to develop a series of "rules" on the basis of these examples and of many others from the composer himself, but such "rules" are never absolute. Furthermore, these interventions are fundamental to the opera and are in no sense "subversive" of it: one can subvert the composer's style by singing the music as written or by paying no heed to what we can learn from such examples, but under normal circumstances the performer is a partner, not an antagonist.

While the principal Rossini variations and cadenzas are for "Una voce poco fa," the new edition also makes available material he introduced for Rosina in the Terzetto (N. 16), "Ah qual colpo." This material, notated in a manuscript of vocal ornamentation found in the Fonds Michotte of the Brussels Conservatory, **A(FM 045)**, has never been mentioned before in the scholarly literature (it is not included in the Ricci volumes and its existence goes unnoticed by Zedda).[21] Rosina's initial period, as written in the autograph manuscript of the opera, concludes with the following material. Notice the absence of an appoggiatura on "son vicina," and the fermata over the last two notes, indicating that a cadenza is required:

e di con - ten - - - to son vi - ci - na a de - li - tar.

Rossini's suggestion from the Fonds Michotte does several things: it replaces the opening arpeggio figuration with lower-note patterns themselves arpeggiated; it modifies the middle of the figuration, including the obligatory appoggiatura on "son vicina"; and it fills in the fermata with a full cadenza:

e di con - ten - - - - - - to son vi -

- ci - na a de - - - - - - - - li - rar.

As I have said before, the inclusion of this material in the new edition is not intended to suggest that Rossini's variations should become "the text," only that they indicate the kinds of interventions that the composer apparently welcomed from his singers.

And perhaps even more important, in the Critical Commentary of the new edition, there is a section prepared by Will Crutchfield, which provides almost seventy-five pages devoted to "Early Vocal Ornamentation" for *Il barbiere di Siviglia*, material that reflects the written practices of singers who actually performed in the opera during the first half of the nineteenth century. Many of these can be dated explicitly.

- In 1821 the French publisher Carli issued two numbers "with all the variants introduced by Joséphine Fodor-Mainvielle [the Rosina] and Jacopo Pellegrini [the Figaro], written by themselves."
- In 1828 Henriette Sontag's variants for London were published by Goulding & D'Almaine in London, with the advertisement that the edition included "the Embellishments & the Graces as sung by Mademoiselle Sontag on the night of her debut at the King's Theatre" (that is, 19 April 1828).
- During the mid-1830s the English singer Adelaide Kemble (the sister of the great actress Fanny Kemble, who later emigrated to America) studied with Giuditta Pasta in Como, then proceeded to sing professionally from 1838 through 1843. The manuscript notebook in which she recorded what she learned is available.
- Rossini's favorite soprano in his French operas, Laure Cinti-Damoreau (who was also the first Contessa di Folleville in *Il viaggio a Reims*), after retiring from active singing, taught at the Conservatory in Paris; she published in 1849 a *Méthode de chant composée pour ses classes du Conservatoire* and developed five notebooks filled with ornamentation, preserved today in the Lilly Library at Indiana University.
- In 1847 the son of the tenor Emanuel García, who was Rossini's original Conte Almaviva in *Il barbiere di Siviglia*, published the second part of a treatise on singing, in which he included what seem to have been

the variants his father sang in the original performance of Rossini's opera and another set of variations for the same piece. According to Crutchfield, "Both sets of variations are well written within the typical vocabulary of the epoch, but one is considerably more brilliant and vivacious, while the other is sweeter and more lingering. García endorses the former: 'one senses clearly that the manner of the second example is too languorous for the character of the rôle.'" Thus García is concerned not only with the technical structure of the ornamentation but also with the overall "affect" they project. He also published several variants for Rosina that he attributed to his sister, Maria Malibran, a singer who frequently sang Rossinian roles and for whom the composer had particular admiration.[22]

In addition to all of this information, Crutchfield tries to develop lessons for vocal performance from instrumental arrangements. Obviously some elements of these arrangements are concerned primarily with showing off the characteristics of certain instruments, but others pertain to more general musical problems and turn out to be fully relevant to the stylistic issues being discussed.

What is fascinating about these examples, Rossini's as well as those of the contemporary singers, is that they make no distinction (other than key) for one vocal type or another. Fodor-Mainvielle was a soprano, and the edition of "Una voce poco fa" published by Carli with her embellishments is in G major, not the original E major, nor even the F major favored by Henriette Sontag or Adelaide Kemble or today's sopranos. But what she performed is stylistically identical to the kinds of variations and cadenzas added by her mezzo-soprano compatriots. This, for example, is the Fodor-Mainvielle cadenza at the end of the cantabile of "Una voce poco fa," transposed from her G major to the original E major:

Notice that there are elements that are clearly characteristic of the vocality of Fodor-Mainvielle: no other singer's version, for instance, makes use of the consecutive trills that she apparently employed to move from F sharp to B near the end of this example, but there is nothing out of style in this

gesture. Or take this more florid example from Henriette Sontag, transposed from her F major to the original E major:

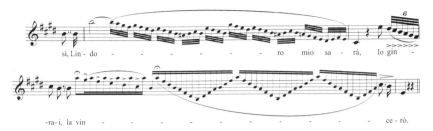

Ms. Sontag obviously relished repetitions (notice how she expanded the
cadence on "[Lin]-do-[ro]" by repeating three figures in the middle of the
run, while adding a group of four notes to the middle figure in a higher
register, and how she dallied with the arpeggiation on her cadenza for "vin-
[cerò]"). From a stylistic point of view, however, these embellishments are
all of a piece, and they are profoundly different from the kinds of variations
that became typical from the 1890s through much of the twentieth century.

The approach to variations for many singers in the twentieth century,
especially coloratura sopranos, was memorialized in an edition of the aria
prepared by Estelle Liebling,[23] which was reflected in the performance
styles of Lily Pons during the 1930s and the late Beverly Sills (a Liebling
pupil) from the 1960s. To my consternation, this publication continues to
be employed even today in many conservatories. What characterizes the
style is an excessive use of the highest pitches in a singer's tessitura, an
approach that emphasizes staccato leaps in the upper register, and a use
of florid passages in places where not a single singer from the first half
of the nineteenth century would have employed such passages. Here, for
example, is Liebling's suggestion for a cadenza to conclude the *cantabile* (I
present these examples exactly as printed in her edition, in Liebling's key
of F major):

Even if the style bears little relationship to anything that would have been
sung during the first half of the nineteenth century, at least the position is
correct. The same could be said of Liebling's suggestion before the reprise
of the cabaletta theme, despite its *piccatate* arpeggios ascending to the high F:

iu fu gui - dar.   Ma,

At the end of the cabaletta, however, Liebling throws at us a conclusion that will always excite the crowd for its high-flying antics, but which is stylistically completely out of place, not only in its individual gestures, but even more in its position:

Ah

Slowing down the drive to the cadence at the end, introducing a cadenza at all in this place, and concluding with a high F: are we truly singing Rossini? or are we pretending that Rosina is a manifestation of the mechanical doll, Olympe, in *Les Contes d'Hoffman* by Offenbach, or of the heroine intoning the Bell Song in Delibes's *Lakmé*? Those are the kinds of operas that provide stylistic sources for the Liebling approach to "Una voce poco fa."

The new edition of *Il barbiere di Siviglia* seeks to provide performers with materials from the first half of the nineteenth century sufficient to make clear what is historically (and stylistically) appropriate for this repertory. Nothing it provides is meant to determine unequivocally what a modern-day singer should do. But the edition does make it clear that the performer is a desirable *partner* in the realization of "Rossini's *Barbiere*," indeed that the opera cannot reach the stage without significant interventions from performers. Such interventions do not in themselves "subvert" the so-called text. What does subvert "Rossini's *Barbiere*" is either of two approaches: playing the opera as written, or introducing models of ornamentation that reflect compositional and performing practices of a much later period. The aim of the new edition of the opera is to provide singers ample proof that their active participation does not require either of these approaches. If, after all that, some singers still choose to deny the Rossini style, that is—to be sure—their prerogative. One asks, only, that they do so knowingly, not out of ignorance.

NOTES

A version of this essay appeared in *Common Knowledge* 17 (2011): 231–46, as part of "Between Text and Performance: Symposium on Improvisation and Originalism."

1. The most interesting and compelling work on transformative stagings has been by David J. Levin. See David J. Levin, *Unsettling Opera: Staging Mozart, Verdi, Wagner, and Zemlinsky* (Chicago: University of Chicago Press, 2007), as well as David J. Levin, "'Va, pensiero'? Verdi and Theatrical Provocation," *Verdi 2001: Atti del convegno internazionale Parma-New York-New Haven,* ed. Fabrizio Della Seta, Roberta Montemorra Marvin, and Marco Marica (Florence: Leo. S. Olschki, 2003), 463–75, with responses by James Hepokoski, Pierluigi Petrobelli, and Clemens Risi. Among the many scholars who have emphasized the role of singers in working *against* "the controlling voice of the composer" is Carolyn Abbate, as cited by Mary Ann Smart in the introduction to the collection of essays she edited, *Siren Songs: Representations of Gender and Sexuality in Opera* (Princeton: Princeton University Press, 2000) 7. There is a series of studies about important divas of the nineteenth century (including Erminia Frezzolini and Rosine Stolz) by Smart herself. See also Susan Rutherford, who in her book *The Prima Donna and Opera, 1815–1930* (Cambridge: Cambridge University Press, 2006) refers specifically to "subversive practices and discourses of representation" in the nineteenth century (18). Important studies in this direction have also been undertaken by Karen Henson (an essay by her is cited in note 3) and others. Nothing said here is meant to denigrate the excellent work accomplished by these fine scholars of operatic performance, even if I believe that they sometimes exaggerate the inherent conflict between a composer's "controlling voice" and the proper work of performers.

2. "E perché in un'opera comica non si potrà fare una cosa leggera e brillante? . . . È scritto bene per la voce: è istromentato leggermente; lascia sentire tutte le parole non disturbate dai soliti contrappunti orchestrali . . . Che male c'è dumque s'è riuscito popolare?!! . . ." The letter is published in *Carteggio Verdi-Boito,* 2 vols., ed. Mario Medici and Marcello Conati, with the collaboration of Marisa Casati (Parma: Istituto di Studi Verdiani, 1978), 1: 224–25.

3. "Mi si domanda inoltre se io ho autorizzato quei tagli! Ah no! ah no! Io ammetto, e senza dispiacere, che le mie opere non si facciano; ma se si fanno, domando sia come le ho immaginate io. Per questo mi rivolgo a voi, mio Editore, ed invoco il contratto che esiste fra noi su questo rapporto. Dichiarate dunque in mio nome alla Direzione dell'Opéra Comique che *Falstaff* deve essere eseguito per intero come lo fu la sera della prima rappresentazione." The letter is published in Franco Abbiati, *Giuseppe Verdi,* 4 vols. (Milan: Ricordi, 1959), 4:544. On Maurel, see Karen Henson, "Verdi, Victor Maurel and *Fin-de-siècle* Operatic Performance," *Cambridge Opera Journal* 19, no. 1 (2007): 59–84.

4. The phrase is from *Song of Myself,* section 51. I quote from Walt Whitman, *Walt Whitman: Complete Poetry and Collected Prose,* ed. Justin Kaplan (New York: Library of America, 1982), 246.

5. Paul Eggert, *Securing the Past: Conservation in Art, Architecture and Literature* (Cambridge: Cambridge University Press, 2009).

6. Philip Gossett, *Divas and Scholars* (Chicago: University of Chicago Press, 2006), 135–42.

7. The letter is printed in *Stravinsky: Selected Correspondence,* vol. 1, edited and with commentaries by Robert Craft (New York: Alfred A. Knopf, 1982), 225–26.

8. Personal communication.

9. I am referring to Nelson Goodman's classic treatment of this problem from

his philosophical viewpoint in *Languages of Art: An Approach to a Theory of Symbols* (Indianapolis: Bobbs-Merrill, 1968).

10. For a sophisticated treatment of this device, see Will Crutchfield, "The Prosodic Appoggiatura in the Music of Mozart and His Contemporaries," *Journal of the American Musicological Society* 42, no. 2 (1989): 229–71.

11. Those who wish to test this assertion should consult the critical edition of *Nabucodonosor*, ed. Roger Parker, *The Works of Giuseppe Verdi*, series I, vol. 3 (Chicago: University of Chicago Press, 1987).

12. Examples from this opera are taken from the critical edition of *Tancredi*, ed. Philip Gossett, 2 vols., *Edizione critica delle opere di Gioachino Rossini*, series 1, vol. 10 (Pesaro: Fondazione Rossini, 1984); see, in particular, 2:464, 606.

13. The manuscript figures as number 170 in The Mary Flagler Cary Music Collection of The Pierpont Morgan Library; see *The Mary Flagler Cary Music Collection* (New York: The Pierpont Morgan Library, 1970), 40. Pasta sang extensively with Rossini during his years at the Théâtre-Italien in Paris (1824 through 1826), and correspondence exists between them also from the 1830s.

14. The example is taken from the critical edition of *La donna del lago*, ed. H. Colin Slim, 3 vols., in *Edizione critica delle opere di Gioachino Rossini*, series 1, vol. 29 (Pesaro: Fondazione Rossini, 1990); see, in particular, 2:858–59.

15. Examples from this opera are taken from the critical edition of *Bianca e Falliero*, ed. Gabriele Dotto, 2 vols., in *Edizione critica delle opere di Gioachino Rossini*, series 1, vol. 30 (Pesaro: Fondazione Rossini, 1996); see, in particular, 1:305–6; 2:1092–93.

16. For a discussion of this incident, see Philip Gossett, *Divas and Scholars*, 239–40.

17. The edition is published as the second volume of *Works of Gioachino Rossini*: Gioachino Rossini, *Il barbiere di Rossini*, ed. Patricia B. Brauner (Kassel: Bärenreiter, 2008).

18. These five manuscripts are identified in the edition as: **A(Beyer)**, variations for the Cavatina Rosina (N. 5) in the private collection of Franz Beyer, Munich, previously published as *Varianten zur Cavatine der Rosina "Una voce poco fa" aus "Der barbier von Sevilla"* by Edition Eulenberg (Adliswil-Zürich, 1973); **A(FM 045)**, a variation for the Cavatina Rosina (N. 5) and several variations for the Terzetto (N. 16) in the Fonds Michotte of the Conservatory of Brussels; **A(FM 331)**, a variation for the Cavatina Rosina (N. 5) in the Fonds Michotte of the Conservatory of Brussels; **A(MI)**, an important series of variations for the Cavatina Rosina (N. 5) in the library of the Conservatory "G. Verdi" of Milan, dedicated in 1852 to the dilettante singer Matilde Juva, sister of Emilia Branca (the wife of the librettist Felice Romani); and **A(PA)**, variations for the Duetto Rosina-Figaro (N. 7), part of a large collection of vocal variants in the Bibliothèque de l'Opéra de Paris, prepared by Rossini before 1839 for Madame de Chambure, née Eugénie Rouget.

19. See Appendix V ("Early Vocal Ornamentation") of the Critical Commentary to the Bärenreiter edition of *Il barbiere di Siviglia*, prepared by Will Crutchfield, 361–421; the quotation is on 393.

20. All musical examples from *Il barbiere di Siviglia* are derived from the Bärenreiter edition.

21. Luigi Ricci, *Variazioni—Cadenze—Tradizioni per canto*, 4 vols. (Milan: Ri-

cordi, 1937–41). See also Gioachino Rossini, *Il barbiere di Siviglia*, ed. by Alberto Zedda (Milan: Ricordi, 1969).

22. For a complete description of these sources, with all bibliographical references, see Appendix V of the Critical Commentary to the Bärenreiter edition of *Il barbiere di Siviglia*. The quotation from Crutchfield is found on 409.

23. The edition, "edited by Estelle Liebling," has the plate number 40448 and appears on pages 81–89 of the album *Arrangements and Editings for Coloratura Voice with Piano* (New York: Schirmer, 1938).

DANA GOOLEY

Enacting the Revolution
Thalberg in 1848

ON MAY 3, 1848, the Viennese pianist Sigismond Thalberg, official court *Kammervirtuos* and one of the most famous pianists in Europe, played a concert in Vienna's *Musikvereinsaal*. The program was standard fare for Thalberg and followed the conventional "mixed" format of its time. Though the detailed sequence is not known, it opened and closed with concert fantasies of his own composition and was interspersed with performances by assisting artists: a violinist, a vocalist, and an actress reading a declamation.

> Thalberg, Fantasy on the Serenade and Minuet from Don
> Giovanni
> De Bériot, Grand duo on motives from "Les Huguenots," with
> violinist Karl Deichmann
> Aria from "Robert le diable" and two songs, sung by Ms. Tuczek
> Thalberg, Barcarolle and etude
> Vieuxtemps, Fantasie-Caprice, with Deichmann
> Declamation by Mrs. Wildauer
> Thalberg, Fantasy on "La muette de Portici"
> Austrian folk-hymn

But the historical context of this concert was anything but standard. Austria, inspired by revolutionary activity in Paris and catalyzed by recent agitation in Pest, was in the midst of its own revolution. It started with the upheavals of the so-called March days, the 13th, 14th and 15th, after which Emperor Ferdinand granted Austria a legal constitution and freedom of speech. Metternich fled to London, and the loathed chief of police Count

Sedlnitzky abdicated. Public enthusiasm after the March days—expressed in mantras of "freedom," "justice," and "order"—was matched only by the city's political chaos. On a nearly daily basis new proclamations were made, new conspiracies hatched, and new plots imagined. The chaos did not let up until the end of 1848, when the counterrevolution completed its work. Thalberg's concert thus took place at a moment when the city's political and theatrical life was in an extremely volatile state. Few contemporary reports suggest anything unusual about the concert, except perhaps that attendance was minimal. But one review, by a young law student named Eduard Hanslick, indicates that something strange happened as the pianist began his encore. After playing a few phrases of "Gott erhalte Franz den Kaiser," Austria's patriotic song since Haydn composed it in 1796, he was rudely interrupted by catcalls and boisterous music outside the hall, and was forced to end his performance on this sour note.

Who were these protesting musicians? And what was it about Thalberg's public identity that might have provoked such an interruption? Was it a commentary on the patriotic song? Hanslick does not identify the protestors or the cause of their protest, but the political stakes will become clearer with a close look at Vienna's theatrical life during the revolutionary months of 1848. Under normal conditions, theatrical performances in Vienna marked themselves off from the "everyday" through strong demarcations of space (the theater), time, and conventions of spectatorship. During the crisis of 1848, however, these demarcations broke down. Vienna's theaters, opera houses, and concert halls became forums where issues of civic and political life played themselves out and put themselves up for affirmation, critique, or negotiation. Public spaces, for their part, were invested with a new sense of theatricality. Political factions staged demonstrations at city squares and other key sites to present the monuments of cultural memory and political authority in a new light—they were put on "stage" for commentary. Observers and participants were pressed to reconsider the meaning of the patriotic song, as its identity was diffuse and multiple—it had been referred to variously as "national song," "national hymn," "Kaiser hymn," "Kaiser song," or "people's hymn." Intentionally or not, Thalberg's performance and encore inserted him into the revolution's carnival of shifting authorities and shifting representations of authority.

RECONSTRUCTING MUSICAL PERFORMANCES of the nineteenth century and of the more distant past, in a way that makes them available for rich performance analysis, can feel like an uphill battle. The lack of video and audio documentation forces us to rely primarily on contemporary newspaper and journal reports, which offer only the barest of facts that a performance analysis would want to take into account. In rare cases, such as opera premieres or exceptionally well-documented performers such as Liszt, Paganini, and Jenny Lind, we can develop a relatively complete impression of a single performance or group of performances, even if this wholeness always remains fictive. But in most cases, including the Thalberg concert under discussion, we have very little documentation. A lack of historical or "archival" documentation for historically distant performances need not be lamented as an unfortunate block. It may be an opportunity as well. As Diana Taylor argues with reference to historically distant Latin American cultures, archival records are just one form of historical memory. Archival memory operates alongside and sometimes in tandem with what Taylor calls "repertoire"—an embodied source of memory consisting of "performances, gestures, orality, movement, dance, singing—in short, all those acts usually thought of as ephemeral, nonreproducible knowledge."[1] The archival record of Thalberg's concert is "thin" by any standard. But when his bodily actions and concert rituals are situated in the horizon of repertoire—the larger, relatively autonomous field of cultural performances to which musical performances belong (and which they may reflect or reconstitute)—it begins to look not thin but overdetermined. As I will argue, his performance evoked other cultural performances—of aristocratic grace, of royal ceremony, and of national patriotism—in ways that were neither intentional nor necessarily consistent with one another.

Historians of the distant past have no simple, unmediated access to repertoire. It must be reconstructed speculatively with the help of archival documents and imaginative gap-filling. As Taylor points out, repertorial memory does not replace or oppose archival memory. Yet the notion of repertoire offers music historians a way of elaborating on the significance of musical performances laterally—that is, through their embodied reflection of parallel forms of cultural performance at a given historical moment—as well as linearly in their historical transformations.[2] By attending to processes of embodied imitation and performative revision, it offers a path that may help get around the nagging problem of archival memory: that documents appear to radically "underdetermine" performance events, partly by filtering out temporal and affective dimensions.

The tendency of this essay, then, is to elaborate Thalberg's concert event through its resonances in the broader field of cultural performances. In the first part I draw on contemporary newspapers and journals to portray the transformed theatrical scene of March, April, and May, which will reveal in part what Thalberg's rabble-rousers might have found objectionable. In the second part I use the Thalberg incident to investigate more broadly the relationship between public virtuosos and political ceremony in the 1830s and 1840s. The recurrence of national and patriotic songs such as Haydn's "Gott erhalte uns'ren Kaiser" and "God save the king" in the concerts of public virtuosos (Thalberg's encore was a typical example) points to deeper affinities between soloistic musicianship and royal or imperial projections of heroism and authority. The virtuoso, operating in the public sphere, absorbed and transformed public roles previously embodied by the king or Kaiser, in a process of performative substitution Joseph Roach has called "surrogation." In the sensitive atmosphere of the revolution, Thalberg's concert, so innocuous on the surface, brought these performative meanings to the surface.

THE REVOLUTION IN VIENNA unleashed energies that radically reorganized the city's theater practices and promoted unusual hybrid rituals combining music, commemoration, mourning, and jubilation. Description of a few of these events will provide background for Thalberg's concert and show how revolutionary performances networked music, stage performers, and the emperor's image to express the revolution's ideologies of freedom and folk. In the immediate aftermath of the March days, the Kaiser hymn showed up repeatedly in theater performances, as actors, singers, poets, and others channeled their efforts toward the cause. When the court opera theater reopened on March 19 with Flotow's *Martha*, one singer left out the opera's Irish folk-melody and inserted in its place the Kaiser hymn (in this case referred to as "national hymn"), at which point "everyone stood up from their seats and joined in with inspiration in the patriotic tone."[3] The week after the 15th also saw a rash of concerts in commemoration of the victims of the fighting. On March 22 and 23 a pair of special concerts was mounted at the Theater an der Wien whose proceeds were dedicated to a monument "for the fallen victims of Austria's three most glorious days of freedom."[4] For this event Karl Meisl wrote a commemorative poem that the audience was instructed to sing to the tune of Haydn's "folk hymn."[5] The orchestra began the concert proper with Beethoven's *Egmont* overture, whose triumphant close was hailed as an "apotheosis of freedom" in which "awakening, battle, victory and the triumph of freedom are painted in proud tones."[6] The curtain opened to reveal a stage decorated with German colors and banners of freedom, and the head of the National Guard stepped forth to deliver inspirational prologue. He was followed by violinist Herr Leonard, who played the "Kaiser song" to instant applause and continued with a set of bravura variations. Next came a patriotic song by

Kucken whose every stanza culminated in the line "Free is my fatherland!," where the audience joined in and applauded. Franz von Suppé contributed a new occasional piece called "Celebratory greeting to Austria's nations." Although one critic found the piece a bit too operatic ("Wälsch") for the occasion, he did admire "the entrance of the *Kaiserlied* in the middle of each strophe," and the audience was excited by the performance by Vienna's most popular opera singer, Joseph Staudigl. Finally, pianist Henri Litolff, who had been concertizing in the city before March, played and conducted his *Symphonie hollandaise* for piano and orchestra, whose finale featured Holland's equivalent of "God save the king."[7]

This mishmash of musical styles—Beethoven overture, virtuoso concerto, national hymn, patriotic student song—was typical of the concerts taking place in Vienna during March, April, and May 1848. Institutions and social habits that normally held these genres apart adapted themselves to the common cause. The most pervasive kinds of music in the public soundscape of the revolution were student songs, men's choirs, and Haydn's song (known variously as "national-hymn," "kaiser-song," and "folk-hymn"). A climactic juxtaposition of these genres took place on April 9 at a lengthy concert of the Men's Choir Society in the *grossen Redoutensaal*. It culminated with Reichardt's setting of "Des deutschen Vaterland," described by a reporter as "the most beautiful song of the German peoples" and sung to the accompaniment of a chorister waving the German flag in front of the stage. After a repetition of the song the whole audience went straight into the *Kaiserlied*. The reporter got so excited as he wrote that he seemed to relive the event: "Yes, Austria loves its Kaiser! Hail to the good Ferdinand!!"[8]

Performances of this kind were not just celebrating but were *enacting* the revolution. Men's choral songs like "des deutschen Vaterland" had been a major source of German cultural identity since 1815, but they lacked political intention or political effect. Only after the March days were these songs so aggressively aligned with the political resonances of the *Kaiserlied*, in performances that in effect married the German people to the emperor through their musical surrogates. During the weeks of the revolution nearly every paean to "freedom" or "nation" in the theaters was combined with a parallel demonstration of "love of Kaiser." This is one sense in which the Viennese revolution differed from its Parisian counterpart: the Viennese were celebrating the bond between emperor and people that they felt had been broken by Metternich's police state. Through rituals combining men's choral songs and the Kaiser hymn, the revolution produced a new cluster of associations for both types of music that suppressed their social and historical differences. Concerts could perform into being, through embodied ritual, the revolution's promise that the interests of the emperor were now with the German people. They created social and participatory experiences where that unity could be felt, not just represented. Revolutionary performances were in this sense driven not by cognition or "ideology," but by social memory and bodily habits attached to the men's-choir tradition and the *Kaiserlied*. As sociologist Paul Connerton puts it in his critique of the "cognitive" bias of traditional social analysis, "Meaning cannot be reduced to a sign which exists on a separate 'level' outside the immediate sphere of the body's acts. Habit is a knowledge and a remembering in the hand and in the body; and in the cultivation of habit it is our body which 'understands.'"[9]

As the initial euphoric celebrations of freedom and commemorative concerts started to fade, public performers began dedicating themselves to more pragmatic revolutionary causes. Braunschweig-based pianist and composer Henri Litolff, in Vienna on tour, devoted his March 22 concert to funding "the construction of a monument for the fallen ones," raising 1,007 florins.[10] Litolff followed up by composing a "March . . . for the heroic student legion, dedicated in brotherhood to the same," which was advertised, published, and immediately performed at further fund-raising events.[11] Several other artists mounted events to provide uniforms for the newly established National Guard, the most important institutional symbol of the revolution. Humorist and critic Moritz Saphir, for example, devoted one of his popular musical-declamatory concerts of mid-April to this fund.[12] Thalberg was thus aligning himself with the revolution's cause by devoting his May 3 concert to the uniforming of the National Guard, raising 895 florins, and making a further cameo appearance the next day for another fund-raiser.[13]

In April, Vienna's theaters became central sites of political contestation and revolutionary symbolization. At the Leopoldstadt Theater several of the upper box seats were removed, and the first tier of boxes was fused with the parterre to symbolize the fusion of classes.[14] The Italian opera house, associated with the aristocracy, was scheduled to open its season April 3, but the performance had to be canceled because the advertising posters were all torn up early in the morning.[15] It is not difficult to divine who was responsible for the vandalism, for the previous day the university students, perhaps the central contingent among the revolutionaries, had abruptly seized the reins of revolutionary celebration. With Professor Endlicher as master of ceremonies, they gathered en masse at University Square and led the procession to the imperial castle, where they discovered that "the ever-beloved Kaiser Ferdinand the benevolent, the brave-hearted, wanted to hear our songs," notably the *Kaiserlied* and "Des deutschen Vaterland."[16] Encouraged by the emperor's goodwill, a group of about five hundred students essentially took over the (Imperial) Theater an der Wien for the next three days and gave performances of a play about German student life by Benedix called "Der lange Israel." Its numerous scenes of student life, drinking, flirting, and singing invited rambunctious participation. When the play's main character sang "Long live freedom, and him who gave us freedom," the whole audience "cried out, all rose from their seats, waved their hats and handkerchiefs and cried out: play the folk-hymn! The folk-hymn! In the middle of the scene! The folk-hymn! Gott erhalte den Kaiser! Hail to Kaiser Ferdinand!!—it was indescribable."[17] The orchestra immediately broke into the hymn, and the students sang with enthusiasm and tears "for the greatest and noblest monarch in the world." At the end of the three days the enthused students proclaimed a new name for the Theater an der Wien: "National-Theater."[18]

In a curious exchange between theatrical and political discourses, Benedix's play, enhanced by the students' participatory realization of it, hatched a new performative political weapon that eventually caught up with Thalberg. In one scene from the play a young man serenades an old hag in song, while the audience is prompted to issue vicious catcalls. This scenario was soon transformed into an effective, carnivalesque ritual of protest called the "mock serenade." In the words of one historian of the Viennese revolution, "Bands of demonstrators would assemble at an agreed-upon hour in front of someone's home or office. A few musicians would accompany the songs, which were often interrupted by catcalls and threats. Mock serenades were given [to] unpopular political figures, for the radicals soon found that these noisy musicales were a simpler method of putting pressure on the government than organizing mob demonstrations."[19] But what was there to protest? All indications up to the middle of April suggest that the students felt their mission to be aligned with that of the Kaiser. In the course of April, however, the radical factions were ascending, turning the revolution on a more anti-monarchical course and winning over the sympathies of the students. The radicals did not accept the constitution as it had been declared on March 15. The problem was less its content than its form: it had been *handed down* to the Austrian people from above, bestowed upon them by the Kaiser. Because the emperor had granted it, he could in theory also rescind it, and there were enough conspiracies in the air to think he might. Radicals wanted a more thoroughly democratic constitution whose fate would be entirely in the hands of elected representatives, leaving no such "sovereign privilege."

The intensifying pressure from political radicals peaked toward the end of the month: "Late in April the radicals inaugurated a violent assault on the government that made their previous attacks pale by comparison."[20] It was in this context that newspapers announced that Thalberg, who the whole time had been away in London, would be returning to Vienna to give a single concert supposedly for the uniforming of the National Guard. One journalist praised the pianist for showing himself a "good, patriotic Austrian" and proudly welcomed him as a Viennese "fellow citizen." But in the tense public atmosphere, with conspiracies running wild, not everyone could be so sanguine or generous. The radical newspaper *Oestereichische allgemeine Zeitung* raised its eyebrows at the suddenness of his return, implying that Thalberg's visit might have had some secret counter-revolutionary motive.[21] Was Thalberg a closet diplomat, bringing counter-revolutionary support from London, or perhaps carrying a message from Metternich to develop a counter-insurgency? Was he merely posing as a national-patriotic artist as a cover? Why was he coming for such a brief period and giving only one concert? The artistically inclined, relatively apolitical *Humorist* came to the pianist's defense: "It is honorable when Thalberg, whose personal connections put him in the narrow circle of the *haute volée*, looks down [*absieht*] and is filled with sympathy for the popular [*Volksthümliche*] as every true artist must be."[22]

Thalberg returned to Vienna at the very peak of intensity of the radicals' mock serenades. The two largest and noisiest serenades took place the night before and the night of Thalberg's concert. On May 2, fifty thousand people "serenaded" the Minister-President Count Ficquelmont. The public suspected Ficquelmont was plotting counterrevolution with the aid of Russia, and in their songs they demanded he return to Russia—all of this couched, of course, in a tone of "valediction." This serenade petered out without response, but it recommenced the night of May 3 (the night of Thalberg's concert). When Ficquelmont failed to emerge from his house to address the serenaders, a second group was sent off to his office in a more aggressive spirit. This time the protesters succeeded: Ficquelmont resigned his position the next day.[23]

With this background in mind we can revisit Hanslick's report on Thalberg's interrupted encore:

At the end of the concert, Mr. Thalberg, recalled by sustained applause, sat down at the piano again and began with the folk-hymn, which was doubtless to be followed by variations. But already during the first bars there was heard suspicious whistling and catcalling from the street—Thalberg suspected the worst and finished with the theme, without variations. And in fact another, very loud concert got underway outside the concert-hall, which, in the manner of a serenade, directed itself to the Imperial-Royal High Police Authority. The public here was much, much more numerous than in Thalberg's concert, yet seemed less cheerful and less given to applause— it whistled [*pfiff*] loudly.[24]

Clearly it was a group of mock serenaders, perhaps even the same group that had harassed Ficquelmont, that disrupted Thalberg's performance. Thalberg's official status as court pianist was probably not sufficient to stimulate a protest of this kind, although it was certainly a contributing factor. The larger issue was that his audience included key members of the royal entourage—the Kaiser's mother, her princes, and the archduchess Hildegard—who were there to display "protection" of the court pianist.[25] (Emperor Ferdinand, however, prudently absented himself.) Police guards were probably posted inside and outside the theater to accompany the arrival and departure of the Kaiser's family, thus provoking the serenaders to their mischief. We can have no idea exactly what the serenaders intended, but the fact that (according to Hanslick) they timed their interruption precisely with the performance of "Gott erhalte" suggests a clever and deliberate calculation. As Thalberg rendered his earnest musical tribute to the Kaiser, the serenaders issued their mock musical tribute to the Kaiser's police, thus foregrounding the common elegiac address of both performances. Hanslick capitalizes on this shared performative substrate: his conclusion humorously plays on the ambiguity of the word "concert" to connect the interior theater space and the exterior public space—to link the artistic and political at a moment when those two were difficult to separate. Amid the anti-monarchic sentiment stirred up by the radicals, Thalberg's performance of the Kaiser hymn may have appeared to be a political statement. There was reason to believe the Kaiser really needed "saving." Just twelve days later, under continuing pressure from the aggressive radical faction, Ferdinand and his family fled Vienna in fear of their lives.

A STRAIGHTFORWARD INTERPRETATION of these events would cite Thalberg's symbolic association with the Kaiser's court, especially his *Kammervirtuos* title, as the origin of the protest. There is no question that this association, reflected in Thalberg's much-noted refined manners, his dress code, and his unruffled performance demeanor, was capable of provoking resistance. When the *Oesterreichische Zeitung* expressed its suspicions concerning his return, for example, it seems to have been based purely on this association. Yet by elevating the symbolic above the performative, this interpretation may overestimate the power of the Kaiser to ground the success of a public performer. Much of the condescension that has been heaped upon Thalberg, starting with Liszt's attacks of the 1830s, stems from the notion that he compensated for a lack of "real" talent with trappings of nobility and imperial protection.[26] Here I would like to elaborate the inverse possibility: that the Kaiser needed Thalberg far more than Thalberg needed the Kaiser. The retreat of royal ceremony from public life after the restoration of the monarchies in 1815 left a gap in the public representation of royal authority, and it cleared the way for the emergence of modern forms of celebrity. Modern celebrity was organized around exceptional skill and individual personality, and it thrived on the resources of print media and public opinion. Of these new celebrities—actors, musicians, writers, lecturers, even detectives and cooks—the instrumental virtuoso resonated best with the conventions of royal ceremony.[27] Thalberg and other virtuosos, by making themselves "kings" and "princes" of their respective instruments and projecting heroic identities in public spaces, bore the residual force of royal ceremony into the bourgeois era and the modernizing city. At a critical moment such as the spring of 1848, when Emperor Ferdinand could not "perform" in public without great risk, and could not guarantee performative efficacy, Thalberg stepped in to do some of that work for him. Thalberg's power in this situation was related to, but not "secondary" to, that of the emperor. On May 3 he stood in for, or "surrogated," the absent emperor.

Cultural historian Joseph Roach uses the term "surrogation" to describe processes of cultural transmission and transformation that take place by means of performance and ritual. Performers and actors surrogate when they conjure up or embody, in substitute fashion, the presence of some important person who has passed away or otherwise disappeared. Through such surrogations, performances can create consoling fictions of continuity and historical tradition. Yet Roach's theorization has a less rosy flip side: "Because collective memory works selectively, imaginatively, and often perversely, surrogation rarely if ever succeeds. The process requires many trials and at least as many errors. The fit cannot be exact. The intended substitute either cannot fulfill expectations, creating a deficit, or actually exceeds them, creating a surplus."[28] Roach thus describes a cultural economy where performance is both conservative, in the sense that it attempts to patch over loss or change, and at the same time transformative, because surrogation involves imperfection, loss of memory, hybridization, and unconscious adaptation.[29]

Surrogation can be distinguished from other forms of cultural transmission in that it operates primarily through performance and embodiment rather than signs or associations. Virtuosos were certainly capable of carrying meanings of the latter, more associative kind. Consider for example the frequent comparison of virtuosos to diplomats. Both were itinerant, international travelers who knew several languages and circulated in high social circles. Critic Carl Gollmick, in a comment that appears to imply Thalberg, bemoaned this aspect of the modern virtuoso: "the overwhelming, untouchable, who circulate only in higher and aristocratic spheres.... Do you see how his face does not express cheerful satisfaction, but how his serious, his sharp features, how his whole disposition recalls the diplomat?"[30] The power of this diplomatic image was strong enough to make another critic stress Thalberg's musical artistry, which made him "more than a minister, more than a diplomat, more than an ambassador."[31] In this case at least, Thalberg's concert performance was analytically separate from his diplomatic image. A similar separation of performance and symbolic image came into play when violinist Ole Bull, concertizing in Paris during its revolutionary events of February 1848, was asked to step into a diplomatic role. He became Norway's representative to the provisional government and gladly accepted.[32] He represented Norway by symbolic association, not through the discourse of his public performances.

Surrogation, by contrast, channels social meaning through the whole affective and communicative fabric of a performance event. Performing virtuosos came to surrogate royal representation after the restorations of 1815, as their spheres of activity shifted away from courts toward the emergent public concert life and its commercial appurtenances.[33] They stepped into a void left by the decline of "baroque" spectacle. Traditional machineries of absolutist spectacle no longer seemed right, acceptable, or convincing for the public projection of royal power. This development varied in character and intensity from place to place. London held onto pompous royal traditions the most tenaciously, with important consequences for the activities of touring virtuosos. In Paris, as Benjamin Walton has shown, the attempts by restored monarchs to mobilize opera as an instrument of propaganda (something opera had always done) ran up against catastrophically embarrassing problems, due to the highly developed commercial and intellectual public sphere of the 1820s.[34]

In Vienna, where authority had been relegated after 1815 to the state and the police, demonstrations of royal pomp were suppressed the most. In the later eighteenth century, the enlightened absolutist program of Maria Theresa and Joseph II had motivated them to sharply reduce public forms of royal and imperial ceremony. They continued to celebrate special occasions such as royal birthdays, but most often within imperial enclosures rather than public spaces. The Viennese emperors who ruled up to 1848 inherited and perpetuated this enlightened absolutist policy with almost no modification. In the words of historian Daniel Unowsky, "During the *Vormärz* [i.e., the 1830s and 1840s], Ferdinand the Good [reigned 1835–48] did not and could not project a majestic aura to his subjects."[35] Virtuosos such as Thalberg, Liszt, and Ole Bull, however, *could* project such an aura, and they absorbed the kinds of charismatic attention that in other places and other times would have been directed toward royals alone.

The retreat of baroque spectacle was counteracted by the emergence of national anthems as a pervasive medium of loyal expression in the early nineteenth century, making these melodies surrogates in their own right. In Austria the key moment was 1796, when Franz Joseph Haydn, impressed by the profound public effect of "God save the king" in London, wrote his famous melody to the text "Gott erhalte uns'ren Kaiser." This text was a literal translation of "God save the king," and Haydn imitated the English anthem's solemn manner as he wrote his melody.[36] These national songs, combining sentiments of loyalty, religiosity, and public virtue, were a powerful new form of propaganda, writing royal ceremony into the bodies of the singing subjects rather than imposing it "from without."

"God save the king" and "Gott erhalte uns'ren Kaiser" were part of a broader historical development. In reaction to the rousing effect of the Marseillaise, composed in 1792, Prussia borrowed the English anthem and wrote new words: "Heil dir im Siegerkranz" immediately became a staple of Prussian national ceremony and remained so for most of the nineteenth century. After the restorations of 1815 "Heil dir im Siegerkranz" became the national hymn of most of the other German states as well: Bavaria, Saxony, Baden, Württemberg, Mecklenburg, Braunschweig, Schleswig-Holstein, and Lichtenstein, and in 1830 it was adopted by the United States with a wholly different text.[37] National songs achieved what baroque ceremony could never do: they evoked royal "presence" in the absence of royalty. They encouraged the social collective to sing and perhaps even affirm its subjection in the theaters of the city, where royal representation was undesirable or difficult to attain. They functioned something like Althusser's interpellation: they hailed the people, the singing collective, as the subject of a monarch while making opaque the structure of authority that lay behind the hailing process.[38]

Instrumental performers turned time and time again to the national songs for their fantasies and improvisations. Indeed "God save the king" was arguably the most commonly treated of all melodies in the first half of the century. As the following list shows, every pianist of note published a fantasy on the tune, often pairing it with the more militant and rousing "Rule Britannia."

J. H. C. Rinck, Variations sur God save the king (for organ, 1820)

C. Czerny, God save the king, mit Variationen (1824?)

N. Paganini, Variationen über God save the king (1829)

J. P. Pixis, Hommage au célèbre Clementi. God save the King varié pour le piano, op. 101 (1829)

F. Kalkbrenner, 'God save the king.' Variazioni di Bravura con Introduzione e Finale per il Pianoforte e Orchestra (1830)

H. Herz, Fantaisie de couronnement, op. 104 (1837)

S. Thalberg, Grande fantaisie sur les airs nationaux anglais God save the queen et Rule Britannia (1837)

A. Dreyschock, Bravour-Variationen über das englische Volkslied 'God save the Queen' für die linke Hand allein (1838?)

F. Liszt, God save the queen (1841–49); Grande paraphrase de concert 'God save the queen' et 'Rule britannia' (1841, incomplete)

In his "Coronation fantasy" (figure 1) pianist Henri Herz went so far as to depict the royal procession and trumpet flourishes in a quasi-narrative manner. Furthermore, Paganini, Kalkbrenner, Moscheles, Mendelssohn, and Liszt all improvised publicly on the anthems or trotted them out for command performances before sovereigns. The prevalence of "God save the king" can be attributed in part to the indispensability of London as a destination for virtuoso tours (more money was to be made there), and in part to the three English coronations that took place in a relatively short period of time: George IV in 1821, William IV in 1830 (where Paganini played for him), and Queen Victoria in 1837.

But opportunity was not the only factor in bringing "God save the king" into the virtuoso tradition. Keyboardists had appreciated the melody as a vehicle of extemporization and variation since the later eighteenth century, and its wide dissemination had practical advantages for the tour-

Fig. 1. Cover page of H. Herz, Fantaisie de couronnement, op. 104 (1837)

ing virtuoso.[39] Liszt, for example, triumphed in England with improvisations on "God save the king" and then reused his ideas in Berlin two years later for "Heil dir im Siegerkranz." Although national songs belonged to the storehouse of familiar and popular materials that virtuosos traditionally treated to variation, fantasia, and improvisation, they were set apart by their elevated, quasi-sacred status. Fantasies on folk tunes and opera melodies refracted elements of an existing bourgeois culture back to bourgeois audiences. "God save" or "Gott erhalte," by contrast, evoked a more spiritualized and less definitely located "presence," not easily contained by the social or affective logic of the concert event. By playing such songs, instrumentalists were plugging themselves into deeply rooted rituals of public life, making themselves into temporary or substitute idols of worship. London audiences rose to their feet as if by an invisible force when Thalberg started the first notes of "God save." Paganini had made a profound effect in Vienna in 1828 with a surprise performance of the Austrian hymn in the presence of Emperor Franz II (reigned 1804–35): he "played the folksong so dear to all faithful subjects, 'Gott erhalte Franz den Kaiser!,' first letting this noble melody sound as the purest music of the spheres in the lightest vibrations of ethereal magic-sounds, and then transforming it with wonderful power back into the true rejoicing-hymn of all peoples united under one Scepter."[40] Just as Paganini's culminating, heroic statement of the hymn stands in for the voice of "all peoples," so does his violin bow evoke images of the scepter, in a deflection away from the emperor's person and onto his "instrument" of power. The fact that Paganini first delivers the melody in ethereal flageolet tones, then moves it toward heroic climax, practically stages an incarnation, a *mise-en-corps* of the spiritual hymn. The intensity of the loyalty expressed at this event surpassed anything Franz II was himself capable of orchestrating.

As quasi-sacred songs, national anthems also brought different expectations from critics and audiences. After hearing Paganini play his solo-violin fantasy on "Heil dir im Siegerkranz" in 1829, Berlin's leading critic pleaded for the integrity of the original melody: "It should only be treated polyphonically; it is a chorale melody which therefore demands at least an orchestra."[41] Paganini took the criticism to heart and furnished a simple orchestral accompaniment for the next performance. Leigh Hunt, however, reacted more vehemently to Paganini's performance of his fantasy on "Gott erhalte" in London (1831):

> It should have been affectionate, but only in such a way as to be compatible with a Hymn, and with the modesty of a religious petition—

fervent, cathedral, deferential, yet at the same time self-collected; *conscious of a presence, before which there is to be no unseemly weakness or overweeningness.* Yet to those who were aware of the nature of the subject, Paganini's chromatical, fond, and manner of playing it resembled a caricature of some morbid loyalist who had got maudlin with the Emperor's wine, and must needs go sighing and dying through the National Hymn.[42]

The tension Hunt articulates between the conventions of virtuoso elaboration and official sanctity appears to have affected Franz Liszt as well. He delayed unusually long before fulfilling his commission for a paraphrase on "God save the queen," and the musical result is filled with dissonances and surprises that are strange even by Liszt's standards, as if resisting the powerful tug of the melody's traditional status.[43]

In the decades before 1848, then, virtuosos were assimilating elements of royal ceremony into their practice and aura, adapting it to public theater while preserving a sense of royal numinosity. Under normal conditions this archaeological layer of the virtuoso's identity, which enabled surrogation, remained absorbed or submerged. The outbreak of revolution in March 1848, however, forced performers, both royal and musical, into new roles. It escalated the need for the emperor to "step forth" into the public domain and demonstrate his new alliance with the people, with freedom, and with the German nation. Royal ceremonies marking the new order were well under way immediately after the March days, yet the Kaiser's relative absence from these ceremonies—a necessary precaution—set processes of surrogation into play. On March 16, for example, the "Imperial royal privileged" Theater an der Wien reopened with a comedy typical of its repertory, prefaced by a ceremony celebrating the revolutionary moment. The ceremony began with a Hr. Lutzberger reading aloud his newly composed poem celebrating freedom of thought (*Geistesfreiheit*) and the Kaiser's favor (*Huld*) over Austria. Applause greeted each strophe of the poem and increased in its fervor. At the conclusion the curtain opened to display a bust of the Kaiser with a garland of laurels allegorizing fame, and according to one report, this game of *fort-da* was repeated several times with the curtain. General excitement generated a spontaneous demand that the orchestra play the "folk hymn," and the entire audience sang along as copies of the poem rained down from box seats into the parterre.[44] There are striking parallels between the morphology of this ritual and that of virtuoso concerts. The soloistic address, the crescendo of intensity, the intermittent surges of applause (in the performance of fantasies and improvisations, climaxes and individual variations would have been applauded), the curtain calls and apotheosis of the "hero," even the shower of poems—all these elements were typical of the concerts of Paganini, Liszt, Thalberg, and their contemporaries (although a single concert might play out this script several times in a row). In 1848, virtuoso concert and royal ceremony shared a ritual form whose *telos* was heroic apotheosis and collective enthusiasm.

Beyond this general structural parallel, Thalberg's concert and the March theater ceremony had another thing in common: the Kaiser's absence. On March 16, political instabilities made him hesitant to appear in public for fear of violence or subversive retaliation. His absence set into motion a series of performative deferrals or surrogations, starting with the poet who purported to voice the ideals of both people and Kaiser. Audience enthusiasm was aroused by the poet but then redirected toward the bust of the emperor. The bust, as a substitute for the emperor's presence, set another deferral into play. The impetus to "bring forth" the bust *several times* from behind the curtain—pure repetition compulsion—concealed an anxiety concerning the absence of the Kaiser. It employed theatrical artifice to insist that he was actually "stepping forth." The Kaiser's glory was then amplified by the singing of the hymn, and distributed into the spectator's bodies through their singing.

As I interpret Thalberg's concert of May 3, political circumstances forced a comparable series of substitutions or deferrals. Ferdinand was absent due to the threats of the radicals and their serenade-demonstrations. His family and entourage may have been sent to the concert not only to support "their" pianist but also to demonstrate support for the National Guard and to defend themselves from suspicion of retreat or counterrevolution. It was not at all clear that the people were "with" them. The concert was poorly attended, and Franz Liszt, no particularly warm friend of Thalberg, sat toward the front of the hall and conspicuously led the applause, as though Thalberg needed "help."[45] Either way, the royal entourage was present as a "stand-in" for the absent emperor. Yet by their presence they also turned Thalberg, the *Kammervirtuos*, into a stand-in. As master of ceremonies he generated audience enthusiasm with his playing, but instead of deflecting this enthusiasm toward the Kaiser's image (in the form of a bust), his performance can be seen as turning his body into the object and image of heroic apotheosis. When it came to playing "Gott erhalte" at the encore, Thalberg reversed this surrogate role; he made himself the "singer" of the *Kaiserhymn*, normally sung by the audience collectively. He thereby strove to redirect the audience's emotion back toward the royal figures and the higher national purpose of the concert. It is here that the mock-serenaders intervened, inverting the elegiac form of the performance, questioning the claim of the virtuoso to speak for the people, and resisting the elocutionary force of the national hymn as a hail to political subordination.

Although my reading concentrates on the internal dynamics of the concert event, the mock-serenaders probably directed their critique at the more general framing elements of the concert. Thalberg's distance from revolutionary affairs was evident in the whole shape of the program. In the revolutionary moment public performers were expected to demonstrate public concern and could be faulted for not doing so. Vienna's main music journal criticized the first concert of the *Gesellschaft der Musikfreunde* (April 4) for its apparent obliviousness: "Why did the Society not choose something suited to the moment [*Zeitgemäss*]? Why did it not put on a mixed concert consisting of pieces somehow linked to the great events that current pulsate feverishly through the fatherland?"[46] Critics and audiences were evidently demanding theater performances and concerts that had the feel of revolutionary celebration. Performers like Litolff, Saphir, Leonard, and Staudigl, as shown earlier, had all made the appropriate adaptations. Thalberg, in dedicating proceeds to the National Guard uniforms, appeared to adapt as well, but in all other respects his program was remarkably "unadapted." Having been away in London, out of touch with the public tone in Vienna, he probably had no idea what alterations needed to be made. His concert included no men's choir, no Egmont overture. Ms. Wildauer's declamation was entertaining and comical, but had no contemporary relevance. His first solo piece, his *Don Giovanni* fantasy, elaborated on two *ancien régime* dances, the serenade and minuet, from an opera that offers an exceptional range of social and affective registers. Did he choose these excerpts to "serenade" the Kaiser's family in the house? Measured against the concert life of April and May, the whole concert had a whiff of political aloofness, and Viennese observers were exceptionally attuned.

The Viennese revolution of 1848, in sum, brought public performance to the fore as a site where new roles and identities could be tested, staged, cheered and affirmed, or mocked and hissed. Theater events and concerts temporarily ceased to be mainly about "works" and became performed experiments, embodied ones, for the new kinds of social and political conditions they expect to bring into being. The revolution did not produce a carnival of radical indeterminacy, but new alliances and new representations of authority were in the making. Participants in theatrical events were reexamining the meaning of the *Kaiserhymn* as well as the meaning of performing heroes. Vienna's civic and theatrical life had become what Victor Turner called an "arena"—a "concrete setting in which [established] paradigms become transformed into metaphors and symbols with reference to which political power is mobilized and in which there is a trial of strength between influential paradigm-bearers."[47] Within this arena, those who sympathized with the revolution suspended the ritualized habits of theatrical spectatorship and produced performances inflected toward specifically revolutionary ends. The revolutionaries were taking advantage of what Turner called the "liminal" potential enclosed within any form of ritualized movement—the "moment when those being moved in accordance with a cultural script were liberated from normative demands"—which opens up the possibility of "formulating a potentially unlimited series of alternative social arrangements."[48] Amid such convergences of the theatrical and the political, a well-established, familiar performer like Thalberg could not escape scrutiny. His May 3 concert brought to the surface aspects of the virtuoso's public identity that had remained submerged for the better part of *Vormärz*. Links between virtuoso performance and royal ceremony—the heroic apotheosis, the "impressing" of the public, the audience's demonstrations of prostration and admiration—could no longer be easily suppressed. The emperor's relative absence from public life, at a moment when his new alliance with the people was being proclaimed, left the cultivation of loyalty to public domain events. Thalberg's misfortune was to have returned to Vienna at a moment when the legitimacy of the emperor, proclaimed so loudly in March and April, was suddenly being called into question.

NOTES

1. Diana Taylor, *The Archive and the Repertoire: Performing Cultural Memory in the Americas* (Durham: Duke University Press, 2003), 20. On how performance studies can productively reframe the interpretation of historically distant events, see the introductory remarks to *Acting on the Past: Historical Performance Across the Disciplines*, ed. Mark Franko and Annette Richards (Middletown: Wesleyan University Press, 2000), 1–3.

2. I accent here the synchronic element of the concept "repertoire," but its diachronic element is equally as important, especially when it is viewed as a medium of cultural memory. Richard Schechner anticipated Taylor's concept when he wrote that "every strip [of performance], no matter how small, brings some of its former meanings into its new context. That kind of 'memory' is what makes ritual and artistic recombinations so powerful." Richard Schechner, *Performance Theory*, rev. ed. (London: Routledge, 1988), 324. Historical musicology currently prioritizes close contextual studies, with clearly demarcated chronological boundaries, presenting a considerable disciplinary block to the study of repertory on its diachronic axis. (On the priority of contextualization, see James Currie, "Music

After All," *Journal of the American Musicological Society* 62, no. 1 [2009]: 157–71.) Musicologists are increasingly exploring intersections of musical and non-musical cultural performance. Maiko Kawabata explores parallels between violin virtuosity and military heroism in "Virtuoso Codes of Violin Performance," *19th Century Music* 28, no. 2 (2004): 89–107. Lawrence Kramer links Lisztian virtuosity to royal ceremony and carnivalesque ballroom dance in *Musical Meaning: Toward a Critical History* (Berkeley: University of California Press, 2004), 68–99. Nicholas Mathew examines Beethoven's ceremonial music in the context of the political culture of the Vienna Congress in "History Under Erasure: *Wellingtons Sieg*, the Congress of Vienna, and the Ruination of Beethoven's Heroic Style," *Musical Quarterly* 89, no. 1 (2006): 17–61.

3. *Wiener allgemeine Musik-Zeitung* 8, no.35 (March 21, 1848): 139. Hereafter WAMZ.

4. WAMZ 8/37, March 24, 1848, 146.

5. WAMZ 8/35, March 21, 1848, 139.

6. WAMZ 8/40, April 1, 1840, 158. One week earlier the same journal (March 24, 1840, 146) described the Egmont overture as a work that "celebrates in tones the death of a hero of justice and freedom."

7. WAMZ 8/37, March 24, 1848, 146. Leonard repeated his piece at Litolff's March 24 concert.

8. WAMZ 8/44, April 11, 1848, 175.

9. Paul Connerton, *How Societies Remember* (Cambridge: Cambridge University Press, 1989), 95.

10. WAMZ 8/40, April 1, 1840, 159.

11. WAMZ "Marsch nach dem Liede: 'Erwacht, o Brüder' von Dr. S. Kapper, für die heldenmuthige Studirenden-Legion komponiert und derselben brüderlich geweiht von Henri Litolff. Für Pianoforte zu zwei Händen" (156). Advertised 8/37, March 24, 1848, 149.

12. WAMZ 8/42, April 6, 1848, 165.

13. WAMZ 8/56, May 9, 1848, 223–24. The status of the "Court Opera Theater" was the subject of heavy debate throughout April. It reopened as the "Opera Theater" on April 29 with Mozart's *Zauberflöte*. See "Brauchen wir eine italienische Oper?" in WAMZ 8/42, April 6, 1848, and WAMZ 8/53, May 2, 1848, 210.

14. *Allgemeine Theaterzeitung*, May 13, 1848, 463.

15. WAMZ 8/41, April 4, 1848, 164.

16. *Allgemeine Theaterzeitung* no. 81, April 4, 1848, 325.

17. *Allgemeine Theaterzeitung* no. 83, April 6, 1848, 334.

18. WAMZ 8/41, April 4, 1848, 164.

19. R. John Rath, *The Viennese Revolution of 1848* (Austin: University of Texas Press, 1957), 165.

20. Ibid., 182.

21. This debate was reported in *Allgemeine Theaterzeitung*, May 5, 1848, 435.

22. *Humorist*, May 5, 1842, 442.

23. Rath, *The Viennese Revolution of 1848*, 182–83.

24. Eduard Hanslick, "Concert des Hrn. Sigmund Thalberg," *Wiener Zeitung* no. 126, May 6, 1848. Hanslick puns on the word "pfeifen" which can mean both

"play [a woodwind instrument]" and figuratively "to hiss" or "to boo." "Am Schlusse des Concerts setzte sich Herr Thalberg, durch anhaltenden Beifall aufgefordert, nochmals an's Piano und begann mit der Volks-Hymne, der ohne Zweifel die brillanten Variationen folgen sollten. Aber schon während der ersten Tacte hörte man verdächtiges Pfeifen und Miauen von der Strasse her,—Thalberg ahnte Unheil und schloss mit dem Thema, ohne Variationen. Und in der That, gerieth man aus dem Concert-Saal unmittelbar in ein anderes, sehr kräftiges Concert, welches, in der Eigenschaft eines Ständchens, der k. k. Polizei-Ober-Direction gebracht wurde. Das Publikum hierbei war noch viel, viel zahlreicher als in Thalbergs Concert, schien aber nicht so beifallslustig und zufrieden,—es pfiff bedeutend."

25. *Humorist*, May 5, 1842, 442.

26. The text of Liszt's famous critique of Thalberg, from the *Revue et gazette musicale* of February 12, 1837, is found in *Franz Liszt: artiste et société*, ed. Remy Stricker (Paris: Flammarion, 1995), 231–35. One of the few writers to approach Thalberg sympathetically is Kenneth Hamilton, *After the Golden Age: Romantic Pianism and Modern Performance* (Oxford: Oxford University Press, 2008), 155–63.

27. On the post-revolutionary production of celebrity performers, see Paul Metzner, *Crescendo of the Virtuoso: Spectacle, Skill, and Self-Promotion in Paris during the Age of Revolution* (Berkeley: University of California Press, 1998).

28. Joseph Roach, *Cities of the Dead: Circum-Atlantic Performance* (New York: Columbia University Press, 1996), 2.

29. Roach developed his theory to account for the cross-cultural flows of the "circumatlantic" world—the sea-based triangulation of relations between Europe, Africa, and North America. In this milieu large ethnic and linguistic gaps weakened the power of writing as medium of cultural transmission and brought performance to the fore. While Roach's theory emerges from questions specific to the circumatlantic context, he also analyzes cultural conditions in central Europe. In the chapter devoted to the death of Thomas Betterton, for instance, he explores how the famous actor's death produced discourses displacing his voice and body to other cultural sites. It is precisely such foregrounding of the performative that took place during the 1848 revolution, and the recurring motifs of Roach's case studies—the affective attachments to the dead, the secularization of official and political functions in theater, the rearticulation of memory, and the theater actor's mediation of collective cultural desires—are all directly relevant to Vienna's performative life after the March days.

30. Carl Gollmick, "Das heutige Virtuosenwesen," *Neue Zeitschrift für Musik* 17, no. 45 (December 2, 1842): 184.

31. "Retour de S. Thalberg à Londres," *France musicale* 2 (1839): 437 ("plus qu'un ministre, plus qu'un diplomate, plus qu'un ambassadeur").

32. Report from Paris in the Leipzig *Neue Zeitschrift für Musik* 1848, col. 251.

33. See Richard Leppert, "Cultural Contradiction, Idolatry, and the Piano Virtuoso: Franz Liszt," in *Piano Roles: Three Hundred Years of Life with the Piano*, ed. James Parakilas (New Haven: Yale University Press, 1999), 252–81; and chapter 4 in Lawrence Kramer, *Musical Meaning: Toward a Critical History* (Berkeley: University of California Press, 2002). See also Jim Samson, *Virtuosity and the Musical Work: The Transcendental Studies of Liszt* (Cambridge: Cambridge University Press, 2003), 66–76.

34. Benjamin Walton, *Rossini in Restoration Paris* (Cambridge: Cambridge University Press, 2007). See especially chapter 2.

35. Daniel Unowsky, "Reasserting Empire: Habsburg Imperial Celebrations after the Revolutions of 1848–49," *Staging the Past: The Politics of Commemoration in Habsburg Central Europe, 1848 to the Present*, ed. Maria Bucur and Nancy M. Wingfield (West Lafayette: Purdue University Press, 2001), 16.

36. A concise account of the origin of this song is found in Hans Otto, "Ein Lied für Franz: Vor 200 Jahren schrieb Haydn seine Hymne," *Concerto: das Magazin für alte Musik* 14, no. 120 (2008): 7–8.

37. A detailed history of the English anthem and its dissemination through other parts of Europe is found in Percy Scholes, *God Save the Queen! The History and Romance of the World's First National Anthem* (New York: Oxford University Press, 1954).

38. Nicholas Mathew argues that these processes of subjection were being transferred to and reconstituted in concert life in Vienna in the 1790s. See "Heroic Haydn, the Occasional Work and 'Modern' Political Music," *Eighteenth Century Music* 4, no. 1 (2006): "This, perhaps, is what makes much of Haydn's music from the 1790s both 'modern' and 'political.' Its new brand of cultural influence, notionally independent from official forms of state power, amounted to a form of consensual and informal control that Gramsci would call hegemony. . . . By this time 'Gott erhalte' was widely portrayed not as a method of enforcing loyalty to the sovereign, but rather as a means of internalizing civic obedience—which Haydn himself supposedly reinforced through the daily ritual of playing his hymn" (24).

39. Forkel's variations on "God save the king" gave rise to an intense controversy with composer and theorist G. J. Vogler, who "corrected" and rewrote them in 1793. Forkel retaliated with a new set of variations in 1813. See Martin Staehelin, "Musikalische Wissenschaft und Praxis bei J. N. Forkel," in *Musikwissenschaft und Musikpflege an der Georg-August-Universität Göttingen: Beiträge zu ihrer Geschichte*, ed. M. Staehelin (Göttingen: Vandenhoeck und Ruprecht, 1987), 9–26.

40. *Allgemeine musikalische Zeitung* no. 31 (1829), col. 110.

41. Ludwig Rellstab reviewing Paganini's April 29 concert in *Vossische Zeitung* no. 101, May 1, 1829.

42. Quoted in Geraldine de Courcy, *Paganini the Genoese*, 2 vols. (Norman: University of Oklahoma Press, 1957), 1:281. Italics added.

43. After his English tours of 1840 a publisher in Hamburg was hounding Liszt for a piece on "God save the queen," but it took him at least three years to come through with it. See his letter of May 7, 1843, in *Liszt Letters in the Library of Congress*, ed. and trans. Michael Short (Hillsdale: Pendragon Press, 2003), 23–34.

44. *Allgemeine Theaterzeitung* no. 67, March 18, 1848, 272. Nicholas Mathew describes similar apotheoses of the Austrian Kaiser's bust in theater and painting around the time of the Congress of Vienna, arguing that such representations belong to an early phase of modern political culture. In Beethoven's popular setting of Kotzebue's *Ruinen von Athens*, for example, Beethoven composed out an apotheosis for the triumphant appearance of the Kaiser's bust from a trap door. See "History Under Erasure," 29–35.

45. This is reported in the memoirs of Liszt's student J. N. Dunkl, *Erinnerungen eines Musikers* (Vienna: L. Rosner, 1876), 20.

46. WAMZ 8/41, April 4, 1848, 162. "Warum wählte der Verein nichts Zeit-gemässes? Warum veranstaltet er nicht ein gemischtes Konzert, aus Nummern bestehend, die doch irgendwie an die grossen Ereignisse anknüpfen, von denen jetzt das Vaterland fieberhaft durchbebet wird?"

47. Victor Turner, *Dramas, Fields, and Metaphors: Symbolic Action in Human Society* (Ithaca: Cornell University Press, 1974), 17.

48. Ibid., 13–14.

JOSEPH ROACH

Cutting Loose

Burying "The First Man of Jazz"

With madness, as with vomit, the inconvenience is mainly
to the passersby.

—JOE ORTON

A NEW ORLEANS JAZZ FUNERAL is a parade you can't watch. Your line of
sight is traversed by the swirling crowd of mourners and revelers called the
"Second Line." They follow the brass band, the corpse, and a logic of their
own. As they approach, the choice you have to make is between standing
on the sidewalk feeling stupid or joining the procession, which before it's
over is as much about dancing as it is about marching. In a "traditional" jazz
funeral, understanding that no two funerals are identical and that traditions change with the times, there are two main parts: the slow and the fast.
A dirge-tempo march to the burial ground with the body comprises the
first part, which in more recent times frequently ends not at the grave but
when the hearse leaves for the distant cemetery. "Just a Closer Walk with
Thee" is a favorite hymn tune for the first part. The second part, with the
deceased no longer physically present, is given over to up-tempo numbers,
especially those with ribald meanings in their lyrics and titles, of which
"I'm Glad Now That You're Dead, You Dirty Dog" is not unrepresenta-
tive of the tradition. The threshold between the two parts is marked by the
defining moment of the whole performance—"cutting the body loose"—
which expresses both grief for the deceased and joy for his (or sometimes
but less frequently her) escape from the sorrows of a sinful world or at least
from Louisiana.

In the mid-1990s the traditional jazz funeral underwent a transformation led by younger musicians playing for their deceased peers, many of
whose violent deaths were attributed to battles over drugs, and those who

mourned them. Emergent ensembles such as the Dirty Dozen Brass Band, the Rebirth Brass Band, and the New Birth Jazz Band reinterpreted the traditional repertoire in terms of rhythm and blues, funk, rap, and hip-hop. The dirge disappeared and the dancing got dirty—nudity, profanity, and flagrant intoxication characterized the behavior of teenaged Second Liners, much to the disgust of the traditionalists. When the great jazzman Danny Barker passed (in New Orleans no one beloved passes *away*), his survivors asked that he not be given the traditional public send-off because he had been scandalized by recent excesses. At that moment in the history of New Orleans jazz funerals, the relationship of "cutting the body loose" to the phrase *cutting loose*, meaning to break out of established behavioral norms, emerged in ways that were suggestive albeit obscure.

Such obscurity—and *double entendre*—are familiar problems to historians of jazz. Experts have on various occasions proposed Arabic, African, Creole, French, Old English, Indian, and Spanish roots in their etymologies, which vainly seek to trace the pristine phonological emergence of jazz out of the hopeless tangle of vulgar tongue-twisters—jass, jasbo, jaser, jaz, chaz, chasse, razz, spasm, and jasm (that is, jism).[1] Even before this African-American musical and kinesthetic style—featuring propulsive syncopation of ragtime and blues materials, polyphonic ensemble playing, improvisation, solo riffs, and dance provocations—had a settled name or myth of origin, commentators and the public had imagined it as both an authenticating practice of African-American culture and a sexual incitement, troubling the Eurocentric boundaries between the sacred and the profane. This analysis typically entails an account of the city of New Orleans as the real and the imagined locus of pure jazz origins, examining how, in the words of Eric Hobsbawm, "'New Orleans' became a multiple myth and symbol: anti-commercial, anti-racist, proletarian-populist, New Deal radical, or just anti-respectable and anti-parental, depending on taste."[2] In the light of Hobsbawm's notion of an invented tradition, I want to examine Michael Ondaatje's *Coming Through Slaughter* (1976), in which the novelist attempts to render the musical life of the city of New Orleans through a combination of fictional and documentary narratives. Ondaatje, using documents from turn-of-the-century New Orleans and quotations from oral histories in the Hogan Jazz Archive at Tulane University, narrates the imagined inner life of "the first man of jazz" Charles "Buddy" Bolden (1876?–1931), the legendary cornetist whose playing is spoken of with awe to this day, even though he never picked up his horn again after going mad in 1907 and never recorded a note.[3]

But I will also read *Coming Through Slaughter* through the experience of living in New Orleans in the 1990s and following the Second Line parades and jazz funerals in those years. A preliminary issue raised both by the novel and by innovations in the traditional jazz funeral during what locals called "the crack wars" concerns the way in which bereavement and loss may be celebrated with festivity and even debauch: from one point of view, it looks like madness; from another, it is a logical expression of ineffable grief. The final issue that I will address, however, concerns the struggle to lay to rest the concept of traditional jazz itself as the very last members of the generation of musicians who carried living memories of Buddy Bolden passed.

The field that lends itself most readily to such an approach is performance studies. Developed as an interdiscipline out of programs in the arts and human science (theater, drama, speech communication, linguistics, anthropology, sociology), performance studies defines as its objects cultural performances of all kinds, from theatrical presentations to rites of passage. Theater historian Marvin Carlson has located a reason for the growing importance of the concept of performance as an analytical tool across the broad spectrum of cultural studies in "the major shift in many cultural fields from the 'what' of culture to the 'how,' from the accumulation of social, cultural, psychological, political, or linguistic data to a consideration of how this material is created, valorized, and changed, to how it lives and operates within the culture, by its actions. Its real meaning is now sought in its praxis, its performance." Moreover, performance is associated not only with doing, but also with "re-doing" (as restored behaviors, as repetitions with revisions), and beyond that with the "self-consciousness about doing and re-doing, on the part of both performers and spectators."[4] Restoration is never perfect repetition: there is always a space, larger or smaller, within the act of re-doing into which invention enters. In that space residual and emergent behaviors contend, and the effects of their struggle spill out into the rest of lived experience.

This property of performance underlies Renato Rosaldo's reinterpretation of ritual, especially mortuary ritual, in *Culture and Truth: The Remaking of Social Analysis* (1993): "Rituals serve as vehicles for processes that occur both before and after the period of their performance. Funeral rituals, for example, do not 'contain' all the complex processes of bereavement."[5] Rosaldo's observation comes at the end of the harrowing first chapter of *Culture and Truth*, "Death and a Headhunter's Rage," in which he explains how his enraged response to the accidental death of his wife made him understand how limited the conception of grief is in "upper-middle-class Anglo-American culture."[6] His purpose was to demonstrate how bereavement reasonably encompasses rage. My purpose is to demonstrate how it also reasonably encompasses the reinvention of tradition through the crapulous excess of youthful self-assertion.

In large measure this complexity of affect in the face of death resonates in the funeral music itself, but that resonance cannot be separated from received ideas that implicate jazz as sexualized expression. Here Ondaatje makes the obvious and familiar narrative move. By opening *Coming Through Slaughter* with scenes of the brothel district of Storyville, he claims the low-down history of New Orleans jazz performance for purposes of predicating his action on Bolden's charismatic capacity to lead a libidinous musical parade.[7] Inside the Storyville parlors, creole and black musicians ("Professors") entertained for tips.[8] On the streets outside, the spasm bands cut loose.

The New Orleans *Times-Picayune* for 17 June 1917, editorializing against "Jass and Jassism," associated "jassism" with "a low streak in man's taste that has not yet come out in civilization's wash" and defined "jass music" as "the indecent story syncopated and counterpointed."[9] Such a description characterizes commonplace attitudes toward "back-of-town" New Orleans. They are evoked with much greater complexity in *Coming Through Slaughter.* In very short, poetic chapters, more like fragments or riffs of oral history interspersed with musically constructed interior monologues from various characters, Ondaatje intimates the larger story of New Orleans jazz through the life of the legendarily gifted but mentally fragile cornetist Bolden: "At 335 Customhouse (later named Iberville), the street he went crazy on, you could try your luck with French Emma's '60 Second Plan.'" As the narrator helpfully explains by citing the archival history of the District, "Whoever could restrain his orgasm with her for a whole minute after penetration was excused the $2 payment."[10]

Bolden's listeners had similar difficulties holding back. In received opinion, filtered through the syncopated prose of *Coming Through Slaughter,* Bolden's mesmerizing riffs captivated passersby and led them away from rival players. Ondaatje has Bolden's fellow bandsman Lewis Mumford recall the crowds of "men that dance to him and the women that idolize him as he used to strut up and down the street." Bolden's image circulates in the sexualized evocation of New Orleans at the turn of the last century, but Ondaatje's character Mumford wants urgently to explain the deep rootedness of this new music in the sacred as well as the profane.

There's about three of us at the window now and a strange feeling comes over me. I'm sort of scared because I know the Lord don't like that mixing the Devil's music with His music. But I still listen because the music sounds so strange and I guess I'm hypnotised. When he blows the blues I can see Lincoln Park with all the sinners and whores shaking and belly rubbing and the chicks getting way down and slapping themselves on the cheeks of their behind. Then when he blows the hymn I'm in my mother's church with everybody humming. The picture kept changing with the music. It sounded like a battle between the Good Lord and the Devil. Something tells me to listen and see who wins. If Bolden stops on the hymn, the Good Lord wins. If he stops on the blues, the Devil wins.[11]

Ondaatje tracks Bolden's path through the streets in ecstatic Second Line parades, the brass marching bands and their choric followers associated with the historic social aid and pleasure clubs that traditionally served as burial societies for African-Americans. At the same time he also acknowledges the sacred musical path that leads to jazz from the "spiritual churches." Although funerals as such are not depicted in the novel, the title *Coming Through Slaughter* refers to the route followed by Bolden's corpse on its final journey back to the city from the madhouse: "Buried in an unmarked grave at Holz Cemetery after being brought from the Asylum through Slaughter, Vachery, Sunshine, back to New Orleans."[12] Putting that procession into the title, Ondaatje invites the reader to understand Bolden's madness as a kind of social death and the narrative as slowly unfolding obsequies for "the first man of jazz."

Buddy Bolden has been cut loose more than once. In 1995 there was a belated jazz funeral for him at the dedication of a plaque to his memory near the site of his unmarked grave. Family members joined local historians, led by Joseph Logsdon of the University of New Orleans, in commemorating the first century of jazz music and in honoring Bolden as one of its founders. The brass band and exceptionally decorous Second Liners processed under the live oaks of Midtown to the treeless paupers' cemetery. Here the more recent graves are marked by wooden boards bearing handwritten inscriptions in paint and felt-tip pen. The siting of the Bolden memorial had to be done by guesswork because the locations of the older graves are forgotten in the successive reburials that compete for spaces in the same overbooked earth. The paths that run between the graves are irregular and unpaved—in fact, unlike the carefully laid-out streets of New Orleans's famous Cities of the Dead, the paths do not necessarily run between the graves but over and among them. And the bodies are in the ground, not above it. The procession broke up as it passed through the maze of the graveyard and reassembled around the new Bolden marker. As the sharp brass band sounds cut through the thick air, the mood of the crowd was deeply nostalgic and only officially festive. Here and there, the band dropped out notes. When a jazz musician intentionally or unintentionally omits tones, leaving empty spaces in the music that the listeners can fill in because they have a pretty good idea about what should go where, he or she is playing "ghost notes." These notes, present to the imagination of the participants because they are partially or even wholly unsounded, at once attempt to honor the past and secure the future by calling them all together in the name of a jazz community.

At this second funeral, as with the publication of *Coming Through Slaughter,* Bolden's story was solemnly retold. The fact that he did not make recordings is the key to a proper understanding of his role. When purists of the 1930s and 1940s revived interest in searching out jazz originals, they discovered a rich vein of oral tradition among the aging musicians of New Orleans who could claim to have heard Bolden play. His memory could be passed along only by description or at best demonstration. Perhaps the most poignant artifact of this search is a recording of Bunk Johnson whistling in what he remembered as the style of Bolden's playing.[13] Most of these notes were ghosts because musical memory without notation is likely to be more creative reinvention than pinpoint reconstruction. In such a moment of performance, when memory returns in the shape of a wish, the hourglass turns, and the replenishing source of the future is rediscovered in the emptying out of the unreconstructable but also the inexhaustible past.

The perceived disappearance of living memory makes people anxious about their origins. The Bolden reburial occurred in the context of both the advent of "crack funerals" and the passing of the last of the old jazzmen who could conceivably have "heard Buddy Bolden play." The funeral of Milford S. Dolliole in 1994 was probably the last of these passings. Born in 1903, "Papa Stack" would have been only four years old when Bolden went crazy and fell silent, but popular sentiment linked him to the first decade of jazz. He was a drummer with the Olympic Jazz Band, the Onward Jazz Band, and the Tuxedo Brass Band. In later years, he played at Preservation Hall, the tourist-oriented venue for the conservators of traditional New Orleans jazz (in fact, the "Bunk Johnson Society" of Stockholm, Sweden, which plays off of old recordings with deadly accuracy, is probably more *authentic* in the strictest meaning of that word). After the Mass of Christian Burial at St. Augustine's in Treme, the Dolliole funeral procession followed the brass band up Esplanade Avenue to St. Louis Cemetery No. 3. The pallbearers and honorary pallbearers were the children and grandchildren of the deceased. It was a jazz funeral that could be described by the word *classic*, if that is taken to mean authentic, authoritative, traditional, enduring, and memorable. After the dirge and the long slow march, the mourners cut the body loose and the Second Line returned to Treme with umbrellas and fancy dance-steps unfurled. Participants speculated that living memory of the piercing sound of Bolden's cornet, which would stop passersby in their tracks a century ago, had finally passed.

Not far away in New Orleans at that time, funerals were being performed in a context of urgency over another kind of loss. Historically depressed by racism, unemployment, and poverty, the Crescent City hit pre-Katrina bottom in 1989–95. The death of scores of young men during an upturn of violence blamed on drugs precipitated a crisis in the community: during those years more "burials with music" were performed in New Orleans than at any time since the 1920s, but many of them in a performance style that most of the mourners at the Dolliole funeral would have disdained.[14] The meaning of the word *performance* is rooted in verbs of doing—to exhibit, to execute, to discharge, to accomplish, or to fulfill— and nouns of things done—shows, rituals, practices, behaviors. What the so-called crack funerals discharged and accomplished, I believe, not unlike jazz music in the 1890s, was an expansion in the range of expression by collapsing the sacred into the profane—what Ondaatje's Mumford called "His music" into "the Devil's music." The traditional ritual was taken apart and rebuilt to serve the more pressing needs of a threatened generation. As parents buried their children, the spectacle of bereavement adapted itself to the cruel inversion of death's usual protocols. As the emergent preempted the residual, it was the peers of the murdered who stepped forward to displace or co-opt the parents with a renovated piety marked by shades and attitude. Stoned Second Liners hijacked funeral processions. They stripped naked, danced lewdly, and spewed beer on one another and over the caskets of the deceased. They marked the line of march by nailing crack bags to the trees and telephone poles. To some this looked like rage and madness—they spoke of it as "social decay." To others it looked like a terrible beauty was being born—they spoke of "dancing it out," meaning that grief was free to take the cathartic form of ecstatic movement, including leaping on top of parked or even moving cars and falling to the ground as if in seizure.[15]

When Darnell "D-Boy" Andrews was buried after being shot dead at age seventeen, for example, the brass band played hip-hop while his friends sprayed beer on the hearse. D-Boy's funeral contrasts vividly with Papa Stacks's. His peers entered the funeral home and took charge of the cortege, which made short work of the dirge. Traditional sensibilities were outraged by these excesses, but less fastidious observers noted that not everyone expresses grief like suburban Presbyterians and not everyone (outside of a war zone) has so much to mourn. There was no doubt about the depth of the emotion expressed. Bereavement is a kind of madness, on which unempathetic passersby might look with embarrassment or even disgust, but which will force its way out somehow through crevices and fissures that performance opens up in tradition.

Along parallel lines, Ondaatje saves the climactic scene of Buddy Bolden losing it for a Second Line parade. In his catastrophic day job as a barber, "the first man of jazz" has already taken a razor and sliced the nipple off Tom Pickett, an apparent rival in love. But the final descent into certifiability happens at a moment when only fellow performers can immediately discern the difference between the music and the madness: "Between Marais and Liberty I just hit notes every 15 seconds or so Henry Allen worrying me eyeing me about keeping the number going and every now and then my note like a bird flying out of the shit and hanging loud and long."[16] If social death can stand in for physical death—and madness is a form of social death—the final procession in *Coming Through Slaughter* is a kind of jazz funeral to mourn and to celebrate what Bolden did and what he might have done. Ondaatje emphasizes the kinesthetic dimensions of the parade. The figure of the woman "who mirrors [Bolden's] throat in her lonely tired dance" seems to represent a spectral version of Storyville itself.

> March is slowing to a stop and as it floats down slow to a thump I take off and wail long notes jerking the squawk into the end of them to form a new beat, have to trust them all as I close my eyes, know the others are silent, throw the notes off the wall of people, the iron lines, so pure and bringing the howl down to the floor and letting in the light and the girl is alone now mirroring my throat in her lonely tired dance, the street silent but for us her tired breath I can hear she's near me as I go round and round in the centre of the Liberty-Iberville connect.[17]

Phrases like "wail long notes" and "jerking the squawk" may be as close as anyone will come to describing Bolden's legendary musical effects on the cornet.

The nostalgia evoked by Buddy Bolden's memory has served a purpose similar to that of ghost notes in summoning jazz communities into imaginary fullness of being. Even as the supposed moment of origin seemed to be receding beyond the grasp (if not the reach) of the jazz purists, a vast space was filling up with its rapidly mutating sounds. The nearly simultaneous development of jazz, the phonograph, and the radio led to the dynamic sonic and kinesthetic diffusion of the music of Bolden's immediate heirs, many of whom were the white purveyors of "Dixieland." This is the story of purity of origins betrayed that Hobsbawm both retails and suspects. In much more recent times, however, the "neoclassicism" championed by Wynton Marsalis has conceived of jazz as the classical music of the Americas, calling for what Scott DeVeaux calls "a careful balance between the modernist ideology of continuous innovation and an insistence on the priority of tradition."[18] Jazz neoclassicism will seemingly fulfill its aspirations when busts of Armstrong and Ellington take their places alongside those of Beethoven and Brahms in the air-conditioned practice rooms of elite conservatories. Meanwhile, back on the streets of New Orleans, inconvenient with madness and vomit, the imperiled first men of jazz are cutting loose.

NOTES

This essay originally appeared in *Issues in Death and Dying*, ed. Robert Harvey (Occasional Papers of the Humanities Institute: SUNY-Stony Brook, 2001).

1. Alan P. Merriam and Fradley H. Garner, "Jazz—The Word," *The Jazz Cadence of American Culture*, ed. Robert G. O'Meally (New York: Columbia University Press, 1998).

2. Eric Hobsbawm, *Uncommon People: Resistance, Rebellion, and Jazz* (London: Weidenfeld & Nicholson, 1998), 242.

3. Michael Ondaatje, *Coming Through Slaughter* (1976) (New York: Vintage Books, 1996).

4. Marvin Carlson, *Performance: A Critical Introduction* (New York: Routledge, 1996), 195.

5. Renato Rosaldo, *Culture and Truth: The Remaking of Social Analysis* (1989) (Boston: Beacon Press, 1993), 20.

6. Ibid., 10.

7. Ondaatje, *Coming Through Slaughter*.

8. Al Rose, *Storyville, New Orleans* (Tuscaloosa: University of Alabama Press, 1974), 103–24.

9. Ibid., 106.

10. Ondaatje, *Coming Through Slaughter*, 9–10.

11. Ibid., 80–81.

12. Ibid., 137.

13. Ibid., 157.

14. Jason Berry, video documentary, *Spirit Tides from Congo Square*, New Orleans, 1998.

15. Ibid.
16. Ondaatje, *Coming Through Slaughter,* 129.
17. Ibid., 130.
18. Scott DeVeaux, "Constructing the Jazz Tradition," *The Jazz Cadence of American Culture*, ed. Robert G. O'Meally (New York: Columbia University Press, 1998), 504.

AIDA MBOWA

Abbey Lincoln's Screaming Singing and the Sonic Liberatory Potential Thereafter

> When she opens her mouth to sing . . . it's perhaps my imagination, [but] I literally have at times seen the sound that comes from her body. I see the sound. I'd not only hear it but see it.
> —MAX ROACH ON ABBEY LINCOLN[1]

> Where shriek turns song—remote from the impossible comfort of origin—lies the trace of our descent.
> —FRED MOTEN ON ABBEY LINCOLN[2]

TO SEE A SOUND, to hear the narrative sung in a scream, is to listen to Abbey Lincoln. With sounds toying with conceptions of music and noise, skirting round the boundaries of annotatability, resisting reiteration, Lincoln disrupted the 1960s New York jazz scene. Having previously sung songs ruminating primarily on love's tribulations or reflecting similar, relatively unthreatening thematic interests, the year 1960 ushered in a radically altered Lincoln. She began to identify with the voices of mass protest and align with a burgeoning politics of Black Nationalism, placing her voice within a body of not only musicians, but also politicians, playwrights, actors, poets, and activists who in retrospect collectively comprised the nebulously-defined Black Arts Movement.[3] Lincoln proceeded to produce music rooted in a quest for a deep political engagement with the black liberation struggles of the time, in large part out of her personal and professional partnership with drummer Max Roach.

In the late 1950s, together with writer-singer Oscar Brown Jr., Roach began to work on a project designed for the 1963 centennial of the Eman-

135

cipation Proclamation.[4] That collaboration fell through, but by the end of 1959, Roach felt he could not afford to stall on a course of action in line with the unprecedented loud and manifold articulations of black grievance. He expedited the project. In 1960, Roach released an album on which he collaborated with other esteemed jazz musicians such as tenor saxophonists Coleman Hawkins and Walter Benton, trumpeter Booker Little, trombonist Julian Priester, and Nigerian conga drummer Michael Babatunde Olutanji. Perhaps most memorably, Roach employed the vocals of Abbey Lincoln. The resultant album was a jazz suite released by Candid Records entitled: *We Insist! Max Roach's Freedom Now Suite*. The live and mediated performances of some of the music on this suite comprise my primary field of analysis.

The suite falls both within and against what was then a burgeoning avant-garde jazz tradition, coming out of lower Manhattan bars and out of late night/early morning experimental jamming sessions.[5] The suite holds five songs: "Driva'man"; "Freedom Day"; "Triptych: Prayer, Protest, Peace"; "All Africa"; and "Tears for Johannesburg." While three of the songs contain conventional lyrics, Lincoln's most memorable contribution is her non-lyrical vocal performance on the track "Triptych: Prayer, Protest, Peace." Lincoln produces sounds of polysemic and polyphonic resonance. Her vocals invite what Fred Moten calls a "bone-deep listening" whose result is the experience of a superfluity of meaning and the animation of additional senses.[6] While analyzing the words of Ralph Ellison's invisible man cogitating Louis Armstrong's music, Moten contends, "Ellison knows that you can't really listen to this music . . . that really listening, when it goes bone-deep into the sunken ark of bones, is something other than itself. It doesn't alternate but *is* seeing; it's the sense that it excludes; it's the ensemble of senses."[7] As such, Lincoln's sounds dissuade a "blind trust of the ear,"[8] to the effect that Roach sees her sounds, Moten hears echoes of Frederick Douglass's Aunt Hester's screams as she was whipped by her slave master, and the bone-deep listener sees and hears the entire ghostly ensemble present in Lincoln's recording.[9] "Perhaps this is my imagination?" Roach asks. Perhaps. But Lincoln's voice works hard to make listeners envision particular moments of black history. Reflecting upon herself and her sound during the original recording and performances of "Protest," Lincoln remarks, "I just want to be of use to my ancestors / It's holy work and it's dangerous not to know that 'cause you could die like an animal down here."[10] For Lincoln, this holy work involves fulfilling the unfinished business of her progenitors. Her project is the evocation of ghosts. And her ghosts are slaves.

There is a stage within Abbey Lincoln's sound upon which she conjures the specters of slavery and its legacy. Not only does Lincoln's voice create a platform to make visible the invisible man, woman, and child of African descent, in the black past and in the black present, she also makes audible the inaudible voices of these apparitions. Lincoln's sounds sketch the site and re-set the stage to dramatize some of the most horrific scenes in the dreadful spectacle at the origin of the formation of African America. She demands that we, her audience, hear her and, through a bone-deep listening, the millions she conjures; that we, too, re-dress African America's originative scenes/redress America's original sin, the repercussions of which she and her people, black people, play out in the aftermath of an unimaginable genesis.

I argue that through the invocation of historic and fictive ghosts prior to and during the "Protest" section of "Triptych," Roach and Lincoln seek to contextualize her scream for freedom. From there I suggest a potential positive outcome to Lincoln's method of using historical invocations for contemporaneous social justice music. I do this by making the case for what I term sonic liberatory potential. To understand this concept one must listen to Frederick Douglass's hope when he hears the slave songs/testimonies of "the dehumanizing character of slavery"—a hope that a sound can make a profound impression in the mind that moves a listener toward action for social justice.[11] Sonic liberatory potential resides in the liminal space between the making of and listening to sounds that unsettle a status quo that would un-hear the iniquities of history; it converges geographies and temporalities to amplify prospective impacts; and it contains the possibility of affecting listeners to the effect of a liberatory impulse (for either the provider or the recipient of the sound). Even though the result of experiencing Lincoln's music varies with each listener, I will reveal the numerous ways Lincoln's sound works to make listeners address some of the inexpressible suffering in black history. Therein lies the sonic liberatory potential engendered by bone-deep listening to Lincoln's screams—an engagement in redress discourse.

As she takes on the burden of voicing her ancestors' grievances, Lincoln engages in the impossible—seeking restitution for the damages done by slavery. Often, when questions of reparations are brought up in one of the most potent arenas, the law courts, they fail to receive substantive attention and success. The primary reasons for which are: the difficulty of showing current material grievances and individuals as the aftermath and afterlife of slavery; the passage of time; and the immateriality of psychic and social trauma (which is potentially slavery's premier legacy).[12] So if, as legal scholar E. Tammy Kim observes, the courts are a "justice-seeking medium" to attend to material and tangible complaints, and if, as Anne Cheng notes, a demand for public recognition allows the transformation of "a marginalized, racialized person from being an object *bearing grief* to being a subject *speaking grievance*" [my emphasis], then when the law fails to redress psychic grievances, artists seek to be heard in what I call "the court of the real."[13] By giving voice to specters, Lincoln pursues their justice. The power of her voice is that it conjures—to borrow Daphne Brooks's expression—ghosts on a record of people who left no record.[14] Her voice brings back the sounds from the plantation, the sounds from the middle passage, in the hopes that this time around, in 1960, almost one hundred years from the retrospectively infelicitous Emancipation Proclamation, these sounds will arraign America for its broken promise to liberate its black citizens.

The Sixth Sense of History or an Ensemble of Ghosts

Moten's theory of "bone-deep listening" is my point of entry into an analysis of the extra-sensory experiences that Lincoln's screams yield. Bone-deep listening is not so much about what to hear as it is about how to hear. For Moten, going bone-deep involves listening so far into history that not only might the middle passage come (in)to mind, but the listener may also activate an "ensemble of senses." He cautions, "Don't just enter the music, but descend into its depths. A bone-deep listening, a sensing of the unbridgeable chasm, seen-said, seen cry unheard but for that bone-deep listening, improvisational vision of invisible performance, that descent into the music, descent into organization, the ensemble of the senses. . . ."[15] In a drug-induced experience, Ellison's Invisible Man begins to see and partake in a sermon on the blackness of blackness while bone-deep listening to Louis Armstrong singing "What did I do to be so black and blue?" He comes out of the hallucination when, like a skipping record, he cannot get an answer to a question on repeat: What is the meaning of freedom?[16] Like Ellison, like Moten, listen to Abbey Lincoln channeling black history, scratching the record to reveal the un-meaning of freedom.

Bone-deep listening is as much about what sound the musician produces as it is about what the listener hears. Just as Jacques Derrida argues that "speech and language are always already taken from a reading," the meaning of music is also always already stolen from the musician in the act of listening to it.[17] This is because once out of the lips and thus control of the producers of the sound, the music becomes readily available to (mis) interpretation. And so variables, including a listener's spatial and temporal proximity to the moment of original production, impact the nature and effect of bone-deep listening to Lincoln's screams. I will elaborate further on the variation of Lincoln's impact with respect to space and time, but first I explore Moten further in the quest for a framework with which to see Lincoln's sound.

In his provocative text *In the Break: The Aesthetics of the Black Radical Tradition*, Fred Moten invites readers to think about, around, and through people or concepts by placing them side by side, in the middle, or on top of other people and concepts. In this way, while briefly meditating on Lincoln's vocal performance, Moten directs us to Frederick Douglass and Aunt Hester, to Saidiya Hartman's *Scenes of Subjection* and to Edouard Glissant, to name but a few.[18] The ensemble of black performances and black history in conversation with Lincoln's screams is sometimes fictive, sometimes factual. When we follow Moten's lead down the trajectory of Frederick Douglass, we encounter a historic theorization of the liberatory potential at the convergence of blackness and audiovisual performance.

In transit, en route to the narrative, we lapse upon Nathaniel Rogers, who in 1844 commented on a speech Douglass delivered with the following observation: "Douglass finished narrating the story and gradually let out the outraged humanity that was laboring in him, in indignant and terrible speech. It was not what you could describe as oratory or eloquence. It was sterner—darker—deeper than these. It was the volcanic outbreak of human nature long pent up in slavery and at last bursting its imprisonment."[19] Rogers describes Douglass's sound as permeating linguistic boundaries, borderline exceeding the form it finds itself within. Significantly, Douglass was one of the first African Americans to win a public voice followed by a voice audible to a literary audience, and therefore inevitably speaking and performing on behalf of the many voiceless to a literary and socio-political realm.

As screaming music, Abbey Lincoln's voice begs a similar description. Yet as we consider Lincoln by way of Frederick Douglass, we read not only Douglass's voice, spoken and transcribed, but also Douglass's literary voice and the voice it animates, that of his Aunt Hester and her "heart-rending shrieks."[20] While Moten considers what it means for Saidiya Hartman to make the conscious choice *not* to engage in a literary re-production of the legendary screams, I consider what it means for Lincoln to engage in an artistic re-production of those screams, or any depicted slave screams for that matter.[21] What is the significance and responsibility of such a choice? We discover the potential inherent in such a decision as we continue to investigate the Douglass lead in search of a theory of a black audiovisual potentiality, and as we arrive at the narrative itself.

In his book, Douglass offers insight into the language and voice of the specters within Lincoln's voice. He analyzes the sounds on slave plantations giving testimony to the latent potential of black sounds.

> They would make the dense old woods, for miles around, reverberate with their wild songs, revealing at once the highest joy and the deepest sadness. They would compose and sing as they went along consulting neither time nor tune. The thought that came up came out—if not in the word, in the sound; and as frequently in the one as in the other. They would sometimes sing the most pathetic sentiment in the most rapturous tone, and the most rapturous sentiment in the most pathetic tone. . . . They would sing, as a chorus, to words which to many would seem unmeaning jargon, but which, nevertheless, were full of meaning to themselves. I have sometimes thought that the mere hearing of those songs would do more to impress some minds with the horrible character of slavery than the reading of whole volumes of philosophy on the subject would do . . . They were tones loud, long, and deep. . . . Every tone was a testimony against slavery, and a prayer to God for deliverance from chains . . . to those songs I trace my first glimmering conception of the dehumanizing character of slavery.[22]

Douglass describes a process of expression whereby the medium of some thoughts must be sound without words. Words were abandoned along with tune and time, but the sounds were always revealing. They unveiled emotions (joy, sadness). Meaning was constituted in the sound itself. For those who were audience to the utterances, the sounds held evidence of the inhumanity of slavery. Douglass asserts these sounds held a greater revolutionary potential than philosophical literature. This is because, particularly in the absence of language, these sounds made a passionate appeal to a listener, these sounds incited emotions.

In addition to the insider-outsider (vocalist-audience) effects of the slave screams, which Douglass describes, screams sometimes served a pragmatic function within slave communities. Glissant makes the case for the ability for noise to signify ("din as discourse") on a slave plantation: "It was the intensity of the sound that dictated meaning: the pitch of the

sound conferred significance . . . since speech was forbidden, slaves cam-
ouflaged the word under the provocative intensity of the scream."[23] Within
a group, screaming was communication. Without the group, with an audience, sounds testified. All those audience to the utterance of these noises
witnessed a case against slavery.

Abbey Lincoln screams. A scream can be a literal testimony of a body
in physical pain. In black history to scream is to defy silencing, and the attempt to erase the very human and necessary noise in response to physical
injury—to whips, to smacks, to the breaking of the body. In her book *The
Body in Pain*, Elaine Scarry argues that pain more than any other phenomenon "resists objectification in language."[24] That is to say, pain, perhaps
more frustratingly so than many other interior states, seeks an "external-
ity," "sharability," that seems to move back away from language.[25] We hear
in Lincoln's vocal expression a release of sound unalloyed to lyrics, akin
to "a reversion to the pre-language of cries and groans, whereby we witness the destruction of language."[26] Thus, considering Scarry and Glissant
alongside each other: screams on slave plantations, represented in literature, represented in musical performances centuries later, contradictorily,
are and are not language.

While Scarry's project unpacks a physical body in pain, and the screams
and cries she refers to arise out of a psychic response to physical agony,
the question remains: What of psychological agony? In the extract above,
Douglass alludes to sounds emerging from particular conditions of the
psyche—"deepest sadness." The psyche in pain? Scarry contends psychological pain *does* have recourse to language and that many artists are
constantly trying to depict suffering. Yet, in *The Melancholy of Race*, Anne
Cheng reveals the shift in character of a psychological pain that cannot
find expression toward that which can. Cheng argues that a "transformation from grief to grievance" is a transformation "from suffering injury to
speaking out against that injury."[27] Thus Cheng elucidates a psychological
pain capable of linguistic expression (grievance) and one incapable of it
(grief). Yet physical and psychological pains are not entirely distinct. Un-
dergirding both Scarry's and Cheng's respective arguments is a question of
the political repercussions of an inability to express pain. This is the notion
that reveals the stakes of Lincoln's screams and the political implications of
Roach and Lincoln's project.

In her explanation of pain's inexpressibility and the political consequences therein, Scarry argues, "the relative ease or difficulty with which
any given phenomenon can be verbally represented also influences the
ease or difficulty with which that phenomenon comes to be politically

represented."[28] In a similar vein, Cheng states, "A traditional method of intervention in the history of racism has indeed been the demand for public recognition. This often takes the form of transforming the marginalized, racialized person from being an object bearing grief to being a subject speaking grievance."[29] Thus, voicing, engaging an audience, making something publically known, denotes the beginning of addressing pain, be it physical or psychological. As such, when Lincoln signifies sounds that evoke a pain without recourse to language in a public forum, she moves toward addressing black, socio-political grief. The impossibility of such a task speaks to the necessity of the form that Lincoln's music takes. In the slippages between communicating a grief, read more easily as grievance in the public sphere, comes the distrust of conventional language. In Lincoln's case, it becomes a distrust of lyrics, harmony, and euphony, and resort to screams, shrieks, dissonance, and irresolution.[30]

At the same time, the song is entitled "Triptych: Prayer, Protest, Peace," and it functions as a movement in three parts. I speak of the dissonance and irresolution in the middle section, "Protest." Yet, the song ends with the hums and coos of Lincoln's voice in the "Peace" part, a suggestion that peace comes after protest. Order is of great import. (And we must not ellipse the context of the production of this song—the midst of the Civil Rights Movement, a turbulent time and period of great social unrest for America's black citizens.)[31] Thus the message that peace can only be heard after protest resonates politically. Particularly in music without lyrics, the names or titles that the artists give to a piece of music go a long way toward shaping meaning for the meaning-making listener. Thus every song is undergirded by the words in the title of the suite: "We Insist!" and "Freedom Now." Each song contains the urgency and reflexivity of the then contemporaneous state of affairs.

"Triptych" is a song about the present. Yet just as sequence within the song is a crucial factor, so too is the arrangement of the songs on the suite. A suite is an ordered set of musical pieces, and as musicologist Ingrid Monson explains, "Triptych" comes after two songs situated within the history of the oppression of black people. The first song, "Driva'man," is a work song with Lincoln singing lyrics that paint the image of brutality on a slave plantation as she produces whip-like sounds on a tambourine, punctuating the end of each line with a smack (*Driva'man de kinda boss* [smack] / *Ride a man and lead a horse* [smack] / *When his cat o' nine tail fly* [smack] / *You be happy just to die* [smack]). Lincoln takes the listener back to a plantation in which the constant sound of the whip, the imminent threat of the whip, begins to punctuate the enslaved body's rhythm and the rhythm of the voice. Within her short and necessary breaths, which follow the violent slap of a tambourine, one hears the pain of black suffering. One hears an insistence on life. Knowing black history in a contemporary moment, or living in proximity to the time and space of the original production of the song, potentially fosters a bone-deep listening through which one sees black history in Lincoln's sound. One hears the sadness spawned by being situated in a genealogy whereby intense physical and psychological torture mark the beginnings of a heritage. One hears a whip. The whip by which humans were driven like cattle: a whip whose slashes sever not only flesh, but also communities, peoples, senses of self/worth; a whip that defines humanity using a language of capitalist economics; a whip that reveals the darker side of mankind—hate.

The second song, "Freedom Day," is a song about the Emancipation Proclamation; Lincoln's lyrics question the actuality or reality of that freedom (*Whisper say we're free / rumors flying must be lyin' / Can it really be?*).[32] "Freedom Day" opens with trembling cymbals followed by the dual dynamism of a triumphant-sounding trumpet and tenor saxophone announcing: Freedom! Rushed beats follow; anxious beats accompanied by Lincoln's voice, legato in distinction to the staccato horns and drums. Roach has an impressive drum solo followed by trumpeting and cymbals. Eventually, Lincoln comes back on vocals, almost undercutting the jubilant sound of the horns and cymbals with her laden voice, a heavy sound, an exhausted and skeptical call for celebration. The song provokes a miscellany of emotions, but ultimately, the song settles on sadness as a listener—aware in hindsight of how black history has unfolded—thinks on the irony of (Abbey/Abraham) Lincoln singing, "free to vote and earn our pay." This song was released five years in advance of the Voting Rights Act. The song is an imagined celebration of a freedom that never came, a freedom day Lincoln and Roach anticipate.

Thus by the time the listener arrives at the third song on the suite, "Triptych," they have experienced an aural journey through a soundscape that sets the scene and serves as a prelude to comprehending the meaning-making engendered by this song. Unsurprisingly, the music set to speak to the contemporaneous moment eschews lyrical articulation. The effect of this setup is to suggest that in order to understand the cries and shouts of black grievance in 1960s America, you must listen closely to the forgotten sounds of suffering from prior critical points in black history.

Consequently, although this song, more than any other song on the suite, attests to the contemporaneous African American situation, it does so having contextualized the call for freedom within the context of the injustices in black history/black memory. But why? Why listen to the past to speak for the present and look to the future?—a collapsing of temporalities congruous with the cross-pollination of the senses. What does it mean for Lincoln to conjure historic/fictive ghosts to make a case for the crisis in the 1960s? Surely, the images of peaceful black protesters hosed, beaten, attacked by dogs, and subjected to the brutalities that occurred during the 1960s provided enough of a referent, of a thing to be signified, without referencing slavery. What does it mean to situate contemporaneous cries within the framework of black history and black performance history?

Making Noise for the Record

A resort to the invocation of history is a move with double potential. On the one hand, Lincoln believed she spoke on behalf of her ancestors, thus she viewed her singing screaming, her voice and hence her body as a ventriloquized vessel in service of a mystical operation—in service of her ancestors: "My instrument is deepening and widening; it's because I'm possessed of the spirit. . . . This is the music of the African muse / I just want to be of use to my ancestors / It's holy work and it's dangerous not to know that 'cause you could die like an animal down here."[33] On the other hand, akin to the sentiment expressed by Saidiya Hartman in her book *Lose Your Mother*, Lincoln and Roach looked to slave plantations as a result of recognizing "the afterlife of slavery"—slavery's legacy. Hartman writes, "If slavery persists as an issue in the political life of black America, it is not because of an antiquarian obsession with bygone days or the burden of a too-long memory, but because black lives are still imperiled and devalued by a racial calculus and a political arithmetic that were entrenched centuries ago."[34] By screaming over furious drumming in front of various audiences during the 1960s, but also, on a record that could permeate living rooms and private spaces around the country and around the globe, Lincoln's voice attempted to activate a sonic liberatory potential.

When it comes to Lincoln, *We Insist!*, "Triptych," and the sounds audible between minutes 3:37 and 4:53 on the suite—that is, the "Protest" segment—the sonic liberatory potential is confounded by, but also enabled through, the fact that the sound is a deliberate reproduction of imagined sounds produced in vastly different circumstances. That is to say, screaming in a concert hall or in a recording studio is incomparable to screaming under a water hose, let alone on a slave plantation. As powerful as it might be, Lincoln's voice does not eclipse that point. Yet, recognizing the forum, hearing and seeing the dissimilarity, begs a series of questions:

What are those sounds? What is she doing? To what effect? That the music provokes these questions allows for a sonic liberatory potential as it instigates a quest to reconcile the disjunction between the lyrics of the preceding songs, the screams on "Triptych," and the words in the title of the suite: "We Insist," "Freedom Now." Such a quest expands the listener's context, potentially arriving back at the ensemble of ghosts Lincoln's voice attempts to represent.

One audience member, poet and activist Kalamu Ya Salaam, reflects upon a 1968 performance of "Triptych" that he attended with the following words.

> I knew about vocalese, the fitting of lyrics to famous jazz solos, but "Tryptich" [*sic*] was several levels beyond because there are literally no words in English to describe specific aspects of our historic and contemporary experiences. Abbey and Max made me believe in time travel, believe in the power of a secular Holy Ghost, a terrible Shiva-force that destroyed you to renew you. I was afraid for her—and for myself also. It seemed as though she might hurt herself. It seemed as if I should do something helpful and not just be a stationary stump while she was going through this. This was not just jazz. This was a religious experience. A new way to live.[35]

The above passage describes a bone-deep listening. Ancestors, pain, history, and the present emerge through Salaam's experience of Lincoln's sound. He elucidates the aforementioned potential of Lincoln's sound by shifting from thinking of the historic, to thinking about her vocal technique, to thinking about action, and then the new world thereafter. Lincoln's screams disturb. They inspire rumination, distort temporalities, and then re-establish a sense of time, which rather than leaving the listener melancholic, unable to take action because he or she is weighed down by the gravity of history, the experience leaves the listener inspired or incited. This mirrors the response elucidated by Ellison's Invisible Man as he listens to Louis Armstrong: "This familiar music had demanded action, the kind of which I was incapable, and yet had I lingered there beneath the surface I might have attempted to act."[36] Action is the result of lingering in a bone-deep listening.

To attempt to put into language precisely what one hears in the 1:16 minutes of "Protest" on the suite would be a self-defeating enterprise, for part of what characterizes listening to the sound is hearing its resistance to language and to notions of song, structure, and genre; even while it resists, it is never outside of a listener's attempts to codify it or translate it.[37] Yet the screams on the record are far more controlled or rather they seem to approach a melodiousness that is absent in video recordings of "Protest."[38]

During the 1960s, Roach and Lincoln toured *We Insist! Freedom Now* both inside and outside of the United States. Videotaped productions reveal the additional performative elements Roach and Lincoln employed to further contextualize their music: facial expressions, attire, gestures, and set designs. One such video is a 1964 made-for-television performance of "Triptych" in the SWF television studio, in Baden-Baden, Germany.[39] The piece begins with "Prayer." Lincoln and Roach are in two separate pens reminiscent of jail cells. Lincoln faces Roach who sits wearing a suit by his drum set. Lincoln stands erect yet relaxed; her body is still, and most of her movement centers around her mouth. The camera privileges a side profile of her face. She wears a long-sleeved blouse and an ankle-length skirt. She wears her hair, which is natural (un-chemicalized), back in an Afro puff—an Afrocentric gesture during the 1960s. She sings "Prayer," and then she takes a step forward and holds onto the bars of the cell. The camera cuts. Lincoln steps up to Roach so that now the audience/camera is inside the cell with them, or rather, they are no longer in the cell but jail bars are visible behind them. "Protest" begins. She clenches her fists, tilts her head upward—gestures of agony. Lincoln's body is not frantic, but her screams involve more elongated, diminuendo cries than on the record or in other recorded performances. When she finishes "Protest," the front side of a jail cell automatically raises entrapping them inside it yet again. She coos, "Peace."

Lincoln's facial expressions and physical gestures broadcast the emotional content of the piece. Her eyes allow her voice to do all the crying; they remain restrained, but extraordinarily sad. During "Peace" Lincoln's eyes become momentarily alive, they seem possessed; but by the end of a grueling emotional journey, we witness silent tears roll down her face. In "Peace," her breathing becomes extraordinarily important, audible and functional. Her breath serves to allow her to recover from the intensity of "Protest," yet it also invokes madness and ecstasy in the midst of a supposed serenity. Though drastically different and radically more tranquil than "Protest," a listener cannot rest easy by the end of "Peace." Remnants of violence cloud her "Peace."

The video renders some of the strongest political elements of the song didactic. The prison motif further reinforces the notion of enslavement/imprisonment, but it detracts from the power of the voice. No longer restricted to sound as the primary means to paint images, Lincoln and Roach create a multifaceted piece of performance art. Particularly in the "Peace" section, Lincoln relies upon her face to emote, choosing various moments not to sing but simply to look at a microphone. She does not have this luxury when audio is the only means of accessing her performance; she must vocally signify things we might see on a video (expressly the gesture of silence; of refusing or being unable to produce sound during a musical performance).[40] Thus, on the audio recording, we hear the sound of a voice stretching and struggling to produce strained cries and screams.

On the record, the pitch and quality of the screams fluctuate in a manner suggestive of over-contemplation. The screams work to distance the listener, which brings them closer to hearing and contemplating "old" sounds stemming from "raw" psycho-physical suffering. Yet the audibility of the production of the sound—such as the audibility of a "safe" scream (probably due to vocal exercises aimed to prevent Lincoln from hurting her throat/herself)—brings the listener back to the present, to the very material circumstances of the contemporaneous, which reinforce the "now" of the suite.[41] Like the successful application of Bertolt Brecht's epic theater technique, the effect of revealing the mechanics of Lincoln's sound production could offer the listener the right perspective in order to think analytically of Lincoln simultaneously inside and outside her performance.[42]

Encountering Lincoln's vocal performance on a record as opposed to a live concert augments the possibilities of her sound. In his book *Phonographies: Grooves in Afro-Sonic Modernity*—a reading of the emergence of modern black subjectivity in relation to sound technologies—Alexander Weheliye observes, "The phonograph emerges as a machinic ensemble (to cross-fade Fred Moten's and Deleuze and Guattari's idioms) that accents the eventness of the (re)production of the source; the source is always (re)produced as an (anti)origin while also appearing as a differently produced occasion in each of its singular figurations."[43] That is to say, the expansion of locations and times brought about by the transportability of the record makes each reiteration, each playing of the suite, an event of its own nature, unrestrained by its dissimilarity to a notion of an original performance.

Weheliye's supposition concedes Peggy Phelan's contention that the recorded performance is something other than the original, and that the original has disappeared, but it sees possibilities in this "something else" that need not pit itself against the live.[44] At the same time, this reproduction, what Weheliye would call a "glaring rupture between sound and vision" as a result of mediatization, augments the possibilities of said sound, for it underscores the intended alienating effect of listening to screaming singing, and it reinforces the obfuscation of spatial and temporal dimensions (although, as I articulated earlier, Lincoln's sound seeks to draw upon the listener's vision in the midst of the rupture of sound and vision that a record makes).[45] For this reason, when Philip Auslander destabilizes the binary between the live and the mediatized by mapping the "electronic ontology of media," I see value in the sentiment driving the quest to defuse performance theorists' proclivity to preference the live over the mediatized.[46]

Weheliye reinforces the fact that with recording and playback technology, the listener can hear a song multiple times and discover new things with every iteration. So when I speak of the possibilities engendered by a recording of "Triptych," I speak of possibilities akin to those Weheliye articulates: "Oralities and musicalities were no longer tied to the immediate presence of human subjects, a situation that occasions not so much a complete disappearance of the human as much as a resounding through new styles of technological folding."[47] Thus, possibilities abound in what Weheliye calls the "ephemoromateriality of recorded sound."[48] However, the greater pertinence of the recording of Lincoln's sounds rests in the potential implications of such sounds on the record.

While cogitating Lincoln as a frontwoman on a record of an ensemble of ghosts, we continue to linger on the question, To what effect? To hear the depths of the resonance of Lincoln's screams, we must consider what is being transmitted in excess of her sound waves, and then realize the significance of recording such a sound. Thus far I have argued for the audibility of some of the ghosts of black history in the screams on "Triptych." Lincoln's screams attempt to represent the impossible: profound psychological grief and intense physical pain in black history. In order to arrive at the sonic liberatory potential in recordings of Lincoln's screams, we need to consider the political implications of Lincoln representing slaves.

While demanding a very tangible, material liberation (desegregation), Roach and Lincoln's project also calls attention to the "incommensurability between pain and compensation."[49] The sounds lament the tragedies of black history; yet in vocalizing irreconcilable injustices, they simultaneously work toward restituting black grief—a move that as Cheng observes occurs through voicing. As I noted earlier, Cheng asserts that a "transformation from grief to grievance" is a transformation "from suffering injury to speaking out against that injury."[50] This speaking out, this voicing, this expressing if not in words in the language of "cries and groans" or in Lincoln's instance the language of shrieks and screams, attests to Stephen Best and Saidiya Hartman's assertion that for the world to become inhabitable again, there needs to be an un-suppression of previously silent grief—redress.

Best and Hartman arrive at the "nuanced conceptualization" of redress discourse through a reading of Ottabah Cuguano's 1787 text, *Thoughts and Sentiments on the Evils of Slavery and Commerce of Human Species*. They define redress discourse through an analysis of the law's relationship to verbal expression.

> A sophisticated understanding captured in the rhetorical distinctions between grievance and grief; between the necessity of legal remedy and the impossibility of redress . . . between the unavoidable form of the "appeal" and its ultimate illegibility and insufficiency . . . between the complaint that is audible . . . and the extralinguistic mode of black noise that exists outside the parameters of any strategy or plan for remedy.[51]

In this description, we arrive at a realization of the importance of the role of sound and the limitations of language within redress discourse. While these words imply that a courtroom might be the appropriate site to seek "legal remedy" for material grievance, they also highlight the futility of the courtroom as a site to seek redress for the immaterial, the intangible, and the psychosocial. It is at this juncture that artists intervene in the project to make black grievance audible by providing a forum to attempt to facilitate a hearing in "the court of the real." In these courts that one might define as social or public spaces of adjudication and redress, Lincoln's voice enacts an un-silencing, a (re)sounding of black noise.

If black noise "represents the kinds of political aspirations that are inaudible and illegible within the prevailing formulas of political rationality . . . [and] . . . always already barred from the courts," then artists such as Lincoln find audience for their sounds in concert halls and other public spaces.[52] At the beginning of 1961, Roach and Lincoln performed the suite at the Village Gate in New York for the Congress Of Racial Equality (CORE); in 1964, *Muhammed Speaks* newspaper advertised, "The Muslims Present an Evening with Max Roach and Abbey Lincoln."[53] The vastly different nature of these political organizations serves to reinforce Monson's observation that the suite and the narratives surrounding it encapsulated "the tensions between the discourses of black nationalism and the mainstream Civil Rights Movement."[54] While live performances in concert halls created these courts of the real, the recording found audience in public forums, too. In 1963, the leading Black newspaper, *The New York Amsterdam*

News, announced: "Max Roach's record album *Freedom Now Suite* is available to 'any fundraising organization requesting it.'"[55] The newspaper goes on to detail the address and phone number of St. Clair studios, where one can obtain the album. This suggests the record can carry Lincoln's political sounds into not only small, private spaces (living rooms and bedrooms), but also larger social gatherings.

The act of recording Lincoln's screams easily warrants aesthetic objections (for selling screaming as singing or as music is a tendentious move). Yet by (re)producing and (re)presenting sounds weighted by the contextualization of black histories, the very act of recording marks a possible intervention. In the court of the real, the recording serves as a public record of previously inaudible sounds, and potential sights. The record seeks to make permanent the narratives that judicial courts and social spaces silence when they fail to redress slavery's legacy. To make a record is to make something seemingly ephemeral such as sound into a material object. To record is to inscribe, and Lincoln's sounds trace violent, long, and loud cries onto the soundscapes of the 1960s. A record is not only evidence of the past, but also in a court, say the court of the real, it is a testament to proceedings. Lincoln's screams testify.

NOTES

1. Max Roach, interview with Ingrid Monson, April 3, 1999, Cambridge, MA, quoted in Ingrid Monson, *Freedom Sounds: Civil Rights Call Out to Jazz and Africa* (Oxford: Oxford University Press, 2007), 254.

2. Fred Moten, *In the Break: The Aesthetics of the Radical Black Tradition* (Minneapolis: University of Minnesota Press, 2003), 22.

3. Ruth Feldstein, "'I Don't Trust You Anymore': Nina Simone, Culture, and Black Activism in the 1960s," *Journal of American History* 91, no. 4 (March 2005): 1349–79, http://www.historycooperative.org/journals/jah/91.4/feldstein.html#REF8.

4. For historical research and information surrounding the facts of the production of this suite, I am indebted to the following sources: Scott Saul, *Freedom Is, Freedom Ain't: Jazz and the Making of the Sixties* (Cambridge: Harvard University Press, 2003); Eric Porter, *What Is This Thing Called Jazz? African American Musicians as Artists, Critics and Activists* (Berkeley: University of California Press, 2002); Ingrid Monson, *Freedom Sounds: Civil Rights Call Out to Jazz and Africa* (Oxford: Oxford University Press, 2007).

5. Moten, *In the Break.*

6. Moten contends: "Jazz is—in the break that is and breaks the climax. Tarrying, lingering, (productive) of bone deep listening." Fred Moten, "Preface for a Solo by Miles Davis," *Women & Performance: A Journal of Feminist Theory* 17, no. 2 (2007): 217–46, accessed March 8, 2009, http://www.informaworld.com/10.1080/07407700701387317.

7. Below is the final section of the extract from Ralph Ellison's *Invisible Man*, which inspires Moten's arguments.

Then somehow I came out of it, ascending hastily from his underworld of sound to hear Louis Armstrong innocently asking,

What did I do
To be so black
And blue?

At first I was afraid; this familiar music had demanded action, the kind of which I was incapable, and yet had I lingered there beneath the surface I might have attempted to act. Nevertheless, I know now that few really listen to music.

Ralph Ellison, *Invisible Man* (New York: Vintage, 1990), 12; Moten, *In the Break*, 67.

8. Moten paraphrases Theodor Adorno's elucidation of Beethoven's "over-arching forms to which the ear could entrust itself blindly" ("Little Heresy," 322) as an "impossible audiovisuality . . . no longer operative blind trust of the ear"; Theodor Adorno, "Little Heresy," *Essays on Music*, trans. Susan H. Gillespie (Berkeley: University of California Press, 2002), 322; Moten, "Preface for a Solo by Miles Davis."

9. In the introduction of his book, Fred Moten explains that as Lincoln screams one cannot but hear the screams of Aunt Hester as detailed by Frederick Douglass in his autobiographical book. I shall return to Moten's supposition shortly.

10. Abbey Lincoln, from notes taken by Fred Moten at the Ford Foundation Jazz Study Group, Columbia University, November 1999, quoted in Moten, *In the Break*, 23.

11. Frederick Douglass, *Narrative of the Life of Frederick Douglass*, ed. David W. Blight, 1st ed. (Boston: Bedford Books of St. Martin's Press, 1993), 47.

12. Stephen Best and Saidiya Hartman, "Fugitive Justice," *Representation* 92, no. 1 (2005): 1–15, accessed June 28, 2012, http://www.jstor.org/stable/10.1525/rep.2005.92.1.1.

13. E. Tammy Kim, "Performing Social Reparation: 'Comfort Women' and the Path to Political Forgiveness," *Women & Performance* 16, no. 2 (2006): 221–49; Anne Anlin Cheng, *The Melancholy of Race: Psychoanalysis, Assimilation and Hidden Grief* (New York: Oxford University Press, 2000), 172.

14. Daphne A. Brooks, "Staring at the Sun: Remixing the Diasporic Drone on TV on the Radio's 'Return to Cookie Mountain,'" lecture given at the University of Southern California, USC Annenberg School of Communication YouTube Channel, accessed March 19, 2009, http://www.youtube.com/watch?v=Sdq9I11MG70.

15. Moten, *In the Break*, 83.

16. Ellison, *Invisible Man*, 9–12.

17. Jacques Derrida, *Writing and Difference*, trans. Alan Bass (London: Routledge, 1981), 178.

18. Moten, *In the Break*, 1–24.

19. Nathaniel Rogers, "Southern Slavery and Northern Religion: Two Addresses," Frederick Douglass and David W. Blight, *Narrative of the Life of Frederick Douglass, an American Slave*, 2nd ed. (Boston: Bedford Books of St. Martin's Press, 2003), 141.

20. Douglass, *Narrative*, 44.

21. Moten, *In the Break*, 1–5.

22. Douglass, *Narrative*, 49–51.

23. Edouard Glissant, "Natural Poetics, Forced Poetics," *Caribbean Discourse: Selected Essays* (Charlottesville: University of Virginia Press, 1999), 123–24.

24. Elaine Scarry, *The Body in Pain: The Making and Unmaking of the World* (Oxford: Oxford University Press, 1985), 5.

25. Scarry elucidates pain's singularity, which she summarizes in her introduction: "Contemporary philosophers have habituated us to the recognition that our interior states of consciousness are regularly accompanied by objects in the external world, that we do not simply 'have feelings' but have feelings for somebody or something, that love is love of x, fear is fear of y, ambivalence is ambivalence about z. If one were to move through all the emotional, perceptual, and somatic states that take an object—hatred for, seeing of, being hungry for—the list . . . would be throughout its entirety a consistent affirmation of the human being's capacity to move out beyond the boundaries of his or her own body into the external, sharable world." Scarry, *Body in Pain*, 5.

26. Ibid., 6.

27. Cheng, *The Melancholy of Race*, 3.

28. Scarry, *Body in Pain*, 12.

29. Cheng, *The Melancholy of Race*, 174.

30. For detailed analyses of musical structures on the suite see Saul, *Freedom Is, Freedom Ain't*, 93–96; Eric Porter, *What Is This Thing Called Jazz?* (Berkeley: University of California Press, 2002), 167–69; Monson, *Freedom Sounds*, 171–81.

31. The Civil Rights Movement, in particular the plight of America's Black citizens, received unprecedented visibility and attention during the 1960s. The same year that *We Insist! Max Roach's Freedom Now Suite* was released, there were sit-ins protesting segregation laws. One particular sit-in at a Woolworths cafeteria in Greensboro, North Carolina, featured as the cover of the suite. This album was released four years prior to the Civil Rights Act of 1964 and the Voting Rights Act (1965), which would attempt to undo, or at least render unconstitutional, laws that discriminated against people for various reasons, including on the basis of race. The album was performed throughout the 1960s, which became increasingly violent as protestors were met with resistance, and those resisting social change were met with more radical protestors.

32. Max Roach, *We Insist! Max Roach's Freedom Now Suite*, United Kingdon, 1990, Candid CDD 79002.

33. Notes by Fred Moten taken during a presentation by Abbey Lincoln at the Ford Foundation Jazz Study Group, Columbia University, November 1999, in Moten, *In the Break*, 23.

34. "I wanted to engage the past, knowing that its perils and dangers still threatened and that even now lives hung in the balance. Slavery had established a measure of man and a ranking of life and worth that has yet to be undone. . . . This is the afterlife of slavery—skewed life chances, limited access to health and education, premature death, incarceration, and impoverishment. I, too, am the afterlife of slavery." Saidiya Hartman, *Lose Your Mother: A Journey along the Atlantic Slave Route* (New York: Farrar, Straus and Giroux, 2008), 6.

35. Kalamu Ya Salaam, *Breath of Life: A Conversation about Black Music*, accessed March 14, 2009, http://www.kalamu.com/bol/2007/03/04/max-roach-abbey-lin coln-"triptych-prayer-protest-peace"/.

36. Ellison, *Invisible Man*, 12.

37. Again, turn to Saul, Monson, and Anderson for analyses of the musical structures of songs on the suite.

38. Watch 1:45 to 3:00 min of a 1964 performance of the *Freedom Now Suite* produced by a German television network and hosted by music journalist Joachim-Ernst Berendt; Pedro Mendez's collection of rare videos, accessed March 19, 2009, http://www. youtube.com/watch?v=2IOz3FeOwGQ.

39. http://www.youtube.com/watch?v=jhLuUoUHOAo, Baden-Baden, Germany, 1964.

40. The image of Lincoln unable to sing as a result of the intensity of a moment is captured beautifully in another performance. See minutes 2:04 and 2:17: http://www. youtube.com/watch?v=2IOz3FeOwGQ.

41. Salaam reflects: "I was afraid for her—and for myself also. It seemed as though she might hurt herself." While he was responding to a live performance of Lincoln's screams, his words support the notion that Lincoln's vocals also inspire thoughts about her technique bringing a listener back to the present, if in fact their thoughts had been transported to a black historic past; Kalamu Ya Salaam, *Breath of Life*, http://www.kalamu.com/bol/2007/03/04/max-roach-abbey-lincoln-"triptych-prayer-protest-peace"/.

42. Bertolt Brecht, *Brecht on Theater: The Development of an Aesthetic*, ed. and trans. John Willet (London: Methuen, 1964), 122.

43. Alexander Weheliye, *Phonographies: Grooves in Afro-Sonic Modernity* (Durham: Duke University Press, 2003), 32.

44. Peggy Phelan, *Unmarked: The Politics of Performance* (New York: Routledge, 1993), 146.

45. Weheliye, *Phonographies*, 29.

46. Philip Auslander, *Liveness: Performance in a Mediatized Culture* (New York: Routledge, 1999), 43–49.

47. Ibid., 7.

48. Weheliye contends that the "interplay between the ephemerality of music (and/or the apparatus) and the materiality of the audio technologies/practices (and/or music) provides the central, nonsublatable tension at the core of sonic Afro-modernity." The false distinction between the ephemeral and the material within the history of the production of black sonic performances, thus, the troubling of the relationships between writing, music, and orality intensified by the increased use of sound technologies engender new "modes of thinking, being, listening and becoming," which warrants his descriptor—sonic Afro-modernity.

49. Best and Hartman, "Fugitive Justice," http://www.jstor.org/stable/10.1525/rep.2005.92.1.1.

50. Cheng, *Melancholy of Race*, 3.

51. Best and Hartman, "Fugitive Justice," 3.

52. Best and Hartman associate their definition of black noise with Robin Kelley's "freedom dream," and with Moten's idea of "the surreal utopian 'nonsense' of a utopian vision, the freedom we know outside of the opposition of sense and

intellection"; see Robin D. G. Kelley, *Freedom Dreams: The Black Radical Imagination* (Boston: Beacon Press, 2002); Fred Moten, "Uplift and Criminality," *Next to the Color Line: Gender, Sexuality, and W.E.B. Du Bois,* ed. Susan Kay Gillman and Alys Eve Weinbaum (Minneapolis: University of Minnesota Press, 2007); Best and Hartman, "Fugitive Justice," 9, 14.

53. CORE presents Freedom Now Suite (poster), January 1961, series 5, box 28, folder 8; "Roach Suite," *New York Amsterdam News* 51 (January 7, 1961), 11, quoted in Monson, *Freedom Sounds,* 159; "The Muslims Present an Evening with Max Roach and Abbey Lincoln," *Muhammad Speaks* 3, no. 25 (August 28, 1964), 14, quoted in Monson, *Freedom Sounds,* 229.

54. Monson, *Freedom Sounds,* 171–72.

55. "Freedom Album May Be Loaned," *New York Amsterdam News (1962–1993),* August 24, 1963. http://search.proquest.com/docview/226800716?accountid=14026.

MARGARET F. SAVILONIS

Got to Get Over the Hump

The Politics of Glam in the Work of
Labelle and Parliament

IN "THE FOUNDATIONS OF GLITTER ROCK," Van M. Cagle cites the "primary themes of flamboyance, style and image construction, polymorphous sexuality, and multimedia montage as performance art" as key elements of the genre, typically associated with David Bowie, Roxy Music, and other white, male, primarily British artists from the early 1970s.[1] Glam, according to Philip Auslander, opened "a safe cultural space in which to experiment with versions of masculinity that clearly flouted social norms."[2] Yet for Black American artists of the same period, the female trio Labelle (Nona Hendryx, Sarah Dash, and Patti LaBelle) and the band Parliament, led by George Clinton, the adoption and adaptation of the visual, if not the musical, style of glam offered a way to challenge conventional representations of not only gender and sexuality but also race. Evolving from standard pop girl group (The Bluebelles) and doo-wop band (The Parliaments) in the 1960s into boundary-stretching rock-funk bands by the mid-1970s, Labelle and Parliament shifted their performance personae in radical ways, blending the flamboyant performance traditions present in the work of other African-American musicians such as Sun Ra, Sly and the Family Stone, and the Commodores with the overt construction of multiple personae facilitated by the conventions of glam. Glam was a vehicle for reinvention, as both acts shed their established mainstream pop identities in dramatic, theatrical fashion, favoring an otherworldly outer space aesthetic that contrasted sharply with the chiffon dresses and neat suits that they had sported throughout the 1960s in their incarnations as The Bluebelles and The Parliaments.

According to cultural theorist bell hooks, "Racist thinking perpetuates the fantasy that the Other who is subjugated, who is subhuman, lacks the ability to comprehend, to understand, to see the working of the powerful."[3] The adoption of the persona of an alien being from another planet, imbued with greater insight than humans, creates an Other who is capable of revealing new truths and presenting new possibilities. Labelle and Parliament, by exaggerating difference in fantastic ways through musical performance, constructed themselves as challengers to established authority and radically reconfigured their status as Others. Both bands worked with costume designers such as Larry LeGaspi, who also designed for KISS, to create their performance costumes and to design the sets and special effects for their live performances. Though not solely responsible for the creation of their "look," for as Hendryx states, "We didn't ask them [Larry LeGaspi and Richard Erker] to make us look like the way we did, it just evolved out of our relationship with them," the performers *are* responsible for the construction of the image, which depends upon the ways in which they embody it in live performance and other media representations.[4] As Simon Frith suggests, "performance is an 'emergent structure'; it comes into being only as it is being performed."[5] The exaggerated performance of identity generates potential for political efficacy through various elements of musical performance, from lyrics and arrangements to the futuristic/spacefolk personae of both bands.

The Politics of Sameness: Girl Groups/Boy Groups of the 1960s

In the 1960s, Nona Hendryx, Sarah Dash, Patti LaBelle, and Cindy Birdsong comprised a traditional "girl group" called the Bluebelles. They recorded songs such as "I Sold My Heart to the Junkman" and "Down the Aisle" that, according to Charlotte Greig, tread "a line between the ultraconventional and the bizarrely avant-garde" as a result of Patti LaBelle's "vocal acrobatics."[6] Despite Greig's characterization of the Bluebelles' performance style as "avant-garde," their repertoire was standard and resembled that of many other groups. According to Nona Hendryx, "The managers pretty much chose the material. We did very standard material . . . we would rework the standard songs into gospel renditions or more soulful renditions. And then we would do our songs about teenage angst, our hearts being broken—you know the stuff!"[7] It was not until the 1970s, when the group transformed into Labelle, sans Cindy Birdsong (who had left to join the Supremes), that their songs would be as challenging lyrically as they were vocally.

Similarly, the physical appearance of the Bluebelles was standard, akin to the look of groups such as the Shirelles, the Chiffons, and the Dixie Cups. The four women wore matching ensembles, simple and elegant, and sported bouffant hairdos (their hair was straightened to conform to the style) that were popular at the time for both black and white women, onstage and off. The clone effect achieved both within individual bands and across the broad spectrum of girl groups reinforces the hegemonic ideology of the United States in the 1950s; the sameness projects a sense of unity and conformity. Photographs and video clips of various girl groups from the late 1950s/early 1960s reveal a pattern that is disturbing in its uniformity: groups comprised of three to four women wearing matching outfits, often ones that represent a white, middle-class fashion sense, sing in harmony and perform synchronized "dances" that are primarily gestural.[8] The overall effect is one of containment, as sexuality is masked by both costume and movement.

Yet sexuality is simultaneously implied by the same elements, as the singers become objects of desire for their audience, idealized icons of femininity. The look of the groups and the kinds of songs they sing reinforce the heteronormativity of American culture; the women are clearly marked as female in appearance, and the songs they sing typically focus on a male object of romantic desire and often include a longing for marriage and family. As Frith notes in *Sound Effects: Youth, Leisure, and the Politics of Rock 'n' Roll*, "The most important function of 1950s teenage culture wasn't to 'repress' sexuality but to articulate it in a setting of love and marriage such that male and female sexuality were organized in quite different ways."[9] Though the Bluebelles began recording in 1962, the kind of group they were, visually and musically, like others in what Gillian Gaar refers to as the "veritable explosion" of girl groups in the early 1960s, had its roots in the 1950s, and the model would not be effectively challenged in the mainstream until later in the 1960s.[10]

The uniformity of the Bluebelles' image ultimately refutes "the multiplicity of cultural, social, and political intersections in which the concrete array of 'women' are constructed."[11] Many of the black girl groups adopted a mainstream white, middle-class aesthetic, appearing with straightened hair and wearing pearls, cardigan sweaters, and prom dresses, serving, to some extent, to mask racial differences through the process of physical assimilation, though "black girl groups were rarely given the exposure their white counterparts received. As Ruth Brown had found in the '50s, radio may have been color blind, but television was not: none of the black girl groups of the early '60s appeared on *The Ed Sullivan Show* no matter how many hits they had."[12] In addition, the idea of a stable category of "women" was reinforced by these representations of sameness. This stable image would ultimately be challenged by the group's transformation into Labelle in the early 1970s, and their choices would conflict with the ideology of white liberal feminism that was emerging in the United States at the same time. Thus, the freedom of glam would provide an avenue for emphasizing not only the politics of racial inequality but also the problems inherent in a feminism that perpetuated the construction of "women" as a unified group.[13]

George Clinton participated in the male version of this scene from 1956 to 1969 as a member of The Parliaments, a group "modeling themselves after groups like the Temptations and the Four Tops."[14] The Parliaments were a doo-wop quintet that produced songs such as "Don't Be Sore at Me," "That Was My Girl," and "Heart Trouble," upbeat ditties reminiscent of those performed by Smokey Robinson and the Miracles or Frankie Valli and the Four Seasons. The Parliaments fit the mold of boy bands from the period: four to five men, dressed in matching suits, singing in harmony and performing largely gestural synchronized dances. Yet they did not have a commercial success until 1967 when they released "(I Wanna) Testify," a song that Clinton notes marked the end of their doo-wop career.[15] That song, "a top three black hit" that "even reached the pop top twenty," shifts away from the swooning string arrangements and lilting vocalizations of the group's earlier offerings, incorporating instead brassier horns, heavier bass, a slower groove, and grittier lead vocals, hinting at the direction in which Clinton and his collaborators would head musically.[16]

As with the Bluebelles, the Parliaments' stage appearance contributed to the construction of their racial identity. Like many black women performers at the time, black men performers straightened their hair to create a particular visual image. According to Clinton, "Everybody who sang doo-wop back in the '50s had their hair done, all those little guys that sang—like Frankie Lymon—had the do. That was part of the stage thing."[17] He goes on to describe the "pretty silky black hair" sported by celebrities such as Nat King Cole, Sammy Davis, and Sugar Ray Robinson, saying, "I think it basically started out with people wanting to look white—but I'm not sure about this 'cause a lot of blacks did it before they even got to America. But let's face it, the more you looked like that back then, the easier everything was for a lot of people."[18] Regardless of Clinton's uncertainty about the intention of those straightening their hair, one must consider the effect of that choice on an audience; straightened hair, combined with the suit-and-tie dress code, creates an illusion of similarity that attempts to obscure racial differences. It signifies control and suggests conformity as the black body becomes manageable. Yet, like the women in Labelle, Clinton and the men from the Parliaments would transform in the 1970s and challenge this construction of conformity by manipulating the conventions of glam.

1970s Transformations: A New Decade, A New Sound, A New Look

Simon Frith contends, "'Performance' defines a social—or communicative— process. It requires an audience and is dependent, in this sense, on interpretation; it is about meanings."[19] Because representation exists, at least partly, in the eye of the beholder, and signifiers change their meanings in different contexts, what one perceives today as an image that reinforces hegemony may have been one that suggested liberation and opportunity in its own time. Assessing the way girl groups "enthusiastically endorsed and pursued . . . mainstream notions of a woman's role, responsibilities and needs in a patriarchal world," Brian Ward argues that "if such sentiments seem staid by the standards of contemporary feminism, they had a rather different resonance in the black community of the early 1960s. The mere fact that young blacks dared to identify with the girl groups' vision of a conventional domesticity, which poverty and racism had so frequently placed beyond their grasp, reflected the hope that fundamental changes in the pattern of racial oppression were at hand."[20] Thus, although the clone motif that existed in girl and boy bands from the late 1950s/early 1960s is problematic in its aesthetic of conventional uniformity, and its assimilative emphasis, the potential for those signs to be read as having potentially affirming effects should not be dismissed outright, though how such images spoke to the "integrationist aspirations of a new generation of blacks" undoubtedly shifted over the course of the 1960s.[21]

As the decade drew to a close, the status quo was challenged with increasing vigor as people agitated more actively for civil rights and against war, and the music scene both contributed and responded to shifts in the cultural landscape. According to Reebee Garofalo, "as the liberal Civil Rights Movement gave way to the more radical demand for Black power, Motown's hegemony over Black pop was successfully challenged by a resurgence of closer-to-the-roots, hard driving rhythm & blues from the Memphis-Muscle Shoals region of the deep South," and studios such as Stax in Memphis and Fame in Muscle Shoals produced recordings from 1965 on that were "raw, basic, and almost angry in tone, as compared to the cleaner, brighter Motown sound."[22] By 1967, this sound began to make its way into the work of the Bluebelles, on their single "Dreamer," and the Parliaments, on "(I Wanna) Testify," marking a step in the groups' impending radical transformations, realized when they metamorphosed into Labelle and Parliament. The changes they made in terms of representation, visually, lyrically, and musically, were deliberate; performers are not oblivious to the power of image. Indeed, Clinton states, "We chose funky costumes so it gives our audience something to think about."[23] According to Sarah Dash, she and her bandmates "came together saying it is time to break this mold. Why do black women all have to look alike because they're singing together? . . . We wanted to change the whole image and the whole mentality of how black women were supposed to represent themselves in this industry."[24] Though one cannot rely solely on the artist's intent, one cannot discount it entirely, either. Members of both groups have acknowledged that they felt a need for a change of style, and they have noted that their new personae and performance style allowed them to infuse their work with greater social consciousness than they had been able to express within their previous genre.

In 1971, Labelle released its first album, *Labelle*. The picture on the cover offers a triptych: each member of the band hangs from gymnastics rings—Hendryx, LaBelle, Dash, from left to right—with Hendryx and Dash upside down. Each woman wears an ensemble made almost entirely of denim, accented by beige suede boots, in LaBelle's case, and a dark brown turtleneck on Dash. The new look shifted their image slightly, as they disposed of the dresses, pearls, and straightened hair, but the band still had what Charlotte Greig refers to as "the downbeat styles of dress favoured by white rock groups."[25] In addition, they had shed what manager Vicki Wickham called their "flakey girl-group image," but they had not yet fully transformed, as the jungle gym poses, though playful, do not convey a sense of self.[26] It was not until around 1973 that the spacey outfits appeared in Labelle's act, and the adoption of glam style changed the band's visual image considerably. Designer Larry LeGaspi created fantastic costumes for Labelle, and their stage act was one of excess rather than containment.[27] Their new look allowed the group to express themselves in a way that challenged traditional notions of femininity and ceased to obscure race.

Their sound also changed as Nona Hendryx's activity as the band's primary songwriter increased; they covered songs by other black artists, such as Gil Scott-Heron's "The Revolution Will Not Be Televised"; and their new producer, Allen Toussaint, wrote songs specifically for them. No longer was Labelle a plaintive girl group pining for love and marriage; many of their lyrics dealt more overtly with sexual desire as opposed to romantic desire ("You Turn Me On"), and they also addressed political themes such as women's rights, race relations, and the government ("Who's Watching

the Watcher?"). Musically, the songs moved closer to funk, featuring prominent horn sections, piano, and percussion.[28] As with their new image, the
new sound of Labelle helped expand the boundaries of gender, sexuality,
and race, reflecting what Nona Hendryx says was the group's desire to seize
"the possibility of changing and moving into the '70s, rather than carrying
the '60s into the '70s."[29]

According to George Clinton, by about 1967, the Parliaments were also
looking ahead: "We saw that it was going to be hard to keep suits alike and
keep routines because it had played out. Even the Temptations had begun
to look nostalgic to us . . . I realized that in order for us to stay there, we
had to come up with another image."[30] The new image meant that they
"stopped fixing [their] hair. [They] didn't have to worry about suits anymore," and included a musical switch to funk, which Clinton defines as "the
midtempo music between rock'n'roll, which was fast, and blues, which was
slow—both of which had become very popular with the white musicians."[31]
Thus the Parliaments transformed from a group that looked and sounded
like a lot of other groups into a series of bands—Funkadelic, Parliament,
and Parliament-Funkadelic—that sounded like few and looked like even
fewer. These choices also helped them foreground black culture by high-
lighting, rather than obscuring, racial differences in their music, lyrics, and
appearance. Thus it seems that both groups were aware of the opportuni-
ties (and complications) that changing their image afforded them and that
their image could reinforce their new messages.

Ultimately, both bands enjoyed greater popularity, both then and now,
in their new incarnations than they did in their girl/boy group forms. Yet
in the beginning, there was some confusion in the mainstream about both,
and Labelle never reached the same level of commercial success as Parliament, nor did they receive the same kind of critical attention as Parliament.[32] In 1973, Labelle released *Pressure Cookin'*, an album that Patti
LaBelle called "their most politically significant record to date," but like
1971's *Labelle* and 1972's *Moonshadow*, the album did not sell well, in La-
Belle's opinion because "the labels didn't understand them . . . and couldn't
promote them properly."[33] The 1974 release *Nightbirds* was more successful; "Lady Marmalade," which reached number one in 1975, brought them
wider attention from critics and listeners, though there was still a general
lack of understanding about the group. Labelle did not fit comfortably into
any category; Greig writes, "White radio stations in the US would not play
LaBelle [*sic*, Labelle] because the group were black; black stations saw the
music as white."[34] Sarah Dash said in 1974, "People haven't found the right
label for us, so they try to ignore us."[35] Patti LaBelle noted at the same

time, "They compare me to Aretha Franklin, Nona to Diahann Carroll, and Sarah to Diana Ross," suggesting the need to define the band in relation to other black female performers, rather than attempting to take them on their own terms.[36]

Similarly, Clinton's efforts were not easily defined. Funkadelic— Clinton's original post-Parliaments band, which released records simultaneously with Parliament's offerings—was, according to Greg Tate, "too wacky for the souled-out splibs and too black for the spazz whiteys who believed hard rock only came in caucasoid and got nothing to do with bloods getting happy feet."[37] In other words, Funkadelic was unpredictable, and the listening audience wasn't quite sure what to make of them. Furthermore, Rickey Vincent notes that when Funkadelic toured with bands such as The Stooges and the MC5, they "still were outcasts—interlopers— black rockers in a white scene" and "didn't quite fit" with the audiences of the "black college circuit in the South and East Coast" either.[38] Some, including Tate, have noted that Parliament took a more radio- and listener-friendly approach than Funkadelic. According to Tate, it was not until the 1975 release of *Mothership Connection* that Parliament "struck the mama load," garnering their first gold record and launching a tour that drove their live career straight through 1980.[39] Clinton's efforts seem to have paid off by 1976, when Neil Bogart of Casablanca Records "authorized Clinton a budget upwards of half a million dollars . . . the largest expenditure ever for a black music act, and all the backing he needed to conceive and construct his massive space-funk-opera extravaganza" for the *P-Funk Earth Tour* in support of the *Mothership Connection* LP.[40]

Flamboyant Sexuality: The Space(wo)man Motif and Glam Aesthetics

The flamboyance associated with glam is most evident in Labelle's onstage personae. A review of their 1974 performance at New York's Metropolitan Opera House notes that their "extravaganza before an adoring audience that arrived in satin, bouclé, lamé, sequins and Christmas tinsel was triumphant. Dressed in costumes that spanned the centuries from medieval courtier and Gibson Girl to futuristic walking suits, they sang, danced and clapped their way through" the show.[41] Such flamboyance and fluidity in dress allowed Labelle to make both gender and race visible in ways that challenged traditional representation. According to Marvin Carlson:

> Traditional representation, committed to resemblance and repetition, attempts to establish and control the "other" as "same" . . . If

Fig. 1. Image of Labelle. Courtesy of Bob Gruen.

performance can be conceived as representation without reproduction, it can disrupt the attempted totalizing gaze and thus open a more diverse and inclusive representational landscape. As [Catherine] Elwes has noted, women performers should "never stay the same long enough to be named, fetishized."[42]

By embodying various kinds of women, from various stages of history (both real and imagined, past and future), through their costumes, Labelle created a present that suggested women have been and can be many things at once. Ideas of multiplicity facilitated by the extravagance of glam suggested new ways of looking; glam allows performers to control the image they project, and change it at will, and enables the performer/object to become a more active participant in the performer/spectator relationship.

The style of Labelle's clothing also challenged traditional representations of gender and sexuality. In his *Rolling Stone* article "Oh, Baby, It's Labelle," Art Harris offers a detailed description of the group's live performance in which the women are variously eroticized, feminized, and androgynized.[43] Sarah Dash's silver metal bra is revealed after she drops the feathers that have been covering it; the feathers add an element of the erotic, and though her breasts are emphasized, the metal cups suggest an impenetrability that blocks the gaze. The combination of elements promotes a complex series of messages about the body that is being looked at and allows Dash to assert power through her femininity. In the same performance, Nona Hendryx "strides out, swishing white feathers from a rhinestone headdress, a tight white knit spacesuit anatomically accented by three black patches. Handcuffs and a riding crop flap against the right hip and seem to beckon: 'Anyone for SM?'"[44] Pictures of Hendryx in this costume reveal that the "black patches" are covered with what appear to be silver metal studs, again suggesting a clash between softness and strength. Also, the headdress that she wears covers her hair completely, de-feminizing her slightly and suggesting a somewhat androgynous body despite the costume's emphasis on her breasts and vagina. In other costumes, when Hendryx does not wear a headdress, one can see that her hair is cut in a short cropped style, so the androgynous effect remains. Hendryx also challenged traditional attitudes about sexuality by voicing her opinions publicly, saying, "I like appealing to both men and women, I have no preferences. I don't limit myself. I'm all sexes. I don't know what a heterosexual or a bisexual or a homosexual or a monosexual is. I don't understand the differences."[45] Thus, Labelle also adopted the polymorphous sexuality that Cagle cites as a key component of glam aesthetics. The women were flamboyant with their sexuality, and their costumes, attitudes, and relationship with their spectators suggest it was a less homogeneous brand of sexuality.

Labelle's lyrics also explore themes of sexuality. Hendryx's composition "You Turn Me On" is a soulful love song that expresses much more than romantic desire for the receiver of the song. Patti LaBelle longingly croons, backed up by Hendryx and Dash supplying harmonies and occasional oohs and aahs, "I come like the pouring rain / Each time you call my name / It's good what you're doin' / What you're doin'" to a lover of unspecified gender.[46] According to Frith, "All songs are implied narratives. They have a central character, the singer, with an attitude, in a situation, talking to someone (if only to herself)."[47] Because the singer of "You Turn Me On" is talking to someone who could be male or female, the audience is less constrained in its identification with the fictional receiver established in the song's narrative; the desire can be read as longing for either a woman or a man.

The members of Parliament also constructed a distinct identity through their costumes. On the cover of *Mothership Connection*, Clinton appears in a skimpy silver spacesuit that covers his head and torso but not the lower half of his body. He wears a diaper with multi-colored tassels, bares his thighs, and sports knee-high silver and black platform boots. Bright red gloves cover his arms, and he boasts clownish makeup, including a red nose. The front cover shows him sitting in the open hatch of a spaceship, legs flung upward, exposing his tasseled crotch; he looks as if he is in the act of snapping his fingers, and his open mouth suggests singing or howling. The image is striking in its simultaneous absurdity, sense of parody, and emphasis on sexuality. Furthermore, his joyful demeanor is directly related to music through the frozen moment of singing and snapping.

The exaggeration of difference created by this image is a powerful comment on the concept of the alienated Other. The color of Clinton's skin, only a small portion of which is showing, is in sharp contrast to the silver and red costume and the silver spaceship. The pose on the back cover, where he sits casually on the edge of the ship as it hovers in an urban alley, backed by a brick building with metal fire escapes, unexpectedly inserts the alien into an identifiable location. The image resonates with the cover of David Bowie's *The Rise and Fall of Ziggy Stardust* (1972). The washed-out tones of the city buildings in both images are juxtaposed with the garish glow of the brightly colored visitors. Philip Auslander notes that the "hand coloring [of Bowie's image] exaggerates the strangeness of his appearance and makes Bowie seem not to belong to the urban landscape in which he appears"; Clinton's persona is even more clearly out of place, as the silver spaceship, radiating bright yellow light, erases any ambiguity about his status as a visitor.[48]

Yet, though seeming to nod at Bowie's construction, the images on *Mothership Connection* offer a different consideration of the outsider's position. The fact that Clinton's "alien" is shown in both outer space and the urban landscape suggests the spaceman's ability to move freely between worlds, and though he may look out of place, he expresses both joy and ease with his identity through his poses. Clinton says, "I was trying to put blacks in places you wouldn't expect to see 'em. I just knew that a nigger on a spaceship would look pretty strange, especially if he looks like he's on a Cadillac."[49] Thus, Clinton merges common stereotypes and campy space caricature to create an identity that challenges the very stereotypes it is representing.

Such images shaped Parliament's live performances as well. In a review of the *P-Funk Earth Tour* mounted by Parliament/Funkadelic in 1976, Maureen Orth and Vern E. Smith write, "Onstage at the Municipal Auditorium in New Orleans, a giant silver spaceship descended from a 40-foot cardboard, blue denim cap. Out stepped an outrageous creature wearing 9-

inch platform boots, fur tails and a flowing Alice in Wonderland blond wig. Ringed behind him was a band and chorus—he called them 'clones'—in costumes that might have been inspired by watching 'Star Trek' on acid."[50] Like Labelle, the members of Parliament, particularly George Clinton, made use of layers in their stage performances, creating a sense of the fluidity of identity. By peeling away costumes to reveal others underneath, often culminating with the revelation of his naked body, Clinton physically symbolizes the construction of identity.[51]

The expression of sexuality in Parliament's case is evident and unabashed, though not necessarily ambiguous or polymorphous, even when Clinton wears feminine markers, such as the "Alice in Wonderland" wig. As Norma Coates suggests, "Rock masculinity . . . is one in which any trace of the 'feminine' is expunged, incorporated or appropriated," and such performances of "hypersexualized masculinity" emerge even in the performances of "glam rockers such as T Rex, Roxy Music and the New York Dolls . . . even while appropriating visual markers such as femininity via dress and make-up."[52] Despite the campy nature of the costumes—feathers, makeup, and gaudy jewelry—the sturdy, masculine bodies and oft-bearded faces of the band undercut notions of ambiguity, androgyny, or effeminacy. Mark Willhardt and Joel Stein describe Clinton's appearance in a fur codpiece as a display of his "sexual bravado, ghetto machismo, and urban styling," reflecting Philip Auslander's suggestion that American glam artists took "pains to insist that any tendency to dress lavishly and use makeup should not be taken as signs of sexual abnormality."[53]

Furthermore, songs such as "Handcuffs," on *Mothership Connection*, establish a heterosexual frame for Parliament's performance personae. The song is addressed to a "Mama" who needs to be controlled by her man. The song asks, "Do I have to put my handcuffs on you, Mama? / Do I have to keep you under lock and key? / Do I have to put my handcuffs on you, Mama? / Now we both know that's not how it should be . . . If I have to keep you barefoot and pregnant / For to keep you here in my world . . . I want to do to you what it is I've got to do."[54] While the song sounds tongue-in-cheek at times, lamenting the need to control the potentially loose female lover, the point here is that, unlike Labelle's more ambiguously sexualized desires to an un-gendered "you," Parliament establishes a clear male/female sexual matrix. In addition, the eventual inclusion of the female opening act The Brides of Funkenstein into live performances, "three gorgeous women, provocatively dressed in tight revealing costumes . . . each of [them taking] her turn wriggling and wailing down [the tongue projecting from center stage into the orchestra], doing her damnedest to outdo her sister,"

establishes a heterosexual frame for Parliament's performances.[55] By calling the women "brides," there is an implied connection between the two
acts that reinforces the heterosexuality of both.[56]

Lyrics also play a significant role in Parliament's identity construction
and provide another way for Clinton and his cohorts to embody multiple
identities. For example, Clinton adopts various personae to flesh out the
sci-fi concept that shapes the albums *Mothership Connection* (1975), *The
Clones of Dr. Funkenstein* (1976), and *Funkentelechy vs. The Placebo Syndrome*
(1977). The hero of *Mothership Connection*, Star Child, is a visitor from another planet who takes control of the radio and encourages his listeners to
relax and enjoy the funk. As a connection to the Mothership, Star Child
offers healing through the "uncut" P-Funk that "not only moves, it can
remove," though he is not the official narrator of the opening song "P-
Funk (Wants to Get Funked Up)," a job that falls to Lollipop Man (alias
the Long-Haired Sucker)—both characters voiced by Clinton. Funk music
and dancing become instruments of liberation that the Mothership offers.
Parliament celebrates black culture by making a distinction between black
and white funk when Lollipop Man says, "Hey, I was diggin' on ya'll's funk
for a while . . . You know, I was down South and I heard some funk, with
some main ingredients, like Doobie Brothers, Blue Magic, David Booie
[*sic*]. It was cool, but can you imagine doobyin' your funk? Ho! W-E-F-U-
N-K, We funk" ("P-Funk").[57] Thus, the "extraterrestrial brothers" are more
privileged, enlightened purveyors and producers of funk who have come to
show the "citizens of the universe" the way. As Star Child takes control in
the album's second track, "Mothership Connection (Star Child)," inviting
listeners to "put a glide in your stride and a dip in your hip and come onto
the mothership," it is clear that moving is no longer something that should
be controlled; letting loose, celebration ("Ain't nothin' but a party, ya'll"),
and expressing oneself are necessary for enlightenment.[58]

Got to Get Over the Hump:
Political Efficacy in the Work of Labelle and Parliament

Labelle's use of glam style clearly broadened the range of representations
available to them as black women in the United States in the 1970s. Yet
they are rarely considered a "political" band, perhaps, in part, because of
what Charlotte Greig argues is a tendency for critics to treat girl groups
with a certain condescension because their songs "were 'all about love'
and therefore rather contemptible. . . . Somehow, when the Beatles or the
Stones sang about love . . . it was fine, but when girls did it, it was evidence

of feeble-mindedness."⁵⁹ Labelle's songs, even the ones about love, can be read as political statements, especially when examined in the context of the choices they made about their image as performers, which challenged traditional notions of femininity, race, and sexuality, and opened the door for female performers who followed.

Sexual politics are undoubtedly present in Labelle's work. "Lady Marmalade," written by Bob Crewe and Kenny Nolan, is the song that remains the most popular and identifiable of Labelle's oeuvre. The song, about a conservative businessman's encounter with a Creole prostitute, sounds like an anthem of sexual liberation. The opening chant, "Hey, Sister / Go, Sister / Soul Sister / Go, Sister" is a supportive cheer, suggesting that Marmalade is a powerful woman in charge of her body and that the singers advocate women taking control in this way.⁶⁰ Unity and identification are implied through the use of the word "sister." Though Marmalade is a prostitute, she is presented as an active initiator rather than a passive receiver. By the song's end, the businessman who has returned to his "gray flannel life" cannot escape memories of his wild encounter with her, her call "Voulez-vous coucher avec moi ce soir?" ringing in his ears.

In 1975, Jean Peters criticized Labelle in the British magazine *Let It Rock*, asking "What fantasies concerning the rampant black woman do LaBelle [*sic*, Labelle] encourage? *Voulez-vous coucher avec moi ce soir?* Do they even know they are singing a New Orleans *vodun mamaloi* song?"⁶¹ As Greig points out, Peters's attitude about the song and Labelle is "typical of the mid-seventies' feminists, who, whilst encouraging what they called 'all-woman bands' in theory, in practice denied female performers access to the same armoury of sex, glamour and glitz that male pop stars were particularly find of using at the time."⁶² Instead of reading the song as potentially liberating, Peters reads it as a negative reproduction of gender and racial stereotypes. The song also raised the ire of people who did not necessarily identify as feminists. CBS would not allow the group to say "coucher" on television, asking them to change it to "dance" instead; a group of black mothers from a church group in Seattle launched a campaign to get radio stations to stop playing the song; and at a private school in Philadelphia, students "were reportedly threatened with suspension if they did not cease and desist from singing the lyrics with abandon in the halls."⁶³

Yet as Nona Hendryx points out, "Dodging something that's real—like prostitution—is ridiculous. I just will not hide in a closet."⁶⁴ By suggesting that the prostitute is empowered, Labelle's performance of the song can be read as a feminist challenge to traditional representations rather than merely a reproduction of stereotypes. One needs to go beyond the lyrics and consider the power inherent in the song's driving piano line, horn section, and Labelle's vocalization. Greig contends that the song was "made in the spirit of high camp," and considering the aesthetics of glam that Labelle adopted in performance, one can read the song as a tongue-in-cheek critique of the eroticization of the exotic Other not only because of the way agency is implied musically in the song but also in the possibility that the three women singing the song are aware of the potential for themselves to become objects of a similar gaze, a gaze that they subvert through their costumes and stage personae.[65]

A video of "Lady Marmalade" aired as a VH-1 Classic exemplifies this performance style.[66] The clip begins out of focus, fading in to reveal Patti LaBelle in a gold top fringed at the shoulders and below her waist with black feathers, accentuated by a black and yellow feather drape attached at her wrists and elbows, circling her like a skirt. LaBelle coyly acts out the persona of Lady Marmalade, "struttin' her stuff on the street," confidently offering her invitation to "give it a go" with a raise of her eyebrows and an extension of her hand, beckoning her potential customer to join her. As the chorus begins, the shot opens up to include Dash and Hendryx, stage right. Hendryx is wearing the aforementioned black and white studded jumpsuit and feather headdress, complete with handcuffs dangling from her left hip; Dash is in a silver bra and wrist cuffs, wearing a skirt of black feathers and silver fabric. All three women move freely, swinging their hips, raising their arms, and smiling broadly; their enjoyment is palpable, as is their control. Eventually, LaBelle removes the feather drape and dances to the space between Dash and Hendryx, and the three pose and strut playfully during the bridge. When the lyrics come back in, the sexual intensity of the performance increases, both vocally and physically, as LaBelle and Dash run their hands along their torsos and Dash sighs into her microphone. Simultaneously, the campy nature of their act increases as exaggerated wrist-flipping and head-tossing accentuate the final delivery of the song's refrain. Throughout the performance, the sensuality of the music and lyrics is embodied in a mischievously erotic way, and the group's revelry leaves no doubt that the women know exactly what they are singing.

"Get You Somebody New," written by Joe Crane, offers a different kind of liberation. The "you" in the song suffers a scathing attack as Patti LaBelle sings the lead vocal with support from her sisters Hendryx and Dash.

LaBelle: If you want somebody to be your slave
Hendryx and Dash: Get you somebody new
LaBelle: If you want somebody that you can save

Hendryx and Dash: Get you somebody new
LaBelle: If you need somebody that you can hurt
Hendryx and Dash: Get you somebody new
LaBelle: I ain't nobody to treat like dirt[67]

In the final moment of the song, the music cuts out, letting the women's voices ring out in unison, "Get you somebody new!" The sense of solidarity provided by the arrangement of the song is an example of what Greig says Labelle took from the girl group fundamentals, "that sense of close friendship and shared experience."[68] Yet the shared experience in this case is not the longing for the love of good man but in the rejection of a bad lover (as in "You Turn Me On," the gender of the "you" in this song is never made explicit).

That solidarity is also evident in Labelle's live performance style. In various clips of Labelle's live performances from the early 1970s, a motif emerges in the ways in which the women negotiate the performance space: the physical shift from isolation to union promotes a powerful representation of community. For example, performing "You Turn Me On" on *Don Kirshner's Rock Concert* in 1974, the women are broken into two groups, with LaBelle downstage left, standing apart from Dash and Hendryx, slightly upstage to the right, the band behind them obscured by low lighting.[69] LaBelle takes the lead vocal, and she removes her microphone from its stand early in the song and begins to cover a lot of ground, moving freely about the stage as Dash and Hendryx remain fixed at their microphones. LaBelle's physical gestures are broad and sharp, while Dash and Hendryx remain contained, swaying slowly. LaBelle eventually works her way to Hendryx's side, and as the three women become a tight unit physically, their voices take control of the song; the instrumentation drops out, leaving the women to sing a cappella, culminating with their powerful command, "Don't . . . Stop . . . What you're doin'," a visceral moment that is heightened by the singers' synchronicity across a series of pregnant pauses and capped by the band's re-entry on LaBelle's signal. The staging, as well as the composition of the song, strikingly reinforces the strength of sisterhood.

The staging of community is also evident in their performance of "What Can I Do for You?," from the same 1974 episode of Kirshner's show, in which the starting configuration of LaBelle to the left of Dash and Hendryx is repeated, though the entire band is visible, and a guitarist joins Hendryx at her microphone.[70] The rollicking, up-tempo song begins with the declaration, "People want truth or nothing at all / People want sincerity and nothing more," and the commitment to the ideas in the song, ultimately a plea for enjoying life, spreading love, and promoting peace, is embodied in the fluid movements of the performers on stage.[71] As in the performance of "You Turn Me On," LaBelle eventually takes her microphone from the stand and closes the gap between herself and the others; shortly after she crosses stage right to join Dash, the rest of the band moves downstage, percussionists playing cowbells and other handheld instruments, until the entire ensemble forms a group downstage center. Hendryx then leads the band into the dancing audience as LaBelle repeats, "What can I do for you? / What can you do for me?" The song's call for unity is reinforced by the staging of it, especially in terms of the physical incorporation of the audience into the performance moment in a role that goes beyond that of spectator.

Labelle's investment in performing politically charged songs is also evident in their cover of Gil Scott-Heron's "The Revolution Will Not Be Televised." Lyrics such as "The revolution will not be right back after a message / about a white tornado, white lightning, or white people . . . The revolution will not go better with Coke . . . The revolution will not be televised" generated criticism in some circles.[72] The song was perceived as racist, and according to Art Harris:

> After shedding her Flash Gordon spacesuit following a stomping, race-around version of "Revolution," Patti surprises the audience by apologizing for the song. She is hurt, she says, that white reviewers in Philadelphia had apparently misunderstood the group's intentions. "They said we were saying to kill Whitey . . . We feel that baddies could be black or white or green or whatever. It has been said that we're a racist group," she is telling the crowd. "But the song deals with the facts of life. We want you to love the next white person and him to love us and if we put our efforts together, maybe we can get the man out of the White House."[73]

Labelle's choice to continue performing the song in spite of such criticism, as with "Lady Marmalade," is in itself a political gesture. Similarly, Patti LaBelle's choice to apologize for the song carries political significance; the demographics of their audience included a wide range of minorities, besides racial minorities, and the gesture includes these others in the pursuit of "the revolution."

When Labelle performed on a music special on NBC in 1974, network executives wanted them to change the lyrics of "The Revolution Will Not

Be Televised"; the song was eventually dropped from the show altogether.[74] Hendryx said in 1975, "I find it sour when people think that 'Lady M' is all Labelle is about."[75] Unfortunately, that identification still holds true for many people, in part because of the way Labelle was defined at the time, from criticism of their lyrics to the refusal of both black and white radio stations to play their music, but also because of the way in which their work has been marketed.[76] For example, the studio version of "The Revolution Will Not Be Televised" appears on 1973's *Pressure Cookin'*, an album that was not released on CD until 2010. Furthermore, Labelle compilations, with the exception of 1997's *Something Silver*, do not include it or songs such as "Space Children" or "Something's in the Air," both of which encourage coalition and revolution. Such omissions contribute to the fact that Labelle is rarely categorized as a politically relevant band.

Parliament, on the other hand, has almost always been considered a political group. According to Mark Willhardt and Joel Stein, "One of the constitutive contradictions to Clinton's funk is that it is a party music that is also, before the fact, an intellectual music."[77] The challenge from Star Child to Sir Nose D'Voidoffunk on *Funkentelechy vs. The Placebo Syndrome* (1977) reads as a challenge from the enlightened funk visitors to the Uncle Toms who "will never dance." Willhardt and Stein write:

> Sir Nose is a takeoff on Sammy Davis, Jr. . . . His sort of side-mouthed "goo-cha-coo" was part of the syndrome of co-opted black cool—too cool to sweat—that Clinton reacted to . . . Sir Nose represents an insincerity antithetical to The Funk, and Sammy Davis, Jr., gave face to the plastic hypocrisy that Clinton abhorred and literally warned against in his personae of Dr. Funkenstein and Star Child.[78]

In "Bop Gun (Endangered Species)," the opening track of *Funkentelechy*, Star Child, backed up by the Brides of Dr. Funkenstein, issues his opening salvo against Sir Nose blending the language of the Civil Rights Movement with the language of soul music.

> BRIDES. On guard!
>   Defend yourself!
>   Movin' right on you, baby . . .
> STAR CHILD. Turn me loose!
>   We shall overcome!
>   Where'd you get that funk from, huh?
>   Turn 'em off

> They're spoilin' the fun
> Let's shoot them with the bop gun[79]

The pulsing beat and lyrical repetition of the call to arms for the "endangered species" to defend itself against "the syndrome"—that is, the non-funky—intensifies as the song progresses, ultimately leading to the song's central chant, "We got to get over the hump," insisting on the necessity for pushing beyond the initial gains of a movement that seemed stalled by the middle of the 1970s. Ward suggests that "as black protest and American racial liberalism entered their own twilight zones, things looked increasingly bleak for black America and the state of race relations."[80] Clinton's construction of intricate mythologies allowed for a critical examination of the socio-political moment in a fantastic way, its playfulness and insistence on the need to cut loose, let go of convention, and embrace the unknown underscoring the sincerity of the desire for change.

The political efficacy of Clinton's myth-making was realized most fully, and spectacularly, in concert. The *P-Funk Earth* Tour, launched in the fall of 1976, provided a spirited coda to the United States' Bicentennial celebrations of the summer. A filmed performance of the October 31 performance in Houston, Texas, begins with a narrator addressing the roaring crowd.

> Funk upon a time . . . The concept of specially designed afronauts capable of funkitizing galaxies was first laid on Man Child, but was later repossessed and placed among the secrets of the pyramids until a more positive attitude towards this most sacred phenomenon— Clone Funk—be acquired. There these terrestrial projects it would wait along with its co-inhabitants of kings and pharaohs, like sleeping beauties, for the kiss that would release them to multiply in the image of the chosen one, Dr. Funkenstein. And funk *is* its own reward.[81]

As the band launches into "Cosmic Slop," led by the diaper-clad, pacifier-sucking guitarist Garry Shider, the camera reveals a stage crowded with outlandishly clad musicians, a steady flow of new bodies entering the space as the song progresses. Finally Clinton appears and takes command, an "afronaut" dressed in a red suit and black cape with gold accents and sporting a loose, bouncy afro, who notes that "we all gonna commence the funk together." After leading the band and the audience through a few more songs, Clinton departs as discreetly as he entered, leaving the others to cool things down with "Children of Productions," a song that celebrates their work as the clones of Dr. Funkenstein, reveling in the fact that they are "gonna blow the cobwebs out your mind."

The delivery of this promised enlightenment is fueled in part by the two characters Clinton next embodies: Star Child and Dr. Funkenstein. Interestingly, in this performance, both of those personae look decidedly less otherworldly than his initial alter ego. Re-emerging to lead the band in "Mothership Connection," Clinton wears no spacey outfit; instead his red skirt fringed with white fur tassels, top comprised of matching tassels, and his straight, waist-long hair ringed by a bandana across his forehead have a Native American inflection. Identifying himself as Star Child, Clinton leads the band in "Mothership Connection," calling on the audience to help "get the Mothership in here," before leaving the reins in the hands of Glen Goins. As the performance nears its climactic turning point, the anticipation for Dr. Funkenstein's arrival is palpable; the promise of the second coming driven by the spiritual revival quality of the calling of the Mothership. Goins leads the trancelike chant "Swing down, sweet chariot / stop and let me ride," his and the other performers' hands raised over their heads in praise, building to his question, "Do you want to fly?" As the speed of the music begins to pick up, the horn section heralds the Mothership's arrival, which descends with engines blasting and lights flashing. Dramatically, Dr. Funkenstein appears in a flash of smoke. In his floor-length white fur coat and matching hat, Funkenstein looks like "an interplanetary pimp"; he immediately seizes command and over the course of the next four songs leads everyone to the promised land as the concert ends in a communal celebration, P-Funk and the opening acts—Bootsy's Rubber Band and Sly and the Family Stone—joining the party.[82]

Perhaps the most striking thing about Clinton's enactment of these various characters in this performance is how he disrupts expectations by bringing the otherworldly back to Earth. The jolly spaceman from the cover of *Mothership Connection* makes no appearance; indeed, that jester quality is not present at all. Though Star Child and Dr. Funkenstein are extraterrestrial visitors, they do not look that different from humans. Their costumes are at once outlandish and identifiable, playing on identifiable visual stereotypes—Native American warrior and urban Black dandy. Yet Clinton challenges the meanings communicated by those images. Because Star Child and Dr. Funkenstein are so clearly in command—of themselves, the band, and the audience—they ultimately resist caricature, and the exaggerated markers of race become positive reinforcements of Star Child's and Dr. Funkenstein's status as enlightened Others.

Thus, Clinton employs the hallmarks of glam—particularly theatricality and image construction—to infuse his musical performances with clear racial politics, as opposed to Labelle's focus on sexual politics, giving Parliament credibility as political spokesmen that Labelle lacks. There is, perhaps, also something to be said about Clinton's control over Parliament as producer, composer, and bandleader. Authoring lends itself to the appearance of agency that those who perform others' work generally lack. Much of the critical work about Parliament has focused specifically on Clinton (a problem that I am ultimately reproducing here) because he is seen as the one in charge. Clinton becomes responsible for the political content of Parliament's work in a way that the women in Labelle do not, despite the fact that Nona Hendryx wrote many of Labelle's songs. Yet if one reads Labelle as authors of their *performance*, even when they are performing songs written by other people, they take on a more powerful position. For both groups, glam offered a way to break free from conventional representations of sexuality, gender, and race (albeit to varying degrees) and allowed for the creation of musical performances—both recorded and live—that challenged established authority and radically reconfigured their status as Others.

NOTES

1. Van M. Cagle, "The Foundations of Glitter Rock," *Reconstructing Pop/Subculture: Art, Rock, and Andy Warhol* (Thousand Oaks, CA: Sage, 1995), 96.

2. Philip Auslander, *Performing Glam Rock: Gender and Theatricality in Popular Music* (Ann Arbor: University of Michigan Press, 2006), 228.

3. bell hooks, "Representations of Whiteness in the Black Imagination," *Black Looks: Race & Representation* (Boston: South End, 1992), 168.

4. Stayce Holte and Duane Wells, "Hey Soul Sister: The Return of the Labelle," *GayWired.com*, May 12, 2008, http://www.gaywired.com.

5. Simon Frith, *Performing Rites: On the Value of Popular Music* (Cambridge: Harvard University Press, 1996), 208.

6. They were originally called The Ordettes. Charlotte Greig, *Will You Still Love Me Tomorrow? Girl Groups from the 50s On* (London: Virago, 1989), 175.

7. Gillian G. Gaar, "Girl Groups," *She's a Rebel: The History of Women in Rock and Roll* (Seattle: Seal, 1992), 53–54.

8. The 1983 film *Girl Groups: The Story of a Sound* provides many clips of bands that look and move in this way. The Ronettes and The Shangri-las, however, often wear pants rather than skirts or dresses, marking them slightly differently, though their choreography is equally restrained. *Girl Groups: The Story of a Sound*, directed by Steve Alpert (Beverly Hills, CA: Delilah Films MGM, 1983), Video.

9. Simon Frith, *Sound Effects: Youth, Leisure, and the Politics of Rock 'n' Roll* (New York: Pantheon, 1981), 238–39.

10. Gaar, "Girl Groups," 31.

11. Judith Butler, *Gender Trouble: Feminism and the Subversion of Identity*, 10th Anniversary ed. (London: Routledge, 1999), 19–20.

12. Gaar, "Girl Groups," 51.

13. Critics such as bell hooks, for example, have argued that mainstream feminist texts such as Betty Friedan's *The Feminine Mystique* (1973) failed to take into account the broad spectrum of women's experiences. Furthermore, in the introduction to the second edition of her text *Feminist Theory: From Margin to Center*, hooks writes, "Nowadays it has become so commonplace for individuals doing feminist work to evoke gender, race, and class, it is often forgotten that initially most feminist thinkers, many of whom were white and from privileged class backgrounds, were hostile to adopting this perspective" (bell hooks, *Feminist Theory: From Margin to Center*, 2nd ed. [Cambridge: South End, 2000], xii).

14. Some sources cite Frankie Lymon and the Teenagers as an inspiration for Clinton and the Parliaments, which is interesting in light of various women interviewed in *Girl Groups: The Story of a Sound*, including Ronnie Spector and Arlene Smith, who cite Lymon as an inspiration for their work. Clinton has also noted that the Isley Brothers were a key influence early in his career (George Clinton, Interview with VH-1, "Q&A with George Clinton: The Big Bow Wow," *Say It Loud: A Celebration of Black Music in America*, December 5, 2001, http://www.vh1.com/sayitloud/georgeclinton.jhtml). Greg Tate, "The Atomic Dog: George Clinton Interview by Greg Tate and Bob Wisdom," *Flyboy in the Buttermilk: Essays on Contemporary America* (New York: Simon & Schuster, 1992), 29.

15. A reworked version of the song, under the title "Testify," appears on Parliament's 1974 album *Up for the Down Stroke*. Clinton, "Q&A with George Clinton."

16. Brian Ward, *Just My Soul Responding: Rhythm and Blues, Black Consciousness, and Race Relations* (Berkeley: University of California Press, 1998), 354.

17. George Clinton, "George Clinton's Hairy Tales," *New Funk Times*, accessed December 5, 2001, http://ourworld.compuserve.com/homepages/PJebsen/nft-hair.htm.

18. Ibid.

19. Simon Frith, *Performing Rites*, 205.

20. Brian Ward, *Just My Soul Responding*, 158.

21. Ibid., 159.

22. Reebee Garofalo, "The Impact of the Civil Rights Movement on Popular Music," *Radical America* 24, no. 6 (1987): 19.

23. Patrick Salvo, "Politics in Pop Music," *Sepia*, July 1976, 69.

24. Gaar, "Girl Groups," 164.

25. Greig, *Will You Still Love Me Tomorrow?*, 177.

26. Ibid., 177.

27. In a 1985 interview with Greg Tate and Bob Wisdom, George Clinton says, when asked about the source of a Zulu costume he wore in performance, "Ain't that a baaad motherfucker, with all them feathers on there . . . Larry Gatsby [*sic*] made that one. He does David Bowie's costumes, too" (Tate, "The Atomic Dog," 34). Earlier in the interview he says, "This business is run by association and money. When you can say . . . Jules Fisher did the spaceships, and Larry Gatsby [*sic*] did the

costumes, you've just associated yourself with the Rolling Stones, the Who, Patti Labelle, *The Wiz*" (Tate, "The Atomic Dog," 33).

28. The music that backed Labelle was played by men.

29. Gaar, "Girl Groups," 163.

30. Clinton, "Q&A with George Clinton."

31. Ibid.

32. Labelle disbanded in 1976, so their career was more short-lived than Parliament's (Funkadelic, Parliafunkadelicment Thang, P-Funk All-Stars, George Clinton), which may contribute to the lack of critical attention given to their work, though their 2008 reunion, which saw the release of a new album and a concert tour, has garnered interest.

33. Art Harris, "Oh Baby, It's Labelle," *Rolling Stone* 3, July 1975, 44.

34. Greig, *Will You Still Love Me Tomorrow?*, 179.

35. Margo Jefferson, "Belles of the Ball," *Newsweek*, October 1974, 113.

36. Ibid., 113.

37. Tate, "The Atomic Dog," 30.

38. *Parliament Funkadelic: Live 1976—The Mothership Connection*, performed by Parliament-Funkadelic. October 1976. Prod. Alan Douglas. Gravity: 1988. DVD. Shout! Factory, 2008. Brian Blum, DVD supervisor; Rickey Vincent, liner notes.

39. Tate, "The Atomic Dog," 30.

40. *Parliament Funkadelic*, Blum and Vincent.

41. They were the "first black rock group to perform" there (Gaar, "Girl Groups," 164). Jefferson, "Belles of the Ball," 113.

42. Marvin Carlson, *Performance: A Critical Introduction* (London: Routledge, 1996), 181.

43. Harris, "Oh, Baby, It's Labelle."

44. Ibid., 42.

45. Ibid., 42–43.

46. *Nightbirds*, music by Labelle, "You Turn Me On" (1974; New York: Epic Records, 1990), CD.

47. Simon Frith, *Performing Rites*, 169.

48. Auslander, *Performing Glam Rock*, 126.

49. Mark Willhardt and Joel Stein, "Dr. Funkenstein's Supergroovalisticprosifunkstication: George Clinton Signifies," *Reading Rock and Roll: Authenticity, Appropriation, Aesthetics*, eds. Kevin J. H. Dettmar and William Richey (New York: Columbia University Press, 1999), 145–72.

50. Maureen Orth and Vern E. Smith, "Dr. Funkenstein," *Newsweek*, November 1976, 102.

51. According to Patrick Salvo, "Bizarre costumes of Parliament/Funkadelic are endless and interchangeable, as group members often improvise" ("Politics in Pop Music," 68–69), so the fluidity of identity is not limited to individual bodies. Indeed, one could argue that the very fluidity of the bands' names—Funkadelic, Parliament, Parliament-Funkadelic, The Parliafunkadelicment Thang—and personnel refuse boundaries.

52. Norma Coates, "(R)evolution Now? Rock and the Political Potential of Gender," *Sexing the Groove: Popular Music and Gender*, ed. Sheila Whiteley (London: Routledge, 1997), 54, 63.

53. Willhardt and Stein, "Dr. Funkenstein's Supergroovalisticprosifunkstication," 154; Auslander, *Performing Glam Rock*, 48–49.

54. *Mothership Connection*, music by Parliament, "Handcuffs" (1975; New York: PolyGram, 1990), CD.

55. Ted Fox, *Showtime at the Apollo* (New York: Holt, Rinehart and Winston, 1983), 306.

56. The Brides of Funkenstein differ from Labelle in another critical way. Descriptions of Labelle's stage performances discuss their movement from the stage into the audience to interact with their fans. On the other hand, Fox's description of the Brides at the Apollo notes that male teenagers from the audience come up onto the stage to join the Brides, and eventually, an older fan, uninvited, rushes the stage and is escorted off. The choice of placement is important. In other words, it is different for Patti LaBelle to initiate an encounter by leaving her space and joining the spectators than for the Brides to have these encounters on the stage, even if they invite the men to join them.

57. *Mothership Connection*, music by Parliament, "P-Funk" (1975; New York: PolyGram, 1990), CD.

58. *Mothership Connection*, music by Parliament, "Star Child" (1975; New York: PolyGram, 1990), CD.

59. Charlotte Greig, "Female Identity and the Woman Songwriter," *Sexing the Groove: Popular Music and Gender*, ed. Sheila Whiteley (London: Routledge, 1997), 168.

60. *Nightbirds*, performed by Labelle, "Lady Marmalade" (1974; New York: Epic Records, 1990), CD.

61. Greig, *Will You Still Love Me Tomorrow?*, 178.

62. Ibid., 178.

63. Harris, "Oh, Baby, It's Labelle," 46.

64. Ibid., 46.

65. Greig, *Will You Still Love Me Tomorrow?*, 179.

66. This video was viewed in January 2009 on YouTube at http://www.youtube.com/watch?v=ZejEpoNiyow&feature=channel_page.

67. *Chameleon*, performed by Labelle, "Get You Somebody New" (1976; New York: Epic Records, 1991), CD.

68. Greig, *Will You Still Love Me Tomorrow?*, 177.

69. *Don Kirshner's Rock Concert* 2.21, December 1974.

70. Ibid.

71. *Nightbirds*, performed by Labelle, "What Can I Do For You?" (1974; New York: Epic Records, 1990), CD.

72. *Pressure Cookin'*, performed by Labelle, "The Revolution Will Not Be Televised" (1973; New York: RCA Records, 2010), CD.

73. Harris, "Oh, Baby, It's Labelle," 43.

74. Jefferson, "Belles of the Ball," 113.

75. Harris, "Oh, Baby, It's Labelle," 46.

76. Case in point: The greatest hits compilation released in 1995 is called *Lady Marmalade: The Best of Patti & Labelle*. Of course, this title also singles out Patti Labelle in a way that the band's albums did not (though, obviously, she is singled out by her surname). Interestingly, however, there has been resurgence in the group's

popularity in the past decade, seeing the release of a new album, *Back to Now* in 2008, and the use of two of their songs in director Lee Daniels's 2009 film *Precious*. One of the tracks, "System," was written by Hendryx around 1976. The song, which Labelle performed on *Don Kirshner's New Rock Concert* in 1976, features shared lead vocals and is a paean to rejecting conformity: "Don't you try to hassle me / Saying what's wrong or right . . . I've got to do what's best for me."

77. Willhardt and Stein, "Dr. Funkenstein's Supergroovalisticprosifunkstication," 146.

78. Ibid., 153.

79. *Funkentelechy Vs. the Placebo Syndrome*, music by Parliament, "Bop Gun (Endangered Species)" (1977; New York: Casablanca Records, 1990), CD.

80. Ward, *Just My Soul Responding*, 357.

81. *P-Funk Earth Tour*, music by Parliament (1977; New York: Casablanca Records, 1990).

82. *Parliament Funkadelic*, Blum and Vincent.

DAPHNE A. BROOKS

"Bring the Pain"

Post-Soul Memory, Neo-Soul Affect, and Lauryn Hill in the Black Public Sphere

[C]ertain figures walk like omnipresent ghosts. Their voices and the things those voices stand for are never far from consciousness, and the mere mention of their names or the mere intimation of the sound of their voices can powerfully focus "feeling" and "mem'ry" in moments of condensed social poetry.

—AARON FOX

Soul to me is a feeling, a lot of depth and being able to bring to the surface that which is happening inside, to make the picture clear. The song doesn't matter. . . . It's just the emotion, the way it affects other people . . .

—ARETHA FRANKLIN[1]

(Up)Hill Battle: Neo Soul Fifteen Years after Its *Miseducation*

"DO YOU LOVE WHAT YOU FEEL?" Pioneering funk and R&B diva Chaka Khan once belted out these words in the 1970s as the disco era was coming to a close, but it is Lauryn Hill, the latter-day reclusive hip-hop/neo-soul genius who has perhaps most powerfully reanimated that musical question to her fans by way of one emotionally trenchant performance in the fall of 2005.[2] Fast-forward to the end of French trickster cineaste Michel Gondry's whimsically galvanizing concert film *Dave Chappelle's Block Party* (2006), and one catches Hill at the height of her affective powers as a singer, delivering a volatile elixir of torment and ecstasy, melancholia and redemptive joy for a rain-soaked crowd swooning along to the pulsating ache of her marvelously stormy vocals. Returning to the stage for a rare reunion with the Fugees, her 1990s hip-hop partners in chart-topping struggle,

180

Hill revisits the group's smash hit cover of "Killing Me Softly," Roberta Flack's epic ode to conflated pleasure and pain, and for a wrinkle in time, reintroduces herself to a pop music world that had long been mourning her absence.[3]

"What ever happened to Lauryn Hill?" became one of the burning pop culture riddles of the new millennium, especially in the wake of the mammoth success of her era-defining 1998 album *The Miseducation of Lauryn Hill* followed by her disappearance from the public eye at the turn of this new century. Before her vanishing act, Hill had been poised to dominate and radically influence a wide swath of pop music culture in the latter half of the '90s. *Miseducation* sold over eight million copies in the United States alone, earned the artist five Grammys, and paved the way for the mainstream success of acts like Outkast and Kanye West. It also captured the hearts of the "rock snob" critical set, as it was only narrowly edged out by Lucinda Williams's back-to-basics *Car Wheels on a Gravel Road* in the annual *Village Voice* "Pazz and Jop" Poll that year. Alongside the debut albums of D'Angelo and MeShell NdegeOcello, Hill's record remains one of the most significant R&B/hip-hop breakthrough albums of that decade. Lauded by critics as one of the most ideologically complex and multidimensional pop music recordings of that era as well, it drew comparisons to *Blonde on Blonde* and *Songs in the Key of Life*.[4]

At the height of her popularity, few would have argued the fact that Hill, like Dylan and Wonder before her, emerged on her album as one of the more ambitious poet-philosophers in popular music culture, an innovative singer-songwriter who translated the desires, concerns, and ambivalences of post–Civil Rights cultural memory into emotionally and spiritually turbulent musicality. Yet with the exception of a controversial and uneven *MTV Unplugged* recording in 2002, a couple of blink-or-you'll-miss-them reunions with her group the Fugees, and a spate of 2010–12 notoriously unpredictable concert gigs, Hill has nearly disappeared from the music world to raise the five children she shares with Bob Marley's fourth son Rohan. Her rare and often erratic live performances have set the blogosphere afire with reports of spectacular concert meltdowns and passionate pleas for a comeback.[5]

An extraordinary Hill return couldn't come soon enough in this new millennium where few artists seem to match Hill's dense, spectacular aura—a kind of energy that draws on multidimensional gravitas and yet transcends Mary J. Blige's oft-lauded "realness"/bling street stylings, Beyoncé's *Cirque du Soleil* electric light orchestrations, and Keyshia Cole's radio-friendly romantic lamentations. Hill had a little bit of all of that going for her on her album (and Blige would herself show up on the record in cameo for the stunning duet "I Used to Love Him"), plus much more during her shining turn-of-the-century moment. Watch her in those final climactic minutes of *Block Party* delivering the chorus of "Killing Me Softly" for the umpteenth time, turning that number into a fresh exhortation and a vocal exegesis on romantic grief and emotional resurrection, and one sees for a fleeting moment the re-emergence of a rousing, risk-taking pop commentator who spoke for an invisible, inter-ethnic generation of young women who had rarely had their personal and social intimacies—romantic hopes, cultural dreams, spiritual desires, and political disappointments—sonically articulated in such viscerally startling registers.

The electric candor of *Miseducation* resonated in a decade that saw women across multiple pop-music genres belting out varying degrees of resistance and revolution, from early 1990s' riot grrrl and alt rock movement artists (Bikini Kill, PJ Harvey, Hole, and the Kims—Deal & Gordon) to high-voltage top 40 power pop (Alannis) and post–Terry McMillan R&B (TLC, Destiny's Child) as the decade wore on. Like female pop singer-songwriters from the previous generation (Joni, Aretha, Carole) or even like old-school, English queer composer and suffragist Ethel Smyth who, as Elizabeth Wood argues, "use[s] music as a sound-form of narrative: as a way to tell truths about life, shape subjectivity, and make audible feelings that are essentially private," Hill's album crystallized the ways in which women artists of that era were engaging sonic forms to articulate the politics and poetics of gendered interiority.[6] Yet what made Hill's record stand out from all that came before it was the rich and deeply realized spiritual dimensions of her lyrics which challenged her listeners to engage with a black female voice that was not just of the body (as black women are so often perceived in popular culture) but of a formidable combination of flesh, mind, and spirit combined.[7]

What follows is an effort to reconsider the lasting impact of Lauryn Hill's one full-length studio album on popular music culture and to think specifically about the ways in which that album and her distinct live performance aesthetics have re-imagined the gendered politics of soulfulness and racialized socio-political affect in relation to the post–Civil Rights black public sphere. In my mind, no popular music artist since Hill has fully encapsulated a politicized aesthetic of feeling more fully, aggressively, and imaginatively than Hill. More still, in the formalistic, vocal, and lyrical expression of that feeling, Hill has reinterpreted the gendered dimensions of post-soul cultural ideologies by shifting the movement's discursive emphasis on male protagonists and masculinist desire (in works by Trey Ellis, Darius James, Paul Beatty, and Colson Whitehead) to black feminist interrogations of gender relationships and spiritually infused identity formations.[8] Nowhere is this revisionist storytelling praxis more audible and visible than in Hill's latter-day live (re)interpretation of "Killing Me Softly (With His Song)" caught on tape for *Block Party*. It is that performance, poised as the emotional climax in Chappelle's urban renewal/soul revival project, which encapsulates and affirms Hill's pivotal role as the iconic voice of post-soul public sphere critical memory and post–Civil Rights cultural insurgency realized. The "feeling and memory" that pulsate through Hill's Brooklyn, one-night-only appearance showcase the ways in which her voice operates as "social poetry" in the grand tradition of soul that Queen Aretha famously outlines above. Hill's climactic live performance that "kills" ultimately generates new ways of theorizing post–Civil Rights identity formations through black female vocalizing and the poetics of sonic affect. Her thick and demanding pop artistry challenges us to look at and listen more closely to the aesthetics of black women's sound(ed) practices in contemporary popular culture and, more broadly, in the fields of performance studies and black studies as well.

When It Hurts So Bad: Gender, (Post) Soulfulness, and the Black Public Sphere

Love is an open wound on *The Miseducation of Lauryn Hill*. It is the source of tremendous despair and pain that ebbs and flows yet still manages to generate great pulsating hope and wonderment in the universe that Hill creates for listeners on her first and only solo studio album. Emotional hurt—ragged, brutal, and unexpected—is a thing of the past, a condition examined by Hill, the sage survivor, as she looks with clarity through a rearview mirror. "I loved real, real hard once / But the love wasn't returned . . ." she sings on "When It Hurts So Bad."[9] The lessons that Hill learns and subsequently administers on her album are both micro and macro, rooted in the truths born out of the most intimate romantic relationships gone awry but reflective of much broader struggles that articulate the very definition of soul music and social conceptions of soulfulness. As defined by a wide array of cultural critics from Brian Ward to Craig Werner, soul takes the ideological elements of the blues and the existential problem of black human struggle and transforms that mortal coil into a combination of spiritual and sensual release—both sacred and profane.[10] It sits at the crossroads of the church and the juke joint. Soul both generates the power to transcend the material conditions in which it is situated and yet is also resolutely of this earth and this lifetime.

If soul is "a useful way of talking about precisely those communicative qualities that exceed the power of language to recapture," as Paul Gilroy observes, then Hill's album and her live performance repertoire bear out this promise of excessive, language-defying communication where "words don't go," as Fred Moten might refer to it. Soul, in fact, is revivified in Hill's repertoire as a kind of sociality that speaks and sounds out *not* "a redemption of our history of suffering . . . but a sign of the impossibility of that redemption." Soul is the audibly realized, affective "site of a kind of ambivalence about the memory of slavery and the desirability and the obligation to forget things which are difficult. Soul suggests," Gilroy continues, "that this suffering is without redemption. . . . It is our open secret."[11]

Let us take a moment here to steer clear of romanticizing black suffering, something Gilroy would surely urge us to do. At the same time, however, we might acknowledge the ways in which Hill, I would argue, more than any other artist of her generation, utilized the aesthetics of sonic philosophical and emotional suffering and melancholia as a way to actualize a critical cultural memory of black women's popular music virtuosity and, more broadly, as a way to articulate 1990s black public sphere politics in a pop music register. Her music generates what Jonathan Flatley cogently refers to as "affective mapping," a kind of "productive" "melancholizing" that "produce[s] its own kind of knowledge" about the historicity of post-soul subjects at the close of the twentieth century.[12] Hill's rich alto—what black music critic Ernest Hardy refers to as a kind of singing "marbled with thick, fat ribbons of sensuality and warmth" and "filled with street wisdom and compassion"—serves as the template for formalistically sounding out affective conditions that exceed language itself. It is that alto, akin to forebears such as Nina Simone, Odetta, and Marian Anderson, which ties Hill to a legacy of black female vocality that archives and translates into sound the condition of suffering to create a double-voiced musical language of ambivalence and amplified corporeal and narrative energy.[13]

Many critics have grappled with the unbearable lightness of being bound up in the classic soul falsetto, and they recognized that gendered register as the site of troubling, laborious (masculine) genius. The falsetto is the place where, to cite Nathaniel Mackey's famous passage from his novel-manifesto *Bedouin Hornbook*, "'the dislocated African's pursuit of a meta-voice' bears the weight of a gnostic, transformative desire to be done with the world." It is a form of vocal expression that articulates and "explores a redemptive, unworded realm."[14] Far less, however, has been made of the alto and contralto voices of black women artists—from Simone and Anderson to comedian Moms Mabley to Hill contemporary MeShell NdegeOcello. That lowdown sound perhaps fails to generate the kind of heated striving, the dangerous ascensions, and the risky/risqué transgressions associated with the falsetto. We expect our black women to descend to the depths of despair while our men (Al Green, Marvin Gaye, Curtis Mayfield, Maxwell) who (sonically) rise are valued for crossing over into the realm of exigent martyrdom, sacrificing their hard-won manhood for the painful heights of gender ambiguity, rehearsing the sounds of emasculating torture as a means of actualizing, in part, a kind of hetero(sexual) healing. Out of this trouble comes "restoration," "renewal," a "new word," a new "world."[15]

But we might listen closely as well to the "wordless" work of a woman's lower vocal registers as it records and reanimates what Moten refers to as "the complex, dissonant, polyphonic affectivity of the ghost, the agency of the fixed but multiply apparent shade, an improvisation of spectrality . . . ." The "ghostly matters" of the black contralto are such that her soundings are often likened to an ineffable history that haunts and yet remains opaque. Paradoxically, she archives the ephemeral dimensions of legacies of subjugation that perpetually and spectrally transfigure in cultural memory and yet which simultaneously accrue a kind of sprawling density by virtue of their very elusiveness. It is in the figure of the contralto where cultural notions of scale, mass, sound, vision, race, and gender oddly converge, where a woman's voice can be likened to that which is mystically "veiled" (as is the case in Pauline Hopkins's 1903 epic *Of One Blood*) and yet can also assume the role of carrying "The Weight" that, for instance, Mavis Staples holds in what was anything but her *Last Waltz*. These types of singers are both of their bodies and elsewhere, perceived as evoking through sound a kind material thickness that is still, however, evocative of "unspeakable" histories that instead must be sung. Their voices compress and translate suffering and sobbing into acousmatic dreamscapes of black historical memory remixed and resounded. They are the figures most often conflated with the "sonic blackness" that voice theorist Nina Eidsheim describes as "a perceptual phantom projected by the listener; a vocal timbre that happens to match current expectations about blackness; or the shaping of vocal timbre to catch current ideas about the sound of blackness . . . ." These women of the lower registers, like their brothers up high, push our imagination, our desires, our quotidian needs to engage with the traces of suffering by challenging us through sound to go to (other) extremes and border regions, to tarry in the boundaries of the elsewhere. By way of their location on these "lower frequencies," they "speak for" us.[16]

They also "speak," as Laurie Stras, like Eidsheim, reminds us, of a history of "racialized sound," one in which "a lower tessitura, especially in women's voices, seems to have been used as a signifier of blackness" in the emerging recording industry of the 1920s, and one in which notions of "blackness" and "sadness" took form in the sonics as "[s]obbing and sighing, yodeling, moaning and wailing glissandi and portamenti." Stras argues that these techniques "all formed part of the blackface artist's portfolio of vocal lore that hypervocalized emotion" that extended onto vinyl during this era.[17] Clearly, these sorts of constructions of sentimental "blackness" have a long and storied history in American popular culture. But rather than capitulating to racially and gender-romanticized assumptions about the putative embodied melancholia of contralto vocalists and black singers in general, I am instead interested in how this tradition of racialized vocal aesthetics re-emerges in the late twentieth-century music of Lauryn Hill less as a marker of authenticity politics and more so as an allusive tool of post–Civil Rights cultural memory. My aim is to shift discussions of the racialized singing voice so as to think less about racial authenticity binarisms (e.g., whether someone sounds "authentically black," or not, by singing contralto) and to think more about the resonance of what Aaron Fox calls "the sounding voice" as "phatic communication," and as "a summarizing symbol of identity and a fundamental medium" of generational "social practice" within the context of what has come to be known as post-soul black popular culture.[18]

We might think of Hill's voice as that of the liminal and lowdown, on having what cultural critic Lindon Barrett calls "a powerful, revisionary force" that can ultimately translate the economy of suffering into an/other musical language.[19] Heard in this way, her contralto singing marks the site of a particular kind of emotional and spiritual transfiguration where excess(ive), dissonant storytelling flourishes and flows on a lower frequency. "When it hurts so bad," Hill sings on her ruminative ballad of the same name, "what you need ironically / will turn out what you want it to be / if you just let it." The (contr)alto singer re-purposes her vocal anatomy by turning the evocation of hurt into collective regeneration.

What did it mean to hear the voice of a contralto on the pop music charts in the 1990s? And what are the ways that that kind of voice, the voice of Lauryn Hill, a voice that fluidly oscillates between alto and contralto— what are the ways that this voice serves as an affective soundtrack for the shifting traumas of the post-soul generation? I would go so far as to suggest that unquantifiable, "ghostly" racial pain is itself perhaps the recurring theme and the core subtext of late twentieth-century black popular culture.

Look no further than comedian Chris Rock's career-defining performance in his aptly titled 1996 *Bring the Pain* concert in order to chart the conflicts, struggles, and deep-water ironies of black social and cultural identity formation in the wake of the Civil Rights movement. Rock used his media platform as a comedian to attack the shibboleths of racial progress, having survived a Brooklyn childhood of post–*Brown v. Board of Education* integration in which racial epithets were still hurled at him from inside (instead of outside) of the classroom. In the post–Civil Rights era, Rock's brand of "racial pain" is perhaps less recognizable than that of previous generations. It is not born out of the impending threat of lynch mob violence but from the flagrant ways that some South Carolinians continue to embrace the Confederate flag. It is not born out of the spectacular abjection of chattel slavery itself but from the casual contemporary disregard for and disdain toward slave reparations—both of which are subjects that Rock would mine on his popular and critically lauded HBO program from the late 1990s.[20]

And it is this *ironic* experience of enduring racial discrimination within what the cultural critic Greg Tate refers to as the era of "legislative racial equality" that generates a kind of racial pain that is itself figuratively reminiscent of the condition of bodily pain that cultural critic Elaine Scarry has influentially outlined and which bears repeating here. Scarry has argued that physical "pain's triumph" is its "absolute split between one's sense of one's own reality and the reality of other persons." For "the person in pain, so incontestably and unnegotiably present is it that 'having pain' may come to be thought of as the most vibrant example of what it is to 'have certainty,' while for the other person it is so elusive that 'hearing about pain' may exist as the primary model of what it is 'to have doubt.' Thus pain comes unsharably into our midst as at once that which cannot be denied and that which cannot be confirmed. . . . Whatever pain achieves, it achieves in part through its unsharability through its resistance to language."[21]

Just as Scarry has famously argued for ways to understand "the difficulty of expressing physical pain," as well as "the political and perceptual complications that arise as a result of that difficulty," then, so too might we consider the ways that artists of this generation, such as Chris Rock and Lauryn Hill in the 1990s, were wrestling formalistically with the limits of expressing post-soul psychic pain and alienation. There is, perhaps, no way to fully articulate the traumas of these kinds of persistent racial tensions that a figure like Chris Rock observes in his material, for like physical pain, racial pain "resists objectification in language." "To have" racial "pain is to have" a kind of "certainty" that can never be fully articulated; "to hear about" racial "pain is to have doubt."[22] Rock's program invoked black socio-political satire and putatively absurdist tactics as reparative work for what theorist Anne Cheng would call the racial melancholic condition that has no cure.[23] *The Chris Rock Show* thus sought to illuminate the unhealing "wound" of blackness in American culture by engaging with its impossible tangibility, making and mining the yokes and the jokes of that impossibility *the* central focus of his humor in the pop culture public sphere.

To be sure, Rock the court jester and Hill the neo-soul singer make for strange bedfellows. Yet I am suggesting that we might consider the compelling ways that, taken together, Rock's late 1990s material and Hill's recordings and performances constitute a poetics of post-soul affect, a structure of feeling that tells us something about the historicity of a generation of black subjects at a particular moment in time. Through performances of post-soul affect, these black artists who were raised in the wake of the Civil Rights movement articulate a recognition (or recognizance) of their own historical formation, as well as their specific affective relation to that recognition.[24]

While Rock used the raw material of black satire to articulate the anxieties and emotional turbulence of the post-soul era through a language of incongruities, Lauryn Hill made (racial) pain palpable in her vocals. In short, she used the vocal tradition of soul itself to provide commentary about that pain. This, then, I argue, is the remarkable innovation of Lauryn Hill's 1990s soul music. Her work produces a kind of sonic critical memory that connects her to a legacy of black female soul singing which, at its core, speaks to the very philosophy of black freedom struggle soulfulness itself, moving besides (to invoke Eve Sedgwick's spatial politics here) redemption to create an alternative space of expressive recognition and subjective reinstantiation.[25] More still, I want to suggest that we consider the ways that Hill's late twentieth-century music "versions" the DuBoisean sorrow songs. That is, her musical aesthetics and particularly her (contr)alto singing does a kind of work similar to that which Flatley describes as "the aesthetic practice" of the sorrow songs, a "practice that originates in and transforms" the melancholic structure of feeling associated with African American subjectivity.[26] "Even as the Songs dwell on loss and disappointment," he argues, "they do so in a collective form that returns insistently to the promise of justice and of the righteous overthrow of an oppressive order."[27]

Hill's posturing on her solo record was undoubtedly "righteous." Like the greats before her (Ray, James, Sam, Al), she proved capable of yoking religious fervor and sagacity with mercurial secularist musings and commentary. Her emergence as a latter-day prophetess steeped in the dual aesthetics of hip-hop and classic-era R&B and soul who was equally capable of wading into moral and spiritual debates linked to black post-soul consciousness both mimicked a kind of masculinist swagger and yet simultaneously marked a significant gender break from Chris Rock's firebrand routines. Like Rock, Hill openly and unabashedly addresses the moral complexities of the post-soul generation on *Miseducation*, perhaps most famously on the album's first single, "Doo Wop (That Thing)," on which she chides her peers for their rampant materialism and nihilistic impulses (women more concerned with "hair weaves like Europeans / Fake nails done by Koreans," as well as the "Money taking, heart breaking . . . sneaky silent men, the punk domestic violence men").[28]

Critics (myself included) have often read Hill's blistering rhetoric on this first single as a sign of the artist's burgeoning social conservatism and her investment in a kind of black self-help ideology that failed to examine the larger socio-political and material infrastructures which have had a lasting impact on black youth culture. And while Hill's much documented, on-stage religious pontificating would surely influence the severe communal (and personal) critiques embedded in the material that she would produce immediately in the wake of *Miseducation*, the album itself moves beyond the impulse to execute moral reform to instead "melancholize" in the form of a black feminist/humanist soul revival. As Flatley makes clear, "melancholizing is something one *does:* longing for lost loves, brooding over absent objects and changed environments, reflecting on unmet desires, and lingering on events from the past. It is a practice that might, in fact, produce its own kind of knowledge."[29] Through the sonic process of melancholizing her own subjectivity and through the aesthetics of black women's soul singing revitalized for a new era, Lauryn Hill produces post-soul knowledge about the world and her place in the world at the dawn of a new millennium.

"Got 'Til It's Gone": Black Feminist Neo Soul, Cultural Memory, and the Pedagogy of Lauryn Hill

Hill's album arrived in the midst of a nostalgic groundswell in black popular music culture.[30] Neo soul flourished in the mid- to late 1990s, first gaining major notice with the release of Philly singer-songwriter D'Angelo's debut *Brown Sugar* in 1995. That album, with its lush, sensuous bass lines, sinuous vocal arrangements that recalled the likes of Marvin Gaye and Bobby Womack, and bright, glorious sparks of gospel-inflected crooning signaled a newfound generational emphasis on recuperating and mixing classic soul's combination of live instrumentation and sacredly profane confessional energy and passion. As *New York Times* music critic Ben Ratliff would observe of this trend, neo-soul artists such as D'Angelo "make a mature music, and a family music, for living rooms, rather than for the streets. In their subject matter there is room for self-doubt, anger, beatitude, whimsy and religion—not just slick come-ons or aggressive bluster. It's increasingly album-oriented as opposed to singles-oriented. Importantly, it marks a gradual return in black pop to the use of instruments instead of electronics."[31]

Neo soul, new(ly) born soul music which took root/route in the post–Civil Rights era, looked to icons like Aretha Franklin and the musical templates of artists like Marvin Gaye, Curtis Mayfield, Donnie Hathaway, and especially Stevie Wonder to revivify the spirit of movement-era, movement-inspired black cultural expression. At its best, neo soul generated for its listeners a gripping form of what I'm calling here sonic critical memory that had the potential to revivify the affective experience associated with the genre. Just as critical memory, according to Houston Baker, "judges severely, censures righteously, renders hard ethical evaluations of the past that it never defines as well-passed," so too does Hill's brand of musical aesthetics draw on the critical memory of soul music culture to do a specific kind of interventionist socio-political work in her performative repertoire.[32] Moreover, Hill's work exemplifies the extent to which the artist situated herself specifically within a black feminist soul music genealogy which, I argue, remains under-theorized.

Few cultural critics have written extensively about the gendered politics of the genre. Scholars such as Brian Ward and Craig Werner have largely produced studies that, while paying great reverence to Aretha, have otherwise tended to champion black male artists as the key architects of soul. Mark Anthony Neal's recent work, on the sexist power dynamics bound up in the work of Bobby Womack and Marvin Gaye, points toward the kinds of cogent critical examinations of the genre that are still much needed. But few critics have rigorously considered soul's centrality as a musical way in which black female performers, Aretha Franklin of course being the most famous, invoked Barthes's grain of the voice, that is "the body in the voice," to mediate and recalibrate the hypervisibility of black female corporeality in the public domain by turning that corporeality, that body in voice, into a phantasmagoric instrument of mobile feeling.[33]

For Franklin, "soul," as she famously characterized it at one time, was to her a "feeling, a lot of depth and being able to bring to the surface that which is happening inside, to make the picture clear." And it was Franklin's brilliant ability to turn that feeling into "moments of amplified meaning" which constituted her greatest work as a soul music artist and that, some have argued, marked her as a feminist cultural pioneer in the context of popular music culture. As Powers observes, "[b]efore feminism coined the phrase, gospel created a space where the personal could be political, and that link is the key to understanding Aretha's social significance." Franklin is, as Powers insists, on songs like "Think," "a reminder of where America learned what" a resistant woman "sounded like," and any resistant women who'd come up since that moment had to admit its influence."[34] In her classic recordings, among them "I Never Loved A Man," "Natural Woman," and "Respect," Aretha Franklin makes the emotional interiority of black subjects audible. Franklin channeled her "celebrated use of melisma (stringing together a series of notes in a single syllable)," a kind of unbridled vocal excess, into a style of vocalizing that insisted on a form of sonic black womanhood that took up social space but that eluded the hegemonic panoptic gaze by shifting the (figurative) weight of the body to sound.[35]

Hill's connections to Franklin and other black feminist musical icons of the Civil Rights and Black Power eras runs deep—beyond the realm of formal collaboration and into the realm of critical memory where a "cumulative, collective maintenance" of a historical "record . . . draws into relationship significant instants of time past and the always uprooted homelessness of now."[36] This is especially apparent on Hill's breakthrough cover of Roberta Flack's 1972 hit "Killing Me Softly With His Song," recorded with the Fugees in 1996, and it is this single which both cleared the way for the *Miseducation* which would follow, as well as Hill's triumphant return to the spotlight in the 2006 film *Block Party*.

In his moving resuscitation of the music of Roberta Flack, R&B critic Jason King has observed of the Fugees' cover of Flack's "rapturous, delicately rendered performance of a song about the process of being enraptured by a delicately rendered performance of a song" that it "cannot—or doesn't attempt to—access the melancholic 'heaviness' of Flack's original."[37] What's missing from this version, King argues, is Flack's unique brand of "gravitas" in her reading of Lori Leiberman's song about "being sensually turned 'inside out' by a guitar-wielding 'young boy' singer."[38] While Flack's recording resulted in a kind of soul music that is indicative of the artist's as well as the soul music genre's perpetual dedication to "making contact and producing getting togetherness," as King refers to it, the Fugees' cover, with its "privileg[ing] of percussive rhythm" over "quiet-fire delicacy," fails to achieve the kind of spiritually transcendent sociality rooted in the track and more broadly in soul's very ethos.[39] Hip-hop's insistence on "bombastic male aggression" and co-Fugee Wyclef Jean's vociferous hypeman background vocals on the track seemingly leave no room for Flack's "politically efficacious" form of soulful "vibeology" to emerge on this track.[40]

I take seriously King's points about the superficial ways in which contemporary R&B and hip-hop artists have of late frequently pursued a nostalgic penchant for the sounds of soulful communitas without fully mining the aesthetic and spiritual substance of such an endeavor. At the same time,

I want to leave room for recognizing the ways in which the Fugees' wildly popular Flack cover might still "engage in the archaeology of living inter-textual tradition" in ways that tap into critical memory's ability to mediate the complicated space between the turbulent cultural past and present.[41] On the Fugees' version of "Killing Me Softly With His Song" we hear Hill lyrically connecting to Flack's bygone pop narrative of the poetics of pain—not racial pain specifically but an aesthetic pain that is both pleasur-able and wrought with agony. Hill and her cohort's "interperformance" of Flack's song allows, then, for a means to showcase an engagement with the fundamentals of soul's ideology, that is, "the continual possibility of getting togetherness against the backdrop of unredeemable suffering and cosmic alienation."[42]

But whereas King reads the song's hip-hop framing devices as detri-ments to the track's ability to sonically articulate the depths of this ideol-ogy, I would suggest that these devices along with Hill's vocal performance both forge a connection with the original and signal its own significant and meaningful uprootedness. While the Fugees' cover strips the original of its "intense attention to dynamics, arrangement, rapturous effects, instru-mentation, and feelingful interaction between vibe-driven instrumental-ists," the very sparseness of their version of the song, the ways in which the gently luxurious arrangements of the original have been here eviscerated in favor of rap aesthetics, points to the tenuous relationship between the post-soul generation's (dis) connections to its cultural past; it does a kind of necessary (if less pleasing to some) critical work to call attention to cultural memory itself.[43] Hill's steady alto anchors the track and carefully echoes Flack's ethereal overdub arrangements and her controlled reading of Li-eberman's lyrics. Save for Flack's "famous scatted bridge" at which point Hill lets loose a brief yet intense melismatic run that pulls the vocals into contemporary top 40 aesthetics, Hill as vocalist remains in harmony with Flack's original, making the soulful past "audible" to a new generation of listeners unfamiliar with the 1972 recording.[44]

Where the track "goes rogue," so to speak, most notably is in its use of "a synth sitar sound," and Wyclef Jean, Praz Michel, and Hill's own rap hype interruptions and chants.[45] As steady as Hill flows as a singer here, Wyclef and Hill's alter-rap-ego "L Boogie" trade banter in the sparse inter-ludes in ways that continuously pull the track into an era shaped by "a post-instrumental, sample-driven generation of music producers."[46] As MC and phantom conductor of the track, Wyclef repeatedly inserts himself into what is an otherwise classic female soul confessional, signaling Hill to sing ("Yo my girl L you got the lyric!") and counting off Hill's repetition of the chorus ("One time! Two times!"). It's a tense dynamic, and one that registers the way that the song itself is caught between two eras, oscillating between two genres. It is a song that in the Fugees' rendering encapsulates the generic and nostalgic displacement of the post-soul generation, and it exemplifies the extent to which Hill as an artist was, from the moment of the group's enormous breakthrough, forced to occupy and mediate multiple representational spaces as a woman MC and as a soul vocalist who emerges as the audible link to the black cultural past. Perhaps most importantly, "Killing Me Softly" is a song that opened the door for Hill to set out on a journey to reposition herself in the world as an urban philosopher in search of new ways to reanimate "getting togetherness," an achievement she would pursue in full on *The Miseducation of Lauryn Hill*.

The stories Hill told on *Miseducation* captured a voice that expressed spiritual longings and socio-political anxieties—urgent, young, gifted, black women's desires and pre-millennially tense concerns. At the same time, Hill, like Wonder, like Roberta Flack before her, was able to transmit a brand of intellectual emotionalism about love as a big Idea in her music that paid homage to some of the great black feminist thinkers of the era, writers like Alice Walker, Toni Morrison, June Jordan, and bell hooks (or even perhaps the French feminist Luce Irigaray). Hill took pop's biggest thematic cliché and transformed it into a centerpiece of schoolhouse rock nostalgia and kitchen table enlightenment on the album. Cosby-meets-*Crooklyn* "classroom" interludes featuring a gaggle of young voices responding to a teacher's questions about love ("How many people in here have ever been in love?" "Tell me about your personal definition of love?" "Do you think you're too young to really love somebody?") weave their way around Hill's songs about adult intimacy, trust, betrayal, despair, and reawakening, turning each story of *how* we love into even bigger tales of *why* we love from our earliest years. Ambitious in its thematic scope and range, Hill's album sought to produce an extended meditation on the personal, the communal, and the cerebrally transformative powers of love as a movement unto itself.[47]

Soul to Soul: Black Publicity, Hip-Hop Urban Renewal, and the Return of Lauryn Hill

But "after the love is gone," how do you (re)ignite a musical revolution?[48] Two years after the release of *Miseducation*, Lauryn Hill abruptly, informally yet very publicly retired from the public eye, gave birth to the first of her five children with Marley, and announced her disillusionment with the recording industry, the media, and her former bandmates. Save for her 2004 *MTV Unplugged* performance and concert recording, Hill has largely shunned the pop world.[49] All of this, then, makes Hill's reemergence in the critically acclaimed documentary *Dave Chappelle's Block Party* all the more startling since it is in this film that Hill, with her former groupmates the Fugees, not only reconnects with the progressive communality that characterized her album but also revitalizes the socio-political utility of soulfulness for a post–Civil Rights generation perched on the edge of Obama's ascendancy.

Shot in Brooklyn in the fall of 2005, *Block Party* is at this point an archival document that captures not only Hill but the comedian Dave Chappelle at what would turn out to be a fleeting turning point in his much-talked-about career. Fresh off the second season of his enormously popular cable sketch comedy series, Chappelle agreed to team with the quirky French indie film director Gondry (*Eternal Sunshine of the Spotless Mind, Be Kind, Rewind*) to document his efforts to organize and stage a daylong block party concert festival in Brooklyn, New York. Echoing the spirit of 1972's legendary concert film *Wattstax* which features a thoughtful and probing Richard Pryor as a key narrator (and note the Pryor shirt worn by Chappelle during the day of the Block Party concert) as well as lesser-known films and events from that same era (*Soul to Soul, Soul Power*), *Block Party* resituates black popular music at the center of an effort to revitalize communal solidarity, and it promotes quotidian collective joy and celebration fostered by the affective energy produced by a series of buoyant, interactive, sweat-inducing sonic performances in a festival setting.[50] Nearly devoid of explicit political discourse save for the incisive protest rap of alternative hip-hop duo Dead Prez and the late-film appearance of Black Panther legacy Fred Hampton Jr., who admonishes the crowd to put their "hands up, eyes open and fists clench . . . say 'power to the people!'," *Block Party* is a film that embraces and executes the concept of black freedom in public space as it is manifested by way of musical performance. Like *Wattstax* before it, it is a work that considers the politics and poetics of civic as well as personal freedoms in the form of a music festival that attests to the lasting value of and communal pleasures found in urban public space. And like *Soul to Soul* and *Soul Power* before it, the film repeatedly stages the scene of live musical performance as a regenerative salve that might rekindle public articulations of black cultural collectivity.

Block Party is indicative of the post–Civil Rights cultural "yearning for a scale of sociality which is denied everywhere. It speaks to the desire for an authentic, face-to-face version of democratic interdependence and mutuality."[51] It also exceeds and complicates the limits of that yearning by literally forming a multiracial counterpublic that is united by black music in the context of the film. Chappelle, the wealthy celebrity, randomly hands out invitations to black and white neighbors, merchants, and strangers for his Brooklyn concert party in his Ohio hometown, offers bus transportation to New Yorkers who line up in Manhattan for the free event, extends a welcome to eccentric white Bohemian Brooklynites and educators of color alike in the area, and hand-picks entertainers: an historically black college marching band, rap superstars (Kanye West), indie heroes (Mos Def), and black feminist neo-soul icons teaming up for the first time on film (Erykah Badu and Jill Scott). This is, indeed, *Chappelle's Show*, but it is also an extravaganza that celebrates and is predicated upon "democratic interdependence and mutuality" fostered by the publicity that is black musical performance.

That Chappelle designates his event as a "party" that sprawls down a street in an urban neighborhood is especially significant since the concert calls attention to the alternative ways of conceiving of soul music as capable of generating not just "the sort of auratic, ambient energy one might expect at a funeral" but a kind of euphoria expressive of life-affirming communality as well.[52] Soul music's ebullient potential is, for instance, in the film best exemplified by the Central State Marching Band's fiercely propulsive cover of Kanye West's hip-hop redemption anthem "Jesus Walks." Fresh off the bus from Dayton, Ohio, the band summons neighborhood residents into the street, into the block party, spreading sound from door to door as West and singer John Legend watch from the sidelines. Gondry interfaces this performance with West's furiously energetic in-concert version of his song, creating an electric circuit between stage and sidewalk, between pop stars and amateur musicians.

This "human interconnectedness and collective intimacy" that courses throughout the film culminates with the magnetic return of Hill and the Fugees as the concert reaches its rousing climax.[53] A sly MC, Chappelle as host first plays the crowd by announcing that while Hill had originally been slated to perform as the headliner for the show, her record label Columbia Records refused to release the rights to use her songs in the film. The solution however? Reunite the Fugees. Backed by the Roots who served as the house band for the entire event, Jean, Praz Michel, and Hill gather themselves for their long-awaited entrance. The camera spies Hill and Praz waiting in the wings while Jean gamely takes to the stage delivering the opening lines of "Nappy Heads (Mona Lisa)," the underground hit off of their first album, 1994's *Blunted on Reality*. Jean as town crier delivers his opening lines ("Round up the posse, Fugee comin round the way!") as Hill chimes in off-stage, punctuating key lines of Jean's battle rap ("You wanna battle swing I bring commanding men like I was king") before he introduces her to the crowd.

This is Lauryn Hill in 2005, looking largely Columbia professorial meets South Orange, New Jersey PTA with a dash of rap rogue thrown in for good measure, all awash in earth tones, flowing linen lines, cream colored kulats, a khaki jacket, and a matching pashmina—with a Yankee cap resting atop her natural locks tipped defiantly to the side. All swagger and conviction, Hill wags her finger at the crowd, self-assured, ready to do battle, and stakes out her space in the flow, reminding her fans of who she is, where she's from, that she "don't wear Jheri curls cause I nah from the West / No disrespect to the West, true indeed / I rock it to the East." Jean and Hill keep time and trade rhymes with playful momentum while welcoming Praz to the stage and into the conversation as well.

The centerpiece of this Fugees reunion and arguably of the block party project and the film itself, the emotional climax, is Hill's virtuosic brilliance as a performer. Jean and Praz initiate the final shift in emphasis in the scene during a conversational interlude between the two that falls in the space between excerpts from the "Mona Lisa" group sequence and the transition into Hill's opening lines of "Killing Me Softly." In reflecting on the group's reunion, Praz scrambles for language to describe the experience of watching Hill perform again. "She was singing . . . 'Killing Me Softly' last night. . . . She was like, we was just like: Goddamn. She's a *beast*. . . . When she started singing 'Killing Me Softly,' I almost wanted to cry." Hill's performance is the film's denouement and its emotional anchor, a return to soulful pain emerging out of musical virtuosity, and an appearance that radiates with "the erotic fusion of Self into Other, the moment where the ensemble on stage format[s] the ensemble in the audience."[54]

Clenching her pashmina like a soul man's towel at this point in the performance, Hill launches into a version of the Fugees' biggest hit accompanied initially by nothing more than Jean's gentle keyboard accents. This "Killing Me Softly" is both rougher and sweeter. Hill punctuates the opening verse with several of her compressed melismas that have the power to suggest powder-keg gravitas without Hill having to ever utilize maximum volume or gross pyrotechnics. Less faithful to Flack's original here, Hill instead works the cadences of the melody more deeply and playfully as the audience, holding fast to her every note, responds vociferously to the metastructure of her performance; notes are greeted with their own squeals, ohs, and ahs as the drama of Hill's vocalizing unfolds. The opening chorus thus establishes Hill's execution of getting-togetherness. Her rippling take on the song's chorus here opens up the volatility of her performance to gospel restlessness as she worries lines and encourages a more aggressive call-and-response dynamic than in the recording on *The Score* album. The pleasure of (re)connecting with the crowd as well as the song is written across Hill's face as she plows through the familiar opening lines of "Killing Me Softly" and listens to the crowd's engagement with her performance. Self and other, audience and performer merge here only to gently divide as Hill shifts into a quietly turbulent re-reading of the opening verse in which she recounts how she "heard he sang a good song / I heard he had a style / And so I came to see him / and listen for awhile," pulling out the end of verses with emphatic runs, ascending scales.

On the one hand, Hill's departure from Flack's "quiet fire" aesthetics in this performance surely calls attention to the ways in which contemporary audiences have become accustomed to and often demand of pop and R&B performers in particular a kind of ornate vocality that musicologist Richard Rischar argues gained popularity in the early 1990s and, in particular, on top 40 radio.[55] But I would argue that Hill's performance stands apart from these sorts of flashy displays of technique by virtue of the economical and unpredictable way that she makes use of the melisma here. In this opening verse, initially free of the hip-hop percussion, the synth sitar, and Jean's hype man chants that weighed the recording down, Hill roves out onto the affective frontier to produce an interpretation of "Killing Me Softly" that bursts at the seams with dramatic power and range. Recalling the aesthetics of her forebear Franklin, Hill emerges in this performance as a method actor, a protagonist responding to the winding emotional journey that Flack's song takes us on. She registers every fear, hesitation, pleasure—the full scale of unmarked (and unrequited) desire embedded in the "Killing Me Softly" narrative, shifting the temporality of Flack's interpretation from a testimonial about an event—a performance—in the past tense to the perpetual present. Hill's "Killing Me Softly" rendition lives out the "killing," demonstrates, executes, performs (in the Austinian sense of the word) the "strumming" of her own "pain," "sings" her whole life through the allusion to "his words."[56] In this moment of exposure, when the song's protagonist feels "embarrassed by the crowd" at having her emotional interiority "read aloud," Hill merges into the figure of both the female spectator whose affective world has literally been turned inside out to that of the performing "young man" who dominates and devastates his audience through the sheer virtuosity of his act.

Such intricately realized aesthetic genius is cause for communal celebration, and so whereas Flack's classic version of the song rests on its own beautifully contained affirmation of the singer-songwriter's ability to tell her story of passionate musical witnessing with intimate and captivating accuracy, the Fugees' "Killing Me Softly" here, in the context of a Brooklyn block party, finally achieves its ultimate utility. With the group's rhythm section joining in now for a reprise of the chorus, with the crowd bobbing and weaving, waving arms in the air, Lauryn Hill (here with what is clearly now her backup group the Fugees) and her rendition of "Killing Me Softly" both explicitly engage with soul's perpetual recognition of psychic suffering (even the pleasurable kind). Her performance allusively reanimates that suffering in a post-soul context, and here at the climax of the concert exemplifies the ways that the (contr)alto vocalist might take the shape of suffering and make our world, at least for a moment and on one rainy day in Brooklyn, thunderously, palpably, invigoratingly (a)new.

NOTES

1. Aaron Fox, *Real Country. Music and Language in Working-Class Culture* (Durham: Duke University Press, 2004), 301. Aretha Franklin, *Downbeat Magazine,* as quoted in Gerri Hirshey, *Nowhere to Run: The Story of Soul Music* (New York: Da Capo Press, 1994), 228. My thanks to the anonymous readers of this piece for their insightful suggestions.

2. Rufus and Chaka, "Do You Love What You Feel," *MasterJam,* UMG Recordings, 1979.

3. *Dave Chappelle's Block Party,* dir. Michel Gondry (Universal City, CA: Universal Studios, 2006), DVD.

4. Ann Powers, "Crossing Back Over from the Sacred to the Profane," *New York Times,* August 1998. Eric Weisbard, "Review of *The Miseducation of Lauryn Hill,*" *SPIN Magazine,* August 1998. Toure, "Review of *The Miseducation of Lauryn Hill,*" *Rolling Stone Magazine,* August 1998. David Browne, "Review of *The Miseducation of Lauryn Hill,*" *Entertainment Weekly Magazine,* September 1998. In 2008, *Entertainment Weekly Magazine* ranked the album at number 2 in the list of the greatest albums of the past twenty-five years.

5. Concert reviews and blog reports of Lauryn Hill's erratic stage behavior date back to the period of her *MTV Unplugged* performance. See, for instance, Toure, "The Mystery of Lauryn Hill," *Rolling Stone Magazine,* October 2003. For recent examples, see, for instance, http://www.rhymeswithsnitch.com/2007/08/lauryn-hill-in-brooklyn.html. La Marr Bruce, "Looking for Lauryn," Critical Karaoke Workshop, Black Performance Theory Retreat, Yale University, May 2009. My thanks to Paul Farber for his insightful comments about Hill's *MTV Unplugged* performance which have enlivened this project. For coverage of one of her more recent shows, see Jon Caramanica, "Worth the Wait? Just Ask Her," *New York Times,* December 29, 2010. See also Rob Harvilla, "Live: Lauryn Hill, Extremely Loud

and Incredibly Close at the Blue Note," The Village Voice Blogs, http://blogs.villagevoice.com/music/2011/01/live_lauryn_hil.php

Harvilla opens his review on a sobering note by declaring that "the bad news always comes first with Lauryn Hill."

6. Elizabeth Wood, "Lesbian Fugue: Ethel Smyth's Contrapuntal Arts," ed. Ruth A. Solie, *Musicology and Difference: Gender and Sexuality in Music Scholarship* (Berkeley: University of California Press, 1993), 164.

7. For more on the spiritual politics of Hill's album, see Powers, "Crossing Back Over."

8. Cultural critics Nelson George and Mark Anthony Neal each examine the politics of "post-soul" culture in their respective works on African-American cultural production emerging in the wake of the Civil Rights and Black Power movements. See also Mark Anthony Neal, *Soul Babies: Black Popular Culture and the Post-Soul Aesthetic* (New York: Routledge, 2002); and Nelson George, *Post-Soul Nation: The Explosive, Contradictory, Triumphant, and Tragic 1980s as Experienced by African Americans (Previously Known as Blacks and Before That Negroes)* (New York: Viking, 2004). For an examination of post-soul writers such as Ellis, James, and Beatty, see Darryl Dickson-Carr, *African American Satire: The Sacredly Profane Novel* (Columbia: University of Missouri Press, 2001).

9. Lauryn Hill, *The Miseducation of Lauryn Hill* (New York: Sony/Columbia Records, 1998), CD.

10. Brian Ward, *Just My Soul Responding: Rhythm and Blues, Black Consciousness and Race Relations* (Berkeley: University of California Press, 1998). Craig Werner, *Higher Ground: Stevie Wonder, Aretha Franklin, Curtis Mayfield and the Rise and Fall of American Soul* (New York: Three Rivers Press, 2005). Craig Werner, *A Change Is Gonna Come: Music, Race, and the Soul of America* (Ann Arbor: University of Michigan Press, 2006).

11. Richard C. Green and Monique Guillory, "Question of a 'Soulful Style': Interview with Paul Gilroy," ed. Richard C. Green and Monique Guillory, *Soul: Black Power, Politics and Pleasure* (New York: New York University Press, 1998). Paul Gilroy, "'After the Love Is Gone': Bio-politics and Etho-poetics in the Black Public Sphere," *The Black Public Sphere, A Public Culture Book* (Chicago: University of Chicago Press, 1995), 53–80. Fred Moten and Charles Rowell, "Words Don't Go There: An Interview with Fred Moten," *Callaloo* 27, no.4 (2004): 953–66.

12. Jonathan Flatley, *Affective Mapping: Melancholia and the Politics of Modernism* (Cambridge: Harvard University Press, 2008), 2.

13. Ernest Hardy, "Too Deep: Aretha-Chaka-Lauryn," *Bloodbeats*, vol. 1, *Demos, Remixes & Extended Versions* (Berkeley: RedBone Press, 2006). For more on Nina Simone, see Ruth Feldstein, "'I Don't Trust You Anymore': Nina Simone, Culture, and Black Activism in the 1960s," *Journal of American History* 91, no. 4 (2005): 1349–79. Tammy Kernodle, "'I Wish I Knew How It Would Feel To Be Free': Nina Simone and the Redefining of the Freedom Song of the 1960s," *Journal of the Society of American Music* 2, no. 3 (2008): 295–317. Daphne A. Brooks, "Nina Simone's Triple Play," *Callaloo* 34, no. 1 (2011): 176–97. For more on Odetta, see Matthew Frye Jacobson, "'Take This Hammer': Odetta, Coffeehouse Publics, and the Tributaries of the Left, 1953–1962," unpublished 2009 ASA Convention paper manuscript. For more on Marian Anderson, see Raymond Arsenault, *The Sound of Freedom: Marian*

Anderson, the Lincoln Memorial and the Concert that Awakened America (New York: Bloomsbury Press, 2010). Gayle Wald, "Soul Vibrations: Black Music in Sound and Space," *American Quarterly* 63 (3) 2011: 673–96. Alex Ross, "Voice of the Century: Celebrating Marian Anderson," *New Yorker*, April 13, 2009.

14. Nathaniel Mackey, *Bedouin Hornbook* (Los Angeles: Sun & Moon Press, 2000), 63. See also Fred Moten, "Black Mo'nin'," ed. David Eng and David Kazanjian, *Loss: The Politics of Mourning* (Berkeley: University of California Press, 2002), 59–76; and his *In the Break: The Aesthetics of the Black Radical Tradition* (Minneapolis: University of Minnesota Press, 2003), 192–211.

15. Moten, "Black Mo'nin'." To be clear, both Moten's and Mackey's brilliant works have been an enormous source of inspiration to me in my thinking about this subject. My aim is to extend the conversation so as to think in specific ways about the work of black women's vocalizing with regard to these tropes. A notable exception to hetero-coded black falsetto performances can, of course, be found in the work of queer disco legend Sylvester. For an exploration of Sylvester in relation to the politics of gender, race, sexuality, and falsetto singing, see Judith Jack Halberstam, "Queer Voices and Musical Genders," ed. Freya Jarman-Ivens, *Oh Boy!: Masculinities and Popular Music* (New York: Routledge, 2007), 183–95.

16. Fred Moten, *In the Break: The Aesthetics of the Black Radical Tradition* (Minneapolis, MN: University of Minnesota, 2003), 196. Avery Gordon, *Ghostly Matters: Haunting and the Sociological Imagination* (Minneapolis, MN: University of Minnesota, 1997). Pauline Hopkins, *Of One Blood, Or, the Hidden Self* in ed. Hazel Carby, *The Magazine Novels of Pauline Hopkins* (New York: Oxford University Press, 1988), 502. Mavis Staples sings "The Weight" in *The Last Waltz*, dir. Martin Scorcese (MGM Pictures, 2002). On "acousmatic blackness," see Mendi Obadike, "Low Fidelity: Stereotyped Blackness in the Field of Sound" (PhD diss., Duke University, 2005). Ron Radano, *Lying Up a Nation: Race and Black Music* (Chicago: University of Chicago, 2003). Emily Lordi, *Black Resonance: Classic Female Singers and the Music of African American Writing* (New Brunswick, NJ: Rutgers, forthcoming). Nina Eidsheim, "Marian Anderson and 'Sonic Blackness' in American Opera," *American Quarterly* 63:3 (2011): 663–64. Ralph Ellison, *Invisible Man* (New York: Vintage, 1980), 581. Gayle Wald, "Soul Vibrations: Black Music and Black Freedom in Sound and Space," *American Quarterly* 63:3 (2011): 673–96. In his study of the country singer's "cry break," Aaron Fox asserts that a "pharyngealized tone . . . can be iconic of the ravaged voice of a character textually narrated as 'crying'. . ." Fox, 276. I am interested in the melancholic atmospheric and spatial resonances associated with (contr)alto vocalists. Descriptions of black contralto singers consistently refer to power and depth as when critics describes "the surging force" combined with the "deep sincerity" of Mahalia Jackson's voice. "Mahalia Jackson Sings: Rouses Town Hall Audience to a Cheering Fervor," *New York Times*, December 23, 1957. Abundant thanks to Jody Kreiman, Marti Newland, and especially Nina Eidsheim for their generous feedback.

17. Laurie Stras, "White Face, Black Voice: Race, Gender, and Region in the Music of the Boswell Sisters," *Journal of the Society for American Music* 1, no. 2 (2007): 214–15. Stras points out that during this period there existed "an abiding fascination for the black female contralto" (214). See also Eidsheim, "Voice as a Technology of Selfhood."

18. Fox, *Real Country*, 272, 273.

19. Lindon Barrett, *Blackness and Value: Seeing Double* (New York: Cambridge University Press, 2009).

20. Chris Rock, *Bring the Pain*, dir. Keith Truesdell (Universal City, CA: Dreamworks, 2002), DVD. *The Best of the Chris Rock Show*, vols. 1 & 2 (New York: HBO Home Video, 2005), DVD. My thinking on Chris Rock's work has been greatly enlivened over the past few years by engaging with Glenda Carpio's marvelous scholarship on black humor. For more on Chris Rock's comedy in relation to slavery and historical memory, see Glenda Carpio, *Laughing Fit to Kill: Black Humor in the Fictions of Slavery* (New York: Oxford University Press, 2008), especially 104–9. See also Bambi Haggins, *Laughing Mad: The Black Comic Persona in Post-Soul America* (New Brunswick: Rutgers University Press, 2007).

21. Greg Tate, *Flyboy in the Buttermilk* (New York: Simon and Schuster, 1992). Elaine Scarry, *The Body in Pain: The Making and Unmaking of the World* (New York: Oxford University Press, 1987), 4. For an examination of pain and the treatment of pain in a racial and socio-historical context, see historian Keith Wailoo's forthcoming study on the subject.

22. Scarry, *The Body in Pain*, 3, 14.

23. Scarry, *The Body in Pain*, 4. Anne Cheng, *The Melancholy of Race: Psychoanalysis, Assimilation, and Hidden Grief* (New York: Oxford University Press, 2001). For more on post-soul diasporic memory and melancholia, see Salamishah Tillet, *Peculiar Memories* (Durham: Duke University Press, 2012).

24. My thinking on this subject has been enlivened by the recent work of Flatley as well as diaspora studies scholar Nadia Ellis. In *Affective Mapping*, Flatley illuminates the ways that affect—and especially melancholia—can serve as a kind of mapping that produces a way in which to understand oneself in relation to history and one's position in the world. "Melancholia," Flatley argues, "forms the site in which the social origins of our emotional lives can be mapped out and from which we can see the other persons who share our losses and are subject to the same social forces" (3). Likewise, in her discussion of "Caribbean soul," Nadia Ellis examines the politics of post-colonial feeling in the works of George Lamming, CLR James, and others. Ellis argues that Caribbean "soul" is a way of describing "affect," the "aspect of subjectivity governed by a conjunction of feeling and thought and . . . also the performance or outworking of that conjunction. . . . West Indian affect," she argues, "during the period of decolonization comes from the West Indian and English subjects' search for belonging, intimacy, ultimately home, in a context where all of those things were muddled and compromised." See Nadia Ellis, *Territories of the Soul*, unpublished manuscript, 4.

25. Eve Sedgwick, *Touching Feeling: Affect, Pedagogy, Performativity* (Durham: Duke University Press, 2003).

26. Flatley, *Affective Mapping*, 107.

27. Ibid., 107.

28. Hill, *The Miseducation of Lauryn Hill*.

29. Flatley, *Affective Mapping*, 2.

30. The heading refers to Janet Jackson's 1997 single "Got 'Til It's Gone," a warmly melancholic pop-neo-soul effort that found the singer dabbling with tropes of nostalgia in order to tell a tale of lost love. Jackson's single sampled a Joni Mitch-

ell "Big Yellow Taxi" chorus loop, and the stylishly haunting video, directed by Mark Romanek, capitalized on apartheid-era South African cultural markers as a means to articulating both cultural as well as romantic melancholia. Janet Jackson, *The Velvet Rope* (Virgin Records, 1997), CD.

31. Ben Ratliff, "Out of a Rut and into a New Groove," *New York Times*, January 23, 2000.

32. Houston A. Baker Jr., "Critical Memory and the Black Public Sphere," *The Black Public Sphere: A Public Culture Book* (Chicago: University of Chicago Press, 1995), 5–38.

33. See Ward, *Just My Soul Responding*. Werner, *Higher Ground*. Neal, ASA 2007 Paper. See also Peter Guralnick, *Sweet Soul Music: Rhythm and Blues and the Southern Dream of Freedom* (New York: Back Bay Books, 1999). Gerri Hirshey has focused more broadly on female artists in the context of what she refers to as the soul music era, but her exploration covers a wider swath of black pop (Motown, girl groups, etc.) than other soul studies. Gerri Hirshey, *Nowhere to Run: The Story of Soul Music* (London: Southbank, 2006). For excellent new work on Aretha Franklin's vocal aesthetics, see Emily Lordi, *Black Resonance*.

34. Ann Powers, "Aretha Franklin," in *Trouble Girls: The Rolling Stone Book of Women in Rock*, ed. Barbara O'Dair (New York: Random House, 1997), 100. For a rigorous analysis of Franklin's breakthrough Atlantic Records debut as well as her vocal virtuosity, see Matt Dobkin, *I Never Loved a Man the Way I Love You: Aretha Franklin, Respect, and the Making of a Soul Music Masterpiece* (New York: St. Martin's Press, 2004). See also Aaron Cohen, *Aretha Franklin, Amazing Grace* (New York: Continuum, 2011).

35. Franklin as cited in Powers, "Aretha Franklin," 92–101.

36. Baker, "Critical Memory and the Black Public Sphere," 7. In 1999, Hill shot a video with Aretha Franklin for her song "A Rose Is Still a Rose" which she wrote for Franklin. The video, which features Hill and Franklin alongside other 1990s black female recording artists such as Faith Evans, Amel Larrieux, and Mary, Mary celebrates intergenerational black female musical collaboration.

37. Jason King, "The Sound of Velvet Melting: The Power of 'Vibe' in the Music of Roberta Flack," ed. Eric Weisbard, *Listen Again: A Momentary History of Pop Music* (Durham: Duke University Press, 2007), 180, 194.

38. Ibid., 180.

39. Ibid., 184.

40. Ibid., 196.

41. Gilroy, "After the Love Is Gone," 57.

42. Gilroy, "After the Love Is Gone," 57, and King, "The Sound of Velvet Melting," 177.

43. King, "The Sound of Velvet Melting," 195.

44. The Fugees, "Killing Me Softly," *The Score* (Sony/Columbia, 1996). King, "The Sound of Velvet Melting," 180.

45. King, "The Sound of Velvet Melting," 194.

46. Ibid., 195.

47. For more on the complexity of Hill's representational persona in the media during this period, see Imani Perry, *Prophets of the Hood: Politics and Poetics in Hip Hop* (Durham: Duke University Press, 2004), 155–90.

48. Musing in 1995 (on the eve of Hill's emergence as a recording artist) on the current state of black music culture and its relationship to the black public sphere, Paul Gilroy would call attention to the ubiquity of "racialised sex" and the black pornographic corporeal in public culture in lieu of an ethics of love and community. In his essay "'After the Love has Gone': Bio-Politics and Etho-Poetics in the Black Public Sphere," Gilroy observes the extent to which "love stories" had ultimately "mutate[d] into sex stories" (69) in black popular music culture in particular, and he "mourn[s] the disappearance of the pursuit of Freedom as an element in black vernacular culture" (59). See also his more recent study *Darker than Blue* which curiously overlooks Hill's work altogether. Paul Gilroy, *Darker than Blue: On the Moral Economies of Black Atlantic Culture* (Cambridge: Harvard University Press, 2011). Gilroy, along with many critics during that period, most surely did not see Hill's solo debut coming right around the corner. Just as well, the critics and publics who so rapidly and passionately embraced her intervention in what was hip-hop and R&B's overwhelmingly "male stage for the theatre of power and kinship in which sound is displaced by vision and words are generally second to gestures" (60) didn't see Hill's subsequent disappearance from the public eye coming either.

49. In 2010, Hill re-surfaced in a rare interview with NPR for the "50 Great Voices" series and reflected on elusive persona. To NPR correspondent Zoe Chace's query about her disappearance, Hill responds by saying that "'there were a number of different reasons . . . but partly, the support system that I needed was not necessarily in place. There were things about myself, personal-growth things, that I had to go through in order to feel like it was worth it." Zoe Chace, "The Many Voices of Lauryn Hill," http://www.npr.org/templates/story/story.php?storyId=128149135.

50. *Wattstax*, dir. Mel Stuart (1973; Burbank, CA: Warner Home Video, 2004), DVD. *Soul to Soul*, dir. Denis Sanders (1971; Miami, FL: Rhino, 2004), DVD. *Soul Power*, dir. Jeffrey Levy-Hinte (2009; Culver City, CA: Sony, 2010), DVD. For more on *Block Party*, see Riley Snorton, "The Artistry of Ethnography in *Dave Chappelle's Block Party*," *The Comedy of Dave Chappelle: Critical Essays*, ed. Kevin Wisniewski (New York: McFarland, 2009), 102–14.

51. Green and Guillory, "A Question of Soulful Style: An Interview with Paul Gilroy," 256.

52. King, "The Sound of Velvet Melting," 193.

53. Ibid., 193.

54. Ibid., 177.

55. Richard Rischar, "A Vision of Love: An Etiquette of Vocal Ornamentation in African-American Popular Ballads of the Early 1990s," *American Music* 22, no. 3 (2004): 407–43.

56. J. L. Austin, *How to Do Things With Words: The William James Lectures Delivered in Harvard University in 1955* (New York: Oxford University Press, 1976).

JASON KING

Don't Stop 'til You Get Enough

Presence, Spectacle, and Good Feeling in
Michael Jackson's This Is It

THERE'S A FANTASTIC MOMENT I can't shake in Columbia Pictures' *Michael Jackson's This Is It*, the 2009 film posthumously cobbled together from raw video footage of Michael Jackson during his final rehearsals. While restaging 1988 synth-funk jam "Smooth Criminal" at Los Angeles's Staples Center, co-director Kenny Ortega asks the wiry pop superstar, who is facing stage front, how he will see an important visual cue on the gargantuan 100 x 30 foot HD 3D screen behind him. With scarcely a moment's hesitation, Jackson replies: "I gotta feel that . . . I'll feel that, the screen behind me."[1]

"I'll feel that": an essential cue in a multi-million dollar live theatrical extravaganza hinges on Jackson's ability to intuitively feel that which he cannot physically see. Ortega seems secure enough to surrender the moment to Jackson's tremendous self-confidence in his own peerless rhythm and timing. No visual proof is required. In the moment in which he'll required to be in the moment, Michael has faith that he'll ride the energy of the moment.

But Jackson's timing is beyond extraordinary. It's extrasensory. As default custodians of improvisational musical traditions, black performers have always been clairsentient futurists, architects of a sentimental avant-garde tradition. The ability to improvise, to think on your feet, is rooted in intuition: gut feeling, muscle memory, the hunch. To feel something is to know it. Black music is *paraperformative*—"feeling beyond" emerges as the way to higher knowledge. Like a precog, Michael Jackson can sense and therefore *know* a future cue he could not physically see on the screen behind him. He bends and manipulates temporality and sculpts the total environment into his vision. Vibrational connectedness to your surroundings—to feel and honor the auratic energy in a space, to be highly present in the moment—is the prerequisite to feeling the future.

Critics have long derided Jackson's heart-on-your-sleeve sentimentality and his schmaltzy pleas for charity on songs like 1991's "Heal the World." But they ignore the implicit relationship between Michael's penchant for feelingful connection and communion with others—his utopian belief in the social whole, multi-oneness, that every thing is present in everything, which is how you'd have to re-read his 1986's charity anthem "We Are the World"—and his clairsentient ability to feel into the future. Jackson's otherworldly perceptual skills, which always already inform and are informed by his immense gifts as a singer, dancer, producer, actor, and stage and studio auteur, explain why director Kenny Ortega confesses in a scene from the extras to the 2010 DVD release of *This Is It* that despite the outsize technological grandeur of the production, at the end of the day "technology didn't run the show . . . Michael ran the show."[2]

Before it became a film, *This Is It* was a planned series of fifty sold-out concerts at London's mammoth O2 Arena, produced by promoter-behemoth AEG Live, and co-directed by Ortega, whose adventurous résumé includes choreographing spectacles like the Olympics and the Academy Awards, and directing the Disney mega-smash *High School Musical* series. Jackson had hoped to make a career comeback with the concerts. He'd neither recorded new material nor toured in years, and had most recently been living in a kind of self-imposed exile in the Middle East with his three young children after having been acquitted in 2005 in a controversial trial centered around child molestation charges. He'd slogged through decades of disastrous press surrounding his bizarre personal life, various financial setbacks, and on-again/off-again prescription drug abuse. For some, Jackson's so-called wackiness had begun to overshadow, if not erode, his sizable musical legacy. The London concerts, set to launch on July 13, 2009, were to consist of newly staged excerpts from Jackson's greatest hits catalog. Fans would vote for the set list in advance. On the morning of June 25, the fifty-year-old singer, in the midst of final dress rehearsals at The Staples Center, unexpectedly passed away from cardiac arrest at his Holmby Hills mansion. Dr. Conrad Murray, hired by AEG Live as Jackson's personal physician, allegedly administered an illegal and lethal overdose of the anesthetic Propofol to the superstar, who reportedly suffered from chronic insomnia. Months later, Murray would be officially charged with homicide, and in November 2011 he was convicted and sentenced to four years for involuntary manslaughter.

The shock of Jackson's death prompted an unprecedented global out-pouring and a veritable tidal wave of media frenzy. In early August 2009, AEG Live cemented a deal with Jackson's estate and Columbia Pictures to help minimize the financial fallout from the canceled concerts. Luckily for all parties involved, AEG had hired commercial director Tim Patterson and collaborator Sandrine Orabona months prior, to document behind-the-scenes rehearsal moments and conduct original interviews with the cast and crew. According to the opening credits, the footage was suppos-edly intended to be used for "Michael's personal library and as original film content for the show."[3] Patterson and Orabona had shot close to 140 hours of raw footage at the time of Jackson's death.[4] Columbia Pictures (a division of Sony) agreed to buy the content for $60 million in order to use it as source material for the proposed theatrical film. By mid-September, concert helmer Kenny Ortega, who had also signed on as film director, had whittled down the raw footage into a manageable 112-minute cin-ematic experience, working closely with Patterson, commercial director Brandon Key, and frequent Ortega-collaborator editor Don Brochu.[5] The patchwork audio, culled from multiple sources, had to be carefully restored by a skilled team that included tour audio supervisor Michael Prince and veteran front-of-house mixer Bill Sheppell.[6]

Michael Jackson's This Is It was released on October 28 to mixed-to-positive critical reviews and robust box office. Domestic sales underper-formed Columbia's expectations. Early hype estimated an unlikely $250 million gross in the first five days. According to website BoxOfficeMojo.com, it ended 2009 as the forty-sixth top grosser with a domestic take of approximately $72 million. The film raked in $260.8 million worldwide.[7] At the time of this writing, *This Is It* holds the record as the highest gross-ing documentary or concert movie of all time (assuming it can be rightfully classified as a concert movie), beating out previous concert film record-holder 2008's *Hannah Montana / Miley Cyrus: Best of Both Worlds Concert Tour*.[8] The February 2010 *This Is It* DVD release, accompanied by newly shot interviews and unreleased footage, also brought commercial success. After his modest 1978 film debut in *The Wiz*, Jackson had several non-starter attempts to establish himself as a box office presence. Ironically perhaps, in death the pop superstar became something of the film star he'd always aspired to be in life.

Because of Jackson's instantiation in sentimental pop spectacle and tab-loid gossip, critics and audiences alike often misread him as a frivolous entertainer rather than a serious auteur. In fact, he spent his adult profes-sional career as both the showman *and* the auteur; or, more to the point, he rendered the dichotomy between the two irrelevant and false.[9] Prior to its release, some feared that *This Is It* would be a hastily assembled hatchet job in which Michael, due to the shady circumstances of his passing, would be portrayed as a drug-addicted aged pop star too feeble and disoriented to move or sing meaningfully.[10] To the surprise of many (perhaps everyone except his die-hard fans) Jackson emerges in the "finished" edit as a remarkably limber and *coherent* showman with clear and forthright artistic and directorial vision.

That's partly because the film completely de-contextualizes the "found" rehearsal footage on which it relies—there's no superimposed voiceover, no times or dates given, no interviews with Jackson even. Instead, the film puts forward a normalizing and revisionist rendering of Jackson: the superstar free from, and absolved of, his infamously controversial baggage. That revisionist rendering is in some ways a refreshing revelation. By returning all the focus to Jackson's inestimable performance skills, *This Is It* indirectly confronts the misconceptions about Jackson's artistry.

But that limited focus also means transgressive aspects of Jackson's star discourse—including his radical androgyny, "queer" paternity, and long history of racial transmogrifications—are suppressed in the world of the film. Decontextualizing the footage reconsolidates the Jackson mythos by re-authenticating the superstar as "normal." The filmmakers in turn market the movie as a must-see revelation of the "authentic" Michael Jackson: a "cleaned up" Jackson might more effectively ascend into franchise nirvana as a merchandising cash cow. As one critic notes, "One can't help but worry that, rather than a bittersweet farewell, the film will merely serve as the opening salvo to a flood of posthumous releases and merchandising that will make Tupac Shakur's estate seem a paragon of restraint."[11]

That said, *This Is It* surprises with effervescent moments of good feeling that exceed the film's conservative attempts to re-script and re-brand Jackson as "authentic" and therefore normal. Few film critics were willing to deal with the staggering phenomenological implications of the project in their reviews. Watching *This Is It*, you're constantly aware that Jackson is far more unreal than real. In fact, he's sort of *out of this world*. During feverish renditions of tunes like "I Just Can't Stop Loving You" and "Billie Jean," Jackson looks like a fierce ghost, a benevolent badass who knows how to expertly craft a spectacular concert even as he can't help getting caught up in the spirit of his own innervating songs. The film's most unforgettable scenes find Jackson shimmying and boogieing in exuberant joy, sharing and flaunting his formidable singing and dancing with his co-worker cast and crew. Some will argue that soulfulness is a dying art at a time when postproduction technologies (like Auto-Tune) have regressed performance expectations. But *This Is It* affirms the recalcitrant power of spirit—of energetic good feeling between artists bent on getting together and sharing together—even in the context of late capitalist techno-megaspectacle.

Spectacle and Non-Spectacle

This Is It borrows its ambiguous title from the unrealized London concerts.[12] The title suggests an unguarded offering, an authentic revelation, laid out in front of you. "It" suggests *thereness* as a response to fans' anticipation, as if to say, "Here you go, this is what you've been waiting for." Kenny Ortega recounts the title's existential origins: "[Michael would] call me up every once in a while or come to visit me on set and he'd say: 'There's nothing out there that has enough purpose behind it for me to want to do it.' Meaning in the live arena. Then, suddenly, I get this phone call and he said: 'This is it.' And during the conversation he said that, like, five times. And I kept laughing and saying: 'You should call the tour *This Is It* because you keep saying it.'"[13]

Jackson long despised the grueling rigors of touring. Since the late 1980s, he publicized each of his solo tours as his last. These pronouncements were always, if nothing else, cunning marketing strategies to entice audiences to buy tickets in record numbers. The title *This Is It* sounded an alarm to fans that there would be no more concerts to follow, as if to say, "You're not getting any more." It also suggests finality, and, by extension, freedom. At the March 5, 2009, press conference at The O2 Arena, Michael referred to the concerts as "the final curtain call." Those portentous words ultimately rang true, albeit not for the intended reasons.

Associate producer and choreographer Travis Payne gives an explanation for the title's ambiguity: "As we went through the process, 'This Is It' began to take on many different meanings. 'This Is It,' a call to action for our planet. 'This Is It,' the last time you'll see me in this scenario. 'This Is It,' the show to come see this summer. Also, 'This Is It' for all of us (dancers) was what we had worked our entire lives to get to. It was a culmination of all those things."[14] Some critics found the declamatory title ironic, given the fact that the concerts never actually took place. With no "there" there, no culmination or climax, the film comes off as immaterial, neither here nor there. In an acidic *Sight & Sound* review, Mark Fisher asks, "Has there ever been a less apt title for a film than *This Is It*? 'This' is very much not 'it'—this film is the making-of feature for a spectacle that never happened."[15] From this perspective the film is nothing more than an unspectacular rendition of a non-spectacle.

The story gets more complex. On October 12, 2009, Sony Records distributed and promoted a posthumous Michael Jackson mid-tempo single also called "This Is It." The single was sold to the public as a "never-before released" recording. In actuality, Jackson first composed and recorded a demo of the song with Brill Building singer-songwriter Paul Anka twenty-six years earlier; the song was intended as a duet for Anka's solo album. According to Anka, Jackson pilfered the mastered tapes from the recording session in 1983 and did not return them until Anka threatened to sue. Anka later placed a version of the tune with R&B singer Sa-Fire in the early 1990s. In the wake of Michael's death in 2009, members of his camp "found" the original 1983 demo recording. "Produced" by Jackson, estate co-executor John McClain, and Mervyn Warren, the recording was retrofitted with new instrumentation and doo-wop background vocals courtesy of Jackson's brothers.[16]

Controversy ensued when Anka did not receive compositional co-credit. Sony promptly turned on its heels and gave Anka 50 percent of the song's profits. Anka, for his part, chalked it up to "an honest mistake."[17] Improbably, Sony deemed it a coincidence that the "found" song from 1983 and the concerts/film from 2009 shared the same title. How could such a blind spot have existed? *New York Times* pop critic Jon Caramanica commented on the affair, "It's probably a reflection of the disarray bedeviling Mr. Jackson's catalog, legacy and institutional memory that no one in his camp seemingly knew, or cared, that this material had already been released in some form."[18] Chaos aside, the song did help boost the sales of the *This Is It* soundtrack album (a double album re-release of Jackson's studio hits featuring the title track, a poem, and a small handful of other unreleased demos) to a solid 1.8 million in domestic sales and 5 million in international sales.

The song's convoluted birthing process parallels the haphazard genesis of the film itself. Both the song and the film force us to contemplate the complex relationships between the spectacular and the mundane, the finished and the unfinished. I recall first hearing "This Is It," released over the Internet in early October 2009. The elementary lite-inspirational chord progressions and uneventful romantic lyric of "This Is It" ("I never heard a single word about you / Falling in love wasn't my plan / I never thought that I would be your lover / Come on please, dear, understand") felt to me brazenly anticlimactic and *un*spectacular, especially given the song's status as the first posthumously released single from the Jackson catalog.[19] "This Is It" was just ho-hum, neither here nor there. In the *Los Angeles Times* Pop & Hiss music blog, Todd Martens goes a step further, calling it "a trifle, and while it's one that certainly won't embarrass Jackson's legacy or break the hearts of fans eager to hear Jackson's voice again, it does bring the fallen pop icon a little back down to earth."[20] The *New York Times*'s Jon Caramanica had little positive to say about the tune, noting, "[It] never fully resolves, working at one melodic and emotional pitch and then fading out." He continues, "But as a musical artifact, it's better as suggestion than song: what I hear here is how Mr. Jackson might have sung these words in a proper studio setting, perhaps in a roomier arrangement with more motion in the rhythm."[21]

It's worth noting that the song does perfectly complement the film for which it was produced. To be sure, the song is mundane and has no real musical resolution, but then neither does the film. (Neither song nor film *could* have a satisfying conclusion. Due to Jackson's death, finality was always already impossible, never an option.) "This Is It" may be little more than a dressed-up recorded demo, a suggestion of what might have been had Jackson lived to see its completion. Truth be told, the film itself is not much more than a slickly edited compilation of rehearsal scenes that only suggests what the O2 performances might have been had the circumstances been different. The song "This Is It" was born from an unreleased demo, a sketch, a trace, an unfinished work-in-progress. It was always already ephemera, never likely intended to be the main event, the finished centerpiece. Its history therefore parallels the history of the film itself. The unfinished rehearsal footage that constitutes the movie was itself ephemera, surplus documentary content, a side dish never intended to be served as the main course. In his *Hollywood Reporter* review, Kirk Honeycutt calls *This Is It* "the first concert rehearsal movie ever."[22] While films like The Beatles' 1970 *Let It Be* have flirted with the rehearsal film format, *Michael Jackson's This Is It* can certainly claim the crown as the first mainstream motion picture in which the exclusive attraction is a rehearsal rather than a full-on concert. In the absence of any sort of culminating performance, the rehearsal process becomes reconstituted as the show itself, the finished product. The part stands in for the whole, as in synecdoche.

As a result, *This Is It* manages to invent a completely improvised film genre, perhaps one never to be repeated again. It's halfway between a flamboyantly spectacular blockbuster (in that it presents scenes from the groundbreaking live theatrical spectacular) and a gritty indie "found footage" reality documentary. In designing his concerts, Michael and the creative team were striving to create the greatest show that had ever been seen. Jackson had long described himself as a "fantasy fanatic," a devotee of the Cecil B. DeMille's school of bigger is always better. He spent much of his post–*Off the Wall* career in monomaniacal pursuit of crossover music as blockbuster entertainment, and he was intent on forever smashing sales records—even his own. *This Is It* proved to be no different. During the film, Jackson talks about his desire to bring his audience "something they've never seen before."[23] The concerts were to break ground on several levels. For one, they were to introduce the world's largest 3D HD screen, supposedly capable of providing an unprecedented immersive live experience. For the staging of "Smooth Criminal," Ortega would use green screen technology to splice Jackson into existing footage from classic Hollywood films. At the end of the screened footage, Jackson was to be filmed jumping through a window; shards of glass would appear to fly into the audience. (Jackson apparently referred to the live 3D experience in upgraded terms as 4D as he intended to break the fourth wall by having the cast move from screen onto stage into the audience.)

Throughout the show, expensive sci-fi style costumes were decked out in unprecedented numbers of Swarovski crystals. Costume co-designer Valdy deployed never-seen-before Phillips Lumalive LED textile technology to illuminate Jackson's fashionable garments on stage. And in another exciting green-screen dance sequence, eleven of Jackson's backup dancers would be filmed performing choreography; they'd be replicated through technology to turn into a virtual army behind him on the screen. Aerialists and massive pyrotechnics that circled the stage perimeter in record time were also part of the plans. And during pro-environment "Earth Song" a menacing on-screen tractor bulldozes a jungle before emerging "out of" the screen to physically appear on the stage. In the 2010 DVD extras, AEG Live CEO Randy Philips confirms that Jackson agreed to perform fifty shows (about twenty had originally been scheduled) only if the Guinness Book of World Records would be on hand to memorialize his achievements, as they had done more than twenty-five years earlier in the immediate aftermath of *Thriller*'s boundary-breaking success.

There is no term that accurately summarizes the Michael Jackson aesthetic, but I'll venture one: *techno-megaspectacle stadium pop soul*. If that descriptor sounds positively "off the wall," you bet it is. At the time of his death Jackson was the sole creator and exclusive custodian of that outsize vision of campy excess: no other artist in recorded music had the clout and the cash—or the cojones, frankly—to deliver a smorgasbord of naked sentimentality, stripped-down soul, James Brown–influenced funk,

Broadway musical theater, inspirational gospel, easy listening schmaltz, B-movie horror, disco cheese, West Coast pop-locking, Henson-inspired puppetry, and whatever else he deemed fit to throw in the pot—all somehow wrapped in the package of sci-fi techno-megaspectacle. Critics have always made an easy target of Jackson's affinity for colossal spectacle. Sean Burns of *Philadelphia Weekly* lambasted the film, calling it "a mechanical, over-choreographed spectacle, drowning out the music with precision timed pyrotechnics, onstage bulldozers, 3-D movies, and even a computer-assisted, black and white machine gun battle against Humphrey Bogart."[24] *Hollywood Reporter*'s Kirk Honeycutt anticipated the by-the-books critical ire: "Make no mistake this was a show intended for a stadium with a dazzling, mixed-media staging. One can even imagine a music critic in London fuming about overproduced numbers that don't trust Jackson's great song catalog to deliver the goods."[25]

In spite of its radical innovations in technology, the O2 shows by and large consisted of a recycled set list, and many of the live stage renditions were relatively low-risk variations on visuals from Jackson's classic music videos. *Sight & Sound*'s Mark Fisher argues:

> If Michael Jackson had lived and managed to perform the 50 (50!) shows planned for the O2 arena in London, they would have been part of the dreary gloss of late capitalism, part of the sense of heavy inevitability and predictability that now dominates the entertainment industry: another super-slick spectacular centered on an ailing pop star long past his best. Yet Jackson's death lends the never-actually performed shows a kind of epic grandeur, now that all the kitschy contrivances, familiar gimmicks and well-rehearsed routines have become the stage set on which the King of Pop's final tragedy was to be played out.[26]

Notably, *This Is It* arrived in theaters two months before the release of James Cameron's acclaimed sci-fi epic *Avatar*, a film that quickly broke box-office records to become the top grossing movie of all time, grossing over $2 billion. Though they're wildly different types of movies, *This Is It* in some ways prefigured *Avatar*'s curious mix of immense spectacle, immersive 3D technology, maudlin sentiment, and back-to-nature themes. I often think of Jackson's proposed concerts as a sort of live UK theatrical analogue to Cameron's sci-fi techno-megaspectacular entertainment. While cultural theorists from Malcolm Gladwell to *Wired* magazine editor Chris Anderson spent years predicting that the widespread availability and accessibility of niche products on the Internet would wipe out hit-driven economics and render the blockbuster irrelevant, *Avatar*'s runaway success seemed to have driven a final nail in those theories' respective coffins.[27]

Jackson's posthumous sales records in some ways did for the music industry what *Avatar* did for the film business. According to *Billboard*, Jackson moved a whopping 8.7 million albums in the year following his death, a remarkable figure considering that by 2009, the industry had long since found itself in a disastrous economic slump, with digital music sales failing to compensate for the concomitant loss in physical (compact disc) sales.[28] The year 2009 became a more modest sales sequel to 1983, celebrated for Jackson's groundbreaking success with *Thriller* which almost single-handedly brought the music industry out of economic doldrums and re-energized sales momentum. In March 2010, Sony entered into a ground-breaking $200–250 million recording contract—the biggest in history to date—with the Jackson estate to issue 10 albums worth of classic album reissues and/or unreleased material.[29] Jackson's resurrection—his "come-back" in death—served as a reminder of the role that "heritage artists" (the industry buzz term for veterans) continue to play in the shaping of the music industry's financial future. The *Independent*'s Pierre Perone comments on Jackson's post-death economic impact, "The music industry, and especially the four major labels, have made a significant shift, and one emblematized by Sony's deal with the Michael Jackson estate: from a model predicated on signing new talent, with all the attendant pitfalls and short-falls that entails, to one where the real money is made maximizing revenue from tried and tested acts by selling their work to an older demographic that buys CDs at the supermarket."[30]

Despite its claims to spectacle status, much of *This Is It* also looks and feels like an unspectacular independent documentary: the original budget for Tim Patterson and Sandrine Orabona's video footage was a whopping $80,000. *This Is It* also shares its aesthetic with the "found footage" genre. On one hand, found-footage films can be experimental films that deliberately decontextualize "found" source material (from existing features films, stock footage, educational films, military films, or anything else), all in the effort to convey a particular meaning that might deviate from the messages originally intended by the source material.[31] On the other hand, found-footage filmmaking can also refer to non-fiction hyper-verité documentaries created from home movies or distressed footage, like Jonathan Caouette's disturbing *Tarnation* (2003) or Harmony Korine's polarizing *Trash Humpers* (2009). And what's more, films like *The Last Broadcast* (1998), *The Blair Witch Project* (1999), *Quarantine* (2008), *Cloverfield* (2008), and *Chron-*

214 · TAKING IT TO THE BRIDGE

icle (2012) help compromise a newly emergent subgenre of found-footage horror. These faux documentaries center around a patched-together edit of raw, amateur footage often shot by deceased victims of some variety of supernatural attack. The film itself *is* the "recovered footage," supposedly found by government officials or other law enforcement officials posthumously. These nimble horror films are often low budget, and produced using DIY filmmaking techniques; or, in the case of J. J. Abrams's *Cloverfield*, they're studio films painstakingly designed to look low budget. The films further distinguish themselves by deploying innovative word-of-mouth and viral marketing campaigns; several films in the genre have emerged as true sleeper hits. *Cloverfield*, for its part, re-imagines a Manhattan monster invasion if the only footage left to document the disaster was culled from an amateur handheld video discovered in the aftermath of the tragedy. The entire film is deliberately shot in single point-of-view, herky-jerky digital video. To ramp up the thrills 'n' chills, films like *The Blair Witch Project* and *Cloverfield* project the illusion that the bleak unfolding action—raw, grainy, and amateurish—is hyper-authentic. In so doing, found-footage films serve to showcase what film critic Karina Longworth has called "the bizarre beauty of degraded low-grade video."[32]

In his *Cloverfield* review, Bruce Newman claims, "The film often sacrifices niceties such as sound quality for authenticity. This may be the first big-budget Hollywood picture in history to go to so much trouble trying to look like crap." He describes the film as an exemplar of voyeuristic Web 2.0 aesthetics: "If this isn't exactly the first YouTube movie, it may be the first to fully discard what snooty scholars refer to as 'film grammar' in favor of a new video-based visual language employed by that Web site, as well as Facebook and MySpace."[33] Though most would not call it a horror film (we'll deal with that in the next section), *This Is It* is like a twisted real-life analogue of the narrative conceit that powers films like *Cloverfield*: it's an edit constructed from valuable "found" handheld video footage (though it was never "lost" per se), more or less rescued in the aftermath of a singular tragedy, in this case the death of Michael Jackson.[34] Many of the same authenticity issues engendered by found-footage films also engulf *This Is It*. The fact that some of *This Is It*'s low-resolution digital rehearsal footage was clearly not necessarily intended for main-event public dissemination certainly enhances the film's claims to realness. In a thoughtful assessment of the found-footage genre, writer Landon Palmer notes that "the requirement of compelling content is probably why this [found-footage] approach has been so popular recently in the horror genre—there's something exciting about *the extraordinary posing as the mundane*."[35]

Many film critics similarly admired the behind-the-scenes mundanity of the rehearsal footage that constitutes *This Is It*, for the voyeuristic "video-based visual language" of the project offered a new lens with which to view Jackson's creative output. Writer Alan Light argues, "The release of a work in progress may have been the only possible way out of the 'bigger is better' addiction that derailed so much of his art."[36] But more to the point, *This Is It* is an unspectacular DIY "found footage" documentary of an unrealized techno-megaspectacle, the London O2 concerts. In that sense, *This Is It* accomplishes the unique and improbable task of bringing Michael Jackson, whose bigger-is-better aesthetic and outsize recording advances made him something of a financial liability to record companies after the mid-1990s, into the twenty-first-century Reality-YouTube-Twitter era. No small feat.

Freaky Ghosts and Inauthenticity

There's no goin' back. See to them, you're just a freak . . . like me!
— THE JOKER, PLAYED BY HEATH LEDGER,
IN *The Dark Knight* (2008)[37]

Who's the freak now? Freaky Boy, Freak circus freak!
— THE MAESTRO, PLAYED BY MICHAEL JACKSON,
IN *Michael Jackson's Ghosts* (1997)[38]

The 2000 theatrical re-release of William Friedkin's 1973 horror classic *The Exorcist* was re-edited to include "lost" footage, re-titled and re-sold to the public as *The Exorcist: The Version You've Never Seen*. Using that marketing ploy as a cue, we might say that *This Is It* attempted to sell the public "The Michael Jackson You've Never Seen." Particularly considering Jackson's lifelong interest in magic, masks, and other forms of subterfuge, one can imagine that the mainstream release of rehearsal footage was not likely his intention in wanting to give fans something they'd never seen before. Jackson spent much of his professional life attempting to carefully manipulate and control his public image. The ethical question arises, Would the superstar have wanted unfinished rehearsal footage in which he was not necessarily at "his best" to be publicly released? Jackson's family initially protested the release of *This Is It*. And a group of ardent fans launched a website, This is Not It.com, to raise public awareness: they believed that AEG Live was using the film to conceal the company's exploitative mistreatment of an allegedly ailing Jackson.

Alan Light confronts these thorny questions of exploitation: "Though often raised in voices of hysteria, these are actually all fair questions, as they are with all outtakes, bootlegs, or posthumously released work by any artist."[39] However, I'm much more interested in the way the producers of *This Is It* attempt to market the film as a singularly authentic revelation of the "true" Michael Jackson. "I think what we want out of this film," said producer Paul Gongaware in scenes from the film's DVD extras, "is for people to see the real Michael Jackson."[40] AEG Live's Randy Phillips confirms Gongaware's authenticity claims, boasting that the film represents "unrestricted access to an unguarded genius."[41] He continues, "There's nothing in it other than the credits that wasn't shot or recorded from March 5, when we did the press conference in London, to June 25, when he died. It's completely authentic. Nothing has been doctored."[42] *This Is It* purports to be an unmediated voyeuristic experience. In other words, the intrinsic authenticity of the found footage—the idea that we feel that we're being allowed to see something we may not have been intended to see—allows the filmmakers to present a unique version of "Michael Jackson Stripped," the celebrity finally exposed for the true artistic genius that we always knew him to be.

The filmmakers want to promote a singular way of seeing Michael Jackson. But the footage is hardly sourced from a hidden camera; there is nothing to suggest that Michael Jackson, who clearly *had* to have greenlighted Tim Patterson and Sandrine Orabona's videography of the rehearsals and backstage material, is not "on" or aware of or performing directly for the cameras. Furthermore, while some of the footage is less than ideal in terms of lighting quality and camera placement, the handheld work is rarely if ever shaky or sub-professional (in contrast to, say, the deliberately amateurish, nausea-inducing *Cloverfield* fictional footage). The fact that a significant portion of the rehearsal video was shot in high definition also suggests that at the very least it was always intended as semi-public or public promotional content (just not necessarily main-event content). As *Hollywood Reporter's* Kirk Honeycutt surmises, "What strikes you is how thoroughly professional, even slick, this footage is. Whatever was it intended for—a making-of doc to accompany the concert DVD, or a television show?—this is no footage rounded up from the crew's cell-phones. Interviews with the cast, musicians and production personnel further underscore a clear intent to go public with this material."[43] Docu-realism serves as evidence of the authenticity of *This Is It's* cinematic rendering of The Michael You've Never Seen Before. Mark Fisher notes, "The roughness of some of the material only adds to its charm, the intimate rehearsal scenes achieving a charge that it's hard to imagine any proper concert film mustering."[44] The filmmakers patched together hours of footage to produce a seamless final edit. While the editing often succeeds at creating coherent musical performances and a convincing-enough "narrative" drive, Ortega's finished product is nonetheless a chaotic mishmash. There's black-and-white footage, color footage, high-definition footage, lower-resolution footage, variable aspect ratios, and split screens. There is no hiding, or even desire to hide, the film's numerous discontinuity issues. High-quality audio surfaces in some parts, and subtitles show up in others where only a single camera operator's stereo mic was used.[45] Finished or mostly finished set pieces, like the newly shot *Thriller* video scenes, are presented alongside scenes that use digital models of set pieces that were never finally realized (like the "Light Man" sequence at the top of the concerts in which Jackson was to emerge on stage out of a video-illuminated full-body casing). The end result at times approximates a higher-end version of a postmodern late 1960s William Greaves flick (not an unreasonable analogy, as Greaves basically pioneered the postmodern meta-film).

Though the songs in *This Is It* are supposedly chronologically sequenced in the set list order in which they were to appear at the O2 Arena, Ortega's movie—full of post-production fades on scenes that don't resolve conclusively on their own—remains a conundrum of disjointed, disfluent, and decontextualized parts, coming and going together like glimpses of scenes from a fever dream, in and out of consciousness, hazy. During one of the opening numbers, "Wanna Be Startin' Somethin," the action cuts between two clearly different performances in which Jackson is wearing different outfits. Yet he's singing what seems to be a singular vocal performance, but it too is likely sewn-together audio. Indeed, the film's temporality is puzzling: there are no dates or times, so we have no idea when scenes are occurring in relationship to each other or where we are in the action at any given moment. (The 2010 DVD extras correct these omissions by adding some dates, albeit haphazardly.) Because the live band and backup singers are attempting to approximate the sound of Jackson's classic recordings in their faithful renditions of the material, it's often hard to tell when and if the onstage singing by Jackson is live or possibly tracked. We're never quite sure what we are hearing at any given moment.

Film critic Sean Burns remarks in his review of the film that "some suspiciously sweetened background tracks don't quite match the lip-sync."[46] Kirk Honeycutt of the *Hollywood Reporter* writes, "The frustration, beyond the greater one—that a tragedy prevented this concert from happening—is not knowing what you're looking at. Where are Jackson and his conspirators at any given moment in the creative process?"[47] In fact, the film is so radically de-contextualized and de-temporalized, it actually manages to produce what must have been an unintended effect: writer Matt Soergel notes, "If you had time traveled into a screening of *This Is It* from, say, 2008, you could watch the entire movie and not know that Michael Jackson is now dead."[48] To be fair, filmmakers dedicate the movie "for the fans" in the opening credits: watching the film presupposes advance knowledge of Jackson's tragic demise. "For the fans" also suggests, implicitly, that nothing that follows the opening credits is necessarily meant to strive for documentary-style "objectivity" (if such a concept even does exist): the film is targeted to the throngs of fans who already love Michael Jackson to re-remember why they love him. Nonetheless, detemporalized editing produces a permanent blind spot so that seeing the totality of the unrealized and therefore "unseeable" O2 concert experience becomes exponentially impossible. The film exists in a kind of permanently broken wholeness: it can't be put (back) together because it was never whole to begin with. Because the film has no definitive, culminating ending (*coitus interruptus*), it approximates the feeling of waking up suddenly from sleep: you're disoriented, blissful, and slightly disappointed that you've just traded in a fantastical alternate reality for the mundanity that is everyday life. Your dream is unrealized.[49]

The film would like us to have faith in its undoctored and unpretentious presentation of Michael Jackson—he's nothing other than what he is. But the finished product is of course highly mediated, and, as such, it may be more valuably inauthentic than authentic. The Jackson estate retained authorial approval of the final edit. The film was required to carry a PG rating, and the terms of their August 10, 2009, contract with Columbia Pictures were purportedly strict: "Footage that paints Jackson in a bad light will not be permitted."[50] Not surprisingly, cast and crew testimonials in the film are, without exception, flattering. Schadenfreude-style footage depicting Jackson messing up or embarrassing himself during rehearsals, if such footage did exist, did not make its way into the final theatrical release. Film reviewer Zach Baron goes so far as to compare the film's inauthenticity to the tortured genesis of the title song.

> Less documentary than closely and manipulatively edited homage to the new-agey "genius" of frequent Michael Jackson collaborator and *High School Musical* auteur Kenny Ortega, *This Is It* is about as honest as the song it's named after—which was co-written with and then stolen from Paul Anka in 1983, sold by Anka to the '80s freestyle starlet Sa-fire in '91 as "I Never Heard," and blithely repack-

aged without acknowledgment to either artist by the Jackson estate earlier this year.[51]

It's also been suggested that we might not have always been seeing the "real" Michael Jackson in the final edit. Even prior to the film's release, word on the street was that the final edit had been constructed using body doubles and previously used bits of audio, due to the paucity of usable footage. Was Michael even really there? The editors claim no such trickery occurred. But in a frothy investigative piece, the *Sun* reporter Gary O'Shea interviewed musicologists and BBC senior studio managers and somehow concluded that some of the audio used in the film to reconstruct songs was at least twenty-eight years old. Jim Kennedy of Sony Pictures responded, "In order to fulfill Michael's vision for his fans and his children . . . the film-makers had to incorporate some pre-existing materials, including vocals, where the rehearsal footage audio was incomplete and/or inaudible. In addition, usage of master recordings (such as 'Earth Song') was credited in the end titles."[52] Whether the footage is real or false—and many if not most concert films augment original audio source material with outsourced sounds to produce the most effective final edit possible—we may never know fully. But the notion that the film could offer us an authentic and knowable and even singular Michael Jackson is a chimera. Michael Jackson's public image is an always already mediated construction. There is no authentically knowable Michael Jackson behind the mask, beyond the multiple discourses that constituted his star text. There are, and have always been, many Michaels. It all depends on how you look.

Ortega's direction honors the circumscribed diegesis of the source footage, limiting the action to the press conference, casting sessions, rehearsals, and soundstages (with the exception of a non-diegetic photo-montage sequence of the Jackson 5). Plenty of compelling material was surely left on the cutting room floor, perhaps to achieve a desired theatrical feature length or to withhold scenes for the DVD release and future commercial repackaging.[53] In contradistinction to the reconstituted backstage melodrama of VH-1's idiotic *Behind the Music* documentary television series, *This Is It* has precious little interest in re-telling the Michael Jackson story. The film offers no voice-over, no personal information about Michael Jackson, no mention of his legal or financial problems, his business dealings or acumen, no mention of his children, and no interviews with Michael. What you see is all you get. For a celebrity who spent most of his professional career overdetermined by discourse, Jackson is completely *under-determined* in Ortega's directorial vision. He exists in a vacuum.

"Under-determining" Michael Jackson has its uses. As reviewer Josef Woodard notes, "What makes *This Is It* such a remarkable achievement, and a surprise to skeptics among us, is that it's an 'inside' job without that insider aftertaste—a raw, real document of this amazing performer at work. No apologia, the film contains none of the incessant nattering, irrelevant punditry, or tabloid spittle following (and preceding) his death."[54] Because we weren't often invited to see Jackson in the process of making his spectacular music (although the hugely popular 1983 *Making of Michael Jackson's Thriller* documentary did singlehandedly revolutionize the behind-the-scenes music video documentary genre), the film emerges as a cinematic valentine to the artistic process. While the racist and primitivist imaginary assumes that performers of color are intrinsically more energetic and spontaneous than their white counterparts—which is another way of saying performers of color don't have to work hard to get good results—watching Jackson painstakingly shape his concert in collaboration with fellow musicians and a superbly talented band and crew is a telling reminder of the incredible labor that undergirds the best of black performance. We're confronted with the compelling results of Jackson's singular lifetime of skilling and practice, from his grueling prepubescent pre-Motown work schedule in Indiana to his brilliant studio and soundstage work to his marathon world tours as an adult solo artist. The film implicitly confirms that Michael Jackson knows how to fiercely "work it" as a performer because he spent his life working hard at it. As a result, the strict focus on performances helps challenge the widespread benign critical indifference to Michael Jackson as musician and artist. While there are tomes of writing and research on The Beatles, Elvis, Dylan, Hendrix, and others, black pop stars like Jackson, Dionne Warwick, Diana Ross, and Whitney Houston are usually denied the same meticulous care and attention. *This Is It* serves, in some ways, as a critical intervention, reconfirming Jackson's artistry and giving us a valuable window into the ways that Jackson's profound sense of discipline manifests in his decisive, auteurist vision.

The film balances Jackson's bigger-is-better approach with a minimalist self-effacing DIY aesthetic. "That's how restrained, how remarkably unsentimental, this exuberant, astonishingly entertaining concert film is," Matt Soergel notes. "It doesn't try to deify Jackson or explain him, and it's all the more moving for that understatement."[55] Journalist Alan Light agrees: "At the most unlikely time, under the most improbable circumstances, *This Is It* accomplishes the single thing that Jackson was unwilling, or unable, to do for the last two decades of his life: It strips away the spectacle, the controversy, the freak show, and it reminds us of the reasons that we first loved him."[56] The film's extreme restraint translates as ingenuousness. It offers cinematic absolution and catharsis for audiences who hope to re-remember Jackson without all the messy complication. As music journalist Greg Tate notes in his 2009 *Village Voice* Michael Jackson obit: "Michael's death was probably the most shocking celebrity curtain call of our time because he had stopped being vaguely mortal or human for us quite a while ago, had become such an implacably bizarre and abstracted tabloid creation, worlds removed from the various Michaels we had once loved so much. The unfortunate blessing of his departure is that we can now all go back to loving him as we first found him, without shame, despair, or complication."[57] Tate's cogent observation confirms co-choreographer and associate producer Travis Payne's take on why the film was made and whom it was made for: "We set out to create a legacy piece, a way to give fans their hero back whenever they wanted."[58]

The obvious danger in creating a decontextualized legacy piece is that Jackson ends up misremembered for posterity. Essentially, the film manages to personify Jackson without ever necessarily humanizing him. We learn nothing of the way that Jackson used his populist art to challenge the way we think about race, gender, class, sexuality, and citizenship, among other markers of identity. Indeed, Jackson's impact on popular culture has been well-documented in decades of terrific works by Kobena Mercer, Philip Brian Harper, David D. Yuan, bell hooks, and Margo Jefferson among others, and doesn't necessarily need regurgitation in these limited pages. But any commemoration of Jackson worth its salt should take into account the challenges he posed throughout his career to questions of identity and the intensely complex geo-historical challenges he himself faced in his rise to pop superstardom.

It's also worth re-remembering Jackson's complex and turbulent relationship to commercial exploitation over the course of his career. In particular, Jackson harbored a love-hate relationship with the two record companies that distributed his material—Motown and Sony. In 2001, in the midst of poor record sales for his *Invincible* album, Jackson organized a scandalous press conference in which he accused Sony CEO Tommy Mottola of racism. Needless to say, Jackson failed to release another original studio album. These darker moments in Jackson's career are wholly suppressed in the film (and not surprisingly so since the film is produced by Columbia Pictures, a subsidiary of Sony). *This Is It* draws on the inherited restraint and modesty of its raw source material to redefine the superstar as context-free and therefore "unmessy," normal, unthreatening, and ripe for commercial annexation. If the film is "for the fans," no viewer ever has to confront anything in the film he or she feels uncomfortable with. Racquel Gates's short essay "Reclaim the Freak" helps identify what may be at stake in our collective mis-remembering of Jackson.

> During his speech at Jackson's televised memorial the Reverend Al Sharpton turned to Jackson's three children and compassionately said, "Wasn't nothing strange about your daddy; it was strange what your daddy had to deal with." But Michael Jackson *was* strange, and to ignore that is to ignore a crucial element of Jackson's persona, the full integration of elements both utterly freakish and heartbreakingly human, the one often working in service of the other. The achingly touching speech that Jackson's daughter, Paris, gave in honor of her father was rendered all the more poignant by the fact that it was the first time we had ever seen the child without her omnipresent veil or carnival mask. It is this duality of Jackson that we must not forget and that we cannot afford to lose. We must, in the wake of his death, *reclaim the freak*. (My italics)[59]

In the face of *This Is It*'s realness claims, it may be far more interesting to consider Michael Jackson in all the ways that he might emerge for us as a freaky, unreal presence. Watching the film in a New York theater on opening night, only four months after Jackson's untimely death, I recall thinking about his presence on-screen as "uncanny." Jackson the post-mortem film star is an apparition, freakishly caught on celluloid, operating in some hybrid space between presence and absence, materiality and immateriality, thereness and not-thereness. In some ways, Jackson's star turn in *This Is It* bears analogy to Australian actor Heath Ledger's post-mortem star turn in 2008 as The Joker in Christopher Nolan's Batman epic *The Dark Knight*. In 2008, twenty-eight-year-old Ledger passed away unexpectedly from an accidental prescription drug overdose only to posthumously receive raves for his creepy, revelatory performance. Just as Jackson's untimely passing transformed *This Is It* into must-see cinema, Ledger's death (in tandem with stellar advance critical reviews) helped make *The Dark Knight* a must-see event and a commercial blockbuster. (*The Dark Knight*, at the time of this writing, is the twelfth highest grossing movie of all time, having earned more than $1 billion dollars at the box office.)

There are other surface similarities between Ledger and Jackson. Both died before their respective times, enshrouded in mystery. Both died from a lethally administered drug overdose in their homes (though Ledger's was self-administered and accidental, and Jackson's was officially a homicide). Though they excelled in mostly different mediums, Ledger and Jackson were both hardworking perfectionists. Both were also insomniacs whose intensely creative energy made it dangerously difficult to "turn off" at night and go to sleep.[60] (Jackson reportedly referred to sleep-inducing anaesthetic Propofol as "milk" due to its chalky appearance.) Both were uncomfortable, albeit to wildly differing degrees, with the darker sides of public adoration.[61] Cultural critics sometimes went so far as to liken Jackson's vitiligo-inflected ghostly pallor and cosmetically enhanced face to Ledger's pancake-faced disfigured Joker character. In reviewing *This Is It,* for instance, Carrie Rickey notes, "When not obscured by fedora, sunglasses and tendrils, Jackson's face, reconstructed and Kabuki-pale, has the shock of Heath Ledger's performance as *the Joker.*"[62]

Film acting is always already a complex simulacrum of the real; recorded performances are ghostly half-lives, traces, of the sources they represent. But the effect of seeing deceased actors deliver revelatory post-mortem work is totally eerie, unsettling—akin to witnessing the walking dead. Jason Solomons of *The Observer* discusses haunting in his review of *The Dark Knight:* "One can't help feeling uneasy about all this. Ledger stalks the film like a *ghost,* partly because he is one now in real life, and partly because up on the screen he's playing a spectral sort of human being, an unknowable, unfathomable violent entity, like a poltergeist."[63] In *This Is It* Jackson is similarly there and not there at the same time, a palpable spirit, magically resurrected. He is *really* post-human, a ghost in the machine. (Spookily, the same late October weekend *This Is It* debuted at number one, the found-footage horror film *Paranormal Activity* made its feature film debut at number 2. That haunted house sleeper, produced on a budget of $10,000, imagines what would happen if a deceased young couple had happened to capture on a digital camera the experience of being stalked by a ghost and then that amateur footage was later recovered. The irony of a Michael Jackson film depicting its own funky brand of paranormal activity and opening on Halloween weekend is not lost on this author.)

But *This Is It* is hardly the first time we've seen Michael Jackson as specter. In *The Triumph,* the 1980 promotional video for The Jacksons' funky single "Can You Feel It," Michael and his brothers play glowing spectral messiahs, beaming over the city, raining down golden hope on the multicultural masses below. In the landmark 1983 John Landis–directed video for *Thriller,* Jackson famously writhed and shimmied as first a werewolf before morphing into an undead zombie. The *Oxford English Dictionary*'s ambivalent definition of "undead"—"Not dead; alive. Also, not quite dead but not fully alive, dead-and-alive"—perfectly captures the uncanny presence of Jackson on screen: he's neither/nor, both/and, in/out.[64]

While some folks already felt Jackson had long since suffered "career death," Greg Tate reminds us that in the latter half of his career Jackson himself already looked like he was not long for this world. "Michael not being in the world as a Kabuki ghost makes it even easier to get through all those late-career movie-budget clips where he already looks headed for the out-door."[65] In the 1997 short film *Michael Jackson's Ghosts*—an incredibly subversive treatise on freakishness and the impossibility of normalcy that deserves critical rethinking—Jackson plays Maestro, a misunderstood "freak" who lives on a hill above a town called "Normal Valley" and transforms into a ghost, terrorizing before ultimately befriending the townspeople. The promotional poster for *Ghosts* depicts a straight-ahead gothic portrait of Jackson, half of his face morphed into a skeleton corpse. Jackson clearly made a career out of performing as if he was half in the here and now and half in some place beyond this mortal sphere. Quite literally, in *This Is It*, he himself is the spectacle, neither here nor there.

Sensual Presence

In *This Is It*, we were given a posthumous vision of Michael Jackson at the most "alive" and spirited we've seen him in years. Still, throughout the film, Jackson and the cast are mostly marking and blocking the concert, not necessarily performing "all out." Jackson apologetically pleads with his cast and crew that he is actively saving his voice, strength, and energy, sketching just enough of an outline of his performances so that his collaborators can develop the show appropriately but no more. Jackson drops and fudges entire lines, and sings off-pitch at others before self-correcting. He continually stops himself from getting too invigorated and caught up in the spirit of his own music, drawing a clear demarcation between the rehearsal and the full-out energy required for a successful arena show.

Toward the middle of the movie, Jackson closes a Jackson 5 tribute medley with a lilting rendition of the 1970 chestnut "I'll Be There." The band drops out as the song comes to a close. In the silent pause, Jackson talks through a spoken tribute that he'll give to his brothers and parents and then he interjects the apology "trying to conserve my throat please so understand" before launching into a tender series of mellifluous vocal riffs on the phrase "I will be."[66] Film critic Kirk Honeycutt notes in his review, "To be clear: No one should expect a concert film. Jackson clearly is conserving his energy, holding back on dance moves and vocal intensity. He is searching for his concert, the way a sculptor chisels away at marble to discover a statue."[67] The tension between control and release in Jackson's artistic process seems to parallel the existential conflict that informed Jackson's personal life, as he often found himself caught between a family obligation to ascetic Jehovah's Witness evangelism and the vision of hedonistic excess he created for himself at his infamous Neverland Ranch.

In another scene, at the close of the ballad "I Just Can't Stop Loving You," Jackson and duet partner Judith Hill riff on the oh-so-appropriate lyric "I just can't stop" to the delighted applause of the backup dancers congregated in the orchestra pit; they've basically become the default private audience during the rehearsal process. Ortega wisely intercuts the scenes of Jackson and Hill doing vocal improvisations with these scenes of the dancers watching from below, fawning in exultation and glee. As the riffing ceases and the song resolves, Jackson says to his adoring crowd: "Now don't make me sing out when I shouldn't sing." Playfully, the band launches into a gospel chord progression, encouraging and egging on the singer to lose himself in the moment. "You better sing!" and "You can allow yourself that one time," they tell the superstar. With a wink in his voice, Jackson politely retorts, "I'm warming up to the moment" and "I really shouldn't."[68]

Jackson's ever-so-feigned attempt to contain the auratic energy that's bubbled over in the venue is instructive. Noticeably, Jackson and musical director Michael Bearden have arranged some of the songs in such a way that they've left deliberate pockets of space, often extending the ending of songs for maximum dramatic effect. In so doing, Jackson leaves room for improvisational moments to occur, for the spirit to come down. Whenever a musician lands on a cue too early, we see Jackson firmly scold him to let the moment "simmer." "You're not letting it simmer," he chides.[69] Jackson's use of a heat metaphor is hardly accidental. He amplifies the electricity of a dramatic moment by leaving pregnant silent pauses in the action—scheduled stops and starts—where the all-important energetic transfer between performer and audience can occur. During the blocking for "Earth Song," for instance, the aforementioned virtual tractor is supposed to come magically "crashing" through the 3D screen to appear as a live prop on stage before closing its menacing "teeth." Jackson, unsatisfied with the rhythm and timing of the blocking, aggressively instructs the action, providing a serious lesson in how to milk a moment for maximum dramatic impact. "The value would be greater," he says, "if you let [the keyboard] rumble . . . let [the mouth of the tractor] stay open . . . let it close in silence [and] when that door opens you start that piano."[70]

I've previously noted how "This Is It" concerts were seen by some as "low-risk" in terms of the heavy reliance on recycled choreography and technological spectacle to wow the audience. But the genuine risk of the shows is much more profound, tied to the suspense created by Jackson in these cultivated improvisational moments where silence and space is left for magic to happen—the proposition of danger without warning. These innervating moments humanize the techno-megaspectacle, and reformat the canned nature of the film medium into a decidedly spirited, human affair. As director and designer Julie Taymor once noted, "Live theater will always surpass media like the Internet. Live theater, when things spontaneously happen, makes audiences feel like something special happened for them. Think of the old circus. There's a feeling that something can go wrong—that there's a danger—because it's live. There's an added thrill that movies don't have."[71] *This Is It* rides on these moments of improvisational danger without warning, and in so doing, it surpasses many other "celebrated" concert films, including the Rolling Stones' corporate, sterile 2007 *Shine a Light*, directed by Martin Scorsese.

Choreographer Travis Payne reminisces that "Michael was the architect of the entire experience. . . . He understood everybody's job and how to equip them to be their best. His intention was to surround himself with the best people he could find, and inspire them to be greater than they thought they could be."[72] Jackson emerges as the auteur, the showman, a vessel for spirit in motion, made palpable. Moving in almost absolute openness and strength, Jackson struts and preens across the stage. His vocals can sometimes sound flaccid in the rehearsal process, but they're remarkable feathery, eagle-like, expressive. During the rendition of "Wanna Be Startin' Something" Jackson directs bass player Alfred Dunbar by scatting the syncopated melody, suggesting the feeling of what he expects from the talented instrumentalist. "It's funk*ier*," Jackson admonishes. Jackson goes on to tell him, "It's not there": he can feel the missing funk. When Dunbar says, "I'm getting there," Jackson retorts, "Well get there."[73]

During a bluesy version of "The Way You Make Me Feel" musical director Michael Bearden plays the opening vamp, searching for the exact tempo and feeling. He hasn't quite hit on it yet. Standing to his left, Jackson slithers and contorts his body and bobs his head as if he can only move to feel if the rhythm is what he's looking for. Jackson wants the groove slower, more groggy—"like you're dragging yourself out of bed," he says. Jackson is looking for subtleties and nuances in the timing that might be imperceptible to most non-musicians. "Don't change so soon," he says. "It should be simpler." Unable to deliver exactly what Jackson wants, Bearden placates the singer—"We'll get the sound"—and reminds him of the importance of soundcheck—"Can't nobody hear what you need to hear." Jackson immediately retorts: "I want it the way I wrote it. I mean like the audience hears it, whatever the record sounds like."[74] In these eyebrow-raising scenes, in which Jackson tells it like it is, as it were, the superstar comes off as a polite badass, uncompromising and tough in his directorial vision but never rude or callous to his co-workers. "With the L.O.V.E." he tells his cast and crew, after giving an order. Jackson owns the stage, and owns the screen.

Beyond his singing, Jackson's on-screen idiosyncratic gyrations are rippling, erotic, and surprisingly supple for his middle age. During the blocking of "Human Nature" and "I Just Can't Stop Loving You" Jackson performs a rehearsed series of queer, hieroglyphic gestures that Dana Stevens of *Slate* hilariously refers to as "bizarre gestural Kabuki."[75] Indeed, Jackson's spasmic, Sarah Bernhardt–size hand and arm movements seem designed for maximum legibility from the back of the O2 Arena; as such, they look incredibly curious on film in close-up shots. And toward the end of the film, Ortega and Payne are on stage discussing their plans for the 3D airplane ending of the concert. (According to the 2010 DVD extras, during the show's finale, a virtual airplane was to land on screen and the cast would enter the HD screen and board the plane. In the final moment of the concert, the plane taxis and "takes off," and appears to fly over the audience, in a magical feat of 3D.) Ortega begins playfully imitating the trademark demonstrative gestures of airline stewardesses running through safety instructions, pointing to exits and putting on masks for the benefit of passengers. Jackson joins in the gesturing—which looks, in this context, strangely reminiscent of voguing—and it's amazing to see his keen eye for physical mimicry. "That's how the stewardesses do it, I love when they do that. I love it," he gushes.[76] Dana Stevens notes, "You realize what a student of bodily movement he really was: Whether from Mick Jagger, Bob Fosse, or a Delta Airlines stewardess, any move he liked was fodder to be incorporated into his signature style."[77]

Some film critics attacked Jackson's "imprecise" directorial language in the film. In one scene, Jackson instructs the musicians to let a moment "bathe in the moonlight": another metaphor to he uses to milk a dramatic moment.[78] Toward the end of the movie, Jackson leads the cast and crew on stage in a ritual hand-locked prayer. His speech, while positive and encouraging, quickly becomes rambling and cliché-ridden. And during a rendition of the Jackson 5's "I Want You Back," the loud volume levels in Jackson's in-ear monitor during performance force him to stop the rehearsal temporarily. "I'm adjusting to the situation," he informs Ortega.[79]

Critics like *Philadelphia Weekly*'s Sean Burns managed to center on this scene, somehow, as proof of Jackson's prima donna insecurity as well as his inarticulateness: "The few times Jackson is actually heard speaking in the movie, he comes off like someone you'd hide from on the subway, unable to articulate a simple request to lower the volume on his headphones without shrieking 'There's a fist in my ear!' Regular communication with fellow human beings was clearly impossible for him by this point."[80]

One wonders if Sean Burns ever attended an actual music rehearsal before. In the absence of an adequate physical language to describe music and sound, musicians often use idiosyncratic terms to get what they want, or they communicate in a way that surpasses the limitations of words to describe that which cannot be easily represented. In the DVD extras, musical director Michael Bearden praises Jackson's musicianship and skill as well as his coherent clarity: "The thing I love about Michael Jackson, though he knows all his vocal parts, he knows all of the background parts that he pretty much did by himself. . . . he still remembers all the rhythms, all the notes, all the intervals, all the everything so when he hears something that's not right *he can tell me exactly what it is*" (my italics).[81] Travis Payne, co-choreographer, flanks Jackson's side for much of the movie even though he barely utters a word. He is clearly instrumental in helping guide Jackson to a better performance, but it appears that the two men share a nonverbal metaphysical form of communication (at least within the world of the film that we're shown). Ortega, who at times seems like the Zach to Michael Jackson's Cassie, is benevolent and respectful, an extremely clear communicator who seems to support Jackson to a fault. In the midst of work, the two men express their love for each on stage more than once.

This sort of highly evolved collaborative listening and feedback—communion if you will—runs throughout the film. Regular, heightened communication with other human beings is not only possible for Jackson, it emerges as the centerpiece of the entire film. The carefully cast, cosmopolitan backup dancers, whom Ortega calls "extensions of Michael Jackson," serve as the immediate audience and are visible in the film. They are portrayed both as participants in the extravaganza and as awestruck fans, stunned and honored to be working with one of their idols. (In fact Payne notes that Michael Jackson cast the dancers based on energy. "Michael's very much about feeling," he says in the film extras. "Michael has to feel that energy, that confidence.")[82] Through slick editing, Ortega cuts away from the stage action to show us the grainy darkened footage of the exuberant dancers in the orchestra pit. The camera positions you to see what Jackson sees from the stage: the dancers throw their arms up in the air, applauding, sending out positive energy back to the stage. We see a visual representation of the electrical current passed between performer and audience, flesh and blood corroborating flesh and blood. "But once he starts dancing with hoofers young enough to be his children, Jackson, who died at age 50, radiates pure energy. It's always a pleasure to watch him move. Just as pleasurable is to see him beam that vitality to dancers and musicians, and see them beam it back."[83]

In the past, I have criticized Jackson for staging class- and status-conscious music videos, like his 1995 "Scream," that enforce a critical physical distance between the superstar as messiah figure and the masses.[84] *This Is It* challenges those class and status implications through the presentation of black performance as labor rooted in shared collective good feeling. For the dancers, the work is labor that is not labor. They appear happy to share the stage with a peerless artist who served as the primary inspiration for the professional work that they do. Jackson's surplus performances—those scenes where he can't help but get carried away by his own grooves—are also about summoning an energy that is rooted in "giving back," even if only for a conservatively bounded moment, to his cast/fans. During the hard-rock performance of "Black or White" Jackson directs Australian guitar phenom Orianthi Panagaris in a fervent guitar solo, instructing her to hold out a screaming guitar note much longer than she intuitively feels comfortable in the moment. Again, Jackson is milking the moment for dramatic impact. (He also would have likely taken a costume change during her extended guitar solo.) "It's time for you to shine," he announces, using his falsetto to demonstrate how he wants her to sculpt the temporality of her guitar solo.[85] It's a telling moment that demonstrates Jackson's generosity of spirit: self-effacing, he wants her to have her moment.

These moments of shared surplus feeling between Jackson and his cast and crew inundate the entire film with radiant good feeling. As Roger Ebert notes in his film review, "These are working people who have seen it all. They love him. They're not pretending. They love him for his music and perhaps even more for his attitude. Big stars in rehearsal are not infrequently pains. Michael plunges in *with the spirit of a coworker*, prepared to do the job and go the distance" (my italics).[86] The film powerfully documents a cross-class artist-to-artist affinity that is rarely seen in the feature film format, much less in everyday life. Through found rehearsal footage, we witness the love and the trust that musicians and dancers have for each other while collectively working toward a spectacular show that is a sum much greater than its moving parts.

The top of the film presents a series of interviews of backup dancers testifying directly to the camera. The footage was clearly shot prior to Jackson's death, as the dancers use the camera as a sort of confessional, speaking directly to Michael, verbalizing their feelings about having been cast in the O2 shows. (We have to presume they'd been given directions by the videographers that Michael would at some point watch the footage.) The last teary-eyed male dancer/interviewee, Misha Gabriel Hamilton, gives the most affecting speech. "I've been searching for something to shake me up a little bit and give me, uh, a kind of meaning to believe in something and this is it."[87] And here we have the film's title, "This is it," redefined as faith itself, unshakable belief, the evidence of things not seen. This is indeed It: the performance, the labor, the work, the camaraderie, the collectivity, the sharing, the collaboration, the energy, the electricity.

The Bluest Magic

> What Black American culture—musical and otherwise—lacks for now isn't talent or ambition, but the unmistakable presence of some kind of spiritual genius: the sense that something other than or even more than human is speaking through whatever fragile mortal vessel is burdened with repping for the divine, the magical, the supernatural, the ancestral.
> —GREG TATE, IN "THE MAN IN OUR MIRROR,"
> *Village Voice* OBIT OF MICHAEL JACKSON[88]

If the film does have a climax, it's Jackson's otherworldly rendition of his 1983 synth-pop masterpiece "Billie Jean." Lighting designer Patrick Woodroffe bathes the stage in blue specials, creating a melancholic vibe. Had the concerts occurred, Jackson would have been dressed in magical remote-control-illuminated tuxedo pants, jacket, ankle socks, and glove. In the rehearsals, however, Jackson appears in a more modest blue and silver dinner jacket. The number itself is minimalist in its execution, a winnowing down of the show's proportions and scale. We're treated to Jackson, standing solitary, on the naked stage. In the DVD extras Ortega describes the bare-bones staging as "a place for [Jackson] to invent."[89] He notes that there is "stuff that should remain sacred," meaning he's left space in this number for Jackson to improvise and to call down spirit through his agile singing and dancing.[90] The arrangement of the live rendition also leaves space for heightened drama and energetic communion. After a full pass of the song, all the instrumentalists gradually fall out, and we're left with drummer Jonathan "Sugarfoot" Moffett powerfully beating out the song's shuffle rhythm in real time.

Grinding and isolating his hips, crotch, shoulders, torso, legs, and neck in impeccable rhythm, Jackson improvises to the muscular groove, and gets carried away, set adrift on blissful funk. He flips the bottom of his jacket up in the air, and kick pushes his leg. He twitches and glides, shuffling his feet, stopping time through rhythm and sculpting the energetics in the concert venue. His movement is a magical mix of pop-locking, mime, Broadway jazz, James Brown and Jackie Wilson funk, and much more. Jackson always claimed that he spent every Sunday, even into his adult career, locked in his bedroom, rehearsing his trademark dancing in worship of a higher spiritual energy. "Sundays were sacred for two other reasons as I was growing up," he once confessed. "They were both the day that I attended church and the day that I spent rehearsing my hardest. This may seem against the idea of 'rest on the Sabbath,' but it was the most sacred way I could spend my time: developing the talents that God gave me. The best way I can imagine to show my thanks is to make the very most of the gift that God gave me."[91] In *This Is It*, "Billie Jean" emerges as a primal scene—Michael Jackson improvising movement to a single percussive groove, with no accoutrements—and it voyeuristically suggests what it must have been like to watch the singer practice those awesome dance moves in his room.

The compelling scene also documents the powerful energetic connection between Jackson and his drummer. Interviewed in DVD extras, Moffett describes the joyous intimacy that constituted his "duet" with Michael. It was "just him and me," he reminisces. "And I played my heart and my soul out to try to evoke an extreme great performance out of him and I would connect with him and I would watch him so closely. He was my dance partner and I will always treasure that. And, um, that's magic and life."[92] Jackson's dancers provide another level of intimacy during the number: they watch from the orchestra pit, once again, in total adulation, enraptured in the moment. Ortega notes in the DVD extras, "You couldn't drag those kids away from being in front of the stage watching Michael. They were there every second they could be—glued."[93]

For James Baldwin sensuality was inseparable from presence. "To be sensual I think, is to respect and rejoice in the force of life, of life itself, and to be *present* in all that one does, from the effort of loving to the breaking of bread."[94] The quality of communion (or soulful getting-togetherness) that emerges most fully in sensual, everyday acts of intimacy, like breaking bread and loving, is also for Baldwin an augmented temporality, a being in and on and past linear time—being "in the moment" as a sensual engagement with the Other. This is yet another way in which Jackson is a brilliant communicator with fellow human beings—he's co-*here*-nt, he's highly in the moment with others. *This Is It* is ultimately a sensual film, one that rejoices and honors the vital life force even as it provides meta-commentary on the phenomenological "problems" of presence and finality. For all the modern talk of 3D and 4D technology as immersion and intimacy, Jackson cultivates intimacy first with his body and soul. Sharing good feeling produces a proximity and depth and scale of immersion that no 3D glasses could ever provide.

As Jackson's breathless "Billie Jean" improvisation ends to spontaneous applause from his private audience, Jackson humbly suggests, "At least we get a feel of it." "God bless you," he continues, responding to the augmenting enthusiasm for his performance. Musical director Michael Bearden, off-camera, mutters into his microphone, "I'm a fan." Ortega walks on stage to congratulate Jackson and announces "Church! . . . The church of rock 'n roll!"[95] It's a slightly odd observation, to be sure, but one that tacitly acknowledges the palpable spirit that has come in the room, summoned by the emotional power of popular music.

Ortega suggests that Michael should drink some water; he's expended a lot of energy. Jackson agrees, we assume, because he melodically sings the line "water." Someone, somewhere, should bring him some, it seems. The image begins to fade, as all things do, and Jackson disappears, somewhere into the blue magical ether.

NOTES

1. *Michael Jackson's This Is It*, directed by Kenny Ortega (2009; Culver City, CA: Columbia Pictures, 2010), DVD.

2. Ibid.

3. Ibid.

4. Blair Jackson, "Michael Jackson's 'This Is It,'" *Mix*, December 2009, 42.

5. Ben Fritz, "'*This Is It*' as His Personal Thriller; Commercial Director Tim Patterson Can Savor His Start-to-Finish Role in Making the Film on *Michael Jackson*," *Los Angeles Times*, November 3, 2009, D.1.

6. Jackson, "Michael Jackson's 'This Is It.'"

7. http://boxofficemojo.com.

8. Scott Bowles, "The Biggest Concert Film of All Time: *This Is It*; Jackson's $101M Surpasses Cyrus," *USA Today*, November 2, 2009, D1.

9. Other critics long ago condemned Jackson outside of the courtroom. For those critics, Jackson's alleged improprieties with young boys (never legally proven) render any discussion of his artistry irrelevant.

10. Also see, for instance, Dana Stevens: "Given that the footage in question wasn't intended for a film but for Jackson's own archive, it seemed inevitable that the result would be an exploitative, thrown-together mishmash, a random bunch of murky home-video snippets padded out with sentimental talking-head interviews

and montages of too-often-seen bits of old MTV videos and tabloid news head-lines" ("The Last Moonwalk: Michael Jackson's Incredibly Moving *This Is It*," *Slate*, October 28, 2009, http://www.slate.com/id/2233842).

11. Andrew Barker, "Jackson's Talent Alive and Well in *This Is It*," *Variety*, November 2009, 64.

12. The complete film title is *Michael Jackson's This Is It*. Throughout the essay I simply refer to the title to *This Is It*, as this is how the film is often referred to even by its own creative team . . . and it's much simpler.

13. Kenny Ortega, "That Was It; *This Is It* Director Kenny Ortega Recalls His Good Friend Jacko," *The Times*, February 2010, 11.

14. Chris Lee, "For Michael, '*This Is It*' Had Many Meanings," *Gainesville Sun*, October 2009.

15. Mark Fisher, "Michael Jackson's This Is It," *Sight & Sound*, January 2010, 66–67.

16. Brad Wheeler, "Paul Anka and the Mystery of the Jackson Jive," *Globe and Mail*, October 17, 2009, A.13.

17. Ibid., A.13.

18. Jon Pareles and Jon Caramanica, "A Jackson Song Arrives, and the Discussion Begins," *New York Times*, October 2009, C3.

19. During the verse Jackson sings the lyric "I'm the light of the world," a self-aggrandizing line that rubbed some critics the wrong way.

20. Steve Jones, "Michael Jackson's 'This Is It': Consensus Is 'It's Not Bad.'" *Miami Times*, October 21, 2009, 1C.

21. Pareles and Caramanica, "A Jackson Song Arrives, and the Discussion Begins," C3.

22. Kirk Honeycutt, "This Is It," *Hollywood Reporter*, October 2009, 20.

23. *Michael Jackson's This Is It*, DVD.

24. Sean Burns, "This Is It," *Philadelphia Weekly*, November 4, 2009, 52.

25. Honeycutt, "This Is It," 20.

26. Fisher, "Michael Jackson's This Is It," 66–67.

27. See Anonymous, "A World of Hits," *Economist*, November 28, 2009, 79, as a response to Malcolm Gladwell, "The Science of the Sleeper," *New Yorker*, October 1999, 48, and Chris Anderson, *The Long Tail* (New York: Hyperion Books, 2006).

28. Gail Mitchell, "Music Biz Insiders Say Sony–Jackson Deal Makes Sense," *Billboard*, March 2010.

29. Ibid.

30. Pierre Perrone, "A Marketable Mystique that the Living Can't Match," *Independent*, March 17, 2010, 10.

31. See Michael Atkinson's "A Universal Movie: Found Footage Films," *Ghosts in the Machine* (New York: Proscenium, 2004), 103–15.

32. Karina Longworth, "Trash Humpers at NYFF," accessed July 3, 2012, http://blog.spout.com/2009/10/02/trash-humpers-at-nyff.

33. Bruce Newman, "'*Cloverfield*' Mantra: If It's Scary, Get It on Video," *Oakland Tribune*, January 18, 2001.

34. A *Los Angeles Times* article discusses videographer Tim Patterson's odyssey to emerge as the editor of the feature film: "Every night after work, he transferred hours of video shot by himself and collaborator Sandrine Orabona to two hard

drives in his home office. The afternoon that Jackson died, Paul Gongaware, a producer of the concert and movie, called him with an urgent request: The footage, which had suddenly become uniquely valuable, had to be delivered to AEG's downtown offices immediately" (Fritz, "'This Is It' as His Personal Thriller," D.1).

35. Landon Palmer, "Culture Warrior: Found Footage Filmmaking," accessed July 3, 2012, http://www.filmschoolrejects.com/features/culture-warrior-found-footage-filmmaking-lpalm.php.

36. Alan Light, "The Resurrection of Michael Jackson: How 'This Is It' Restores an Icon's Magic," accessed July 3, 2012, http://music.msn.com/the-resurrection-of-michael-jackson/story/feature/.

37. *The Dark Knight*, directed by Christopher Nolan (Burbank, CA: Warner Brothers Studios, 2008), DVD.

38. *Michael Jackson's Ghosts*, directed by Stan Winston (New York, MJJ Productions, 1997), DVD.

39. Light, "The Resurrection of Michael Jackson."

40. *Michael Jackson's This Is It*, DVD.

41. Ray Waddell, "That Was That and *This Is It*," *Billboard*, November 2009, 24.

42. Ibid., 42.

43. And videographer Sandrine Orabona also notes that her filmmaking approach assumes public dissemination: "I have a habit of approaching everything I document as if it's going to be seen by the largest audience—both technically and creatively even when I'm part of a small two person crew" (quoted in Paul Cashmere, "Interview: Sandrine Orabona, Videographer for *This Is It*," accessed July 3, 2012, http://www.undercover. com.au).

44. Fisher, "Michael Jackson's This Is It," 66–67.

45. The song's famously funky and highly recognizable bass line sounds remarkably visceral played on movie theater speakers or high-quality home audio speakers; we rarely get to hear Jackson's music played in these settings.

46. Burns, "This Is It," 52.

47. Honeycutt, "This Is It," 20.

48. To be fair, the opening credits do give away the film's "trick" ending.

49. Carrie Rickey provides a gustatory metaphor: "Watching this footage is comparable to being in the kitchen, savoring the smells and sampling tidbits, as a banquet is being prepared, but not getting to see it—or taste it—as it is served" ("Michael Jackson's Moves Are the Star of 'This Is It,'" *Philadelphia Inquirer*, October 30, 2009, W4).

50. Anonymous, "Jackson Concert Film in the Works," accessed July 3, 2012, http://news.bbc.co.uk/2/hi/8186995.stm.

51. Zach Baron, "*This Is It*: Michael Jackson Goes Out with a Whimper," *Miami New Times*, November 5, 2009.

52. Anonymous, "Michael Jackson—Jackson Movie Uses Old Material," accessed November 16, 2009, http://www.contactmusic.com.

53. For instance, "Stranger in Moscow," a rendition of the plaintive 1995 *HIStory* album cut, is not included in the film's final edit.

54. Josef Woodard, "Last Rites for the 'It' Man," *Santa Barbara Independent*, November 5, 2009, 77.

55. Matt Soergel, "Long Live the King of Pop: Michael Jackson Film Is a Tri-

umph in an Unsentimental, Exuberant, Musical Way," *Florida Times Union*, October 30, 2009, J6.

56. Light, "The Resurrection of Michael Jackson."

57. Greg Tate, "The Man in Our Mirror," *Village Voice*, July 1, 2009, 13.

58. Light, "The Resurrection of Michael Jackson."

59. Racquel Gates, "Reclaiming the Freak: Michael Jackson and the Spectacle of Identity," *Velvet Light Trap* 65, no. 1 (2010): 3.

60. See Terry Gilliam, quoted in Peter Biskind, "The Last of Heath," *Vanity Fair*, August 2009, 82: "Says Gilliam, [Heath] desperately wanted to sleep. And he finally got the big sleep."

61. See Brian J. Robb on Heath Ledger: "He also claimed he hated being the center of attention, especially when it didn't relate to his work. 'It's the worst part of the job. It's a surreal experience to be hounded, or followed, or recognized. But at least I'm not Michael Jackson'" (Brian J. Hobb, *Heath Ledger: Hollywood's Dark Star*, 2nd ed. (Medford, NJ: Plexus, 2010), 95). Clearly, Ledger was highly aware and respectful of the fact that he'd never quite reached Jackson's superstar heights.

62. And just as postproduction editing and flown-in parts may have made *This Is It* possible, Heath Ledger died halfway into shooting in his last film, Terry Gilliam's *The Imaginarium of Doctor Parnassus* (2009). To complete the picture, recognized actors like Johnny Depp stepped in to "finish" Ledger's performance. Due to circumstance, the film wears its constructedness and inauthenticity on its sleeve.

63. Jason Solomons, "Heath Is Where the Heart Is: A Posthumous Oscar Seems to be Already on the Cards but, Asks Jason Solomons, Does *Heath Ledger's* Joker Justify the Hype?," *Observer*, July 20, 2008, 3.

64. *The Oxford English Dictionary*, s.v. *undead*.

65. Tate, "The Man in Our Mirror," 13.

66. *Michael Jackson's This Is It*, DVD.

67. Honeycutt, "This Is It," 20.

68. *Michael Jackson's This Is It*, DVD.

69. Ibid.

70. Ibid.

71. David Rockwell and Bruce Mau, *Spectacle* (New York: Phaidon Press, 2006), 105.

72. Light, "The Resurrection of Michael Jackson."

73. *Michael Jackson's This Is It*, DVD.

74. Ibid.

75. Stevens, "The Last Moonwalk."

76. *Michael Jackson's This Is It*, DVD.

77. Stevens, "The Last Moonwalk."

78. *Michael Jackson's This Is It*, DVD.

79. Ibid.

80. Burns, "This Is It," 52.

81. *Michael Jackson's This Is It*, DVD.

82. Ibid.

83. Rickey, "Michael Jackson's Moves Are the Star of 'This Is It,'" W4.

84. Jason King, "Form and Function: Superstardom and Aesthetics in the Music Videos of Michael and Janet Jackson," *Velvet Light Trap* 44, no. 1 (1999): 80–96.

85. *Michael Jackson's This Is It*, DVD.

86. Roger Ebert, "Jackson's *This Is It* a Fitting Finale," *Chicago Sun Times*, October 30, 2009, http://www.suntimes.com/.

87. *Michael Jackson's This Is It*, DVD.

88. Tate, "The Man in Our Mirror," 13.

89. *Michael Jackson's This Is It*, DVD.

90. Ibid.

91. Michael Jackson, "My Childhood, My Sabbath, My Freedom," posted on http://www.beliefnet.com/Faiths/2000/12/My-Childhood-My-Sabbath-My-Freedom.aspx.

92. *Michael Jackson's This Is It*, DVD.

93. Ibid.

94. James Baldwin, *The Fire Next Time* (New York: Vintage International, 1963 [1991]), 43.

95. *Michael Jackson's This Is It*, DVD.

MARIA M. DELGADO

Carles Santos
"Music in the Theatre"

CARLES SANTOS HAS BEEN A FEATURE of Catalonia's avant-garde music scene since the mid-1960s, when he began collaborating with the artist and poet Joan Brossa. For over forty years now, working in the intersections between opera, art, and theatre, he has been involved in interdisciplinary ventures that have sought to find new paradigms of music performance. Based between Barcelona and Valencia and juggling a linguistic register that incorporates both Catalan and its Valencian variant, his has been a trajectory that has moved through liminal linguistic, geographic, and conceptual spaces, probing the multifarious ways in which music might serve as an organizing principle for stage action.

EVEN THOSE UNAWARE of his maverick music theatre spectacles may have heard his compositions during numerous ceremonies of the Barcelona Olympic Games in 1992 or heard his film scores for Pere Portabella's films or his compositions for Comediants and other theatre troupes. A versatile iconoclast, he transcends the term "composer." Resident musician at the Lliure since 2003, an accomplished pianist, visual artist, photographer, and filmmaker whose numerous cinematic projects include *El pianista i el conservatori/The Pianist and the Conservatory* (1967), *La cadira/The Chair* (1968), and *LA RE MI LA* (1979), the discourses and textures of all these art forms infuse his theatrical creations. Born in Vinaròs in the province of Valencia in 1940, Santos locates himself as "heart and soul a Catalunyan [*sic*],"[1] positioning his work within a specific Catalan Mediterranean sensibility which is too often dismissed as "bizarre" or categorized under the blanket term "surreal"[2] but which Santos refers to as "particular."[3]

Trained as a pianist at Barcelona's Conservatori Superior de Música del Liceu, he made his reputation as a concert pianist before moving on to specialize in contemporary music in the early 1970s. During the late 1960s Santos had spent time living in New York, where John Cage was to prove a decisive influence. Cage is referenced in many of his productions, most conspicuously *La meua filla sóc jo* (*I Am My Own Daughter*) (2005). This features a direct reference to Cage's 1952 piece "4'33"" through the sequence that reproduces the American composer's 4 minutes and 33 seconds of silence. His recordings of works by Karlheinz Stockhausen, John Cage, and Anton Webern in 1975, and his direction of the Grup Instrumental Català (GIC) at the Joan Miró Foundation between 1976 and 1979, situated him within an avant-garde forging new methodologies in their breaks with established musical structures and codes.[4]

Since 1978 he has been associated almost exclusively with his own compositions, although he remains passionately attached to a classical music tradition, acknowledging the importance of working with classically trained musicians and singers and of playing Bach or Brahms every day ("it's good for the pianist and good for the person . . . it's not good to cut with tradition").[5] As a performer he is far more interested in engaging with an audience than with ensuring that his music is consecrated in printed or recorded form.[6] His interdisciplinary approach to music has seen a wave of collaborations across fine art museums and galleries, concert halls and theatrical venues. These have involved a long-standing association with the Grup de Treball (Working Group), whose members included the artists Antoni Tàpies and Joan Ponç, and ventures with the filmmaker Pere Portabella. These include the films *Vampir-Cua de Cuc/Vampire-Worm's Tail* (1970), *Pont de Varsòvia/Warsaw Bridge* (1989), and *Die Stille vor Bach/The Silence before Bach* (2007), a series of shorts about Joan Miró made between 1970 and 1974, and the cinematic sequences in *El compositor, la cantant, el cuiner i la pecadora* (*The Composer, the Singer, the Cook and the Sinner*) (2003), where film is used rhythmically to comment on the onstage action.[7]

The avant-garde poet, dramatist, and painter Joan Brossa, a figure who is both evoked in Santos's autobiographical theatre production *Ricardo i Elena* (2000) and directly referenced through the assessment of his legacy in *Brossalobrossotdebrossat* (2008), was a regular associate of Santos's in the 1960s.[8] Their collaboration on performance pieces like *Suite bufa* (*Comic Suite*) (1966), where Santos played Josep Maria Mestres Quadreny's score, and on *Concert irregular*, premiered in 1968 to commemorate the seventy-fifth birthday of Joan Miró and with a score composed by Santos,[9] was to launch the latter on a theatrical journey which was to be consolidated during the 1980s and 1990s with a series of music theatre productions beginning in 1983 with *Minimalet-minimalot*.[10] It has been a search for a per-formance language for music that moves beyond the parameters of concert recitals or operatic rendition that has fuelled Santos's own evolution from pianist to choreographer-director.

This essay provides an introduction to his work, dealing with five of his most emblematic productions—*L'esplèndida vergonya del fet mal fet* (*The Splendid Shame of the Deed Badly Done*, 1995), *La pantera imperial* (*The Imperial Panther*, 1997), *Ricardo i Elena* (2000), *El compositor, la cantant, el cuiner i la pecadora* (*The Composer, The Singer, the Cook and the Sinner*, 2003), and *Brossalobrossotdebrossat* (2008)—while contextualizing their motifs, themat-ics, and musical concerns, where appropriate, within a broader body of work. Santos's productions often self-consciously emulate and reference each other both musically and visually. The choice of productions will al-low for the mapping of patterns and echoes while arguing for the particular resonances of these pieces within Santos's extensive oeuvre.[11] The essay will indicate how Santos's theatrical work has been marked by unease with reductive or conclusive categorizations and the need, in his own words, to follow Cage's trajectory in seeking to "make music visible."[12]

"More Opera Than Theatre"? Instruments and Impediments

Que conste que yo no hago teatro musical. Eso es otra cosa. Lo mío es música en el teatro, entendido como vehículo comunicativo.[13]

(Let it be clear that I don't do musical theatre. That is something else. What I do is music in the theatre, understood as a communicative vehicle.)

Santos's work has been described as "more opera than theatre, more like an animated sculpture than a show, more like circus than dance."[14] While he has described *Sama samaruck suck suck* (2002), first presented at Paris's Parc de la Villete in March 2002, as "ópera-circo"[15] (opera-circus), and it draws significantly on the iconography of traditional circus acts—contortionists, acrobats, trapeze artists, tightrope walkers, jugglers, cyclists—the piece is organized musically as a sound score. Music provokes the fundamental questions that underpin all his productions: "Can the scenario become a great stage? Can literary language be substituted by musical language? Can the musician become a character-actor?"[16] It is always the point of origin for all the stagings, and never used simply to illustrate what is happening onstage: "We don't use music to underline anything. Music can be seen: it is there, in images."[17]

The score is the start. I have one idea in terms of theatrical structure and then the score comes, and then everything comes together at once. When I start rehearsals, 40 per cent is not yet written, but I get to know the people and that helps me to finish the piece. I keep things open in rehearsal to allow for feedback but there is no improvisation in performance. The piece and the rehearsals finish together.[18]

Music is always the pivot around which his lavish productions hinge but the process of physicalizing the aural has entailed the entwining of different forms, all of which explore the performative and communicative elements of musical performance. "The pleasure of playing and giving pleasure playing"[19] are central to an understanding of Santos's theatrical language of transformation, where words transcend their literal meaning to offer alternative discursive configurations. His spectacles are structured around a series of vignettes or *tableaux vivants*, like the endless stream of hair emerging from a hole in the wall pulled by a man in figure-hugging PVC plastic dungarees, or the woman clad in pink tied to a windmill and spun around like the hands of a clock, or Antoni Comas's seafarer, ship perched on his head, seemingly trapped behind a table by endless chrome forks in *L'esplèndida vergonya*. Santos has summed up the text of *L'esplèndida vergonya* as "sung using different phonetic effects and expressions of the voice,"[20] and these find their visual analogy in the patterns created onstage. Santos has often referred to the voice as an "exceptional" but "underused instrument," and his percussive use of voice, "not what you would call melodic . . . [,] is based a lot on rhythms" negotiating a relationship between "sung sounds" and textual lyrics.[21] There is often little narrative cohesion to Santos's works, for he eschews storytelling in favor of using music to "explain something more"[22] with onstage actions choreographed to provide a visual commentary on the music or what Santos sees as "a different way of giving a concert."[23] It is in the words of the critic Pablo Meléndez-Haddad as if his work provides an alternative to the established operatic libretto, which he replaces with a sonic variation on the musical text.[24]

The titles of the productions are often playful and alliterative.[25] Santos has referred to music as the medium of sensuality,[26] and this is evident in the tone of most of his productions. In *La pantera imperial*, like the earlier *Cena Bach* (*Bach Supper*) of 1996 forged from the music of Johann Sebastian Bach, the seductive qualities of Bach's compositions were made corporeal through the performers' rituals of tender and lewd allure. Patterns and shifts in the music found their counterpoint in the physical gestures and moves of the performers. In *La pantera imperial,* as with Santos's 1996 production *Figasantos-Figotrop,* the sensuous qualities of the music were reflected and commented on by the onstage antics. Music for Santos is theatre to be seen as well as heard,[27] and it may be for this reason that he asks his audience to dispense with intellectual preconceptions and allow themselves to be guided by the spirit and poetry of the piece.

Often instruments become protagonists in the unfolding stage dramas. In *L'esplèndida vergonya,* a wandering pianola opened the production, its high C penetrating the darkness with alarming persistence. Dominating the spectacle's final sequence too, it swerved around the stage like a demon possessed. The pianola also provided an alternative stage for an alluring Venus-like mermaid who lies on it with languid candor. Words are not necessarily clear carriers of meanings but rather, as *Ricardo i Elena*'s Latin libretto makes clear, malleable semantic sounds where form usurps content as the primary mode of communication. It may be the imagery of the production that remains with an audience, but it is the music which generates the images—images which "arise oneirically from the modalities of his [Santos's] music, a uniquely maverick interpretation of rhythm, timing and resultant atmosphere."[28] These images often relate to and play with musical motifs, as with the mermaid who emerged tied to a grand ticking metronome in *L'esplèndida vergonya,* the trapeze that featured in *Ricardo i Elena* and *Sama samaruck suck suck* as a visual analogy for the metronome, and the battering and dismantling of pianos and pianolas which is such a feature of most of Santos's theatrical work.[29]

Santos also constructs instruments from the materials of our domestic encounters. In *El compositor,* structured around eighteen musical vignettes,[30] the habitually somber "Eia, mater, fons amoris" from *Stabat mater* was rendered by sixteen gigantic steel saucepans lit in sumptuous shades of red and displayed like organ pipes—a homage perhaps to Víctor García's 1976 production of Valle-Inclán's *Divinas palabras* (*Divine Words*) but also a playful reference to Rossini's culinary skills. The pans simmered on a giant hob like a symphonic Rossini chorus. *El compositor* opened with the sound of a drop of water falling onto a box strategically positioned on the empty stage. Lit by a faint spotlight, the water hissed as it fell onto the heated surface, disappearing into a faint cloud of steam. The repeated amplified sound of drop following drop, falling from the ceiling, offered a metronome against which the score was adeptly positioned. The concentrated rhythmic pulse accelerated, the drops coming more quickly to provide something in the manner of what the the *Times*'s Richard Morrison saw as a Rossini *accelerando* but which might also be judged as an overture to the piece.[31]

The tempo provided by the sound of falling water also suggested something of the soundscape of Bill Viola's *The Crossing* (1996), with the drops intensifying into a steady stream and then a symphonic flood of water. The sudden opening of a flap at the front of the box witnessed Antoni Comas's Cook pop out like a jack-in-the-box, a dismembered head emerging from a giant oven singing a fragment of the Count's "Ah, il più lieto, il più felice" from Rossini's *Il barbiere di Siviglia*. This image, positioning the Cook as part-Rossini and part-Count, both commented on the intersections between biography and intertextuality that can be traced in the authorial text and provided an enactment of the turbulent emotions experienced by the Count at that narrative point in the opera. As the Cook retreated back into the oven as abruptly as he emerged, we were confronted with the brutal image of a man returning to his inferno.[32]

Moments of Rossini's life were evoked and referenced through the production—as with the falsetto solo in the final sequence recalling the composer's singing of Desdemona's "Willow Song" to the Prince Regent at Brighton Pavilion in 1823, the use of "Quelques mesures de chant funèbre: a mon pauvre ami Meyerbeer," his final composition, to close the production, and the repeated culinary analogies. The sexual intrigues and complications between the Composer (Santos), the Singer (mezzo Claudia Schneider), the Cook (Antoni Comas), and the Sinner (soprano Alina Zaplatina) echoed the plotline of *Le Comte Ory*. Santos, however, rejected attempts to impose a plot onto the piece: "lo importante es la música que se despliega al gusto de las gotas"[33] (what's important is the music which opens out to the taste of the drops). "Las gotas son el equivalente escénico de la nota musical. . . . Caen como metronomes"[34] (The drops are the scenic equivalents of musical notes. . . . They fall like metronomes). As with the trapeze in *Ricardo i Elena* and *Sama samaruck suck suck*, the drops offered an organizing motif. Reappearing as objects to be caught by the mezzo and soprano as they sing, they shaped the structure and content of the piece. As Clémence Coconnier has delineated, drops are present in the singing.

> The word games, the speech games and onomatopoeias are like drops in the lyrics, exaggerating the material nature of the body and also its sounds. Drop by drop the piece unfolds. . . . A trickle of *Barbiere*, a dash of *Stabat mater*, a few operatic duets and arias, a string sonata that Rossini wrote at the age of 12: from the first image of the drop of water to the end (it is also the last piece written by the composer), Santos makes us taste the rhythm of Rossini.[35]

Fig. 1. Surmounting obstacles: Antoni Comas sings with his head in water in Carles Santos's *La pantera imperial*. Photo Carles Santos, courtesy of the Companyia Carles Santos and the Teatre Lliure.

Indeed, as with *L'esplèndida vergonya*, in *El compositor,* water functions both as a musical and visual motif.[36] Portabella's black-and-white film in the third sequence shows water drenching the human body to the sound of the storm music of *Il barbiere di Siviglia* and *La Cenerentola;* Antoni Comas's tenor sings while gargling the water being poured over him; the singers and dancers slip and slide on the wet stage; a corseted singer is positioned like a trapped mermaid on the piano singing a Rossini aria. Water is the quintessential bodily fluid, the life force but also its opposite, that which impedes it. Repeatedly in *El compositor, La pantera imperial,* and *L'esplèndida vergonya,* Santos references his 1987 aquatic choral opera, *Tramuntana Tremens,* as singers are obliged to perform while immersed in water (see figure 1). Impediments frequently feature as part of the conditions of performance in Santos's work.[37]

La pantera imperial, an earlier prototype for *El compositor* in its musical approximation to a composer's work, placed Bach, the point of origin for so much Western music, under Santos's scalpel. The production's title alluded

244 · TAKING IT TO THE BRIDGE

to the centrality of the piano in all Santos's work—made manifest in the piece through its physical and strategic positioning on the stage as clavichord, pianola, and piano. "With piano or without piano there is always the piano,"[38] Santos has asserted. It is both a companion and an adversary, both subject—dancing across the stage as a wayward pianola—and fetishized object of desire. A source of pleasure and pain, it is played, battered, and caressed. Santos often configures the instrument as a prosthetic limb, a configuration indelibly bound up with his own movements: recognition of the implications of the two to three hours he spends in daily practice. Not insignificantly, the poster image for Santos's retrospective at the Fundació Joan Miro in 2006 showed him tied to the cross of a grand piano.

From his earliest theatrical pieces, like *Beethoven, si tanco la tapa, què passa?* (*Beethoven, if I Close the Lid, What Will Happen?*, 1983), where the audience was recurrently shown a performer draping herself lasciviously over both Santos and the piano while he continued playing as if impervious to her allures, the piano has dominated his theatrical visions. In *Brossalobrossotdebrossat* it is the central stage prop, an environment linked to a stairway of books that links the literary and the musical in both conceptual and concrete ways. In *Ricardo i Elena*, the piano is embraced and accosted by a dancer in black. The Imperial Bösendorfer on which Santos plays at home is described by the composer as a grand black panther that is difficult to master.[39] In *La pantera imperial* the piano functioned as the instrument through which the various pianists attempted to make sense of the enigma that is Bach. Moving away from the earnestness that surrounds much Bach interpretation, Santos offered a performed commentary on the responsibilities, struggles, and pleasures of reading Bach. Bach is for Santos the "Bible for any musician, the musical Shakespeare. Through it your spirit is uplifted."[40] *La pantera imperial* repositioned fragments of Bach's oeuvre anew within a Santos prologue and finale. Framed by an imposing three-sided wall of forty suspended synthetic Bach busts (which also had a little of Santos's own facial profile about them), the performer-musicians grappled with the impossibility of a definitive rendition and the weight of the composer's authoritative presence. The space, constructed a little like a boxing or wrestling ring, functioned metaphorically to provide a visual analogy for the struggle for tonal supremacy which is very much central to Bach's preludes and fugues. Santos effectively visualized the harmonic tensions played out in the music. The combative encounters produced by this quest were graphically illustrated through the brutal exchanges rendered before us: the gyrating platform on which tenor Antoni Comas sought to play the clavichord, the soprano trying to find her voice in the midst of a deafening racket, Comas attempting to sing with his head repeatedly submerged in a bowl of water, a mad pianola interrupting the stage and attacking the performers seated at the piano or chasing two pianos around the stage, the harpsichordist spinning around on a revolving platform while playing a prelude, a singer struggling across the stage weighed down by a Bach bust fixed to her back, or Santos kneeling with his arms stretched out in the form of a crucifix while playing Bach on two pianos. Against seemingly insurmountable obstacles, the musical tensions were wittily played out. In exploring practices that extend beyond those associated with the written word, *La pantera imperial* asked significant questions around how the process of making and performing functions in the transmission of knowledge in musical performance.

Visually as well as musically, the layers of previous interpretations proved a constant point of reference in *La pantera imperial*. The sweeping of debris from the stage after each scene offered a brilliant analogy for Santos's own process of acknowledging the weight of the past in shaping the present. Costumes were abrasively eclectic, a hybridization of periods, textures, and styles. Mariaelena Roqué, the designer who collaborated with Santos on the dramaturgical and visual shape of the productions until 2010, has acknowledged the role played by the fantasies of Dalí, Picasso, and Gaudí in crafting the costumes for *La pantera imperial*.[41] But such influences run alongside styles that traverse three centuries and draw on fabrics developed in the textile industry that fuelled Catalonia's industrialization in the nineteenth century and utilized habitually in both opera and circus, the two art forms referenced in all of Santos's music theatre work. Crinolines were refashioned alongside thigh length boots, tight bodies, breeches, tailcoats, and eighteenth-century ruffles. Eighteenth-century pigment dyes and fabrics used in bullfighting suits of lights were juxtaposed with Lycra corsets derived from a Vivienne Westwood model. Transparent fabrics allowed for the refraction and reflection of light in ways that highlighted the facets of characters that were equally translucent, fleeting presences.[42] Part of the disarming quality of Santos's theatre is based on a celebration of discordance—both musical and scenic. Colors and textures often clash; objects appear undersized or oversized, costumes occupy a disproportionate relationship to the body. It is part of a strategy of distortion that undermines habitual scenic configurations. If Santos's music theatre relies on the textures, smells, tastes, and colors of the everyday, they are reconfigured in ways that question habitual modes of theatrical representation.

Identity and Culture

Much of Santos's work revolves around modes of representation. It is as much about recognizing how national identities are forged through wider cultural discourses. Valencian dishes and dialects are commented on in *Ricardo i Elena* as prawns vie for attention across a giant back wall with rice that at a certain angle might be tiny maggots—a reminder both of the life/death cycle and of Valencia's emblematic dish, *paella*. In *Brossalobrossotdebrossat* Santos examines the oeuvre of Joan Brossa. The twenty scenes present no unifying concept of the man or his work but rather enter into a dialogue with his literary writing, his imagery, and his persona. While there is no specially composed score, the process of staging fragments of Brossa's work is in itself shown to be a form of composition for the stage—as seen in the opening scene where actors Mònica López and Jose Maria Mestres provide a rendition of Brossa's 1963 *Variaciones para una puerta y un suspiro de Pierre Henry* (*Variations on a door and a sigh by Pierre Henry*). The focus is on rendering Brossa's writings as if they were a score,[43] presenting them in ways that contextualize them within further musical tropes and paradigms (as with Brahms's *Lied*, Wagner's overture to *Tristan and Isolde*, and the projections of Busby Berkeley's choreography and the Marx Brothers' *A Night in Casablanca* (1946)—the latter juxtaposed with an interview with Brossa). The projection of an Arabic reading of Brossa's *La xarxa* (*The Net*) further serves to reposition Brossa within a broader avant-garde than Catalan scholarship has previously allowed.

Indeed through his trajectory Santos's own irreverent positioning and dismantling of motifs and stereotypes from Catalan culture stands alongside intertextual references from the operatic, musical, and cinematic repertoire beyond Catalonia—the title of *El compositor* cites both the Spanish title of Alessandro Blasetti's *Too Bad She's Bad* (1955) (*La ladrona, su padre y el taxista*) and Peter Greenaway's *The Cook, the Thief, His Wife and Her Lover* (1989). The presence of the Sabadell Lider Camera within *La pantera imperial* was a graphic recognition of the Catalan choral tradition which has shaped Santos's musical grounding as decisively as Cage or Stockhausen. Santos has also acknowledged that the phonemes he sings have their point of origin in the onomatopoeias that are so characteristic of the Catalan language.[44] The imagery of the Mediterranean is palpably located in much of his work with maritime references (the ships, the man dressed as a prawn, the seafarers, the mermaids, aquatic blue and gold hues), featuring heavily in *L'esplèndida vergonya* and *Tramuntana tremens*.[45]

A significant number of Santos's key collaborators are also Catalan or Barcelona-based. Santos's collaborations with singers, actors, dancers, dramatists, and artists have allowed for an exchange and absorption of new styles and an evolution of his stage language. His process of writing/composing during rehearsals, allowing space for feedback and input from the performers and musicians whom he sees as part of an organic team, questions a conception of musical composition which views the score as the means toward an end where the input of singers lies solely in the interpretation of the annotated notes. He may come into rehearsals with a score written, but the extensive two- to three-month rehearsal period involves substantial performer input. The versatility of Santos's performative team—whose musical skills often appear matched by acrobatic dexterity—has proved a distinctive feature of his music theatre. His regular team of collaborators includes Venezuelan designer Mariaelena Roqué (credited as co-director on *El compositor* and co-director of the Companyia Carles Santos), Catalan choreographer Toni Jodar, Catalan tenor Antoni Comas, Barcelona-based mezzo Claudia Schneider, and dancer Ana Criado. Roqué, in the words of Barcelona's former mayor, Joan Clos, dresses Santos's music.[46] Roqué is a constant presence in rehearsal, watching and listening to the performers, and only crafting the costumes in response to what she witnesses.[47] Costumes need to be both functional and emblematic, part of the color-coding that shapes the rhythm—both musical and visual—of each production.

Santos's work is often centrally concerned with playfully interrogating cultural stereotypes and the way these are promoted through musical tropes. While it has often been positioned by the British critical establishment around Spanish prototypes—"if Salvador Dalí and Pedro Almodóvar choreographed a dream, it might look like this"[48]—few have dissected the specificity of the references noted. The *zapateado* (flamenco tap-dance) through which Bach was interpreted in *La pantera imperial* positioned the spectacle within an innovative prism of relocation which recognized the ways in which Spain's cultural formation has remained inextricably linked to flamenco. *La grenya de Pasqual Picanya, asessor jurídic-administratiu* (*The Loco of Pasqual Picanya* [*Legal and Administrative Adviser*], 1990) features Santos drinking from a *botijo* (a jug with spout and handle) and serves, alongside the copious culinary motifs in Santos's work, to reflect on the analogies between musical and gastronomic consumption.

Making good music is a pleasure. Eating well is a pleasure. The pleasure of eating music or of making music to eat is a great pleasure. A musical work for the pleasure of eating. An eating of music. I ask

you, are eating and listening to music two pleasures or a single pleasure?[49]

The conspicuous excess of Santos's aesthetic may also have served as a
factor in drawing parallels with Spain's most prominent cinematic export,
Pedro Almodóvar. The *Guardian*'s theatre critic Michael Billington, recognizing the construction of *L'esplèndida vergonya* around a series of recurring
visual motifs marked by a fetishization of the female form, a kitsch costume
register, and visual saturation, summarized it as "a mix of Robert Dhery's
famous revue, *La Plume de ma Tante* with a Pedro Almodóvar movie and
a bit of *Hellzapoppin'* thrown in."[50] Certainly both Almodóvar and Santos may acknowledge the influence of the Spanish grotesque or *esperpento*
(from Goya to Picasso), but it may be that foreign critics' equation of the
two is based on a heavily generalized reading that likens their unfixing of
sexual and performative identities and their theatricalization of sex while
failing to consider the cultural specificity of the visual references employed
by each director.

Sex and Pain

José Miguel G. Cortés, director of Castelló's Espai d'Art Contemporani
(contemporary art gallery), defines Santos's work as revolving around two
axes which may appear contradictory but are actually complementary: sex
and pain.

> Carles Santos manifests his relationship with sex in a way which
> is . . . light-hearted. . . . Through it, he achieves a deconsecration
> and a vulgarization of sex, presenting it in unthinkable images or
> situations, where the borders of the body (both physical and psy-
> chological) are transformed. . . . In this attempt, he cross-dresses and
> pluralises the identities of his characters turning them into poly-
> morphic subjects, freed from fears and taboos.[51]

In *L'esplèndida vergonya*, two naked men could be glimpsed through a fridge
door that opened and closed with alarming speed. *Sama samaruck suck suck*
was structured toward a musical crescendo that had distinctly sexual connotations. Santos's organization of *La pantera imperial* provided graphic
examples of his view that "there is an orgasm in Bach every 24 bars."[52] *El
compositor* was ordered around sexual encounters that propelled the piece
forward both musically and visually. Sex was both a physical act and a cho-

reographed routine, with the Cook and Singer appearing to dance on the bed through their copulation, the corporeality of the enactment providing what Joyce McMillan viewed as "the links between the power of great music and the basic impulses of our own bodies."[53] Indeed, such imagery may also function as a discreet commentary on the syphilis that plagued Rossini in his final years, resulting in severe depressions and mental instability.

In *La pantera imperial* cumbersome restrictive costumes were discarded by the performers, falling like petals onto the floor of the stage. The constricting and constraining attire of performance was shed like a second skin to liberate the body. The costumes which littered the floor, alongside the shoes and shoeboxes meticulously laid out by the performers, provided further indications of the debris of performance which was continuously swept from the stage. In addition, the white shoeboxes may also have obliquely commented on the pronounced infant mortality rate of Bach's immediate family.[54] One of the performers standing primly at the front of the stage ponderously recited biographical information about Bach and his epoch, but, increasingly drowned out by the music around her, she became a largely irrelevant figure. It was in the music and the stark imagery that moments of Bach's life, music, and legacy were played out. And it was through the prisms of pain, and discipline, that the associations were made manifest.

Pain is intrinsically linked by Santos to artistic creation. The poster to *La pantera imperial*, designed by Santos, features a semi-clenched hand with a miniature of Bach contained in the palm, while the fingers are decorated with burning cigarettes pierced by long painted talons. It is a simile for both the pain—strain, injuries, the sacrifices produced by the discipline involved—and the pleasure of playing. The object of gratification contained in an antiquated frame (Bach) is simultaneously coveted and endangered. Often in his productions, artists are forced to work in conditions that defy logistical expectations.[55] *El compositor* seems to comment repeatedly on Rossini's comparison of a tenor exerting himself to reach a high C or D with the sound of a capon's throat being slashed.[56] Antoni Comas's tenor sings while tightly bound in a laced corset that curtails and imprisons. In *Sama samaruck suck suck* too a soprano sings while flying through the air held by a harness. In the musical rendition of *Lisístrata*, presented as part of Valencia's Biennale in June 2003, the title protagonist sang while driving past on a motorbike speeding at 100 kilometers an hour. In *L'esplèndida vergonya*, a violinist suspended in the air played upside down with breathtaking virtuosity. An opera singer with a tiny galleon perched on his head sang while placed on a wardrobe that floated through the air alongside a pair of enormous black stilettos and a sturdy fridge. But these objects, which often clashed and crashed against each other, like a giant mutant mobile, proved more than just aesthetic reminders of a world where incongruous items rest cheek by jowl: rather they functioned alongside the more conventional instruments to provide a percussive soundtrack for the production, and a means of acknowledging the diverse influences that come together in artistic creation.

Santos as Subject: *Ricardo i Elena*

Santos himself is often a regular performer in his post-operatic productions. In *La pantera imperial* he commented on his own role as a celebrated concert pianist when he animatedly played Bach on two pianos clad in a well-worn tailcoat that evoked the attire of traditional musicians. In *El compositor,* taking the role of the composer—and thus drawing analogies with Rossini—he sat at a baby grand piano that animatedly squirted water at carefully positioned bust-cum-urinals of Beethoven, Verdi, and Wagner. This may have been a comment of sorts on Rossini's often non-acknowledged influence on these later composers, but it may also, as Mark Fisher was to shrewdly note, have reflected Santos's view that Rossini "pisses all over them."[57]

Santos has argued for his onstage presence as a means for the composer to face the public and defend his work.[58] In *La meua filla sóc jo* he turned to the narrative plotting of naturalistic drama but here twisted through the prisms of a Wagnerian mythology, opening with four pregnant mythical beings giving birth to a single child. While the visual imagery of the women and their names offered a nod to the German composer, their operation of remote-controlled cars pointed to a more direct link to the consumerist culture of the new millennium.

Ricardo i Elena too juggled references to the personal and the mythical, with Santos both the subject of the production and the author of its execution.[59] While the naming of *Ricardo i Elena* after his parents suggested a marked autobiographical slant, Santos did not judge the piece as specific to his particular familial circumstances.[60] Rooted in the austere post–Civil War climate in which he grew up in a family of doctors, *Ricardo i Elena* is rather "una aproximación a la posguerra a través de un conducto musical"[61] (an approach to the postwar years refracted through a musical idiom) and an attempt to musically reclaim an era, the 1940s, tinted in black and white, like the films of the period.[62] Ricardo and Elena are simply representative of a particular generation who were parents in a black-and-white era that found it difficult to adapt to the demands of technicolor. Santos's choice to craft the piece in Latin is worth considering here. Latin may be a "dead" language but is also highly musical, holding the roots of present Romance languages as well as liturgical music. Here it functions as a statement on both the religious framework of the characters' lives and the non-communication which lies at the heart of *Ricardo i Elena* where much is said and cited but little is listened to: a state which Santos views as "vivir en una soledad compartida" (living in a shared solitude) which many couples settle for after lengthy periods of shared existence.[63] The Latin libretto in *Ricardo i Elena* may sound exquisite but is often shockingly mundane— Elena (Claudia Schneider) screeching out a list of tasks for Ricardo (Antoni Comas) in Scene 2, Ricardo talking of Elena's Catalan roots in Scene 3, the discussion of who's going to eat what by Ricardo, Elena, and the servant/ housekeeper Donaxona in Scene 7. It is precisely Santos's ability to fuse the sacred and the mundane (both musical and visually) that makes *Ricardo i Elena* such a disarming piece of theatre.

The piece was not fixed in a particular era, but references to the 1940s—including the design of the furniture—suggested an affiliation to that decade. Childhood memories and encounters were woven into the framework of the piece but flashbacks served, as in black-and-white films of the period, to provide images of recalled moments and imagined instances. There were clear nods to particular visual characteristics of the area in which Santos was brought up, like the ornamental tiles from the Vinaròs Hermitage which frame Elena's bed. It is, according to Mariaelena Roqué, about taking certain visual and symbolic elements that can provide a subtle taste of past places and moments.[64] These moments, however, were not merely visual but also musical, as the production was filled with references to composers who enjoyed a presence in Santos's youth like Robert Schumann (1810–56) and Lorenzo Perosi (1872–1956), whose Credo from the *Missa Pontificalis* was included in the piece. As with *Brossalobrossotdebrossat*, it was as much a study of the formative influences that shape consciousness as a corrosive commentary on artistic commodification.

As with *La pantera imperial* and *L'esplèndida vergonya*, *Ricardo i Elena* was marked by an absence of narrative cohesion. Rather it was organized around a series of episodes revolving around a theme. This was eloquently announced in the opening scene as a man was seen walking precariously across a high tightrope hung with a cross. As he carefully made his way from one side of the stage to another we were given a stark image of artistic creativity trying to keep a steady balance in a world contaminated by commercial imperatives and marked by the remnants of a religious sensibility which infuses even society's most secular members. Individuals were introduced, disembodied voices projecting through the darkness, suspended in a black void of nothingness. Lit individually from above, they functioned like symbolic icons singing out remnants of religious requiems in adoration and celebration of a greater being that cannot be quantified and that defies the rampant materialism glorified by contemporary culture.

Spirituality and materialism were locked in combat for the show's one-hour duration. Seated at a Victorian harmonium, a symbol of the bourgeois turn-of-the-century drawing room, three performers played a delicate trio, serving to conjure images of the middle-class society where music functioned as a means toward revealing hidden desires which the codes of respectability sought to keep under wraps. Santos, born during the difficult post–Civil War years, may here have been commenting on his own childhood spent during this religiously oppressive period. The production harks back to earlier epochs, not merely through its Latin libretto and its musical associations ranging from the medieval to the contemporary, but also through the visual emblems employed in the various sequences. At one point toward the end of the performance, paintings were dangled before us like falling snow. These symbols of artistic acquisition displayed in glorious excess in the family home were here brutally dislocated and crumbled to the floor in an image which recalled the melting clocks of Dalí's "The Persistence of Memory" (1931). The cultural encounters in *Ricardo i Elena* demonstrated consumerism and spirituality as the antagonists over which artistic (and perhaps even domestic) wars are fought.

In conditions of physical and emotional containment and constriction, tenor Antoni Comas and Santos were obliged to "produce" music, a testament to the resilience and discipline which marks their craft. Carles Santos engaged in a duet with temptation (or perhaps inspiration?) in the form of a woman dressed in black (the habitual *femme fatale*) whose caresses of the piano become both the dangerous other which he, as a musician, has to learn to harness and the muse which motivates him. This is a motif of much of Santos's work and relates to the axes of sex and pain considered earlier in the essay.[65] In *L'esplèndida vergonya*, a violinist is dangled by his feet, flying through the air as he continues to play while, in the production's closing moments, Uma Ysamat's mermaid soprano, precariously placed over a church window, sang defiantly while drizzling the stage with water emerging from her crotch. In *El compositor* a similar image was recycled as Antoni Comas's Cook sang lying on his back on the floor, his head wedged in a Perspex box on which the Sinner (Alina Zaplatina) squatted as she sang, massaging a huge prosthetic phallus that ejaculated at a timely moment.

Gender, Art, and Performance

Santos's work often deconstructs established gender imagery, placing women in positions of narrative agency rather than as chattels of exchange. Frequently his work comments on the religious and secular iconography that has marked gender construction over the past five hundred years. Santos's female protagonists are "sacred and diabolical"[66] subjects who function as agents of change and action. Sex is often a violent act, charged with eroticism and danger, but gender roles are often reversed with women (both literally and metaphorically) on top. In *L'esplèndida vergonya*, a woman clad in a red bikini forced the contents of a phallic tube into the mouth of a man being dragged along the floor with his head trapped in a glass cage. In *Ricardo i Elena* the battle for sexual supremacy was realized in a series of complex encounters between Santos and the woman in black, and Ricardo and Elena, who all, during the seventh sequence, engaged in a series of violent verbal and physical diatribes that culminated in an impassioned sexual encounter on a piano stool.

All of Carles Santos's work revolves around enacted conflicts. In *La pantera imperial*, pianos jostled over space with busts of Bach suspended around the parameters of the stage, providing a wrestling ring to contain the struggle (see figure 2). In *Ricardo i Elena* the conflict was somewhat more complex as religious icons vied with symbols of domestic stability. Accompanying the disruption of musical harmonies came images of visual dissonance. Audiences were witnesses to a violent and rapid juxtaposition of the tensions that have been at the heart of artistic debates since the Renaissance. In the fifth sequence, a dancer, clad only in a loose-fitting red loincloth, straddled a suspended cross as she climbed over rosary beads in her ascent toward the skies. Sexually provocative, she functioned as a constant reminder of the delicate line between erotic and religious iconography. If *L'esplèndida vergonya* merged sexual and religious imagery in its final sequence of a woman urinating while dangling from a church window, in *Ricardo i Elena* the links were played out even more emphatically. Acrobats dangling across turning bells, trapped as within a time capsule, served to remind the audience that all religious music is as much linked with repression as with liberation—a point made also by the Lieder Camera in *La pantera imperial* as they offered the Crucifixes from the B Minor Mass with outstretched arms in the form of a cross.

The whole process in *Ricardo i Elena* seemed to remark on the ways in which religion fosters the culture of repression and surveillance that forms the cornerstone of the bourgeois society exposed in the production. In the

Fig. 2. The wandering pianola performs against the many busts of Bach-cum-Santos in Carles Santos's *La pantera imperial*. Photo Carles Santos, courtesy of the Companyia Carles Santos and the Teatre Lliure.

final episodes of the production, this society of vigilant surveillance finally imploded upon itself. This was here displayed through the hard metallic post-industrial objects—a chair, a standard lamp, an upright piano, a coffee table marked by two heavy books—vying for supremacy. As they clashed and collided in a macabre dance for domination, we were reminded of how repressive discontents come back to haunt the psyche. This led to a situation in the tenth sequence where Ricardo, envisaged as a medieval religious zealot, was transformed into a smartly dressed business executive, stunningly achieved through a double trapeze act which both unclothed and then reclothed the performer—a direct homage to Joan Brossa and his Striptease pieces written in the 1960s and further referenced in *Brossalo-brossotdebrossat*. Along the production's journey from the trappings of ritual to the trappings of commerce, the emblematic suit served as the perennial symbol of the formality of contemporary buy-and-sell culture.

In the final sequence, as Carles Santos was flanked at the piano by his parents—an image of control and surveillance—the audience were presented with an image of the anti-Christ as the dancer dressed in red re-appeared on a suspended cross. But to view the production in merely religious terms misses the strong domestic vein that characterized it. The fourth sequence opened with Santos's mother Elena giving birth to Carles upon a bedstead—reminiscent of Federico García Lorca's *El público* (*The Public*, 1930–31)—vertically suspended across a fresco of tiles from the local Vinaròs Hermitage, firmly establishing the piece's credentials as a theatrical exploration of domestic dynamics and the tensions between the private and the public spheres. In the seventh sequence, as Comas's Ricardo and Schneider's Elena expressed disapproval at their son's relationship with Joan Brossa, we were provided with some indication as to Santos's formative influences. Rather than clear autobiography, these were moments from a recalled childhood: snippets of conversation, imagined moments, reconstructed instants all framed within a larger tapestry of religious and artistic exploration where the private and the public are irrevocably intertwined.

Santos, "Performance," and Post-Operatic Music Theatre

While Santos may claim that his work is never about provocation but rather about a process of investigation and expression, the provocation of discussions around the purpose, role, and boundaries of opera and music theatre have been at the very forefront of his stage productions.[67] Conventions of performance are often dissected and interrogated, as in *El compositor*, where the duets from *Semiramide*, sung by a mezzo and soprano, consistently omitted the final note, teasing the audience who were repeatedly deprived of closure (and climax). The extract from *Zelmira*'s "Cara, deh, attendimi" cabaletta was sung excruciatingly slowly by Comas's Cook as a means of signaling both its mathematical construction and its demands on the human voice. Santos refused to have *Ricardo i Elena* categorized as "performance," viewing it instead as an opera staged in theatres.[68] My own classification of Santos's theatrical work categorizes it within the realms of the post-operatic in consistently interrogating the bounds of opera's conventions and formal practices. Moving away from nineteenth-century dramaturgical models, composition takes place across both musical and scenic registers. Santos, like his European contemporaries Heiner Goebbels, Christoph Marthaler, and Helmut Lachenmann,[69] draws on diverse musical and visual influences in the pioneering of new vocal modes. Whereas Goebbel's citations may be more obviously pop-based, as with the Beach Boys in *Hashirigaki* (2000), and Marthaler's compositions may seem more observably grounded in the context of post-1989 German unification and traditions of Germanic cabaret, both share with Santos a fascination with envisaging how elements that might once have been seen as the unique preserve of opera can be reconfigured in ways that allow for a reflection both on opera as a historical phenomenon and on contemporary post-operatic music theatre practices that frame the operatic within other aural modes and tropes.[70]

While Marthaler may have been judged more overtly political in his commentary on German history and national identity, Santos's theatrical productions demonstrate no less of a fascination with the processes of cultural memory, historical appropriation, and the mythologization of artistic endeavor. His own work as a graphic artist—evolving from the LP/CD covers and posters conceived for his own stage work and recordings—has further allowed for the branding of Santos across the performative arts to the visual arts. While parallels can be drawn with Pina Bausch's subversion of the norms of classical ballet or Tadeusz Kantor's reassignment of objects toward non-figurative ends, Santos's theatrical discourse is governed by a sensibility where concepts of the musical and visual avant-garde intersect with autobiography, literature, mythology, and the wider Iberian cultural context in which he lives and works.

Although the Companyia Carles Santos folded in early 2010, following the personal and professional separation of Santos and Mariaelena Roqué, Santos has continued to work with the theatrical registers established by the company between 1984 and 2009. Indeed, *Chicha Montenegro Gallery* (2010), co-produced by the Lliure and realized with a number of his regular performer-collaborators, confirms his commitment to an aesthetic where the paratheatrical, music, and memory intersect. With an *a capella* structure and a constant visual tension between the vertical and the horizontal—as performers fly across the stage and writhe along the floor—*Chicha Montenegro Gallery* offered a contemplation of a Godot-like absent other who haunts the characters that populate the production's varied vignettes. Chicha is alter ego and muse, friend and foe: the mysterious other that exhilarates and excites the artistic imagination.[71] It may be over thirty-five years since Santos first appeared on the Catalan music scene, but *Chicha Montenegro Gallery* demonstrates a continuing fascination with the ways in which music can be enacted through the physical and material language of the stage.

NOTES

This article is developed from two earlier publications on Santos: "Making Music Visible: The Theatrical Work of Carles Santos," *TheatreForum*, no. 20 (2002): 3–12; and "Composing for the Stage: The Music Theatre of Carles Santos," *Contemporary*

Theatre Review 17, no. 3 (2007): 278–301. This article has benefited greatly from the suggestions of the late David Bradby, David George, and Richard Pettengill. Thanks are due also to Carles Santos and Mariaelena Roqué for speaking to me at length about their work in July 2006.

1. Carles Santos, quoted in Christopher Bowen, "Christopher Bowen Witnesses an Operatic Feast in Barcelona," *Scotsman* (Magazine supplement) (May 1996), 18. Significantly, however, Valencia has been keen to "appropriate" him with high-profile commissions for the 2001 Biennale—a *fanfarria* (musical fanfare) composed for 2001 musicians—and the 2003 Biennale—a musical rendition of Aristophanes's *Lysistrata* (*Lísistrata*). For further details on these productions, see Empar Marco, "La Bienal de Valencia arranca con La Fura y la fanfarria de Carles Santos y 2.001 músicos," *La Vanguardia* (June 12, 2001), 42; and Javier Vallejo, "El amor y no la guerra," *El País* (Babelia supplement) (June 7, 2003), 20.

2. See, for example, Marc Lambert, "*L'esplèndida vergonya del fet mal fet*," *The List* (August–September 1996), 41; and Mark Fisher, "*The Composer, the Singer, the Cook and the Sinner,*" *Guardian* (August 31, 2004), 18.

3. Lambert, "*L'esplèndida vergonya del fet mal fet*," 14.

4. For further details on his early work see Maryse Badiou, "Carles Santos, veinte años de riesgo," *El Público*, 48 (September 1987), 15–17; and Manuel Guerrero, ed., *Carles Santos: Long Live the Piano!*, Exhibition Catalogue (Barcelona: Fundació Joan Miró/Generalitat de Catalunya, 2006), 73–160.

5. Carles Santos, quoted in Christopher Bowen, "Surrealism as a Way of Life," *Scotsman* (Festival insert) (August 1996), 3.

6. See Ferran Bono, "Carles Santos da una vuelta de tuerca a Rossini en Torrent," *El País* (Comunidad Valenciana supplement) (April 23, 2004), 9.

7. On collaborations with the dancer Cesc Gelabert and the conceptual artist Frederic Amat, see Delgado, "Composing for the Stage," 281.

8. For English-language introductions to Brossa, see Joan Brossa, *Words Are Things: Poems, Objects and Installations*, Exhibition Catalogue (London: Riverside Studios, 1992); Jordi Coca, "Brossa and the Others," *Contemporary Theatre Review* 17, no. 3 (2007): 446–52.

9. *Suite bufa*, a musical action written with music by Josep M. Mestres Quaderny was first performed by Santos, Anna Ricci, and Terri Mestres at the SIGMA Festival in Bordeaux in 1966. His first stage composition for Brossa was *Concert Irregular*, premiered to commemorate the seventy-fifth anniversary of Joan Miró's birth in 1968.

10. While the Companyia Carles Santos's first production was *Arganchulla, Arganchulla Gallac* (1987), Santos had been creating music theatre pieces since *Minimalet-minimalot*.

11. The first four productions have toured extensively both within Spain and beyond. *L'esplèndida vergonya* opened at the Mercat de les Flors before going on to the Hebbel Theatre Berlin in 1995, the Edinburgh International Festival in 1996, and Strasbourg's Music Festival in 1999. *La pantera imperial* was first seen at Frankfurt's Künstlerhaus Mousonturm in 1997 before securing international performance dates at Berlin's Hebbel Theatre (1999), Milan's Teatro dell'Arte (1999), Lyon's Théâtre National Populaire (1999), the Buenos Aires Festival (1999), and Brazil's Filo Londrina (2000), as well as a British tour encompassing the Brighton, Salisbury, and Manchester Festivals and Warwick's Arts Centre (1999). Since

opening at Barcelona's Teatre Nacional de Catalunya in March 2000, *Ricardo i Elena*'s European engagements have included dates at Paris's Odéon-Théâtre de l'Europe (2000), Berlin's Hebbel Theatre (2000), Belfast's Waterfront Hall (2000), Nice's Centre Dramatique National (2001), and Edinburgh's International Festival (2001). *El compositor* was first seen at the Teatre Nacional de Catalunya in November 2003, before touring to the Théâtre National de Tolouse (2003), the Edinburgh International Festival (2004), Perpignan's Salle Trenet-Palais des Congres (2005), Naples's Teatro Mercadante (2005), and five Dutch venues (2005). *Brossalobrossotdebrossat*, perhaps because of its subject matter, has had less international exposure; it opened at Girona's Centre d'Arts Escèniques de Salt in April 2008 and has subsequently played at a range of Spanish venues including Barcelona's Teatre Lliure and Madrid's Teatro de la Abadía (2008).

12. Joyce McMillan, "Basque Drama," *Scotland on Sunday* (Festival insert) (August 25, 1996), 3.

13. Carles Santos, quoted in Luis G. Iberni, "Carles Santos estrena el musical *Ricardo y Elena*. 'Es una venganza contra mis padres'," *ABC* (El Cultural section) (March 5, 2000), 64–66 (65).

14. McMillan, "Basque Drama," 3.

15. Cover to program for "*Sama samaruck suck suck*. Ópera-circo de Carles Santos en la Nave de Sagunto," Generalitat Valenciana/Ciudad de las Artes Escénicas, September 2002.

16. Marta Cureses, "Santos Index," *Carles Santos*, Exhibition Catalogue (Castelló: Espai D'Art Contemporani de Castelló, 1999), 227–35 (227).

17. Carles Santos, cited in Clémence Coconnier, "A propósito de *Sama samaruck suck suck*," essay in the program for *Sama samaruck suck suck*, 20–24 (23).

18. Carles Santos, cited in Bowen, "Surrealism as a Way of Life," 3.

19. Carles Santos, "In Conversation with Ruth Mackenzie at the Edinburgh International Festival" (August 1996).

20. Carles Santos, quoted in Lambert, "*L'esplèndida vergonya del fet mal fet*," 41.

21. Carles Santos, quoted in Neus Miró, "A Conversation with Carles Santos," *Carles Santos*, Exhibition Catalogue (Castelló: Espai D'Art Contemporani de Castelló, 1999), 241–45 (243).

22. Carles Santos, quoted in Josep Ruvira, "The Artistic Dimensions of Carles Santos," *Carles Santos*, 227.

23. Ibid., 225.

24. Pablo Meléndez-Haddad, "Estéril y aplaudida provocación," *ABC* (November 6, 2003), 51.

25. For concrete examples of this, see pages 243–44 and 246 of this article.

26. See Miró, "A Conversation with Carles Santos," 248.

27. See Bowen, "Surrealism as a Way of Life," 3.

28. Catherine Lockerbie, "Surrealism and Spoof," *Scotsman* (August 24, 1996), 17.

29. For further details on the dismemberment of the piano in Santos's installation art and photographs, see note 38.

30. Twelve of these were a compilation of Rossini's "greatest hits" juxtaposed with lesser-known material from his youth, while six further pieces were compiled by Santos as homage to the Italian composer.

31. "Edinburgh Theatre: *The Composer, the Singer* . . . ," *The Times* (August 30, 2004) (unpaginated cutting from Edinburgh International Festival Press Office). The idea of the drops as a minimalist overture is also tackled by Agustí Fancelli, "Una gota de agua," *El País* (November 6, 2003), 39.

32. The term *inferno* is also used by Joan-Anton Benach when commenting on the opening episode; see Joan-Anton Benach, "Una filigrana desde el corazón de Rossini," *La Vanguardia* (November 6, 2003), 54.

33. Anonymous, "Carles Santos recrea la música de Rossini a partir de una gota de agua," *El País* (Comunidad Valenciana supplement) (December 16, 2004), 6.

34. Bono, "Carles Santos da una vuelta de tuerca a Rossini en Torrent," 9.

35. Clémence Coconnier, "A Drop and Rossini," essay in the program for *El compositor, la cantant, el cuiner i la pecadora*, Edinburgh International Festival, August 27–30, 2004.

36. On the maritime imagery of *L'esplèndida vergonya*, see pages 240, 241, and 246.

37. For further examples of this in *La pantera imperial* and other productions by Santos, see pages 241, 244–45, and 249–50 of this article.

38. Carles Santos, quoted in Lynne Walker, "Bach to the Here and Now," *Herald* (August 12, 1998), 16. The piano was the point of origin for Santos's retrospective, "Visca el piano!" (Long Live the Piano!) at the Fundació Joan Miró between June 30 and November 5, 2006, featuring dismembered, battered, and reconfigured pianos collected under the title "Pianos intervinguts" (Tampered Pianos) as well as celluloid prints and images of Santos practicing, his Imperial Bösendofer grand piano transferred from his Vinaròs home, and the errant, wandering pianola from *La pantera imperial*. For further details, see *Carles Santos: Long Live the Piano!*, ed. Guerrero, 45–72.

39. See Walker, "Bach to the Here and Now," 16.

40. Carles Santos, quoted in Walker, "Bach to the Here and Now," 16.

41. See ibid., 16.

42. See Mariaelena Roqué, "Going and Coming Back," *Mariaelena Roqué desvesteix Carles Santos*, Exhibition Catalogue, ed. Jaume Maymó (Barcelona: Institut de Cultura, Museu Tèxtil i d'Indumentària/Ajuntament de Barcelona, 2006), 271–305 (286–87).

43. Ana María Dávila, "Carles Santos reivindica al Joan Brossa más 'incómodo y atípico' en su nuevo espectáculo," *El Mundo* (April 25, 2008), 68.

44. Vicente Ponte, "The Sounding Body (Regarding Carles Santos)," *Carles Santos*, Exhibition Catalogue (Castelló: Espai D'Art Contemporani de Castelló, 1999), 235–40 (238).

45. For further information on these Catalan influences, including nods to Dalí's work and the art-deco décor of modernist Barcelona, see Delgado, "Composing for the Stage," 289–92.

46. Joan Clos, untitled foreword, in *Mariaelena Roqué desvesteix Carles Santos* (Barcelona: Ajuntament de Barcelona, 2006), 267. An exhibition held in 2006 at Barcelona's Textile and Clothing Museum titled "Mariaelena Roqué undresses Carles Santos" documented the breadth of their collaboration, with examples provided of her costumes and her working methods. Clos's observations are taken from the foreword to the exhibition catalogue.

47. For further details, see Maria M. Delgado, "Barcelona's Grec: A Change of

Name and a Change of Direction," *Western European Stages* 18, no. 3 (2006): 85–96 (96).

48. John Peter and Adrian Turpin, "*The Composer, the Singer, the Cook and the Sinner*," *Sunday Times*, September 5, 2004 (Edinburgh International Festival Press Office cutting).

49. Carles Santos, quoted in Cureses, "Santos Index," 232. For further details on the gastronomic references in Santos's work, see 378–80, 384–86.

50. Michael Billington, "*The Splendid Shame of the Deed Badly Done*," *Guardian* (G2 supplement) (August 28, 1996), 11.

51. José Miguel G. Cortés, "Introduction: Carles Santos in the EACC," in *Carles Santos*, Exhibition Catalogue (Castelló: Espai D'Art Contemporani de Castelló, 1999), 215–17 (216).

52. Quoted in Neus Miró, "A Conversation with Carles Santos," *Carles Santos*, 241–45 (241).

53. Joyce McMillan, "Rossini's Sensory Overload," *Scotsman* (S2 supplement) (August 30, 2004), 4.

54. See also Richard Morrison, "Flip your Wig to Crazy Dude Bach," *The Times* (September 1, 1998), 15.

55. See pages 243 and 252 for examples of this in *La pantera imperial* and *El compositor.*

56. Cited in Rodney Milne, "Variations on an Enigma," essay in the program for *El compositor, la cantant, el cuiner i la pecadora*, Edinburgh International Festival, August 27–30, 2005.

57. Mark Fisher, "*The Composer*," 18.

58. See Bono, "Carles Santos da una vuelta de tuerca a Rossini en Torrent," 9.

59. His solos too interrogate the relationship between authorship and performance. For further details see Delgado, "Composing for the Stage," 294.

60. Anonymous, "Carles Santos estrena en el TNC una ópera sentimental en latín sobre la posguerra," *La Vanguardia* (March 11, 2000), 47.

61. Ibid., 47.

62. Carles Santos, quoted in Justo Barranco, "Carles Santos prepara para el Nacional *Ricardo y Elena*, una obra inspirada en su juventud," *La Vanguardia* (August 20, 1999), 42.

63. Santos, cited in Iberni, "Carles Santos estrena el musical *Ricardo y Elena*," 65. It may also provide a link to his 1986 collaboration with Gelabert, *Desfigurat*, which juggled medieval Gregorian thematics.

64. See T. Monago, "El 'latín macarrónico' de Carles Santos," *Diario de Sevilla* (February 24, 2001), 52.

65. For further details see pages 248–50 of this essay.

66. Cortés, "Introduction: Carles Santos in the EACC," 216.

67. See Sara Sans, "Pulso ciudadano. Carles Santos," *La Vanguardia* (Vivir en Tarragona supplement) (May 30, 2000), 2.

68. See R.T., "Carles Santos concibe una pequeña ópera en latín y en blanco y negro," *El País* (November 17, 2000), 60.

69. Lachenmann's "thunderous musical style" has been compared to Santos's. See Glenn Loney, "The Edinburgh Festival 2004: Cutting Edges and Dull Blades," *Western European Stages* 16, no. 3 (2004): 65–70 (69).

70. For further information on Goebbels and Marthaler see Nicholas Till, "Street Fighting Mensch: Heiner Goebbels," *The Wire*, no. 229 (March 2003), 46–60, and Marvin Carlson, *Theatre Is More Beautiful than War: German Stage Directing in the Late Twentieth Century* (Iowa City: University of Iowa Press, 2009), 116–38.

71. For further details see Delgado, "Relocations, Reworking, Reopenings: Catalans in Madrid, Argentines in Barcelona," *Western European Stages* 23, no. 1 (2011): 13–30 (14–16).

INGRID MONSON

Tchekisse
Neba Solo's Senufo
Counterpoint in Action

NOTORIOUSLY DIFFICULT TO CAPTURE and communicate, the experience
of performance has always eluded the conventions of the scholarly article.
Charles Seeger despaired of this situation by declaring that at the heart of
musicological study lies the *linguocentric predicament:* the incommensurability between "music knowledge and feeling in music" and "speech knowledge of and feeling in music"[1] which results in a strange dilemma.

> To talk about music we have to use the full armament of verbiage . . .
> and much more, replete with universals and particulars, concepts
> and percepts, abstractness and concreteness, feeling and imagina-
> tion, and so forth; yet to know that there is no evidence whatever
> that the music compositional process, whether precomposed or
> composed in the act of singing or of playing an instrument, operates
> in any such terms.[2]

Some thirty years after Seeger's musings, advances in multi-media computer and internet-based technology offer rich possibilities for lessening—
although not eliminating—the gap between the analysis of music and its
sensory experience. In this essay, I experiment with internet-based media
examples (video, audio, image) as a means to explicate and analyze the performance of Neba Solo's *Tchekisse*, in what I hope is a musically compelling
way. Although the divide between text and sensory experience remains, the
use of performance material to explain and interpret other performance
material is at the heart of the endeavor. I first introduce Neba Solo, who is

a phenomenal bala[3] (wooden xylophone) player and composer from south-eastern Mali. I continue with an explanation of his composition *Tchekisse*, drawn from several video-recorded performances gathered during my ethnographic work in Mali, primarily in 2005. Media examples are viewable at http://nebasolo.com/ingridmonson/Senufo_Counterpoint.html, and they are essential to the narrative of the essay. I follow the performance with a broader cultural context for Neba Solo's work and conclude with some thoughts on musical scholarship in a more accessibly multi-media age.

Neba Solo

Souleymane Traoré, whose professional name is Neba Solo, was born in Nebadougou, Mali, in 1969, and is one of the most celebrated musicians in Mali. In 1995 he won the first prize in the bala competition at the Dundunba Top festival held in Koutiala, Mali (figure 1). Since then he has become a major star in Mali and performed internationally in France, the United States, and Korea. The overwhelming success of his recording *Can 2002* (2001) led to his being named Chevalier de l'Ordre National du Mali in 2002, and in August 2009 he was named an Officier de l'Ordre National du Mali, an even greater honor. He has several other albums, including *Kenedougou Foly* (1997), *Kene Balafons* (2000), a collaboration with an Iranian Trio Chemirani entitled *Falak* (2003), and more recently, *Neba Kady* (2008).[4]

To provide an analogy from an American perspective, he's something like the Charlie Parker and Charles Mingus of the Senufo bala. Like Parker he is virtuosic and a true original, whom all the younger bala players strive to emulate. Like Mingus he's a composer who invents all the instrumental parts and aurally transmits them to his band. His song lyrics comment on contemporary social and public health issues such as vaccination, AIDS, female excision, protecting the environment, and political corruption. He views part of his mission as sensitizing people to important ethical and political issues of the day, as well as alerting them to what they can do to keep themselves healthy.[5]

Souleymane Traoré was raised in the village of Nebadougou, twenty-five miles northeast of Sikasso, at the southern tip of Mali (figure 2). Sikasso is Mali's second largest city. The Kenedougou region, as the area around Sikasso is known, is one of Mali's richest agricultural areas (known for cotton, rice, millet, corn, vegetables, and fruit) and has the country's highest annual rainfall (55 inches per year). Sikasso—historically a trad-

Fig. 1. Neba Solo holding trophy from the Festival Triangle du Balafon.
Photo by Ingrid Monson.

ing crossroads inhabited by both Jula merchants and Senufo people—was
also the seat of the Kenedougou Kingdom, a late nineteenth-century state
known for its resistance to the Samory Touré, and later the French.

As a child, Neba Solo herded cattle and learned to be a farmer as well
as a musician. He did not attend school but became literate as an adult
through taking a course on how to write Bamanankan, which he speaks
in addition to Senufo and French. His father, Zano Traoré, was a well-
respected village musician and *donso* who very early on recognized his son's
extraordinary talent.[6] As a child, Neba Solo learned all of the instruments
used in the Kenedougou region—including bala, tchatchara, karinyan, ka-

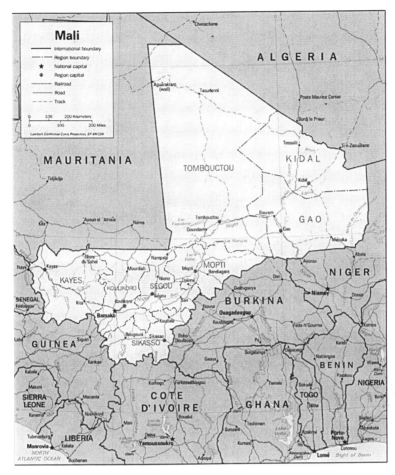

Fig. 2. Map of Mali. Source: University of Texas Libraries.

melngoni, and bara drum. As a teenager, he and his older brother Ousmane formed a group that played for celebrations, festivals, dances, naming ceremonies, and other social events at villages throughout the Kenedougou region. Souleymane's reputation quickly spread by word of mouth, and soon people were asking each other whether they had heard the Solo from Neba (*Solo* is a common nickname for *Souleymane*). Soon everyone was calling him Neba Solo. Although his music sounds "traditional" to Western ears by virtue of its acoustic instrumentation, it actually represents a professionalization and modernization of traditional Senufo music.[7]

Captivated by the bass lines of Alpha Blondy's reggae recording of *Je-*

Fig. 3. Neba Solo making a bala. Photo by Deborah Foster.

rusalem, the eighteen-year-old Souleymane had an epiphany as he walked through the streets of Bamako. What if he were to build a bigger bala with more bass notes and develop a new ensemble style featuring more prominent bass lines? What if he were to change the traditional tuning of the pentatonic bala so that it would be compatible with the tunings of other Malian instruments, such as the six-stringed kamelngoni? By Senufo tradition, undertaking this experiment required asking for his father's permission. Zano Traoré granted Souleymane a period of time in which to develop his ideas that would culminate in a recorded example of the new style. If his father was pleased, he would give his blessing to his son's musical direction. Souleymane added three bass notes to the bala's traditional seventeen keys and also experimented with various tunings (figure 3). First and foremost, he wanted to expand the role of the bass in the music. His new version of traditional Senufo tunes, with an expanded texture and new tuning, ultimately earned the approval of both his father and local audiences. National observers credit him with revolutionizing the place of the bala in Mali.[8]

The new style reconfigured the musical ensemble. Instead of three balas—one for bass, one for treble, and one for accompaniment—Solo used two balas. The accompaniment parts are distributed between the two instruments as follows. His brother Siaka Traoré, on the treble bala, gener-

Fig. 4. Neba Solo group performing. Ntogonasso, Mali, 5 March 2005. Instruments visible: bass bala, treble bala, bara drum. Photo by Ingrid Monson.

ally improvises melodies with his right hand while playing accompaniment parts with the left hand. Neba Solo, on the bass bala, usually improvises bass lines with his left hand and plays accompaniment parts with his right hand (figure 4).

The interplay between the two brothers creates a rich contrapuntal texture among interlocking parts. What is remarkable in performance is their variety of ways of modulating from one configuration of parts to another, often with sections of increasing tempo. This new contemporary sound for the bala modernized an instrument that had been dismissed by urban dwellers as a primarily village instrument that was not suitable for modern (professionalized urban) music. Indeed, to understand the respect in which Neba Solo is now held, one needs to know that when he first came to Sikasso many dismissed him as a player of the *fali gala bugula* (ribs of a donkey). When the group was scheduled to play at the anniversary of Radio Kene in Sikasso, the director of the station, Daouda Mariko, took one look at the balas and bara drums (signs of the village) and asked them to leave the stage. They began to play offstage, winning over both the audience and the director, who later became one of Neba Solo's chief advocates.[9] In this sense, Neba Solo has become a figure of particular pride for the people of Kenedougou who live in the dozens of small villages surrounding Sikasso.

Tchekisse

Tchekisse is a love song and a dance, Neba Solo's arrangement and development of a traditional Senufo song. The lyrics speak of a young woman who excuses herself to take a walk after dinner: she longs to hear the sound of her beloved's voice as he waits for her. So far, the piece is based on a song traditionally sung by young women of marriageable age.[10] Then Neba Solo abruptly turns to the topic of work, more specifically, the flute that calls people to work, especially those who are reluctant to work. In order to be part of the family (the Senufo family), he reminds his audience, you must work. Even if you can't farm, you must do something else. You must get up in the morning and do something constructive. Neba Solo explains that he likes to include additional messages in his love songs—to have two messages at once. *Tchekisse* continues by describing the feelings of tremendous longing experienced when a lover must travel or go away for an extended period of time: "Don't forget me, think of what we have done together; think always of me." After he has sung the lyrics, Neba Solo invites people to dance Tchekisse, the name of a particular step. "Nyans an fe," he calls. "Dance with your big beautiful behinds . . ."

What I am calling *Senufo counterpoint* refers to the musical texture accompanying the song. I use the Western term, with all its possible misinterpretation, to draw attention to the importance of the combination of parts in this music, and the bala players' aural awareness of the independent melodic parts of each of their hands as well as their combination.

Listen to the opening of *Tchekisse* as recorded on Neba Solo's album *Can 2002* (Media Example 1, http://nebasolo.com/ingridmonson/Senufo_Counterpoint.html). An introduction featuring a melody in parallel octaves and the opening phrases of the song in stop-time leads to a melody in the treble bala that cues the entrance of the full band. Each bala then begins a basic pattern, which serves to establish the rhythmic framework (*ncintoige*) of the first section of the piece, in this case the rhythm of the cultivators. The instruments heard are the treble and bass bala, tchatchara (a pair of large shaken rattles), low and high bara drums, drum set, and karinyan (a metal scaper).

A series of video and audio examples will convey the component parts of *Tchekisse*, some principles of variation, and the place of improvisation in the group's performances of the piece. There are two large sections in the composition, a medium-tempo first section during which the lyrics are sung and a faster second section, featuring up-tempo improvisational solos, section breaks, and spectacular synchronized dancing. Media Examples 2 and 3 show Neba Solo demonstrating the treble and bass bala parts that define the rhythmic feel of the first section. In the treble part (which Siaka Traoré plays in performance), notice the triple subdivision and how an interlocking of the left and right hands produces the melody (Media Example 2). The bass part interlocks with the treble melody and establishes a strong bass line (Media Example 3). Culturally, the bass and treble are thought of as a mother and her children. The authority of the mother is emphasized in the Bamanankan proverb *n'i ye min men baladenw da, balamba de y'a fo* (Whatever you hear in the bala children's mouth, it is the bala mother who has said it).

Replay the treble part and clap your hands (or tap your foot) where you perceive the beat. Do the same thing with the bass part. When I've presented these examples to live audiences in the United States, people frequently place the beat of the treble pattern as in Media Example 4; for the bass part, like Media Example 5. These points match the places I first heard the beat when learning these bala patterns. The listener placing the beat of the treble pattern as in Media Example 4 takes the highest note of the pattern as the beat-inducing accent. Students of African and African diasporic musics will not be surprised to learn that the beat as performed by the Neba Solo group resides in another location.

Now listen to where Neba Solo places the beat (with his foot tap) as he plays this variation of the bass pattern (Media Example 6). He taps his foot in a 2:3 relationship to the right-hand part of his pattern. Listen also to Media Example 7 in which I clap the correct placement of the beat for the treble part. This beat matches where the dancers step. The beat comes one eighth-note to the left of where I heard it when learning the pattern. It is not that the beat placement is "natural" to the Senufo and "unnatural" to us; rather it is a compositional decision by Neba Solo. Mr. Traoré explained to me that in order to keep people from easily imitating him, "I often seek to complicate the piece so that those who are in the process of imitating have a problem playing it exactly like me. . . . I often take weak note and make it the basis of the beat."[11]

In notation the alignment of the parts can be represented as in figure 5. Figure 6 shows the same passage in TUBs notation, which makes the tied notes in the right hand of the bass look less awkward.[12] In fact, there is nothing awkward about playing the part once the interlocking of the hands is mastered. In teaching bala parts, Neba Solo often corrects by showing a student the places where the two hands come together (the white-headed upward arrows in the bass part of figure 5), which then serve as important physical points of orientation for the player. Some intervals are also labeled to show that the two-handed points of attack in these patterns are on perfect intervals: P8, P5, P4. The dotted line in the lower part shows how one of the few imperfect intervals occurs successively rather than vertically. Of course, the pentatonic scale (interval vector 032140), with its greater preponderance of fourths, fifths, and seconds plays into this. As I learned these parts during my fieldwork, I found myself noticing ways in which the interlocking parts in many ways conformed to the pedagogical principles of Western counterpoint: points of arrival on consonances, the frequent use of contrary motion, and the melodic character of each interlocking part. For me, one of the intriguing things about the music of Neba Solo is its fabulous cross-rhythms that are at the same time tuneful, a quality characteristic of music from Mali more generally. Such music goes a long way toward undermining the erroneous idea that African music concerns only rhythm.[13]

Both repetition of key patterns and their variation play central roles in the development of the performance: in Media Example 8, Mr. Traoré demonstrates a variation of the bass part. Another key aspect of this music in performance is the seamless movement from one bala pattern to another as time unfolds. There is also often an exchange of roles between the brothers as the shifting from one bala idea to another takes place. Watch and listen to Media Example 9, where Neba Solo moves from a variation of the bass pattern to an upper register accompaniment pattern that continues by migrating smoothly down an octave. Take note of the higher register pattern: in the concert footage to come of Siaka Traoré's improvised solo on treble bala, it serves as the accompaniment to a peak moment in his solo.

Let's experience the opening of a performance of *Tchekisse* that took place on 5 March 2005 in Ntogonasso, Mali (Media Example 10). The occasion was a Unesco/Radio Kayira tour dedicated to AIDS education. This is a rough version of the opening, as the female vocalist Djelika Gantiege has trouble synchronizing in octaves with Neba Solo's lead vocal. In performance studies, it seems important to present not simply exemplary performances but also those where the difficulties and challenges of consistency in performance break through. After all, a few minutes later this same performance features a remarkable treble bala solo by Siaka Traoré. In Media Example 11, we hear Neba Solo complete the lyric of *Tchekisse*, and the treble bala begins to improvise. Two moments may stand out: when Mr. Traoré begins a repeating pattern that seems to increase the tempo (but does not), and toward the end of clip when he pauses and then begins playing intensely in octaves. At this point begin to listen for the upper register bass bala accompaniment part that we saw Neba Solo demonstrate in

Fig. 5. Notation of treble and bass bala parts. Transcribed by I. Monson.

	12	1	2	3	4	5	6	7	8	9	10	11	(12)
Bala T R		E 1	G 2		E 1			1 e	G 2		E 1		
Bala T L	b 4			D 5		A 3		3 a		D 5			(b 4)
Bala B R	B 4		G 2		E 1	A 3	A 3		G 2		E 1	B 4	B 4
Bala B L			B 4				E 1		A 3	A 3	D 5		
PULSE		x			x			x			x		

Fig. 6. TUBS notation of the treble and bala parts.

Media Example 9. The flow between song, solo, and accompaniment forms a key dimension of the aesthetic pleasure in Neba Solo performances.

Watch Media Example 12 to see concert footage of the entire first section to *Tchekisse* from a performance that took place in Karangana, Mali, on 4 March 2005 (the day before the Ntogonasso performance). A large public courtyard, bounded by a four-foot-high concrete-block wall, serves as the open-air concert hall: the performance space is typical for a small town or large village in Mali. A cleaner musical opening is heard in this rendition. You will notice some visual clutter at the beginning, however: three men take turns photographing Neba Solo in performance. The emcee for the Radio Kayira tour (in the green, blue, and yellow patterned shirt) actually takes a picture of his friend standing right next to Neba Solo with no apparent concern that he might be disturbing the performer. Neba Solo shows no apparent irritation, since such occurrences are common in Mali, no matter how renowned the performer: even in more formal concert spaces in the capital city of Bamako, audience members often take the stage to dance, be photographed with, or in some cases hug the performer.[14] The boundary between performer and audience in Mali is generally far more porous than in the United States.

Musically, Siaka Traoré's solo on the treble bala (beginning at 2:44) differs considerably from the one in the Ntogonasso performance, although certain elements remain constant: moving into a riff figure (3:10) that cross-cuts the time in a way that seems to increase the tempo; the rising figure following it (3:19); and the playing in octaves that cues Neba Solo's shift into his high-register accompaniment part. In both performances the first section builds up excitement through moving from one patterned idea to another, variation, and improvisation. Drawing material from more than one performance makes apparent both the advantages and drawbacks of recorded media: the performance in Ntogonasso is better lit (thanks to the presence of professional videographers from Malian television), Siaka Traoré's solo is more inspired, but the performance of the lyrics to the song is more compelling in Karangana. When selecting media to include, audio and visual considerations can be at cross-purposes. I didn't use the opening of the Karangana performance because of the distraction of the photographers in the visual frame, yet despite its clear visuals, the Ntogonasso performance included one of the most problematic song openings and also one of the most compelling treble bala solos.

So far, we've only seen material from the first section of *Tchekisse*. The second section quickens the tempo considerably, as the virtuosic synchronized dancing of the brothers Bocary and Ibrahim Dembele leads to the climax of the piece. Their choreography unfolds over the contrapuntal fabric created by the bass and treble balas, featuring solos by both. In Media Example 13, Neba Solo demonstrates some of the accompanying parts he uses in section two. He plays a constant accompaniment part with the right hand and a varied bass part with the left: this provides an example of what is meant by Neba Solo playing accompaniment with the right hand and improvising bass parts with the left. Note that he plays a 3 against 4 pattern with the left hand at the same time that he doubles the number of strokes with the right hand. In full performance footage from a concert at Sanders Theatre at Harvard University on 10 November 2005 (Media Example 14), notice that Neba Solo's improvising left hand and steady right hand pattern are matched in inverse by Siaka Traoré. He plays a repeating ostinato in the left hand as he moves from riff figure to riff figure with his right hand, developing a solo as he goes. Many of these riffs stay constant from performance to performance, but their timing and order do not. When the dancers begin a step where they kick each other's feet in time, the band moves to a new riff figure (2:07) that ultimately leads to Neba Solo's solo on the bass bala, accompanied by a spectacular treble riff on the higher-pitched bala. From here, Neba Solo signals the re-entrance of the vocal, which is done in stop-time: the bass bala temporarily drops out as Neba Solo sings the lyric. A call from the leader's bass bala signals the approaching coda as the dancers pause. When they begin their intricate footwork again, a final burst of energy from the group leads to the close.

Cultural Context

In my broader project, Neba Solo's life and music serve as a kind of aural and interpretive focus that sheds light on a number of cultural, musical, and interpretive issues in the fields of African studies, ethnomusicology, anthropology, and globalization studies. Among these are the relationship between tradition and innovation, the impact of digital technology in the twenty-first century, the role of music in social commentary and public health education, and the role of global ambitions in the local musical imagination.

The fact that Neba Solo is Senufo in a predominantly Mande Mali provides an important cultural context for understanding the significance of his reconfiguration of the pentatonic bala. Mande heritage is widely celebrated in Malian national culture through the history of the great Mali Empire of the thirteenth to sixteenth centuries and its founding figure Sunjata Keita. The prestige form of Mande music in Mali is *jeliya*—the music of the jeliw, or griots.[15] Jeliw are hereditary musicians, one of several occupations of the *nyamakalaw*, the hereditary artisanal strata of society, which also includes blacksmiths, leatherworkers, potters, and orators known as *funew*. Jeliw musicians have the hereditary right to play certain instruments including the kora, ngoni, and mande bala (which is heptatonically rather than pentatonically tuned). Jeliw and other artisans play complex roles in Malian society. They are simultaneously respected, for their cultural gifts and role as mediators, and disparaged, for their right to demand money from people at social occasions. They are also known for their spiritual powers, that is, their knowledge of the secrets of *nyama* (the Bamanankan word for life force), which can be deployed for good or evil. The Mande bala plays a powerful role in the *Sunjata*, the founding epic of Mali. Sunjata's ability to defeat the Sosso king Soumarou Kante was made possible by Sunjata's jeli Balla Fasséké—who discovered the secret chamber housing Soumarou Kante's spiritual objects, including a magical heptatonic bala—and also by Sunjata's half sister Nana Triban, who revealed the white cock as Kante's taboo spiritual item. Balla Fasséké's bala later became an important instrument of *jeliya*.

The pentatonic bala played by Neba Solo holds a far humbler place in the symbolic imaginary. Found in southeastern Mali, Côte d'Ivoire, and Burkina Faso, it is considered a village instrument, not played by hereditary groups of musicians with special rights. When I mentioned to jeli musicians in Bamako that I was studying bala with Neba Solo in Sikasso, one said to me, "His bala has only five notes; ours has seven." In other words, prestige should be on the side of studying Mande bala and *jeliya*. When I mentioned this conversation to Neba Solo's brother Zico, he remarked, "Well, Neba Solo can do things with five notes that they can't do with seven!"

One reason for my interest in Neba Solo is that the music of southeastern Mali is perhaps the least studied of the major musical genres in Mali. Although there have long been historic links and overlaps between the Mande, Fulbe, Jula, and Wasulunke in this economically vital region of Mali, its history and culture are not well studied. Nevertheless, pentatonic music from southern Mali has become quite prominent in national musical culture, and internationally as well, through the Wasulu music of Oumou Sangare, Mali's most famous female singer, and the music of hunters.

All this lends significance to Neba Solo's prominence in Mali. To travel with his band is like being with a rock star. He is one of the favorite musicians of Amadou Toumani Touré, the former president of Mali, and was often invited to play at state functions. Indeed, when the president of the Congo visited Mali in 2007 and heard several musical groups including famous jeliw, it was in the end only Oumou Sangare and Neba Solo, neither of whom are jeliw, that he invited to perform in the Congo.

Increasingly, scholars are emphasizing that Mande heritage alone does not account for the richness of Mali's music. Instead, it coexists within a wider array of ethnic and regional styles that have collectively shaped what Eric Charry has termed a sahel-savanna music culture.[16] Included here are the musical cultures of the Tuareg, Soninke, Bamana, Fulbe, Bozo, and Senufo: when one talks about the the culture of the Kenedougou region, one is talking not only about Senufo culture per se but about its many overlaps with the cultures and languages nearby. Although Neba Solo is not a jeli, when he performs certain songs, he utilizes many performative aspects of *jeliya* in communicating with his audience—most notably, circulating through the audience and exhorting members of his audience to live up to their culture and traditions, and do the right thing. He is often invited to perform at prominent social events in Bamako, for families who are not Senufo or from the Kenedougou region. In other words he has cross-ethnic appeal in a multi-ethnic society.

The Performance Visualized

In presenting *Tchekisse* my strategy has been to use solo video footage of the different parts to explicate their role in larger ensemble trajectories that are partly composed and partly improvised. A common feature of music-analytical argumentation is the parsing of the performance (or work) into constituent parts, which then are made to function as signs of a larger musical process (or form). Since music is so multidimensional—comprised of intricate combinations of timbre, rhythm, pitch, pace, attack, and dynamics—singling out particular parts in a performance necessarily imposes a hierarchy of value, a necessarily reductive interpretive framework that, nevertheless, provides a window onto a key aspect of the musician's craft: understanding the central elements of sound and bodily coordination that make possible the navigation from one musical event to another, in ways that can never be predicted entirely from the constituent elements alone. In using Neba Solo's demonstration of the different parts, I've observed a classic ethnomusicological desideratum of taking the performer's hierarchy of musical elements as a point of departure, so providing an interpretation of the performance that focuses on its aural events.

As Nicholas Cook has argued, however, musical events are never alone, but rather embedded in relationships among sounds and their various representations.[17] The visual components of performance seen on the video recording add color, motion, dance, gesture, facial expression, and audience reaction to the multidimensional space that music coordinates. By seeing the dancers, for example, viewers unfamiliar with the beat conventions of the rhythmic feel of *Tchekisse* can find the right place by simply matching the steps of the dancers with their feet or hands, which is how young children often learn. As they do so, they may adjust their perception of the location of the beat. When a young bala player has difficulty finding a pattern, Neba Solo's teaching strategy is to ask them to hold their sticks limply as he plays their arms for them, thus inculcating the bodily feel of the note placement. Finding the beat, in a rhythmically complex musical structure, seems more daunting in the abstract than when cued by a multiplicity of visual and aural events. These multisensory cues to perception of the auditory whole still require the experiencer to develop aural representations of the whole and part that aid in navigating musical and performance space more generally.

I have called the conscious focusing of sensory attention that can yield differing experiences of the same event *perceptual agency*.[18] I had in mind the multiple auditory representations that can arise as a product of focusing on a variety of parts of the musical texture—the "two side" of a two-against-three polyrhythm, the composite or resultant pattern produced by a four-against-three polyrhythm, the bass line in a jazz ensemble, or the piano voicings comped in relationship to an improvised saxophone solo. Moving from one aural focus to another—say from the bass to the soloing instrument—can yield different experiences of the same event. Yet this process seems hardly restricted to the aural domain. Focusing visually on various elements of the performance as well as hearing them would also seem to provide potential grounds for alternative understandings of this multi-faceted performance.

One final remark. Although the video footage was all recorded from live performance, its "liveness" evaporated the moment the record button disengaged. All forms of recording, it seems to me—whether writing, audio recording, video recording, or photography—fix their objects, sensory modality differences notwithstanding. Auslander's observation that the live and the mediatized are mutually dependent seems apt here.[19] Our ability to video-record performances offers the possibility of presenting our explanations of music in a more musical and corporeal fashion; nevertheless, the divide between experience itself and our interpretations of it remains. This is cause neither for celebration nor for mourning, but is a recognition of the complex human counterpoint—visual, audio, tactile, historical, symbolic—that music always carries with it.

LIST OF MEDIA EXAMPLES

Media examples are at http://nebasolo.com/ingridmonson/Senufo_Counterpoint. html. All media recorded by Ingrid Monson, except where indicated.

Media Example 1. Audio clip. Neba Solo, opening of *Tchekisse*, Can 2002. Bamako, Mali, March 2001, Mali K7 SA. Recorded by Mali K7 SA.
Media Example 2. Video clip. Neba Solo demonstrating treble bala part to first section of *Tchekisse*. Sikasso, Mali, January 2005.
Media Example 3. Video clip. Neba Solo demonstrating bass bala part to the first section of *Tchekisse*. Sikasso, Mali.
Media Example 4. Audio clip. One possible beat placement for the treble part.
Media Example 5. Audio clip. One possible beat placement for the bass part.
Media Example 6. Video clip. Neba Solo demonstrating the bass pattern with beat placement. Sikasso, Mali.
Media Example 7. Audio clip. Treble pattern with correct beat placement.
Media Example 8. Video clip. Neba Solo demonstrating variation of the bass bala part.
Media Example 9. Video clip. Neba Solo moving from one bala part to another.
Media Example 10. Video clip. Neba Solo group performing the opening to *Tchekisse*. Ntogonasso, Mali, 5 March 2005.

Media Example 11. Video clip. Siaka Traoré performing improvised solo on *Tchekisse*. Ntogonasso, Mali, 5 March 2005

Media Example 12. Video Clip. *Tchekisse*, section 1. Karangana, Mali, 4 March 2005.

Media Example 13. Video clip. Neba Solo demonstrating bass bala parts to the second section of *Tchekisse*.

Media Example 14. Video clip. Neba Solo group performing *Tchekisse*. Sanders Theatre, Harvard University, 10 November 2005.

NOTES

1. Charles Seeger, *Studies in Musicology, 1935–1975* (Berkeley: University of California Press, 1977), 47.

2. Ibid., 41.

3. The instrument is also known as the balafon, the French word for the instrument. In Bamanankan (Bambara in French) the instrument is known as the *bala;* to play it is *bala fo,* literally to make the bala speak.

4. Neba Solo, *Neba Ka Di* (2008); *Can 2002* (Bamako, Mali K7 SA 2001); *Kene Balafons* (Cobalt 9295, 2000); *Kenedougou Foly: La Nouvelle Vague Du Balafon* (Cobalt 09281-2, 1997); Neba Solo and Trio Chemirani, *Falak* (Cobalt 09352-2, 2003).

5. The information about Neba Solo presented here is the product of three research and teaching trips to Mali (three weeks in 2002, four and a half months in 2005, and six weeks in 2007).

6. *Donso* is the Bamanankan word for hunter, a concept in Mali that is much broader that the term *hunter* implies. The hunter is also a healer, seeker, and repository of deep cultural knowledge. See Lucy Durán, "Women, Music, and the 'Mystique' of Hunters in Mali." In *The African Diaspora: A Musical Perspective,* ed. Ingrid Monson (New York: Garland, 2000), 137–85.

7. Interview with Neba Solo, 12 January 2005, Sikasso, Mali.

8. Interview with Neba Solo and Yacouba Traoré, 12 January 2005, Sikasso, Mali; Kassim Traoré, *Bamako Hebdo,* 8 August 2009. http://www. maliactu.net/index.php?option=com_content&view=article&id=2977%3Aremise-de-decorations-aux-artistes--neba-solo-officier-de-lordre-national-du-mali-&Itemid=99 (accessed 23 November 2009).

9. Interview with Neba Solo, 16 February 2005, Sikasso, Mali.

10. Interview with Neba Solo, 15 January 2005, Sikasso, Mali.

11. Interview with Neba Solo, 12 April 2005, Sikasso, Mali.

12. TUBS (Time Unit Box System) notation was developed in ethnomusicology by James Koettig. Each box represents a fixed unit of time. In Koettig's usage an X denoted a rhythmic event and a blank box a rest. Here, I've placed pitch names that correspond to the transcription in each box, as well as the number of the bala keys, which enable it to be used as a kind of tablature. The numbers indicate the eighth notes of the staff notation. There are two principal advantages to TUBS rhythms in the notation of complex polyrhythms: (1) a particular subdivision of the rhythmic events (duple or triple) need not be imposed, and (2) a pattern can be arranged to begin on any time unit without having to adjust the notation with ties and visually confusing displacements.

13. In *Representing African Music: Postcolonial Notes, Queries, Positions* (New York:

Routledge, 2003), Kofi Agawu argues passionately for not reducing African music to rhythm.

14. When Oumou Sangare performs she is often hugged by audience members on stage.

15. In Bamanankan, the singular form is *jeli*, the plural *jeliw* (pronounced jel-ee-ou).

16. Eric Charry, *Mande Music: Traditional and Modern Music of the Maninka and Mandinka of Western Africa* (Chicago: University of Chicago Press, 2000), 291.

17. Nicholas Cook, *Analysing Musical Multimedia* (Oxford: Oxford University Press, 1998), 23, 270.

18. Ingrid Monson, "Hearing, Seeing, and Perceptual Agency," *Critical Inquiry* 34, no. S2 (2008): S36–S58.

19. Philip Auslander, *Liveness: Performance in a Mediatized Culture* (New York, Routledge, 1999).

ROGER MOSELEY

Playing Games with Music (and Vice Versa)

Ludomusicological Perspectives on
Guitar Hero and *Rock Band*

> I wonder about the future, when not so many people are playing *Guitar Hero* or *Rock Band* any more. The many guitar controllers made of plastic: where do they go? Have you seen that, in Africa, some countries accept e-waste from Europe? I saw so many CD and cassette players. I really don't like that kind of situation.
> —MASAYA MATSUURA[1]

CENTURIES FROM NOW, one might imagine, archaeologists combing land-fill sites in Africa in search of clues concerning musical culture at the beginning of the millennium will be confronted with bewildering evidence. The organic materials from which traditional instruments are currently made will have decayed, their metal turned to rust. If not irreparably damaged, the delicate circuit boards of the digital audio workstations on which early twenty-first-century music is created and recorded will have been frozen in obsolescence; the binary code enciphering their musical operations, etched in concentric rings on hard disk platters, will need to be decrypted. In any case, all such remnants will be dwarfed by mountains of undersized plastic guitars, preserved in excellent condition owing to their petrochemical composition. Manufactured in China, they will be found to have traveled all over the globe—particularly to North America—en route to their final resting places.

Organologists of the future might puzzle over the musical function of these stringless and pickup-less pseudo-chordophones, for it will quickly

279

become apparent that they have never been capable of generating any sound beyond the clatter of five brightly colored buttons on the neck and the click of a rocker switch in the middle of the body: they lack even a MIDI interface. Were they toys for children, mere models of "real" guitars, or fetish objects that transmitted the bardic lore of ancient "rock 'n' roll"? Did they represent an electronic evolution of the electric guitar, or were they aligned with the revolution of early digital musical culture? Did their ubiquity signify a democratization or a debasement of musical skills and values? Most intriguing of all, how were they played, and what kinds of musical experience did they enable?

At the height of their popularity in 2008, the *Guitar Hero* and *Rock Band* franchises seduced millions of players with the promise of the ultimate in rock-star verisimilitude.[2] By the end of 2010, however, players had begun to relegate their plastic instruments to the attic in what will perhaps prove to be the first legs of their journeys to African landfill sites such as those observed by Masaya Matsuura, the Japanese musician and game developer who has been hailed as a founder of the "rhythm-action" genre of digital games.[3] By pondering the ultimate fate of *Guitar Hero* and *Rock Band* peripherals and their unintended environmental consequences, Matsuura tacitly draws attention to the complex economic and cultural forces that both shape and issue from the West's insatiable appetite for novel forms of entertainment. From the vantage point of an imaginary future, we might gain perspective on the vertiginous rise and decline of these games over the course of the last decade. But beyond that, we might also begin to map out larger historical and geographical networks that locate *Guitar Hero* and *Rock Band* within an epistemological and technological trajectory connecting Athanasius Kircher's Rome, Jacques de Vaucanson's Lyon, Charles Babbage's London, and Matsuura's Tokyo to Cambridge, Massachusetts, home of Harmonix Music Systems, the games' original development studio. Before we proceed, however, a short description of these games and the type of musical gameplay they enable will be in order for the uninitiated.[4] For this purpose, *Rock Band 3*, developed by Harmonix and published by MTV Games in 2010, will represent the ten *Guitar Hero* and *Rock Band* games released for digital game consoles between 2005 and 2010.[5]

Rock Band 3 invites up to seven people to form a band in order to "perform" rock songs from the 1960s to the 2010s via a game console, a television, and plastic peripherals in the form of microphones, guitars, a two-octave keyboard, and a drum kit. On guitar, drums, and keyboard, the games demand rhythmic accuracy and manual dexterity: players watch

Fig. 1. Promotional image featuring the *Rock Band 3* gameplay interface, reproduced courtesy of Harmonix Music Systems. The lyrics and relative pitches for three vocalists scroll from right to left along the "staff" at the top of the screen, while color-coded "gems" travel toward the four instrumentalists (from left to right: guitar, drums, keyboard, and bass). The guitar and keyboard are depicted in "Pro" mode, discussed in note 64. The vertical bar on the left indicates how well each member of the band is playing; the current collective score and star rating are on the right. (Image © 2010 Harmonix Music Systems, Inc.)

color-coded "gems" travel toward them via "note tunnels" that constitute a form of animated tablature, melding a piano roll with the iconography of a guitar fretboard and the multi-dimensionality of a journey through both space and time (see figure 1).[6] Players react either by hitting the appropriate color-coded drums or keys, or by holding down the relevant colored buttons on the neck of the guitar and activating the "strum bar," when the gems cross a threshold at the bottom of the screen. Using a karaoke-style microphone, the vocalist attempts to hit the pitches indicated by horizontal lines across the top of the screen, although he or she is free to switch octaves (and phonemes) at will. The band's collaborative performance is quantified in points and reflected in the on-screen crowd's reaction: play well and they will respond enthusiastically; play poorly and boos will ring out. At the successful completion of each song, the game presents players with metrical evaluations of their rendition, summarized by a star rating akin to those dispensed by music critics. The group's "career" progresses through numerous set-lists and venues across the world until global rock-stardom has been achieved (or the console has been powered down for the night).

The enormous commercial success that *Guitar Hero* and *Rock Band* enjoyed between 2006 and 2009 was as unexpected as it was dramatic. Faced with the unlikely transformation of the concept from an obscure, expensive, and impractical digital game into a multi-billion-dollar pop-culture phenomenon, commentators grasped for superlatives.[7] The *New York Times* hailed *The Beatles: Rock Band* as "a cultural watershed," "a transformative entertainment experience," and quite possibly "the most important video game yet made."[8] For many rock stars and guitar teachers, conversely, the proliferation of plastic guitars was an insulting commoditization that trivialized the rock-star ethos and its discourses of authenticity, rebellion, and individualism.[9] In 2008, Alex Rigopulos, co-founder of Harmonix, alumnus of the MIT Media Lab, and one of *Time Magazine*'s 100 most influential people of 2008, asserted, "We're at the beginning of a . . . revolution of music now where playing with music [rather than listening to it] is what people are going to expect to do with music that they love."[10] Few dared to disagree, for better or for worse, especially since MTV's acquisition of Harmonix in 2006 had lent powerful corporate backing to the notion that revenue streams from digital games might even save the entire recorded music industry. By the end of 2009, however, the multi-billion-dollar bubble was deflating fast: music-based game sales were down by $784 million on the previous year.[11] Although macroeconomic factors doubtless contributed to this state of affairs, the game publishers' exploitation of their franchises also led to accusations of overkill.[12] MTV's parent company Viacom disposed of Harmonix in 2010, thereby restoring the studio's independence, and Activision announced the closure of its *Guitar Hero* division the following year.[13]

Despite the unprecedented and transformative impact that technological innovations have had on music over the last two centuries, the period is also littered with the detritus of futures that never came to be. Alongside Johann Nepomuk Maelzel's wildly successful metronome, for instance, languishes his ill-fated panharmonicon.[14] Moreover, when a new technology manages to grip the imagination, it rarely does so in quite the manner envisaged by those behind it: think of the saxophone, the phonograph, or the Hammond B-3 organ. From this perspective, perhaps it was the very clarity of the future promised by *Guitar Hero* and *Rock Band* that so quickly reduced them to yesterday's vision of tomorrow. At the same time, their rise and fall adheres to the template of a classic rock narrative: the arc charting their fortunes traces that of the indie band whose meteoric commercial success elicits disdain from elitists and accusations of "selling out" from its devoted fan-base, precipitating a rapid return to obscurity. Just as the games' popularity grew in large part through the buzz created via online communities, viral marketing, and other forms of memetic transmission (including old-fashioned word of mouth), so did their fortunes wither owing to the same relentless pursuit of novelty on the part of consumers and the saturation of the marketplace that was fueled by ruthless competition between the games' publishers.[15] There is no doubt that *Guitar Hero* and *Rock Band* were thoroughly enmeshed in the labyrinthine networks of (re)mediation through which twenty-first-century economic and social capital circulate, as Kiri Miller has shown; she has also demonstrated however, that first-person encounters with these games are characterized by an intense immersion in the moment.[16] The engrossing experiences that they afford hints at a deep relationship between the absorptive and ephemeral attributes of musical performance and digital gameplay. In this essay, I will explore the terms on which that relationship might be articulated under the rubric of "ludomusicology."

To the best of my knowledge, the digital-game researcher and music theorist Guillaume Laroche coined the Graeco-Latin word "ludomusicology" in 2007.[17] Whereas Laroche's deployment of the term has reflected a primary interest in music *within* games, I am more concerned with the extent to which music might be understood as a mode of gameplay. In my view, ludomusicology involves the study of both the musically playful and the playfully musical. Bringing music and play into contact in this way offers access to the undocumented means by which composers, designers, programmers, performers, players, and audiences interact with music, games, and one another. It promises to account for competitive behavior, the acceptance and evasion of protocols and constraints, the pleasures of rhythmic bodies in motion, and the dizzy delight taken in exhibitions of virtuosity. Ludomusicology is thus more concerned with performativity—with discourses that, in Austinian terms, do what they say—than it is with the text-based preoccupations of representation, meaning, and interpretation.[18] In other words, ludomusicology recognizes that music and digital games are not merely to be read, seen, or heard, but *played*. Music, from this perspective, constitutes a set of cognitive, technological, and social affordances for behaving in certain ways, for playing in and with the world through the medium of sound and its representations. For their part, digital games offer rules—which is to say possibilities bound by constraints—for entering into relationships with the world that are simultaneously material and imaginary, real and virtual.

Guitar Hero and *Rock Band* serve as excellent test cases for ludomusicology because they explicitly conflate the playing of games and of music.

They thus provide an opportunity to investigate how concepts and terminology associated with digital games might illuminate musical artifacts and practices.[19] To demonstrate the scope of ludomusicological inquiry, I will first consider what musical performance and digital gameplay have in common as alternatives, supplements, or antonyms for "work." Drawing on an influential taxonomy developed by anthropologist and sociologist Roger Caillois, I will outline a conceptual framework for the types of musical play that *Guitar Hero* and *Rock Band* invoke and combine before considering the material elements that enable them. The games' controllers draw on the rhetoric of toys in order to invite playful engagement; at the same time, they serve as interfaces between the digitality of computer code and of players' fingers, thereby translating dexterous performance into the terms of information theory and cybernetics. As both toys and machines, these guitar controllers undermine the discourse of authenticity so central to rock music's mythology, instead forcing players to confront the recursively mediated quality of their ludomusical experiences.

How do the hardware and software of these games configure the interactive possibilities for those who engage with them? Players of *Guitar Hero* and *Rock Band* shuttle between the roles of the traditional performer and the contemporary listener, for whom to "play" means to trigger the reproduction of a performance by pressing a button on an electronic device. Playing the "guitar" thus entails playing the music *back* via the interaction of fingers and buttons, but it also involves playing *along with* it. Multiple implications of "recreation" are apt here: as well as connoting the pleasure and entertainment derived from playful activity, the term connotes the games' reproductive aspects and the extent to which they inspire players both to play according to the rules and to create anew via disruptive play, hacking, and the modification (or "modding") of both software and hardware. The complex and diverse manifestations of recreation that emerge from ludomusical engagement with *Guitar Hero* and *Rock Band* can be traced back to a range of North American, European, and Japanese sources, objects, and traditions. By charting this nexus and revealing connections that reach across both space and time, I hope to suggest how a ludomusicological approach might inform the study of disparate musical texts and practices.

From Work to Play: Definitions and Taxonomies

Exploring the motives and purposes of human play has preoccupied anthropologists, sociologists, cognitive scientists, economists, philosophers, psychologists, and educators.[20] Within Western culture, the issue of how play and work mutually define, exclude, and complement each other has been a central concern, as a glance at definitions of the two words in the *Oxford English Dictionary* confirms. To paraphrase: work is obligatory while play is voluntary; work moves objects via effort and exertion, while in play they oscillate and revolve freely; work transforms things from one state into another via laborious construction, while play involves quicksilver shifts between states; work is tiresome while play is pleasurable; and work is real while play is make-believe. Perhaps most relevant in this context, work has to do with the production of the plastic fine arts—and, of course, the *musical* work—whereas play has to do with the enactment of drama, on the one hand, and musical performance and *re*production, on the other.

The markedness of this binarism, and in particular the elevation of work over play in moral, religious, and economic spheres, was noted by Max Weber, who accounted for it in terms of the rise of Protestantism and capitalism.[21] In *Die rationalen und soziologischen Grundlagen der Musik*, Weber subjected the history of European art music to similar treatment: he argued that while the rational, systematic basis of literate "art" music held great potential for composers, conductors, and audiences from the nineteenth century onward, it did so at the expense of improvisatory, informal styles of play.[22] Weber's historical reflections registered the discursive influence of *Musikwissenschaft*, according to which music was treated primarily as a textual medium, and pride of place was reserved for the reified musical work and its associated ethic. Perhaps this is unremarkable in light of the discipline's philological heritage, but its effects have been far-reaching. The imposing figure of Beethoven embodies the values of this system: his compositional labor, painstakingly documented by copious sketches and manifested through *thematische Arbeit*, has been privileged over the performer's responsibility to play the carefully tallied score.[23] Such musical works have been curated in an imaginary museum, to cite Lydia Goehr's resonant formulation, as canonical objects to be venerated rather than as pretexts for playful performance.[24]

In his 1958 book *Les jeux et les hommes*, Caillois echoed Weber's argument that the reasons for valuing work over play were moral and economic, since "play is an occasion of pure waste: waste of time, energy, ingenuity, skill, and often of money. . . . Nothing has been harvested or manufactured, no masterpiece has been created, no capital has accrued."[25] For Caillois, as for Weber, play was at odds with the commitments to productivity, utility, and hard work typical of industrialized societies. The uncertainty surrounding the outcome of play, its governance according to arbitrary rules, its focus on the pleasures and challenges of the moment, and its celebration of novelty, fantasy, and make-believe defy the moral rigor of work. But, as Caillois went on to argue, these attributes of play might also enable it to be construed as the most profound of pursuits. This belief has a long and distinguished history stretching back to Plato's Athenian sage in the *Laws*, who asked, "What, then, will be the right way to live? A man should spend his whole life at 'play'—sacrificing, singing, dancing."[26] Framed this way, play is not mere escapism from the daily grind but rather its ultimate purpose: humans work in order to be able to play.

Hans-Georg Gadamer observed that "the word 'Spiel' originally meant 'dance'. . . . The movement of playing has no goal that brings it to an end; rather, it renews itself in constant repetition."[27] Gadamer's formulation suggests an aesthetic connection between inutility and Immanuel Kant's notion of "purposiveness without purpose" that locates the beautiful in a realm beyond the reach of utilitarian function or explanation. Following Kant, as Claus Pias points out, Friedrich Schiller conceived of this realm as a space for interplay between life and form, power and law, nature and reason, through which "a state of the highest reality" could be attained.[28] For Schiller, the *Spieltrieb* (or play instinct) drove the pursuit and unification of aesthetics, happiness, and moral perfection: "Humans only play when they are in the fullest sense of the word human beings, and *they are only fully human when they play*."[29] In their different ways, then, Plato, Kant, Schiller, and Gadamer perceived work to be a necessary prelude to the rituals of play, embodied through motion, rhythm, and pattern.

In his influential book *Homo Ludens*, first published in 1939, Johan Huizinga directly challenged the cultural valorization of work over play. Huizinga noted that the display of skill, the pleasure in testing the limits of one's own abilities and those of others, and sometimes even the endangerment of one's safety and well-being for no apparent reason pervade many societies, often to an extent which defies utilitarian explanation.[30] Going further, Huizinga asserted that a culture's most vital elements—its religious, philosophical, political, and artistic fields—should be understood as fundamentally playful in that they foreground theatricality, competition, challenge, virtuosity, and improvisation.[31] These characteristics shed light on the linguistic and conceptual parallels between music and games. In many ancient and modern languages, the verb "to play" is applicable to both: Huizinga speculated that "it seems probable that the link between play and instrumental skill is to be sought in the nimble and orderly movements of the fingers."[32]

Despite—or perhaps owing to—its boldness, Huizinga's thesis runs the risk of essentializing play and understating the degree to which it is socially embedded. While play has undoubtedly suffered as work's marked antonym, merely inverting their hierarchical relationship fails to address the historical and social contingency of each term. In *The Adventures of Tom Sawyer*, Mark Twain encapsulated the difficulty of distinguishing between the two with striking simplicity: "Work consists of whatever a body is *obliged* to do, and . . . Play consists of whatever a body is not obliged to do."[33] The notion of obligation that articulates Twain's opposition of work and play can be understood in many ways, depending on whether one adopts an economic, sociological, or psychological perspective. There is nothing intrinsic about a given activity that defines it as either "work" or "play": it is categorized as such according to the values, functions, and imperatives assigned to it within a given society or ideology, as well as by the psychological profiles of the individuals involved. The very conditions and characteristics that make play enchanting—motion, rhythm, repetition, and the challenges posed by rules—can be identical to those that make work tedious and arduous, as any professional athlete will testify.[34] In a musical context, Twain's maxim warns against mapping work and play onto the activities of composers and performers/listeners respectively. While taking account of the economic and sociocultural formations that construct the work/play dichotomy, we will thus have to look beyond them in order to identify the material and phenomenological conditions under which music becomes playful and play musical.

Play's resistance to definition has proved to be one of its defining qualities, but this has not precluded attempts to name and classify its manifestations. In *Les jeux et les hommes*, Caillois refined Huizinga's identification of play's components and attributes, enumerating six central characteristics: freedom (play must be voluntary), separateness (play takes place in what Huizinga called a "magic circle" that is marked off from everyday life even as it constitutes part of it), uncertainty (the outcome must not be known in advance), unproductivity (the object of a game is not to produce goods or capital, although it may redistribute them, as is the case with gambling), regulation (whether by rules, customs, or taboos), and fictiveness (play unfolds in a subjunctive mood, "as it were" rather than "as it is").[35] In accordance with what he termed his "diagonal" orientation, Caillois also proposed a taxonomic system according to which games can be understood in terms of four basic categories (or certain combinations thereof): *agôn* (games of competition, from chess to gladiatorial combat), *alea* (games of chance, such as roulette or certain card games), *mimicry* (playful activities involving simulation or make-believe, such as theater, charades, or masked

Table I. Classification of Games

	AGÔN (Competition)	ALEA (Chance)	MIMICRY (Simulation)	ILINX (Vertigo)
PAIDIA ← Tumult, Agitation, Immoderate laughter	Racing, Wrestling, Etc. Athletics } not regulated	Counting-out rhymes, Heads or tails	Children's initiations, Games of illusion, Tag, Arms, Masks, Disguises	Children "whirling", Horseback riding, Swinging, Waltzing
	Boxing, Billiards, Fencing, Checkers, Football, Chess	Betting, Roulette		Volador, Traveling carnivals, Skiing, Mountain climbing, Tightrope walking
Crossword puzzles LUDUS →	Contests, Sports in general	Simple, complex, and continuing lotteries*	Theater, Spectacles in general	

Kite-flying, Solitaire, Patience

N.B. In each vertical column games are classified in such an order that the *paidia* element is constantly decreasing while the *ludus* element is ever increasing.

* A simple lottery consists of the one basic drawing. In a complex lottery there are many possible combinations. A continuing lottery (e.g. Irish Sweepstakes) is one consisting of two or more stages, the winner of the first stage being granted the opportunity to participate in a second lottery. [From correspondence with Caillois. M.B.]

Table 1. "Classification of Games," reproduced from Roger Caillois, trans. Meyer Barash, *Man, Play, and Games*, 36.

carousing at the Venetian carnival), and *ilinx* (activities involving vigorous motion that induces disorientation or vertigo, such as dancing the tarantella or riding on roller coasters).[36] Caillois's categories, along with examples of games that fall into each, are represented in table 1.

Caillois proposed this taxonomy as a corrective to what he saw as Huizinga's narrow focus on play as *agôn*. The categories of *alea*, *mimicry*, and *ilinx* were posited to reflect the pecuniary and arbitrary aspects of play, its social formations and rituals, and its unruly kineticism. Caillois thus aimed to deepen and complicate Huizinga's fundamental insight into the importance of play by showing it to be more than the rehearsal or enactment of antagonistic conflict.

In musical terms, the competition associated with *agôn* is brought to the fore in contests based on skill and popularity, from the mythical duel between Apollo and Marsyas to the historic clash between Mozart and Clementi, and from the song contest in Wagner's *Die Meistersinger von Nürnberg* to the television show *American Idol*. *Agôn* is also a feature of certain musical genres or idioms, from the "dozens" (the African-American tradition of head-to-head improvised verbal sparring that contributed to the rise of battle rap in the late 1970s) and the trading of improvised jazz solos to the classical concerto (which typically pits the heroic soloist against the massed forces of the orchestra). The vast majority of digital games inculcate or reflect *agôn*: it is particularly prominent in first-person shooters and sports games, but can be found in any game featuring multi-player modes, adversarial artificial intelligence, or high-score tables. *Guitar Hero* and *Rock Band* facilitate individual and co-operative competition between rival players (both locally and online) in which the player or band with the higher score prevails. Moreover, *Guitar Hero III: Legends of Rock* infuses the *agôn* of the musical contest with the digital-game convention of the "boss battle," a titanic encounter that pits the human "guitarist" against a computer-controlled opponent.[37] In a Faustian finale worthy of Niccolò Paganini, the game culminates in a virtuosic duel with "Lou the Devil" to the strains of "The Devil Went Down to Georgia."[38]

Caillois's category of *alea* accounts for games in which players abdicate their agency to the vagaries of chance. Its musical manifestations are relatively rare, and are more often found in compositional strategies than in playful performance: from this perspective, eighteenth-century musical dice games rub shoulders with aleatoric compositions by John Cage, Karlheinz Stockhausen, and Pierre Boulez.[39] The only relevant aspect of *Guitar Hero*, however, is the randomly allocated "power-up" (a temporary gameplay aid) that the player can earn during boss or multiplayer battles.

By contrast, the category of *mimicry*, or simulation, offers many possibilities for parsing the complex and ambiguous ways in which *Guitar Hero* and *Rock Band* negotiate between fantasy and reality.[40] Chief among these is the degree to which the games' miniaturized plastic guitars encourage imaginary role-playing by fostering the illusion that the player is "playing" a rock star, even as they convey an ironic awareness of the absurdity of the conceit. Caillois points out that this type of contradiction is more apparent than real, since the pleasure of *mimicry* lies in playful imitation rather than serious deception: "The child who is playing train may well refuse to kiss his father while saying to him that one does not embrace locomotives, but he is not trying to persuade his father that he is a locomotive."[41] In other words, the child simultaneously is and is not a locomotive, just as the actor is and is not Hamlet.[42] The subjunctivity of *mimicry* sidesteps the oft-rehearsed arguments over whether plastic guitars are "real" or "fake": to insist on the distinction in a ludic context is as meaningless as it would be to argue over the toxicological effects of the "poison" taken by Leonora in a production of *Il trovatore*.[43]

The category of *ilinx* is most directly applicable to the kinesthetically thrilling experience of musical performance. For Caillois, *ilinx* is centered on testing the limits of the player's embodied control and proprioception, as exemplified by activities such as rolling down hills to induce dizziness, certain drinking games, or bungee jumping.[44] Its emphasis on risk-taking and the loss of self-possession allies *ilinx* to the exhibition of musical charisma and virtuosity, the disorienting effects of which are often transmitted to the audience (as in the case of those who swooned in the presence of Liszt or The Beatles). *Ilinx* is also associated with certain musical genres: the unpredictable rhythmic dislocations and boisterous humor of a Beethoven scherzo, for example, burlesque the staid eighteenth-century minuet by infusing it with a heady dose of *ilinx*. In the context of *Guitar Hero* and *Rock Band*, players may incorporate *ilinx* as part of their rock-star *mimicry* by performing such feats as playing the guitar behind their heads, or with their eyes closed. The games themselves encourage such exuberant behavior by allowing players to activate "Star Power" or "Overdrive" (modes in which the player's score is temporarily multiplied) by screaming into the microphone, crowning a drum fill with a climactic strike on the pad representing the crash cymbal, or thrusting the guitar into a vertical position, which is registered by a motion sensor in its body.

Across all four of Caillois's categories, a perpendicular axis of play registers the degree of *paidia* (the player's childlike delight in defying or ignoring constraints, and the pleasure taken in tumult, improvisation, and contrary behavior) as opposed to *ludus* (the player's willing submission to the non-negotiable rules that govern the pursuit of games, and the pleasure taken in confronting—or ingeniously circumventing—arbitrary and recurrent obstacles). As examples of *paidia*, Caillois lists somersaults, scribbling, pulling threads, and deliberately holding up queues, while crosswords and anagrams are representative of *ludus*.[45] This continuum reflects the social mediation of the player's psychological approach as much as it characterizes activities themselves: even chess, which for Caillois is paradigmatic of *ludus*, can be played with a devil-may-care or willfully disruptive attitude that introduces an element of *paidia*.[46] However, certain compositional approaches (and, to varying degrees, the performative modalities they suggest or mandate) are more readily identified with one than the other: the serial technique and Sudoku-like construction of Webern's Concerto op. 24, for instance, are redolent of *ludus*, while the spirited badinage of Poulenc's song "Couplets bachiques" veers toward *paidia*.[47]

The *ludus* of digital games lies in the arbitrary rules, stringent conditions, and harsh consequences with which they traditionally confront the player: the awarding of three "lives" at the outset of a game, for instance, or the punishment of infractions with instant "death." While all manner of games depend on rules, digital games differ from their predecessors in the extent to which they simultaneously enact and enforce rules according to their intrinsic mathematical structures: the computational power behind the digital game allows it to act as architect, interface, opponent, and referee.[48] Recent games aimed at a broader audience have taken great pains to conceal the cold logic that underpins them, presenting players with a user-friendly veneer of *paidia*. One of the secrets of *Guitar Hero*'s initial success was the degree to which its plastic guitar and artfully casual presentation promised the *paidia* associated with rock music while appearing not to demand the investment of time, energy, and concentration typical of *ludus*: the game affects to take care of the hard work for its players by serving as their virtual manager, roadie, teacher, and fan base.[49]

The notion that game players could reap the virtual rewards of superstardom without putting years of effort into mastering an instrument proved unpalatable to many rock musicians. Stemming in part from the stakes invested in professional musical performance, their criticism was based on the tacit assumption that playing the electric guitar—itself once commonly disparaged as a waste of time and "genuine" musical talent—is a worthwhile and productive pursuit. Its terms ironically transposed, the culturally dominant work ethic thus re-asserted itself against the unabashed play ethic of the digital game. Both despite and owing to the aura of rebellious *paidia* that surrounds it, rocking out can be a serious business, as bands—and brands—such as The Beatles know only too well.

It is thus hardly surprising that Noel Gallagher of the band Oasis explicitly rejected the parallels between music and games: "I always tell kids playing a guitar is not a video game; there is no level to get to."[50] However, by bemoaning the fact that players of *Guitar Hero* and *Rock Band* partake of "the guitar-playing experience . . . without . . . having to put anything into it," rock musician John Mayer revealed a fundamental sense in which he *does* conceive of music as a game.[51] By charging game players with breaking the unwritten rules governing musical pedagogy and performance in order to get more for less, Mayer in effect accused them of cheating, a notion that makes most sense when framed ludically.[52] From the valved horn to Auto-Tune, controversies over the use and abuse of technological assistance in the creation and performance of music have typically been framed within discourses of authenticity: the term certainly resonates throughout *Guitar Hero* and *Rock Band*.[53] But we might also consider these debates in the light of music's *ludus*, the game-like sense in which it operates according to rules that impose arbitrary constraints on its players. Why, for instance, is it admirable for a two-handed pianist to tackle the demanding solo part of Ravel's Piano Concerto for the Left Hand *come scritto*, but ignoble if she avails herself of her right hand at particularly tricky moments? Although doubling her manual resources at the keyboard might well increase the chances of an accurate performance, any benefits would likely be negated by the audience's perception of her behavior as somehow unsporting.

Mayer's dismissal of *Guitar Hero* and his condescension toward "the masses" who play it evinced a brand of elitism often displayed by "hardcore" gamers: in both cases, a sense of superiority derives from a mastery over—and thus an investment in—the rules and obstacles that deter "casual" players.[54] Committed *Guitar Hero* aficionados soon discover that playing the game on its higher difficulty levels requires a considerable investment of time and labor.[55] Many such players strip away all traces of *paidia* in favor of scrutinizing and exploiting the game's rules and mechanics in order to maximize their scores. Some calculate the optimal junctures at which to activate "Star Power" or "Overdrive" within each song and do so with the press of a button rather than the *ilinx*-fueled brandishing of the guitar, which jeopardizes the player's "combo" (a streak of flawless execution that leads to higher scores).[56]

Conversely, there will always be those who refuse to conform to the game's *ludus* and take delight in playing according to their own rules.

Throughout the technological realm, members of hacking and "modding" communities perform ingenious alterations on software and hardware. Both *Guitar Hero* and *Rock Band* have been subjected to a bewildering array of such projects, from the conversion of guitar controllers into functional MIDI instruments to hacks allowing for the insertion of the player's own choice of music into the games.[57] Far from frowning on such transgressive tendencies, Matt Boch of Harmonix actively encouraged them: the punk rock–inspired do-it-yourself ethos of their exploits fed back into official development, contributing both to the content and to the counter-cultural image that the games purveyed.[58]

In the case of both music and digital games, the *ludus-paidia* dialectic encapsulates many of the tensions and ambiguities that performance brings to the fore. A central paradox lies in the fact that while both music and games are celebrated for the freedom of expression they are perceived to facilitate, the acquisition and manifestation of this freedom depend upon a complicated, inflexible set of rules and conventions. The years of practice through which an individual such as Mayer develops proficiency in playing the guitar require perseverance in the face of severe conditions and constraints, whether self-imposed or enforced by the authoritarian figure of the teacher. Success thus calls for a strong commitment to the principles of *ludus*, even—or especially—when the music that emerges is heard to convey *ilinx* or *paidia*. The *paidia* of punk rock, for example, may have been rooted in its rejection of the elaborate *ludus* governing the composition and performance of progressive rock, but punk's anti-establishment aesthetic enacted its own form of *ludus*, exemplified by the mandate that no more than three chords per song were necessary. Likewise, the symbiotic relationship between the rational, *ludus*-governed world of the computer and the *paidia*-inspired counter-cultural hacking and modding communities bears out Eric Zimmerman's claim that play "exists both because of and also despite the more rigid structures of a system."[59] The joy of *paidia* and the illicit pleasures of cheating are inextricable from the regulatory discipline of *ludus* and the sober principles of fair play.

Caillois's modular taxonomy offers a useful means of naming playful musical practices for which a vocabulary has hitherto been largely lacking.[60] But the identification of elements is merely the first step in accounting for the particular forms that such practices can assume through processes of representation and mediation. In order to articulate more precisely what musical play involves in *Guitar Hero* and *Rock Band*, we will have to take account of the material objects that enable and constrain it.

Instruments of Mediation

The plastic peripherals of *Guitar Hero* and *Rock Band* constitute the prime interfaces between the ludic and the musical: they simultaneously serve as controllers and instruments, mediating between the player, the game, and the music. Placing *Guitar Hero*'s iconic controller (a version of which is shown in figure 2) alongside the standard Xbox 360 controller (illustrated in figure 3) reveals some obvious similarities. Whereas the resemblance of *Guitar Hero II*'s Gibson X-Plorer to its real-world counterpart is morphological rather than functional, its kinship with the Xbox 360 controller is both. In particular, four of the X-Plorer's five brightly colored fret buttons can be found arranged in a diamond formation on the Xbox 360 controller: the lineage of both devices passes through the red, yellow, blue, and green buttons of *Simon*, the iconic electronic memory game designed by Ralph Baer and Howard Morrison and released by Milton Bradley in 1978, and its arcade precursor *Touch Me*.[61]

Going further, the colors of game controllers' buttons can be traced back to Milton Bradley's personal commitment to the nineteenth-century ludic and pedagogical theories of Friedrich Froebel, the German founder of the Kindergarten movement.[62] As a strong advocate of Froebel's concepts, Bradley formulated the standard shades of red, yellow, blue, green, orange, and purple still used today in the production of Froebel's series of *Spielgabe* (play gifts) for young children.[63] By featuring these colors prominently both on-screen and off, *Guitar Hero* thus embedded itself in a long tradition of toys and games, ensuring that suitably "literate" players would instinctively grasp its mechanical and ludic configuration. But this accessibility came at the cost of credibility with those among the non-gaming audience for whom the controller's toy-like appearance confirmed preconceptions that the digital-game medium and constituency were irredeemably childish.[64]

It is indeed the guitar's toy-like nature that identifies it as a vehicle for *paidia* (a word used by Plato's sage when advocating for the importance of play), which means "childish play, pastime, or amusement."[65] Perhaps this explains in part the discrepancy between the miniaturized plastic guitar and the real/imaginary counterpart invoked by its skeuomorphic pegs and Gibson branding. The "reality gap" opened up between the player and the rock star is analogous to the temporal gap that the "toy" guitar opens up between an adult player and his or her childhood, a time span also reflected by the games' retro-flavored set-lists. Cumulatively, they cover half a century of blues, rock, metal, and country music, constituting a veritable soundtrack of modern North American history (and thus a history of

Figs. 2. (L) White Gibson X-Plorer controller for *Guitar Hero II* (Microsoft Xbox 360); (R) Standard Microsoft Xbox 360 controller.

the modern North American soundtrack). The cheerful naïveté of *Guitar Hero, Rock Band,* and their controllers invokes nostalgia for imaginary bygone days when life was simpler and music better, thereby creating a space in which the full-grown player can shamelessly enjoy the pleasures of make-believe and *mimicry*.[66] Giorgio Agamben's insight into the historicity captured by the banal materiality of the toy applies here: "What the toy preserves of its sacred or economic model, what survives of this after its dismemberment or miniaturization, is nothing other than the human temporality that was contained therein. . . . The toy is a materialization of the historicity contained in objects, extracting it by means of a particular manipulation."[67] Many adult players of *Guitar Hero* and *Rock Band* manipulate their controllers not to relive the past but to recall the prospect of a future that never came to pass.

Situating the *Guitar Hero* guitar within an organological context illuminates other aspects of its form and function. Viewed this way, the electronic "guitar" represents a continuation of the process by which the electric guitar displaced its acoustic forerunner during the second half of the twentieth century. Steve Waksman has shown that much of the controversy surrounding the rise of the electric guitar lay in the extent to which its sound was disembodied, produced by amplifiers and effects pedals rather than plucked by the performer's fingers.[68] The *Guitar Hero* controller extends this process of sonic devolution, divesting the last acoustic traces from the instrument itself by delegating the (re)production and processing of sound to the game console, to which it relays the player's input in almost precisely the same manner as a standard controller. Indeed, it is possible to play *Guitar Hero III* with a standard Xbox 360 controller: the game even awards the player "achievements" for satisfying certain conditions while doing so.[69] By eschewing strings in favor of buttons, the *Guitar Hero* controller digitizes the electric guitar; the guitar, in other words, becomes a keyboard. The digitality of its buttons facilitates the algorithmic modulation of the player's more or less dexterous input into musical output via a cybernetic relationship with the software.

In order to investigate how and why rock's digitization took this particular form, a brief detour to Tokyo will be necessary. In 1997, the Japanese entertainment corporation Konami released *BeatMania*, an arcade game that presents players with a five-note keyboard and a turntable as input devices with which to match rhythmically ascending or descending symbols on the screen to a sequence of songs and tracks.[70] The success of *BeatMania* led Konami to dedicate what became known as their Bemani division to the development of games that explored the common ground between gameplay, music, and rhythmic entrainment.[71] These games share fundamental gameplay and interface elements while varying the form and function of the player's input device.[72] In *BeatMania*'s successor, *Dance Dance Revolution*, players match the on-screen symbols by activating the corresponding panels of a metal dance pad: the *ilinx* and *paidia* thus induced helped make the game an international smash hit.[73]

The next arcade games in the Bemani series were *GuitarFreaks* and *DrumMania*, released in 1998 and 1999 respectively, and the two could be connected to enable cooperative and competitive play. Collectively, these games contain practically all the conceptual and mechanical elements found in *Guitar Hero* and *Rock Band*, from the peripherals to the fundamental principles—and many specific details—of the software design.[74] It is thus unsurprising to discover that Eran Egozy, co-founder of Harmonix, was influenced by the Bemani series, as well as by Masaya Matsuura, when he and Rigopulos visited Tokyo in 1999: "There was a fairly pivotal moment over there when we saw this form of music gameplay—in games like *BeatMania* and *PaRappa* and *Dance Dance Revolution*—that was really compelling and addictive. We thought that maybe we should be the music company that takes these types of ideas . . . and brings them to the U. S."[75] In a reversal of the stereotyped process according to which Japanese industry merely copies and refines Western innovations, *Guitar Hero* and *Rock Band* turn out to be imitations of Japanese "originals." Although *Rock Band* appears to have been modeled on the classic Anglo-American four-piece outfit, the game's guitars, drums, and microphones can all be traced back to Japan's arcades and karaoke bars.[76] But, of course, the dynamics of global mediatized culture were already at play in the design of Komani's Bemani games, as they had been in karaoke itself. While their soundtracks typically focus on Japanese pop, techno, and associated electronic genres, *GuitarFreaks* and *DrumMania* clearly allude to "analog" Western musical instruments and traditions.

It is thus perhaps less useful to think in terms of "originals" and "copies" than to reflect on how concepts, practices, and objects are transformed through transmission within and across musical cultures. In this light, we might consider the multiple meanings of the word "score" insofar as it refers to the quantification and summation both of a game and of a musical composition. In Bemani games as well as *Guitar Hero* and *Rock Band*, both the musical score (the charted gems, or notes, that approach the player through space and time) and the ludic score (measured in points) regulate players' reproductive accuracy: the former prescribes while the latter motivates and evaluates. *Rock Band*'s musical score for guitar and drums operates as a form of tablature, in that the five fret buttons or drum pads are represented on screen as they appear (or feel) to the player; in Peircean terms, the actions to be taken are represented iconically rather than encoded symbolically. At the same time, the procession of notes resembles nothing more than the unspooling of a player-piano roll, an early version of which was invented by Claude-Félix Seytre in 1842 (illustrated in figure 3). The games' scrolling "note tunnels" depicted in figure 1 are visually and kinetically analogous to Seytre's spooling "music belt," while his "music disk" could be construed as a "prophetic relic" (to borrow Alan Liu's terminology) that indexes the optical disks on which *Guitar Hero*, *Rock Band*, and their music are stored and distributed.[77]

Such parallels suggest that the broader history and sociology of music in both Japanese and Western contexts can offer illuminating perspectives

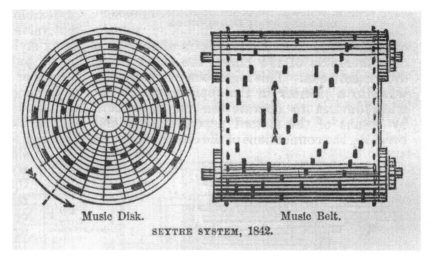

Music Disk.   Music Belt.

SEYTRE SYSTEM, 1842.

Fig. 3. Seytre's "music disk" and "music belt," reproduced from *Appletons'
Annual Cyclopedia and Register of Important Events of the Year 1885, 615.*

on the ludic concepts that the games invoke and evoke. It is worth pointing out that Egozy of Harmonix is an accomplished clarinetist who regularly performs chamber music, and also that the domestic setting in which
Guitar Hero and *Rock Band* are collaboratively played—typically a spacious
living room, given the high cost and logistical demands of the requisite
hardware and software—is more characteristic of *Hausmusik* than it is of
the classic garage rock band.[78] The same could be said of the games' emphasis on the reproduction of (more or less) canonical musical texts with
the greatest possible fidelity, particularly in the case of *The Beatles: Rock
Band*.[79] Rigopulos himself has made the historical connection between *Rock
Band* and earlier technologies of musical recreation: "When there were no
record players, [there were] people in the house who knew how to render
sheet music into music on their pianos. I see what we are doing now as
a massive historical throwback."[80] Again, the divergent meanings of "recreation," pertaining to faithful reproduction on the one hand and leisure
activity on the other, find common ground on the field of play.

Depictions of mechanized representational systems capable of prescrib-
ing (or transcribing) musical performance can be extended from the water
organ designs depicted by Athanasius Kircher in his *Musurgia universa-
lis*, published in 1650 but based on a sixteenth-century instrument at the
Villa d'Este in Tivoli, to the "piano roll" viewing mode commonly found

in the MIDI sequencing software used for contemporary music production.[81] From Kircher to Harmonix, all such systems binarize notation in that their musical data consists of arrays of bits that signify either a note or its absence. As David Suisman has observed, the concept of Seytre's music belt was derived from earlier developments in the pre-history of computing: Jacques de Vaucanson's design and Joseph-Marie Jacquard's execution of the automated loom head in Lyon had been conceived along similar lines, as were the punch cards that Charles Babbage designed for his speculative "analytical engine" in London.[82] From this angle, *Guitar Hero* and *Rock Band* expose the degree to which music notation is a form of information technology that transcodes sight into sound, script into action. The colored gems the games send toward the "guitarist" are converted by fingers into a form of binary: the five fret buttons offer thirty-one input combinations which, depending on the selected difficulty level, operate algorithmically when triggering the reproduction of the music. The player's fingers—literally, the digits—thus compute the outcome. If successful, the corresponding portion of the recording is played back; if not, a chastening "clunk" sound is followed by an awkward silence until the next gem offers the possibility of redemption.[83] Unwittingly, the successful player becomes an expert decipherer, a fact that has not gone unnoticed by neuroscientists and cryptographers.[84]

The operation of the software is itself predicated on the same technological foundation. Binary logic governs the thousands of lines of code that are compiled, executed by the console's central processing unit in order to enact and enforce the game's *ludus*, and modulated into audio-visual output that facilitates the players' *paidia*. The player, the instrument, the software, and the hardware thus form a nexus through which cognitive and musical responsibilities are digitized and distributed according to an ever-shifting balance between uncertainty and redundancy.

From these multiple perspectives, the *Guitar Hero* controller can be understood to combine the morphology of Konami's *GuitarFreaks* guitar, the topography of the keyboard, the mechanicity of the piano roll, and the cybernetic logic of *Simon*, encoded and adorned by Froebel's cheerful colors. It thus synthesizes elements from Kindergarten, the bourgeois parlor, Japanese arcade culture at millennium's end, and—above all—the post-war military-industrial complex in the United States that gave rise to digital games in general, and to *Simon* in particular. (Ralph Baer was working for Sanders Associates, a defense contractor, when he developed it.)[85] While this might seem jarring, it is entirely commensurate with the history of both toys and digital play: consider bows and arrows, cap guns, and *Call of Duty* in the light of Friedrich Kittler's assertion that "the entertainment industry . . . is an abuse of army equipment."[86] Inflecting this perspective with Agamben's historicity, we might suggest that as weapons age, they become more toy-like. In the case of the axe, at least, *Guitar Hero* seems to bear this hypothesis out.

Genuine Fakery

Matt Boch of Harmonix has alluded to the problematic ontology of the plastic guitar by pointing out the ambiguity of its central strum bar. Understood in terms of a "real" guitar, its singularity would imply that the instrument has only one (imaginary) string, but its function in the game—particularly in relation to the playing of "chords"—makes matters more complex: "What does the strum bar represent? Is the strum bar the pick dragging across the strings? Is it the strings? Is it the pick and the strings? It's none of those things."[87] Boch's questions suggest that the game controllers be conceived not as real guitars *manquées* but as haptic devices whose primary function is to prompt the gestures and sensations associated with John Mayer's "guitar-playing experience." They can be understood not only within the context of guitar history, technology, and virtuosity outlined by Waksman, but also in relation to the parallel history of air guitar, a realm of musical make-believe and fantasy that Caillois would classify as characteristic of *ilinx* as well as *mimicry* and *paidia*. To (mis)appropriate Jean Baudrillard's terminology, the guitar controller is best understood not as a simulation of its real-world counterpart but as a simulacrum, a representation of the air guitarist's imaginary instrument.[88]

Rock music has always given rise to debates over authenticity, whether they circulate around Elvis Presley, glam rock, nu metal, or emo.[89] The central issue lurking behind them is always the contingency of the reality at stake, and—more important—who has the power to define and lay claim to it. By presenting their players with simulacra, *Guitar Hero* and *Rock Band* offer them the opportunity to redefine what is real. In Lawrence Grossberg's diagnosis of the postmodern predicament, "[the] only possible claim to authenticity is derived from the knowledge and admission of your own inauthenticity. . . . The only authenticity is to know and even admit that you are not being authentic, to fake it without faking the fact that you are faking it."[90] *Guitar Hero* and *Rock Band* are emblematic of a tendency to soften rock's hard edges by satirizing its excesses with tender irony: the plastic guitar domesticates and infantilizes the phallic potency of the electric guitar in the spirit of films such as *This Is Spinal Tap*, *Wayne's World*, and

School of Rock. By freely admitting their inauthenticity, both plastic and air guitarists generate pleasure from the knowing, creative manipulation of artifice, paradoxically delivering a "real" experience. Through the double logic of *mimicry*, they represent the concept of the "genuine fake."

Guitar Hero and *Rock Band* thus question the tenets of authenticity even when presenting the music of a band widely perceived to epitomize them. In September 2008, Metallica released their album *Death Magnetic* as downloadable content for *Guitar Hero III* and *Guitar Hero: World Tour.* This version of the album has been called "definitive": according to many fans and industry professionals, it sounds better than the CD release owing to the latter's excessive compression.[91] But buyers of *Death Magnetic* via *Guitar Hero* are required to play the game flawlessly in order to hear all the music recorded by Metallica: moreover, players will also hear the reactions of the in-game crowd while contributing their own musical elements in the form of improvised drum fills, vocal additions to (and timbral deviations from) James Hetfield's master tracks, and modulated guitar sounds via the effects switch and vibrato arm. Even an attempt to reproduce the album as faithfully as possible will thus transform it into a cover version.

If live performance is to be understood as an index of authenticity, however, it could be argued that a play-through of *Death Magnetic* by four *Guitar Hero* players is in some ways *more* authentic than Metallica's own recording. Like most contemporary rock music, the tracks on *Death Magnetic* were recorded piecemeal and subjected to extensive digital manipulation; they thus only rarely and partly reflect the band's continuous collective performance, whereas a rendition of the album via *Guitar Hero* and its instruments obliges players to play (along with) entire songs in real time.[92] In such a scenario, who is "real," who is "faking," and can anyone be accused of cheating?

In *Liveness,* Philip Auslander asserts that "initially, mediated events were modeled on live ones. The subsequent cultural dominance of mediatization has had the ironic result that live events now frequently are modeled on the very mediatized representations that once took the self-same live events as their models."[93] In this light, it is telling that Harmonix was acquired by MTV in 2006: Alex Rigopulos himself drew parallels between the two companies' transformation of musical culture.[94] Just as MTV revolutionized popular music in the 1980s by representing it as a (tele)visual medium rather than as a primarily auditory phenomenon, so *Guitar Hero* and *Rock Band* add an extra sensory dimension by introducing haptic interactive elements in concert with audiovisual stimuli. Instead of watching a band on television, players virtually *become* a band on television: by showcasing an adoring crowd fixated on the on-screen antics of the players' customized avatars, the game intimates that the television is watching the player rather than vice versa. Although the animations are canned and the music pre-recorded, the performance in the living room is unmistakably live. Adding a recursive twist to Auslander's formulation, then, we might propose that *Guitar Hero* and *Rock Band* enable live performances predicated on the reproduction of pre-recorded music tracks via input devices that invoke tropes associated with live rock performance that themselves draw on an iconographic repertoire transmitted via music video, which was itself founded on the reification of earlier live performance.[95] The *Guitar Hero* and *Rock Band* controllers thus (re)mediate between the ludic and the musical, the live and the recorded, and the "fake" and the "real."

Bearing the Japanese origin of these controllers in mind, the pedagogy and performance of Western art music in Japan offer intriguing parallels to the discourses of authenticity, originality, and mechanization that attended the reception of *Guitar Hero* and *Rock Band* in North America and Europe. Addressing the perception of a "robotic" performance style associated with Shin'ichi Suzuki's method of violin instruction, Robert Fink contends that American parents were troubled by the notion that their children were striving for no more than "the 'mindless' reproduction of a mechanical reproduction."[96] Noel Gallagher and John Mayer's phobic reactions to *Guitar Hero* reprise those anxious parental reactions with uncanny precision. They represent both a fear that the changing rules of the musical game threaten to strand them on the wrong side of a generational and technological divide, but also an aversion to the mechanical and the jejune.[97] The suturing of buttons onto a guitar arouses scornful laughter from those who perceive "something mechanical encrusted on the living," to recall Henri Bergson's resonant phrase.[98] As Miller and her subjects eloquently demonstrate, the perception of mechanicity in *Guitar Hero* and *Rock Band* is filtered through ethnic, gendered, and sexualized stereotypes.[99] They stem in part from the games' ludic logic, instrumental configurations, and Japanese associations, which challenge common assumptions concerning rebellion, authenticity, and ethnicity in relation to rock.

As Fink suggests, however, Suzuki's philosophy and method can be understood in very different terms, notably those provided by Zen Buddhism.[100] "Do not play; let the bow play," proclaimed Suzuki. Rather than interpreting the motto as a mechanistic repression of individuality, we might place it in ludic dialogue with Gadamer's observation that people are played rather than playing, that "all playing is a being-played."[101] As we have seen, while games and music allow for the expression of personal and social identity, their *ludus* also involves elements that enchain players to rules and protocols, an experience that can nonetheless feel liberating rather than coercive. While games are constructs, they in turn construct the subjectivity of their players. This chiastic relationship between game and player reflects a ludic invertibility and reciprocity: in Schiller's words, play configures a relationship between the material and the formal so that "the operation of the one at the same time confirms and limits the operation of the other."[102] *Guitar Hero* and *Rock Band* allow the willing player to become the instrument of the game: in Suzuki's terms, he or she does not play but lets the strum bar play. If all goes well, the song will play too.

Margaret Robertson has drawn attention to the parallels between a musical score and the machine code of a digital game: "Creators devise an experience, and commit it to code. The code then sits there, lifeless, until a performer picks it up. Then, through a complex tool which requires substantial manual dexterity to master, the performer interprets the experience the creator devised. No two people will play the code the same way. Some players will perform better than others. Some will get stuck and give up before the end."[103] Although both musical notation and game code exist in a literary form, they are not primarily texts to be read but rather programs for courses of actions to be taken.[104] This helps explain why, when discussing *Rock Band*'s effect on how players experience music, Rigopulos declared that "the instruments reprogram you."[105] On the one hand, we might consider the potential of this concept to account for how musicians organize and process information in the course of training and performance; on the other, we might follow Suzuki and Gadamer by exploring how musical culture and literature program, reprogram, and even debug the people who engage with them.

As I suggested above, connections between digital games and musical experience could start with the transferal of terminology: what might it mean to conceive of chamber music as "multi-player co-op," of Chopin's "Minute" Waltz as engaging "speed run" mode, or of Liszt's *Réminiscences de Don Juan* as a "single-player mod" of Mozart's eight-player opera?[106] More broadly, a ludomusicological approach to Western art music might help trace its capricious shuttling between the drastic and the gnostic, to echo Vladimir Jankélévitch and Carolyn Abbate.[107] Rather than conceiving of texts and performances in terms of works and renditions, we might think of a score as describing and constituting the ludic rules according to which music is to be played. The insights yielded by the experience of play in the digital age might thus be brought to bear on what has now become known as the analog era, a retronym that conceals the extent to which both "digital" and "analog" concepts and practices co-existed before the two terms were forced into binaristic opposition.[108]

Conversely, ludomusicology might bring new—or freshly old— historical and cultural perspectives to bear on Robertson's claim that *all* digital games "have a music about them," and that "common to them . . . are [the] elements of performance, rhythm, interpretation and difficulty."[109] In *Donkey Kong: Jungle Beat*, the game that prompted her article, the player controls the simian protagonist's movements using the "DK Bongos" con- troller developed for Namco's rhythm-action game *Donkey Konga*.[110] Other ostensibly non-musical games have turned guitar controllers into instru- ments of the player's will, transforming "musical" input into visual and ki- netic on-screen output.[111] Approaching such games from the perspective of performance might help reveal why, in the opinion of legendary Nintendo developer Shigeru Miyamoto, "those directors who have been able to in- corporate rhythm . . . in their games have been successful."[112]

Both digital gameplay and musical performance are fugitive phenom- ena: to adopt Hans Ulrich Gumbrecht's formulation, they undo themselves as they emerge.[113] Oscillating between categories, they simultaneously rely on and evade the terms that seek to define them. Game play emerges through the interaction between players and objects, on the one hand, and the rules and constraints that regulate their motion, on the other. Musical play takes place in the spaces that open up between sign and sound, instruc- tion and execution, the permissible and the imaginable. It is from these in- terstices of the material and the epistemological that the discipline of ludo- musicology might emerge as a way to bring insights yielded from studying musical performance to bear on how ludic experiences are constructed and represented, and vice versa. Ludomusical play can be conformist or trans- gressive, erotic or violent, virtuosic or rudimentary, since players operate both within and against the technological and ideological constraints that define the rules of sonic engagement. By making these rules legible, ludo- musicology sets out to register—and perhaps even to navigate—the flux between script and improvisation that characterizes the experience of play- ing both music and digital games.

For all the depth, complexity, and sheer fun that they offer, *Guitar Hero* and *Rock Band* afford only a tantalizing glimpse of what twenty-first- century musical games might become and how they promise to reconfigure musical theory, practice, pedagogy, and creativity. Matsuura's gloomy vi- sion of their environmental consequences, conversely, reminds us that the freedom of play comes at a cost, that its formations are never ideologically neutral, and that to lose ourselves in the pleasures of a ludic present may put the future at risk. Ultimately, however, play refuses to be pinned down: neither utopian nor apocalyptic, literate nor oral, digital nor analog, finite nor infinite, play twists and splices binaristic continua into Möbius strips. While its precise significance may elude our grasp, we can perhaps make a first move toward registering the delights, dangers, and transformative potential of both music and games by acknowledging in earnest the importance of being playful.

GAMES CITED

AaaaaAAaaaAAAaaAAAAaAAAAA!!! A Reckless Disregard for Gravity. Developed by Dejobaan Games. Watertown, MA: Dejobaan Games, 2009.

The Beatles: Rock Band. Developed by Harmonix. Redwood City: Electronic Arts/MTV Games, 2009.

BeatMania. Developed by Konami. Tokyo: Konami, 1997.

Boom Boom Rocket. Developed by Bizarre Creations. Redwood City: Electronic Arts, 2007.

Dance Dance Revolution. Developed by Konami. Tokyo: Konami, 1998.

DJ Hero. Developed by FreeStyleGames. Santa Monica: Activision, 2009.

Donkey Kong: Jungle Beat. Developed by Nintendo. Tokyo: Nintendo, 2004.

Donkey Konga. Developed by Namco. Tokyo: Nintendo, 2003.

DrumMania. Developed by Konami. Tokyo: Konami, 1999.

Fret Nice. Developed by Pieces Interactive. Torrance, CA: Tecmo, 2010.

Frequency. Developed by Harmonix. Cambridge, MA: Sony Computer Entertainment, 2001.

GuitarFreaks. Developed by Konami. Tokyo: Konami, 1998.

Guitar Hero. Developed by Harmonix. Mountain View, CA: RedOctane/MTV Games, 2005.

Guitar Hero: Metallica. Developed by Neversoft. Santa Monica: Activision, 2009.

Guitar Hero: Warriors of Rock. Developed by Neversoft. Santa Monica: Activision, 2010.

Guitar Hero: World Tour. Developed by Neversoft. Santa Monica: Activision, 2008.

Guitar Hero II. Developed by Harmonix. Mountain View, CA: RedOctane, 2006.

Guitar Hero III: Legends of Rock. Developed by Neversoft. Santa Monica: Activision/RedOctane, 2007.

Guitar Hero V. Developed by Neversoft. Santa Monica: Activision, 2009.

Karaoke Revolution. Developed by Harmonix. Segundo, CA: Konami, 2003.

Lego Rock Band. Developed by Harmonix and Traveller's Tales. Burbank: Warner Bros./MTV Games, 2009.

Mirror's Edge. Developed by EA Digital Illusions Creative Entertainment. Redwood City: Electronic Arts, 2008.

PaRappa The Rapper. Developed by NanaOn-Sha. Tokyo: Sony, 1996.

Quest for Fame. Developed by Virtual Music Entertainment. Ōta: Namco, 1999.

Rock Band. Developed by Harmonix. Redwood City: Electronic Arts/MTV Games, 2007.

Rock Band 2. Developed by Harmonix. Redwood City: Electronic Arts/MTV Games, 2008.

Rock Band 3. Developed by Harmonix. Redwood City: Electronic Arts/MTV Games, 2010.

Rock of the Dead. Developed by Epicenter Studios. Pomona: Conspiracy Studios and UFO Interactive, 2010.

Simon. Developed by Ralph H. Baer and Howard J. Morrison. East Longmeadow: Milton Bradley, 1978.

Taiko no Tatsujin. Developed by Namco. Ōta: Namco, 2001.

Touch Me. Developed by Atari. Los Angeles: Atari, 1974.

NOTES

1. Brandon Sheffield, "Marching to His Own Drummer: Masaya Matsuura's Thoughts," posted March 6, 2009, http://www.gamasutra.com/view/feature/3955/marching_to_ his_own_drummer_.php.

2. The original *Guitar Hero*, developed by Harmonix for Sony's PlayStation 2 game console and released in 2005, met with relatively modest success; the greater impact of its sequel, *Guitar Hero II*, attracted the involvement of industry behemoths and rivals Activision Blizzard and Electronic Arts, leading to the bifurcation of the games' concepts, mechanics, and other intellectual property into two competing franchises, *Guitar Hero* and *Rock Band*, published by Activision and EA respectively. For a complete list of games in both franchises and a succinct account of their operation, see Kiri Miller, *Playing Along: Digital Games, YouTube, and Virtual Performance* (Oxford: Oxford University Press, 2012), 86–93.

3. For a brief description of Matsuura's career as musician and game developer, see Tristan Donovan, *Replay: The History of Video Games* (Lewes: Yellow Ant, 2010), 281–83. On the heavy human and environmental toll on Africa that has been exacted by Western demand for videogames, see Nick Dyer-Witherford and Greig de Peuter, *Games of Empire*, 215–29. Throughout this essay, I use the term "digital game" rather than "video game" not only as a corrective to oculocentric discourse but also to acknowledge both the nature of the electronic medium and its interfacing with thumbs and fingers.

4. For an excellent overview of *Guitar Hero* and *Rock Band*, and a comprehensive ethnographic study of the diverse ways in which they have been played, see Miller, *Playing Along: Digital Games, YouTube, and Virtual Performance*.

5. *Rock Band 3* was released for Microsoft's Xbox 360, Nintendo's Wii, and Sony's PlayStation 3 consoles in 2010; other iterations of the franchises have been released for handheld devices including Nintendo's DS, Sony's PlayStation Portable, Apple's iPhone, iPod touch, and iPad, and the Android mobile operating system.

6. On the representation of musical time and space in digital games, including *Guitar Hero*, see Peter Shultz, "Music Theory in Music Games," *From Pac-Man to Pop Music: Interactive Audio in Games and New Media*, ed. Karen Collins (Aldershot: Ashgate, 2008), 180–84. As well as playing together in the traditional sense, guitar heroes and rock bands can play online, both collaboratively and competitively. To

adopt David Borgo's terminology, the musicking that these games enable hovers between the second and third order ("Beyond Performance: Transmusicking in Cyberspace," this volume).

7. In January 2009, it was announced that Neversoft's *Guitar Hero III: Legends of Rock* had become the first digital game to surpass $1 billion in sales (Kris Graft, "Activision: *Guitar Hero III* Passes $1b," posted January 9, 2009, http://www.edge-online.com/news/activision-guitar-hero-iii-passes-1b). On the economic impact of *Guitar Hero* and *Rock Band*, see the unsigned article "Playing Along," *Economist*, October 11, 2008, 89; and Jeff Howe, "Here It Goes Again," *Wired*, March 2009, 19–20.

8. Seth Schiesel, "All Together Now: Play the Game, Mom," *New York Times*, September 6, 2009, http://www.nytimes.com/2009/09/06/arts/television/06schi.html.

9. For examples of rock luminaries' negative reactions to the games, see Judy Berman, "Rolling Stones, Pink Floyd Hate *Guitar Hero*, *Rock Band*, Teenagers in General," posted September 8, 2009, http://blog.limewire.com/posts/25764-rolling-stones-pink-floyd-hate-guitar-hero-rock-band-teenagers-in-general/.

10. James Brightman, "Interview: Alex Rigopulos on *Rock Band 2*, Competing with *Guitar Hero*, and Evolving the Music Genre," posted July 24, 2008, http://www.gamedaily.com/articles/features/interview-alex-rigopulos-on-rock-band-2-competing-with-guitar-hero-and-evolving-the-music-genre-/?page=3.

11. Antony Bruno, "Sales of Music Video Games Plummet in 2009," posted December 18, 2009, http://www.reuters.com/article/idUSTRE5BH5DS20091218?type=technologyNews.

12. See Jesse Divnich, "The Divnich Debrief: Roadblocks in the Music Genre," posted July 20, 2009, http://www.industrygamers.com/news/the-divnich-debrief-roadblocks-in-the-music-genre/; Matt Matthews, "Analysis: *Guitar Hero* vs. *Rock Band*—Beyond the Numbers," posted October 23, 2009, http://www.gamasutra.com/php-bin/news_index.php?story=25739; Ben Reeves, "MTV Games Lays Off 39 Harmonix Employees," posted December 10, 2009, http://gameinformer.com/b/news/archive/2009/12/10/news-mtv-game-s-layoff-39-harmonix-employees.aspx; Jim Reilly, "Layoffs at Radical, Neversoft—Luxoflux Closes," posted February 11, 2010, http://xbox360.ign.com/articles/106/1068657p1.html; Brendan Sinclair, "Analysts Blame 2009 Slump on Music Genre, Lack of Innovation," posted January 15, 2010, http://www. gamespot.com/news/6246485.html; and David Wesley, "Too Much of a Good Thing: Explaining the Decline of *Guitar Hero* and *Rock Band*," posted October 28, 2009, http://performancetrap. org/2009/10/28/decline-of-guitar-hero-and-rock-band/.

13. See Leigh Alexander, "Activision Dissolves *Guitar Hero* Business, Refocuses on Digital," posted February 9, 2011, http://www.gamasutra.com/view/news/32946/Activision_Dissolves_Guitar_Hero_Business_Refocuses_On_Digital p.php and Leigh Alexander, "Report: Harmonix Sold for Just Under $50," posted January 4, 2011, http://www.gamasutra.com/view/news/32271/Report_Harmonix_Sold_For_Just_Under_50.php.

14. It is telling that despite Maelzel's musical and ludic efforts to animate the mechanical, such as the panharmonicon (for which Beethoven wrote his battle sym-

phony *Wellingtons Sieg*, op. 91) and the chess-playing "automaton" known as the Turk, his lasting achievement—the metronome—did quite the opposite: it mechanized the human.

15. For an example of these dynamics (and the extent to which they can be manipulated), see Steven E. Jones, *The Meaning of Video Games: Gaming and Textual Strategies* (New York: Routledge, 2008), 69–96.

16. Miller, *Playing Along: Digital Games, YouTube, and Virtual Performance*, 85–151. On the logic, operation, and political import of such networks, see Alexander R. Galloway and Eugene Thacker, *The Exploit: A Theory of Networks* (Minneapolis: University of Minnesota Press, 2007).

17. On Laroche's initial ludomusicological activities, see Tasneem Karbani, "Music to a Gamer's Ears," posted August 22, 2007, http://www.uofaweb.ualberta .ca/arts/news.cfm?story=63769; I independently hit upon the term in 2008 (see Roger Moseley, "*Rock Band* and the Birth of Ludomusicology." Paper delivered at the Annual Meeting of the Society for Ethnomusicology at Wesleyan University, Connecticut [2008], and at "Music and the Moving Image," New York University [2008]). The term "ludomusicology" is partly derived from ludology, itself a recent neologism attributed to Gonzalo Frasca, who defines it as a "discipline that studies game and play activities" (Gonzala Frasca, "Ludology Meets Narratology: Similitude and Differences between (Video) Games and Narrative," accessed June 19, 2012, http://www.ludology.org/ articles/ludology.htm). "Ludomusicology" has gained currency in recent years, as was borne out by the founding of the Ludomusicology Research Group UK in 2011 (http://www.ludomusicology.org).

18. Ian Bogost's *How To Do Things With Videogames* makes this Austinian point both via its title and through Bogost's acknowledgment of music's parallax relationship with gameplay (30–36). Ian Bogost, *How To Do Things With Videogames* (Minneapolis: University of Minnesota Press, 2011), 30–36.

19. A burgeoning community of scholars has framed the relationship between music and digital games in creative, pedagogical, ethnographic, and theoretical contexts: see Juha Arrasvuori, *Playing and Making Music: Exploring the Similarities Between Video Games and Music-Making Software* (Tampere: University of Tampere, 2006); Shultz, "Music Theory in Music Games"; Miller, "Jacking the Dial: Radio, Race, and Place in *Grand Theft Auto*," *Ethnomusicology* 51, no. 3 (2007): 402–38; Kiri Miller, "Schizophonic Performance: Guitar Hero, Rock Band, and Virtual Virtuosity," *Journal of the Society for American Music* 3, no. 4 (2009): 395–429; David Sudnow's pioneering *Pilgrim in the Microworld: Eye, Mind, and the Essence of Video Skill* (New York: Warner Books, 1983) (especially in conjunction with his account of learning how to improvise jazz piano, *Ways of the Hand*); McKenzie Wark, *Gamer Theory* (Cambridge: Harvard University Press, 2007), 126–50. Digital-game critics and developers have also recognized the correspondences between music and games: see Ollie Barder, "Symphony of Play," posted November 24, 2009, http:// www.escapistmagazine.com/articles/view/issues/issue_229/6806-Symphony-of-Play; J. C. Herz, "Making Music Without the Instruments," *New York Times*, January 20, 2000, G17; Margaret Robertson, "One More Go: *Donkey Kong: Jungle Beat*," posted January 7, 2009, http://www.offworld.com/2009/01/one-more-go-donkey-kong-jungle.html.

20. For a comprehensive summary of scholarly approaches to play, see Brian Sutton-Smith, *The Ambiguity of Play* (Cambridge: Harvard University Press, 1997).

21. Max Weber, *Die protestantische Ethik und der Geist des Kapitalismus*, ed. Dirk Kaesler (Munich: C. H. Beck, 2004). For an extension of Weber's concept of rationalization to the realms of play and leisure, see Thomas S. Henricks, *Play Reconsidered: Sociological Perspectives on Human Expression* (Urbana: University of Illinois Press, 2006), 78–108; Victor Turner, "Liminal to Liminoid, in Play, Flow, and Ritual: An Essay in Comparative Symbology," *From Ritual to Theatre: The Human Seriousness of Play* (New York: PAJ Publications, 1982), 37–41.

22. Max Weber, *Die rationalen und soziologischen Grundlagen der Musik* (Munich: Drei Masken Verlag, 1921).

23. In this context, Beethoven's disdain toward the violinist Ignaz Schuppanzigh when he dared to mention the difficulty of a passage in one of the "Razumovsky" Quartets, op. 59, is telling: "Do you think I care for your wretched fiddle when the spirit speaks to me?" Heinrich Schenker, "Genuine and Sham Effects," *Der Tonwille: Pamphlets/Quarterly Publication in Witness of the Immutable Laws of Music*, ed. William Drabkin, 2 vols., 2:115–16 (Oxford: Oxford University Press, 2003).

24. See Lydia Goehr, *The Imaginary Museum of Musical Works: An Essay in the Philosophy of Music* (Oxford: Oxford University Press, 1992). Within historical musicology, playfulness has rarely been acknowledged as a meaningful aesthetic stance beyond the contexts of twentieth-century modernism (outlined by Andrew Westerhaus in "Stravinsky and the Ludic Metaphor," PhD diss., University of Chicago, 2012) and avant-garde, counter-cultural, or experimental movements such as Dada and Fluxus.

25. Roger Caillois, *Les jeux et les hommes: le masque et le virtige* (Paris: Gallimard, 1958), trans. Meyer Barash, *Man, Play, and Games* (Urbana: University of Illinois Press, 2001), 5–6.

26. Plato, *Complete Works*, trans. Trevor J. Saunders, ed. John M. Cooper and D. S. Hutchinson (Indianapolis: Hackett, 1997).

27. Hans-Georg Gadamer, *Truth and Method*, trans. W. Glen-Doepel, Joel Weinsheimer, and Donald G. Marshall (London: Continuum Books, 2004), 104.

28. Claus Pias, "The Game Player's Duty: The User as the Gestalt of the Ports," *Media Archaeology: Approaches, Applications, and Implications*, ed. Erkki Huhtamo and Jussi Parikka, 164–83.

29. Emphasis in original. Friedrich Schiller, *Briefe über die ästhetische Erziehung des Menschen*, ed. Artur Jung (Leipzig: Teubner, 1875), 57.

30. *Homo Ludens* appeared in German in 1939 and was published in English in 1955; all citations refer to the latter version. Johan Huizinga, *Homo Ludens: Versuch einer Bestimmung des Spielelementes der Kultur* (Amsterdam: Pantheon, 1939). Translated as *Homo Ludens: A Study of the Play Element in Culture* (Boston: Beacon Press, 1955).

31. Hector Rodriguez, "The Playful and the Serious: An Approximation to Huizinga's *Homo Ludens*," *Game Studies* 6, no. 1 (2006), http://gamestudies .org/0601/articles/rodriges.

32. Johan Huizinga, *Homo Ludens*, 42. According to Huizinga, languages that feature a "playfully homologous" relationship between music and games include Japanese and Greek as well as French, German, and English (43).

33. Capitalization and emphasis in original. Mark Twain, *The Adventures of Tom Sawyer* (New York: Penguin Putnam, 2002), 21.

34. Just as work can be pleasurable, so can games become a slog: players of

role-playing games talk of "grinding" (engaging in mindlessly repetitive in-game activities) in order to "level-up" their characters and facilitate progress (see Steven Poole, "Working for the Man," posted October 27, 2008, http://stevenpoole.net/trigger-happy/working-for-the-man/). Such nominally playful activities are sometimes outsourced as paid labor.

35. Roger Caillois, *Les jeux et les hommes: le masque et le virtige*, trans. Meyer Barash, *Man, Play, and Games*, 9–10.

36. Roger Caillois, *Les jeux et les hommes: le masque et le virtige*, trans. Meyer Barash, *Man, Play, and Games*, 11–36. Caillois drew the term *mimicry* from biology, where it describes the sharing of perceived similarities between species. In his essay "Mimicry and Legendary Psychasthenia," Caillois interprets the *mimicry* of insects as non-utilitarian, as a playful luxury rather than a Darwinian adaptation for survival, as described in Thomas S. Henricks, "Caillois's *Man, Play, and Games*: An Appreciation and Evaluation," *American Journal of Play* 3, no. 2 (2010): 157–85, 4. On Caillois's notion of "diagonal science" and his complex relationship with Huizinga, surrealism, the animal world, and the sacred, see Claudia Mesch, "Serious Play: Games and Early Twentieth-Century Modernism," *From Diversion to Subversion: Games, Play, and Twentieth-Century Art*, ed. David J. Getsy (University Park: Pennsylvania University Press, 2011), 60–72.

37. On boss battles, see Clive Thompson, "Who's the Boss?," *Wired*, posted May 8, 2006, http://www.wired.com/gaming/gamingreviews/commentary/games/2006/05/70832. Tellingly, the introduction of agônic conflict in *Guitar Hero III* was coeval with the outbreak of economic competition between Neversoft, Harmonix, and their respective publishers.

38. In *Guitar Hero III*, "The Devil Went Down to Georgia" is Steve Ouimette's cover version of the original song by the Charlie Daniels Band in which Johnny, a young fiddler, bests the devil in a violin-playing contest. On the satanic iconography of rock music, and heavy metal in particular, see Robert Walser, *Running With the Devil: Power, Gender, and Madness in Heavy Metal Music* (Middletown, CT: Wesleyan University Press, 1993).

39. On musical dice games, see Neal Zaslaw, "Mozart's Modular Minuet Machine," *Essays in Honor of László Somfai on His Seventieth Birthday: Studies in the Sources and Interpretation of Music*, ed. László Vikárius and Vera Lampert (Lanham, MD: Scarecrow Press, 2004), 220–26.

40. Digital games facilitate and draw upon *mimicry* in many forms, from the fantasy world of the role-playing game (which often also involves the operations of *alea*, in keeping with its dice-rolling origins in table-top games such as *Dungeons & Dragons*) to the "realism" of the sports management simulator.

41. Roger Caillois, *Les jeux et les hommes: le masque et le virtige*, trans. Meyer Barash, *Man, Play, and Games*, 21.

42. For an alternative perspective on this dichotomy, see Philip Auslander's adaptation of Erving Goffman's theories concerning performer-audience relationships in "Jazz Improvisation as a Social Arrangement," this volume. Philip Auslander, "Tryin' to Make It Real: Live Performance, Simulation, and the Discourse of Authenticity in Rock Culture," *Liveness: Performance in a Mediatized Culture*, 2nd ed. (London: Routledge, 2008), 73–127.

43. See Hans-Georg Gadamer, "The Play of Art," *The Relevance of the Beautiful*

and Other Essays, trans. Nicholas Walker, ed. Robert Bernasconi (Cambridge: Cambridge University Press, 1986), 127–28. Despite their sonic and social disparities, both opera and certain sub-genres of rock music, such as glam metal, share an intense engagement with play through *mimicry:* in addition to their musical intensity, both feature masks, costumes, pyrotechnics, and other theatrical accoutrements that collectively entreat the audience to suspend its disbelief.

44. First-person digital games are best at imparting the sense of motion and disorientation typical of *ilinx:* examples include EA Digital Illusions Creative Entertainment's parkour-inspired *Mirror's Edge* and Dejobaan Games' vertigo-inducing *AaaaaAAaaaAAAaaAAAAaAAAAA!!! A Reckless Disregard for Gravity. Mirror's Edge*, developed by EA Digital Illusions Creative Entertainment (Redwood City: Electronic Arts, 2008). *AaaaaAAaaaAAAaaAAAAaAAAAA!!! A Reckless Disregard for Gravity*, developed by Dejobaan Games (Watertown, MA: Dejobaan Games, 2009).

45. Roger Caillois, *Les jeux et les hommes: le masque et le virtige*, trans. Meyer Barash, *Man, Play, and Games*, 28–30. It should be noted that the sense in which Caillois deploys *ludus* ("game" or "play" in Latin) is at odds with the English adjective "ludic," which connotes undirected and spontaneous playful behavior: confusingly, these are precisely the characteristics that Caillois ascribes to *paidia*.

46. For example, a player might recklessly sacrifice her queen for the pleasure of watching the game unravel (or simply to annoy her *ludus*-oriented opponent). Bernard Suits defines such players as "triflers" who recognize the rules but not the goals of a game (Bernard Suits, *The Grasshopper: Games, Life, and Utopia* [Peterborough, Ontario: Broadview Press, 2005], 58–60).

47. See David Cohen, "Webern's Magic Square," *Perspectives of New Music* 13, no. 1 (1974): 213–15. As its title suggests, the *paidia* of "Couplets bachiques" is mixed with a good measure of drunken *ilinx*.

48. For a theoretical overview of the constitutive, operational, and implicit rules that enable and constrain gameplay, see Katie Salen and Eric Zimmerman, *Rules of Play: Game Design Fundamentals* (Cambridge: MIT Press, 2004), 101–5, 141–49.

49. These features distinguished *Guitar Hero* from Harmonix's previous rhythm-action game *Frequency*, which traded on the synergy between its comparatively esoteric electronic soundtrack and its futuristic presentation: while these attributes enhanced its appeal for technophiliac gamers, they restricted its mass-market potential. On the factors behind the rapid expansion and diversification of the digital-game audience in recent years, in which the success of *Guitar Hero* and *Rock Band* played a major role, see Jesper Juul, *A Casual Revolution: Reinventing Video Games and Their Players* (Cambridge: MIT Press, 2010).

50. Robin Murray, "Noel Gallagher on *Guitar Hero:* Not a Fan, It Seems," posted February 3, 2009, http://www.clashmusic.com/news/noel-gallagher-guitar-hero.

51. Quoted in Brian Hiatt, "Secrets of the Guitar Heroes: John Mayer," posted June 12, 2008, http://www.rollingstone.com/news/story/21004549/secrets_of_the_guitar_heroes_ john_mayer/print. Rigopulos has cheerfully admitted the element of truth in Mayer's complaint, going so far as to specify the game's algorithmic input/output ratio: "A game like *Rock Band* gets you maybe 50 percent of the way [toward the experience of musical performance] with 3 percent of the effort" (quoted in Daniel Radosh, "While My Guitar Gently Beeps," *New York Times*,

August 16, 2009, http://www.nytimes.com/2009/08/16/magazine/16beatles-t
.html?pagewanted=all).

52. In the world of digital games, cheating does not necessarily imply dishon-
esty or deception: circumvention of a game's prevailing rules may or may not be enabled and sanctioned by its developers (see Julian Kücklich, "Forbidden Pleasures:
Cheating in Computer Games," *The Pleasures of Computer Gaming*, ed. Melanie
Swalwell and Jason Wilson (Jefferson, NC: McFarland, 2008), 52–71). Suits defines
the cheat as the trifler's counterpart: she acknowledges the goals but not the rules
of a game (Bernard Suits, *The Grasshopper: Games, Life, and Utopia*, 60).

53. See Trevor J. Pinch and Karin Bijsterveld, "'Should One Applaud?': Breaches
and Boundaries in the Reception of New Technology in Music," *Technology and Culture* 44, no. 3 (2003): 536–59.

54. "I mean, what would you rather drive, a Ferrari or one of those amusement-
park cars on a track?" (Mayer, quoted in Brian Hiatt, "Secrets of the Guitar Heroes:
John Mayer").

55. The games themselves acknowledge this by incorporating "practice" modes
in which players can tackle troublesome passages at a reduced tempo. *Rock Band 2*
even features a dedicated "drum trainer" mode, which instructs the player according to the principles of traditional drumming pedagogy. For the *ludus*-averse, *Rock
Band 2* also introduced a "no-fail" mode in which the show always goes on, no matter how shambolic the performance.

56. Such players congregate online at the ScoreHero forum (http://www.score
hero.com/ forum/), where they exchange arcane strategies and techniques in pursuit of ever-higher scores. See Miller, *Playing Along: Digital Games, YouTube, and
Virtual Performance*, 137–41.

57. See the project undertaken by the Guitar Zeros ("The Zero Guide") and
www. scorehero.com forum user Reptiliack's tutorial for inserting new tracks into
the PlayStation 2 version of *Rock Band* (Reptiliack, "How to Get Custom Songs
Into *Rock Band*," posted May 26, 2008, http://rockband.scorehero.com/forum/
viewtopic.php?t=9189).

58. "I'm super-proud of the online community that has popped up around [the
peripherals]. I think they're an awesome and relatively cheap project box for doing
all sorts of crazy, different things. We're hoping to see people plug these things
into their computers, and perform in their band with them" (Matt Boch, quoted in
Chris Dahlen, "Interview: Harmonix Music Systems," posted July 17, 2008, http://
www.avclub.com/articles/harmonix-music-systems,14273/). The potential for
compositional creativity, previously the exclusive domain of hackers and modders,
was officially enabled by the MIDI-based Music Studio mode of *Guitar Hero: World
Tour* and was extended by the establishment of Harmonix's Rock Band Network,
a "system that [allows] bands, studios and record labels to create and sell playable
game content from their master recordings using the same professional tools used
by our developers" ("Coming Soon," accessed June 19, 2012, http://creators.rock
band.com/statichome).

59. Eric Zimmerman, "Narrative, Interactivity, Play, and Games: Four Naughty
Concepts in Need of Discipline," *First Person: New Media as Story, Performance, and
Game*, ed. Noah Wardrip-Fruin and Pat Harrigan (Cambridge: MIT Press, 2004),
159. Jon Dovey and Helen W. Kennedy frame the same insight in politicized terms,

asserting that digital gaming is simultaneously the "prodigal son of the military/industrial/capitalist complex and its illegitimate and unruly child" (Jon Dovey and Helen W. Kennedy, *Game Cultures: Computer Games as New Media* [Maidenhead: Open University Press, 2006], 36).

60. Despite its virtues, Caillois's ethnocentric perspective on play both limits and over-extends the scope of his taxonomy; moreover, it could be argued that his categories cannot account for the complexities of technologically mediated play. Sutton-Smith's seven "rhetorics" of play (outlined in Brian Sutton-Smith, *The Ambiguity of Play*, 9–12) draw upon a broader range of intellectual and cultural resources; see also Salen and Zimmerman's succinct but powerful definition ("play is free movement within a more rigid structure," Katie Salen and Eric Zimmerman, *Rules of Play: Game Design Fundamentals*, 304).

61. Among other peripherals, this shared ancestry incorporates the controller for the Japanese version of the Super Nintendo Entertainment System, released in 1990, as well as *Simon*, which was based on the arcade game *Touch Me*, released by Atari four years earlier. Although *Simon* was a memory game, it is telling that its primary-colored quadrants emitted musical pitches that collectively constituted a C-major triad.

62. On Froebel, see Joachim Liebschner, *A Child's Work: Freedom and Guidance in Froebel's Educational Theory and Practice* (Cambridge: Lutterworth Press, 2006).

63. See Milton Bradley, *Color in the Kindergarten: A Manual of the Theory of Color and the Practical Use of Color Material in the Kindergarten* (Springfield, MA: Milton Bradley, 1893).

64. Successive iterations of the *Guitar Hero* and *Rock Band* guitars have become ever-more "realistic" in appearance as ever-greater authenticity has been claimed for the games themselves, culminating in the painstaking attention to detail that characterizes the music, instruments, iconography, and historical presentation of *The Beatles: Rock Band* (documented by Radosh in "While My Guitar Gently Beeps"). Beyond that, Fender produced both "simulated" and "hybrid" six-string guitar controllers (licensed from Mustang and Squier respectively) for use in *Rock Band 3*, released in 2010. These controllers offer players the chance to develop "actual musical skills" through the introduction of accurately tabulated "Pro" modes: the invocation of professionalism serves to distinguish such serious pursuits from the casual dabbling of the amateur, thereby reconstructing a work/play dichotomy within the game itself. In 2011, Ubisoft pursued this tendency to its logical conclusion by releasing *Rocksmith*, an "authentic guitar game" that connects to any electric guitar: players thus "really" perform the game's songs, within the ambit of an adaptive difficulty system. *Rocksmith*'s very title evokes artisanship rather than heroism, work rather than play.

65. Henry George Liddell and Robert Scott, rev. Henry Stuart Jones, *A Greek-English Lexicon* (Oxford: Clarendon Press, 1940), s.v. παιδιά. Plato's use of the term reflected his conception of humans as playthings of the gods and of ritual as a "game" played out in the gods' honor. *Paidia* (play or game), *paideia* (education or culture), and *paides* (children) share the same etymological root.

66. For a polemical diagnosis of this cultural condition, see Simon Reynolds, *Retromania: Pop Culture's Addiction to Its Own Past* (New York: Faber and Faber, 2011).

67. Giorgio Agamben, "In Playland: Reflections on History and Play," *Infancy and History: The Destruction of Experience*, trans. Liz Heron (London: Verso Books, 1993), 80. The "toyness" of the plastic guitar is brought to the fore in *Lego Rock Band*, developed by Harmonix in collaboration with Traveller's Tales, which "mashes up" primary-colored franchises in order to appeal simultaneously to children and to their nostalgic parents.

68. Steve Waksman, *Instruments of Desire: The Electric Guitar and the Shaping of Musical Experience* (Cambridge: Harvard University Press, 1999). See also André Millard, ed., *The Electric Guitar: A History of an American Icon* (Baltimore: Johns Hopkins University Press, 2004).

69. "Achievements" contribute toward every Xbox 360 player's "Gamerscore," a cumulative tally of his or her accomplishments in all games played and thus an index of skill, devotion, and free time.

70. Later iterations of *BeatMania* expanded the keyboard's range to seven keys. The two-octave keyboard peripheral introduced with *Rock Band 3* draws directly upon this lineage; likewise, FreeStyleGames' *DJ Hero*, a spinoff from the *Guitar Hero* franchise, is indebted to both *BeatMania* and *Frequency*. Its innovation lies in the degree to which its soundtrack, centered on turntablism and mash-ups of electronic music, hip-hop, and pop, reflects the archetype of the DJ whose musically creative activities revolve around the selection and combination of pre-existent elements rather than focusing on the composition and performance of "original" material.

71. By 2010, the Bemani division had released thirty-nine different arcade cabinets since the original *BeatMania* (cited in the unattributed article "Rhythm Attraction—The Rise of the Beatmatching Business: How Rhythm-Action Topped the Charts," *Edge* 211 (February 2010): 74).

72. On Japanese arcade culture in general and rhythm-action games in particular, see Brian Ashcraft and Jean Snow, *Arcade Mania! The Turbo-Charged World of Japan's Game Centers* (Tokyo: Kodansha International, 2008), 50–65; Chris Kohler, *Power-Up: How Japanese Video Games Gave the World an Extra Life* (Indianapolis: BradyGames, 2004), 132–64. For broader cultural context and commentary, see Joseph Tobin, ed., *Pikachu's Global Adventure: The Rise and Fall of Pokémon* (Durham: Duke University Press, 2004); Larissa Hjorth and Dean Chan, eds., *Gaming Culture and Place in Asia-Pacific* (New York: Routledge, 2009).

73. See Joanna Demers, "Dancing Machines: *Dance Dance Revolution*, Cybernetic Dance, and Musical Taste," *Popular Music* 25, no. 3 (2006): 401–14; Jacob Smith, "I Can See Tomorrow in Your Dance: A Study of *Dance Dance Revolution* and Music Video Games," *Journal of Popular Music Studies* 16, no. 1 (2004): 58–84. Smith describes the bifurcation of *Dance Dance Revolution* communities into "tech" and "freestyle" contingents. In Caillois's terms, tech players focus on *agôn* and *ludus* while freestylers exhibit *mimicry* and *paidia*. Miller discusses similar types of ludic attitudes to *Guitar Hero* and *Rock Band* in *Playing Along: Digital Games, YouTube, and Virtual Performance*, 127–29.

74. The Aerosmith-themed *Quest for Fame*, developed in the United States by Virtual Music and initially released for PC in 1995, merits a mention here, particularly since an arcade version was manufactured by the Japanese company Namco as a rival to Konami's Bemani games in 1999. There is no evidence, however, that it directly influenced either Konami or Harmonix.

75. Maggie Overfelt, "How 'Horrendous Failure' Led to *Rock Band*," posted September 3, 2009, http://money.cnn.com/2009/09/03/smallbusiness/harmonix_ rock_band_startup_story/index.htm. *PaRappa The Rapper,* a "rhythm-action" game developed by NanaOn-Sha under Masaya Matsuura's direction, was released in Japan for the PlayStation in 1996. According to Rigopulos, "the release of *PaRappa* was a life-changing event for me—it wasn't the first rhythm-action game, but it was the first great one, and it altered Harmonix's trajectory" (quoted in "Rhythm Attraction—The Rise of the Beatmatching Business: How Rhythm-Action Topped the Charts," 71). Harmonix also gained invaluable experience by collaborating with Konami in developing and localizing the Japanese *Karaoke Revolution* digital-game franchise for the North American market; see Randy Smith and Greg LoPiccolo, "All the Way to 11," *Edge* 194 (November 2008): 74–75.

76. While imitation might be the sincerest form of flattery, Konami responded by suing Harmonix for patent infringement; see Chris Kohler, "Konami Sues Harmonix Over *Rock Band*," posted July 10, 2008, http://www.wired.com/ gamelife/2008/07/konami-sues-har/. By early 2011 the case had reached settlement, details of which had not been made public.

77. Liu defines prophetic relics—or reverse skeuomorphs—as "epistemological rather than instrumental stitches between past and present. They are an index or placeholder (rather than cause or antecedent) of the future" (Alan Liu, "Transcendental Data: Toward a Cultural History and Aesthetics of the New Encoded Discourse," *Critical Inquiry* 31 [2004]: 72). For a historical perspective on the piano roll as "software" and the ontological and legal uncertainty to which it gave rise, see Lisa Gitelman, "Media, Materiality, and the Measure of the Digital; Or, the Case of Sheet Music and the Problem of Piano Rolls," *Memory Bytes: History, Technology, and Digital Culture,* ed. Lauren Rabinovitz and Abraham Geil (Durham: Duke University Press, 2004), 199–217. For a complementary perspective that situates the piano roll and *Guitar Hero* in the context of "re-performance," see Nicholas Seaver, "A Brief History of Re-performance," MSc diss., Massachusetts Institute of Technology, 2010.

78. A full set of instruments and software for *Rock Band* initially retailed for approximately $200. The private, domestic setting of the typical North American *Guitar Hero* experience contrasts with the vibrant public spaces of the Japanese arcades in which *BeatMania, Dance Dance Revolution,* and *GuitarFreaks* are usually played; the exoticized fascination such spaces can exert on the Western imagination is reflected in Sofia Coppola's film *Lost in Translation* (2003). Although rhythm-action games are played domestically in Japan and publicly in North America, the converse is the prevailing norm (see Miller, *Playing Along: Digital Games, YouTube, and Virtual Performance,* 129–41; Shinichiro Kumano, "Konami: Jōshiki wo kutsugaesu ongaku gēmu dai-hitto, Kanren shōhin nado tamen-tenkai," *Nikkei bijinesu,* February 15, 1999, 61–64).

79. *The Beatles: Rock Band* removes the improvisatory elements present in *Rock Band 2* (such as freestyle drum fills and cadenza-like "Big Rock Endings") and prohibits singers from substantially reducing the levels of the original vocal tracks.

80. Quoted in Daniel Radosh, "While My Guitar Gently Beeps." In this vein, Miller draws a telling analogy between *Guitar Hero* notation, transcription, and gameplay and the culture of four-hand amateur pianism in the nineteenth century (Miller, *Playing Along: Digital Games, YouTube, and Virtual Performance,* 105–6).

81. Kircher's design for an elaborate water organ is reproduced in Siegfried Zielinski, *Deep Time of the Media: Toward an Archaeology of Hearing and Seeing by Technical Means*, trans. Gloria Custance (Cambridge: MIT Press, 2006), 127. See also the eighteenth-century conception of a "machine that shall write Extempore Voluntaries" as described in John Freke, "A Letter from Mr. John Freke F. R. S., Surgeon to St. Bartholomew's Hospital, to the President of the Royal Society, Inclosing a Paper of the Late Rev. Mr. Creed, concerning a Machine to Write Down Extempore Voluntaries, or Other Pieces of Music," *Philosophical Transactions (1683–1775)* 44 (1746–47): 446; and V. D. de Stains's representation of barrel organ notation in *Phonography*, plate VII (V. D. de Stains, *Phonography; Or the Writing of Sounds*, 2nd ed. [London: Effingham Wilson, 1842], 190–91). The keyboard peripheral released alongside *Rock Band 3* makes explicit the game's "piano roll" notational lineage and provides a more conventional input device for interacting with it: for players, guitar parts and keyboard parts are interoperable (see Justin Haywald, "What *Rock Band 3*'s Pro Keyboard Can Teach You About Real Music," posted August 17, 2010, http://www.1up.com/ do/reviewPage? pager.offset=0&cId=3180908&p=).

82. See David Suisman, "Sound, Knowledge, and the 'Immanence of Human Failure': Rethinking Musical Mechanization through the Phonograph, the Player-Piano, and the Piano," *Social Text* 28, no. 102 (2010): 19; Gerhard Nierhaus, *Algorithmic Composition: Paradigms of Automated Music Generation* (Vienna: Springer, 2009), 39–43; Lisa Gitelman, "Media, Materiality, and the Measure of the Digital; Or, the Case of Sheet Music and the Problem of Piano Rolls," *Memory Bytes: History, Technology, and Digital Culture*, ed. Lauren Rabinovitz and Abraham Geil, 203–4.

83. Despite or owing to their efforts, the Guitar Zeros' conversion of *Guitar Hero* controllers into functional MIDI instruments accentuates the disparity between the MIDI-like digital latticework of the games' interfaces and the analog modulations of the electric guitar itself: the former binarize—and inevitably fall short of—the latter. See Jaron Lanier, *You Are Not a Gadget: A Manifesto* (New York: Knopf, 2010), 7–10.

84. See Hristo Bojinov et al., "Neuroscience Meets Cryptography: Designing Crypto Primitives Secure Against Rubber Hose Attacks," https://www.usenix .org/conference/usenixsecurity12/neuroscience-meets-cryptography-designing-crypto-primitives-secure.

85. On the relationship between digital games and the military-industrial complex, see Patrick Crogan, *Gameplay Mode: War, Simulation, and Technoculture* (Minneapolis: University of Minnesota Press, 2011); Claus Pias, "The Game Player's Duty: The User as the Gestalt of the Ports," *Media Archaeology: Approaches, Applications, and Implications*, ed. Erkki Huhtamo and Jussi Parikka, 164–83. On Baer's involvement with the military, see Steven Karras, ed., *The Enemy I Knew: German Jews in the Allied Military in World War II* (Minneapolis: Zenith Press, 2009), 131–49.

86. Friedrich Kittler, *Gramophone, Film, Typewriter*, trans. Geoffrey Winthrop-Young and Michael Wutz (Stanford: Stanford University Press, 1999), 96–97.

87. Chris Dahlen, "Interview: Harmonix Music Systems." *Quest for Fame* featured a similarly ambiguous "V-Pick."

88. Jean Baudrillard, *Simulacra and Simulation*, trans. Sheila Glaser (Ann Arbor: University of Michigan Press, 1996).

89. See, for instance, Hugh Barker and Yuval Taylor, eds., *Faking It: The Quest for*

Authenticity in Popular Music (New York: Norton, 2007); Philip Auslander, "Tryin' to Make It Real: Live Performance, Simulation, and the Discourse of Authenticity in Rock Culture," *Liveness: Performance in a Mediatized Culture*, 73–127.

90. Lawrence Grossberg, "The Media Economy of Rock Culture: Cinema, Post-Modernity, and Authenticity," *Sound and Vision: The Music Video Reader*, ed. Simon Frith, Andrew Goodwin, and Lawrence Grossberg (London: Routledge, 1993), 185–209.

91. Victor Godinez, "Metallica Fans Say *Guitar Hero* Versions of *Death Magnetic* Songs Beat Those of the CD," posted September 25, 2008, http://www.popmatters.com/pm/article/metallica-fans-say-guitar-hero-versions-of-death-magnetic-songs-beat-those-/. See also Ian Shepherd, "Metallica['s] *Death Magnetic* Sounds Better in *Guitar Hero*," posted September 15, 2008, http://mastering-media.blogspot.com/2008/09/metallica-death-magnetic-sounds-better. html.

92. The tired arm of an expert player testifies not only to the repetitiveness of certain riffs but also to the superior efficiency of copying and pasting in Pro Tools compared to human-powered techniques of replication. For footage of the recording of *Death Magnetic* that features Pro Tools and click tracks, see *The Making of Metallica's* Death Magnetic, directed by Metallica (bonus DVD with Metallica, *Death Magnetic* Box Set Limited Edition, Vertigo 00602517804609, 2008).

93. Philip Auslander, "Tryin' to Make It Real: Live Performance, Simulation, and the Discourse of Authenticity in Rock Culture," *Liveness: Performance in a Mediatized Culture*, 73–127.

94. Chris Kohler, "Full-On *Rock Band* Makes Jamming Follow-Up to *Guitar Hero*," Wired, posted September 14, 2007, http://www.wired.com/gaming/gamingreviews/magazine/15-10/mf_harmonix?currentPage=all.

95. To add one final twist, in 2008 VH1 Classic broadcast *Rock Band 2: The Stars*, a "reality" show along the lines of *Big Brother*. Living in a mansion under the threat of weekly elimination, participants vied with one another for the title of the best *Rock Band 2* player: criteria relating to both *ludus* (technical accuracy and high scores) and *paidia* (energy and attitude) were applied by judges Alice Cooper and Sebastian Bach.

96. Robert Fink, *Repeating Ourselves: American Minimal Music as Cultural Practice* (Berkeley and Los Angeles: University of California Press, 2005), 221. From a different perspective, Paul DeGooyer of MTV Games has compared *Rock Band* to the Kódaly Method of music instruction, particularly its pedagogical approach to rhythm (cited in Daniel Radosh, "While My Guitar Gently Beeps."

97. Gallagher has admitted, "I've never played *Guitar Hero* myself. I suppose I'm a bit old-fashioned" (Robin Murray, "Noel Gallagher on *Guitar Hero:* Not a Fan, It Seems").

98. Henri Bergson, *Laughter: An Essay on the Meaning of the Comic*, trans. Cloudesley Bereton and Fred Rothwell (New York: Macmillan, 1921), 37.

99. Miller, *Playing Along: Digital Games, YouTube, and Virtual Performance*, 141–49.

100. Robert Fink, *Repeating Ourselves: American Minimal Music as Cultural Practice*, 226–33.

101. Shin'ichi Suzuki, *Young Children's Talent Education and Its Method*, trans. Kyoko Selden (Van Nuys, CA: Alfred, 1996), 51; Hans-Georg Gadamer, *Truth and Method*, trans. W. Glen-Doepel, Joel Weinsheimer, and Donald G. Marshall, 106.

102. Claus Pias, "The Game Player's Duty: The User as the Gestalt of the Ports,"

Media Archaeology: Approaches, Applications, and Implications, ed. Erkki Huhtamo and Jussi Parikka, 164–83.

103. Margaret Robertson, "One More Go: *Donkey Kong: Jungle Beat*."

104. In Kittler's formulation, "code is the only language that does what it says": it is performative in the strict sense of the term (paraphrased in Alexander R. Galloway, *Gaming: Essays on Algorithmic Culture* (Minneapolis: University of Minnesota Press, 2006), 5). Nicholas Cook has made an analogous point in the context of chamber music: "to think of [a Mozart quartet] as a 'script' is to see it as choreographing a series of real-time, social interactions between players" (Nicholas Cook, "Music as Performance," *The Cultural Study of Music*, ed. Martin Clayton, Trevor Herbert, and Richard Middleton (New York: Routledge, 2003), 206).

105. Chris Kohler, "Full-On *Rock Band* Makes Jamming Follow-Up to *Guitar Hero*."

106. It is suggestive that Lang Lang's 2011 album commemorating Liszt's bicentennial year is entitled *Liszt: My Piano Hero*.

107. Vladimir Jankélévitch, *Music and the Ineffable*, trans. Carolyn Abbate (Princeton: Princeton University Press, 2003), 77–79. Carolyn Abbate, "Music—Drastic or Gnostic?," *Critical Inquiry* 30, no. 3 (2004): 505–36.

108. Ian Bogost, *Unit Operations: An Approach to Videogame Criticism* (Cambridge: MIT Press, 2006), 27–28.

109. Margaret Robertson, "One More Go: *Donkey Kong: Jungle Beat*."

110. *Donkey Konga* was adapted from Namco's *Taiko no Tatsujin*, an example of a Japanese rhythm-action game that does not draw upon Western iconography and organology: it features a controller in the form of a taiko drum.

111. See, for instance, *Fret Nice*, developed by Pieces Interactive (Torrance, CA: Tecmo, 2010); *Boom Boom Rocket*, developed by Bizarre Creations (Redwood City: Electronic Arts, 2007); *Rock of the Dead*, developed by Epicenter Studios (Pomona: Conspiracy Studios and UFO Interactive, 2010).

112. Steven Poole, *Trigger Happy: Videogames and the Entertainment Revolution* (New York: Arcade, 2000), 187.

113. Hans Ulrich Gumbrecht, *Production of Presence: What Meaning Cannot Convey* (Stanford: Stanford University Press, 2004), 113–14.

DAVID BORGO

Beyond Performance

Transmusicking in Cyberspace

- An ensemble of thirty performers prepares to improvise music together. With only basic conceptual sketches agreed upon beforehand and a language of improvised conducted gestures to guide them, this performance already carries a considerable degree of risk. Add to this the fact that the musicians and their respective audiences are physically located in three distinct venues spanning nearly 3,000 miles and the notion of "creating music together in the course of performance" may appear to enter the realm of impossibility.

- On the street, a young woman with conspicuous white cords dangling from her ears appears lost in the music she alone is hearing, and yet somehow also deeply engaged in and by her surroundings. At times she turns her entire body in response to loud sounds in her environment. At other moments she dramatically taps, shakes, and rotates the device she is holding. Sometimes she whispers garbled words, hums strange melodies, or uses objects and surfaces in her surroundings to create percussive sounds and rhythms. It is hard not to wonder what she is hearing and what compels her to these unusual activities.

- A visitor to an otherwise sedate museum is asked to remove his shoes, don a brightly colored robe, and wear a blindfold. With assistance he enters a ritualized space full of unusual and disorienting sounds and sensations. Others who are similarly dressed saunter and even dance about, variously pulled together or swept apart as if by magnetic or other invisible forces. In reality, each participant is honing in on a personal "sound signature" that can modulate in response to one's own actions, to the proximity of others, or to the subtle prodding of a hidden computer operator. These strangely clad and sight-impaired individu-

319

als appear to be participating in a form of collective composition, and, some might even say, collective consciousness.

WHAT DO THESE THREE moments of "musicking" have in common? Although it can be argued that practices related to these were in evidence, often in some nascent form, prior to the digital revolution or the emergence of "cyberspace," their immersive, interactive, multi-modal, and spatially extended dimensions are in other ways quite new. Collectively they seem to tug at the very seams of our orthodox notions of music performance, that is, a localized and shared experience involving some variety of well-understood action-sound couplings unfolding in linear time.[1] Perhaps because of this potential dissonance with conventional understandings of music performance, discussions surrounding newer forms of music engagement tend to polarize rather quickly.

Are these newer technologies and practices democratizing the musical experience, opening the floodgates of creativity on a mass scale? Or do they invite a sort of "mass amateurization" that robs music of its former depth and required discipline? Do newer technologies afford more immersive, intense, and deeply personal engagements with sound? Or do the considerable technological investments and the ever-present worry of industrial manipulation actually make the music less direct, less engaging, somehow less "real"? Are we experiencing new possibilities for combining sonic exploration and social interaction, perhaps glimpsing emergent properties and decentralized behaviors that are difficult for humans to intuit or imagine? Or do these practices actually increase isolation and dependency and potentially decrease music's diversity? Can we reconcile our conventional notions of "presence" and "effort"—aspects central to Susan Fast's argument in favor of the "live" concert event that begins this volume—with these new musicking scenarios?

The slippery notion of "technology" may be the most common inroad to discussions about how music is created, consumed, experienced, and ultimately perceived in the contemporary moment (at least among the relatively affluent), but both "technology" and "music," despite the ease with which we use these concepts in our everyday lives, are remarkably polysemous terms. Computer science pioneer and occasional professional jazz guitarist Alan Kay once described technology as "anything that was invented after you were born." Kay's light-hearted comment highlights rather perceptively how "technology," as a notion, is inextricably linked to a user's frame of reference. Martin Heidegger framed the issues with considerably more nuance in his 1954 essay "The Question Concerning

Technology." For Heidegger, technology involves "the manufacture and utilization of equipment, tools, and machines, the manufactured and used things themselves, and the needs and ends that they serve. . . . The whole complex of these contrivances is technology."[2]

Similarly, the word "music" is used in a variety of different, overlapping, and imprecise ways. As a purely physical phenomenon, music involves sound waves traveling through a medium of air. Music as heard and understood, however, involves human perceptual faculties and cognitive processes, all of which have co-evolved through perception-action cycles in tandem with a shaping environment (involving biological and cultural affordances), such that the notion of "music to my ears" signifies much more than a physiological response.[3] The term "music," for English speakers at least, is also frequently conflated with various forms of musical inscription, including notation (as in "Do you have the music for tonight's performance?") and recordings on various analog and digital media (as in "Do you want to see my music collection?" or "What music do you have on your iPod?"). This semantic confusion extends ontologically to the regulative conception of a musical work. Lydia Goehr reminds us, "Speaking about music in terms of works is neither an obvious nor a necessary mode of speech, despite the lack of ability we presently seem to have to speak about music in any other way."[4]

Christopher Small coined his well-known neologism "musicking" to combat these and other recalcitrant notions and to refocus our attention on music as social activity.[5] In ways not dissimilar to Heidegger's, however, Small's theorizing was provoked by a perception that traditional values (in Small's case those regarding musical collectivism and spontaneity) were rapidly receding in the wake of Western commercialism and consumerism. Small's notion of musicking—"to take part, in any capacity, in a musical performance, whether by performing, by listening, by rehearsing or practicing, by providing material for performance (what is called composition), or by dancing"[6]—offers a wonderfully integrated approach to exploring musical sounds, conceptions, and behaviors, but recent digital technologies, and the network infrastructure on which they communicate, have reconfigured the musicking landscape in ways that could not have been easily anticipated.

Elsewhere I have begun the process of bringing Small's notion of musicking into the twenty-first century.[7] Here I would like to expand on this earlier work by introducing the notion of "transmusicking," a turn-of-phrase inspired by the provocative, poetic, and at times utopian-tinged writings of "transarchitect" Marcos Novak, a professor and director at transLAB at the University of California, Santa Barbara. In brief, I am less interested here in musicking that uses newer technologies primarily for the creation of conventional musicking products, practices, and occasions. I am more interested, instead, in approaches that explore the unique affordances of digital and network technologies. As the prefix *trans-* implies (from Latin meaning "across, beyond, through"), I am also keenly interested in how these new musicking approaches might be at once a transmutation or transgression of previous conventions and expectations while remaining interwoven within the existing social, cultural, political, and commercial matrix.

Recent decades have witnessed the emergence of a variety of activities that could (in part or in full) productively fall under the banner of transmusicking, including virtual music, network music, generative music, reactive music, interactive music, navigable music, telematic music, and sound art, to name only a few. These practices and communities differ in significant ways, but they often share an orientation that questions presupposed boundaries between composers, performers, and listeners, or those between music conceived as product or process. Rather than seeking to generate a shared experience—a customary goal of much conventional music performance—transmusicking practices frequently accept or aim to produce a more diffuse engagement in which everyone has a different experience, or subsequent experiences are dramatically different. The "performative" activity associated with transmusicking is often interactive, immersive, even co-creative, and it frequently involves a distributed or co-located aspect. As early as 1992 Marcos Novak argued:

> Music has been previously understood as something that occurs in linear time, that can be understood as a single object in time . . . it is possible to stop seeing music as singular, as a street between point a and point b, and to start seeing music as multiple, as landscape, as atmosphere, as an n-dimensional field of opportunities.[8]

According to Novak, "Music has exceeded both sound and time, and it has been permanently altered by the introduction of space and inhabitation into its range of speculation."[9]

Obviously a survey of several decades worth of emerging transmusicking is beyond the scope of a short essay, and some excellent introductory texts can be found elsewhere.[10] Instead, I focus here on the three "performances" sketched out at the start of the essay, interspersing them with more theoretical discussion of musicking in the cybernetic era.

Telemusicking

Inspired by a dinner conversation with composer and accordionist Pauline Oliveros at the Guelph Jazz Festival, contrabassist Mark Dresser began investigating the potential of telematic performance in late 2007.[11] In November of that year, he organized a telematic performance involving a distributed ensemble of nearly thirty musicians drawn from research groups at Stanford, UCSD, and Rensselaer Polytechnic Institute, Oliveros's home institution. The three ensembles—and various sub-groupings of them—performed structured improvisations together, often utilizing soundpainting, the versatile interdisciplinary conducted sign language developed by Walter Thompson.[12] The performers, with Dresser and Sarah Weaver as the primary conductors, developed complementary palettes of soundpainting gestures in the weeks leading up to the event, based on the idea of translating metaphorical imagery into specific musical textures. Dressers recalls that the musicians "used SKYPE, iChat, iVisit, Google Docs (and when all else failed cell phone) to develop every aspect of the metaphoric palettes" in a distributed and collaborative fashion.

In addition to its wonderful ability to structure large improvising groups, using Thompson's soundpainting language for this first co-located performance was also a way to minimize the effects of latency. Latency, in general, is the time lag between when something is initiated and when its effects are detectable. In networked performances latency can be introduced at many stages, but ultimately the speed of light is a non-trivial upper limit to how fast our networks can communicate over long distances. Making more bandwidth available is the (relatively) easy part of improving a network; reducing latency is considerably more difficult, and removing latency is impossible.[13] With soundpainting (and other similar conducted approaches for structuring improvisation) there is already a certain unavoidable latency between the time at which a gesture is initiated and when other performers perceive, interpret, and respond to it. The soundpainting language can be used to create music with a shared pulse and meter, but it is often exploited, as it was during this performance, for its ability to coordinate textural and timbral developments.

A second telematic event presented on February 13, 2008, was organized by Dresser around the question of "whether or not a telematic ensemble could successfully play 'in time' together." This performance was co-located between three California institutions to reduce the distance that signals would need to travel. The distributed ensemble included seven musicians: Dresser, Philip Larson (voice), Michael Dessen (trombone), and

Billy Mintz (drum set) at the Center for Research in Computing and the Arts (CRCA) at UCSD; Myra Melford (piano) and David Wessel (electronics) at the Center for New Music and Audio Technologies (CNMAT) at UC Berkeley; and Chris Chafe (cello and celleto) at the Center for Computer Research in Music and Acoustics (CCRMA) at Stanford. The performance featured a set of new compositions written by group members to explore ensemble playing in challenging rhythmic and metric situations and to facilitate collective improvisations.

Reflecting on the experience, Dresser felt that the latency was negligible, equivalent to the adjustment that musicians automatically are accustomed to when performing in a space with somewhat 'wet' acoustics." Telematic performance, at least at this geographic remove, proved for Dresser to be "somewhere between live performance and playing in an isolation booth in a recording studio." Although this performance helped to demonstrate that within a certain geographic radius audio latency could be reduced to almost negligible levels, audio is only one component of a fuller telemusicking experience. The current "weak link," according to Dresser, is the audio-visual synchronization, since high-quality video requires much greater bandwidth.

Given the considerable technical requirements and challenges, why would anyone care to perform music at distant locations? There are of course practical concerns that make telemusicking a potentially attractive proposition for touring musicians (and this was an important impetus for Dresser's initial explorations). In her opening essay, Susan Fast focused on the (pleasurable) anticipation generated by wading through traffic and waiting in lines in order to attend a concert in person, but for touring musicians who have grown weary of (or less able to) travel (especially in a post-9/11 world), telemusicking might offer some desirable advantages. Beyond the everyday pragmatics, simply staying connected to and developing artistic collaborations with international colleagues always poses substantial challenges. Pauline Oliveros writes, "It is heartening to think that I can connect with my many friends throughout the world and strengthen our relationship with global culture. The ability to link with partners around the globe with less and less latency is an exciting development to say the least."[14] Despite these potential benefits, Dresser stresses, "Let's be clear, telematics is not a substitute for live performance. It is another format and perhaps even another venue, with its own properties. As plug and play systems develop and the integration of video and audio quality improve, those potentials will reveal themselves."

So what might these potentials be? In an article titled "The Telematic Music System: Affordances for a New Instrument to Shape the Music of Tomorrow," Jonas Braasch, a colleague of Oliveros at RPI, argues against the early euphoric belief held by many in telematics research that "we could virtually teleport ourselves to a distant location with such realism that we would lose our awareness of the enabling technology."[15] Instead, he insists that we must create new and better design goals for telematic music collaborations by treating telematic systems as a new class of musical instruments or as a unique environment, focusing on the affordances that the telematic system introduces rather than trying to circumnavigate current system limitations. In his own telematic projects, Braasch often explores issues of privacy and cultural exchange: the former since one may not always be fully aware of one's co-participants in a telematic environment (as individuals can move in and out of frame) or know for certain how (or even if) one is being seen and heard at a co-located space; and the latter since, as Braasch sees it, the impulse to telemusick also has much in common with the impulse to travel to or discover unknown terrain. In addition to audio-visual transmissions, Braasch also notes that haptic and olfactory senses could play an important role in telemusicking situations.

Addressing telepresence research in general, cognitive scientist Andy Clark writes, "We should not simply assume that the most effective use of these technologies lies in the attempt to re-create, in detail, the same kinds of personal contact and exchange with which we are currently familiar." If we do, Clark believes, "they will almost certainly continue to disappoint."[16] In an article titled "Not Being There," computer music researcher Miller Puckette expresses similar misgivings about what we might call orthodox telemusicking involving video screens and the explicit goal of a "transparent" distributed performance. "If you see someone on a screen," Puckette writes, "does that mean the person is really thousands of miles away, or just in a nearby closet?" Puckette describes an early project with which he was involved, Lemma 2, that chose instead to send audio analysis rather than sound across the network in a way that allowed performers to trigger instruments, samples, or sound generators at the co-located space while also simultaneously having their own instruments played by "ghost" performers. Rather than present a static video perspective, the Lemma 2 musicians broadcast video from individual head-mounted cameras while a series of interactive visual scenes, designed by Vibeke Sorenson, presented computer-generated graphics incorporating inputs from local and remote performers. "Because the relationships between local and remote instruments, and between sound and graphics, were constantly shifting," Puckette writes, "the perceived presence of the remote performers was enigmatic rather than didactic." Interestingly, Puckette concludes that distributed performance technologies may be most useful at the rehearsal stage, since they "promise to encourage bolder experimentation with or by performers . . . over a longer span of time than might be possible physically, given the hyperactive schedules we all now enjoy."

It may be that once "plug and play" systems become more accessible and reliable (as Dresser, Oliveros, and others envision), the "always on" aspect of a globally connected telemusicking community will, in and of itself, offer significant (and potentially revolutionary) creative rewards. But Clark usefully summarizes three main problems with mainstream (or, as he calls it, "vanilla") virtual reality: (1) perception is not passive; (2) even if you add moving and acting, the day of full, multisensory, high-bandwidth, real-time, two-way interaction via telepresence remains distant; (3) even full telepresence, thus achieved, might be more a crutch than a shoe. The last point references an article by Jim Hollan and Scott Stormetta titled "Beyond Being There," in which the authors argue that crutches are designed to remedy a perceived defect and shoes to provide new functionality.[17] Ultimately they wish to avoid scenarios in which new telecommunication technologies are tied to an agenda of attempting to imitate one medium of communication—an already well-known type of engagement—with another. Clark, following their insight, argues that "a few relatively simple kinds of tele-interaction might yield a more robust sense of presence than a failed attempt to re-create the full gamut of human 'intercorporeality.'"[18] We may be best served by looking for the transformative rather than the replicative potential of these new technologies, exploring ways to expand and reinvent our sense of presence, body, agency, interaction, and identity.

Beyond Being There

It is easy to understand the allure of real-time musicking-at-a-distance. For millennia, musicking seemed to be both site- and time-specific. Sounds, after all, can only travel so far before they are no longer heard, and, as Walter Ong famously observed, they exist only when they are going out of existence ("When I pronounce the word 'permanence,' by the time I get to the '-nence,' the 'perma-' is gone, and has to be gone").[19]

But to look at musicking read large is to look beyond sounds to embodied and social action. As a helpful illustration, we can envision musicking practices as falling within a two-by-two matrix, with one axis for time and one for space. The temporal axis moves from "synchronous" to "asynchronous," and the spatial axis moves from "local" to "remote." This gives us four quadrants: "local and synchronous," "local and asynchronous," "remote and synchronous," and "remote and asynchronous."

The foundational paradigm of musicking, I argue, is an incorporating knowledge-practice, by which I mean it involves the entire complex of perception-action cycles related to sound production/reception that encode into bodily memory through repeated "performances" (and here I am using the term to encapsulate all of the activities Christopher Small includes in his conception of musicking). As such, this *first order* of musicking predominantly involves activities that are local and synchronous (and often synchronized as well). However, first order musicking is also "local and asynchronous" to the extent that bodily memory is engaged and re-engaged over time and develops in a surrounding socio-cultural context (e.g., a mentor-student relationship or a community of practice).

Second order musicking involves material inscription in some fashion. By inscription I mean the act of placing the mark of one thing within the fabric of another. Despite their different specific affordances, music notation and recording share this material dimension of inscription (whether one "carves" atoms of paper or particles of magnetic tape). As a result, second order musicking offers the potential to move us further in both the asynchronous and remote dimensions for several reasons: (1) musical inscriptions can be constructed over considerable expanses of time (both with pen and paper and now with multi-track recording); (2) a significant period can elapse between the time of inscription and the time of "performance" (when additional first order musicking takes place, perhaps by playing from a score or by listening/dancing to a recording); (3) the asynchrony of creating material inscriptions can afford distributed collaboration (although this may or may not be emphasized for cultural reasons, and it also can be a key component of synchronous musicking); and (4) material inscriptions, in tandem with distribution/broadcast technologies, afford the dispersal of sounds and scores to remote locales.

Although some (especially those wishing to defend the live event or oral music culture) might argue that musical inscription affords these things at the expense of its "agility"—similar to how when one travels by car or airplane it is possible to get to farther places faster, but there are also more places that one cannot go—I tend to agree with David Waller that "the modality of music transmission is neither inherently restrictive nor inherently liberating. If it seems otherwise that is because the modality is nested in restrictive or liberating attitudes and practices of a particular culture or subculture in which individuals participate (or not)."[20]

The one quadrant of our musicking model left relatively untouched in this brief account is "remote and synchronous"; something that, until quite recently, would seem to defy the laws of physics. Telematic musicking does represent a significant leap forward in our attempt to fill this elusive quadrant. Potentially more important to realize, however, are the ways in which transmusicking, as I am using the term here, can explode this binary space-time matrix. In the digital and networked realm we see the beginnings of a *third order* of musicking, one that offers new affordances and appears to circumvent many of the previous constraints associated with the first and second orders in ways that can be at once powerful and problematic.

Briefly, third order musicking takes advantage of the near immateriality of bits and the near instantaneous transmission of digital information. If first order musicking is constrained by its locality and temporality—by the way in which physical sound waves disperse and dissipate and the way in which physical bodies interact—and second order musicking is limited by the materiality of its inscriptions—score paper and albums still take up shelf space after all and are costly to duplicate and disseminate—then third order musicking appears to transcend, or at least transgress, some of these spatial and material constraints. In the third order (to borrow a phrase from Paul Miller), sounds become unbound.[21]

Third order musicking still involves musicking as an incorporating knowledge-practice, and it takes advantage of previous music inscription practices as needed—each of these paradigms overlaps and should therefore not be pitted against one another—but it also benefits from completely new ways of accessing, visualizing, and manipulating musical data.[22]

To be clear, "going digital" by itself is not enough to produce transmusicking. It must also change how we create, engage, share, and, ultimately, understand music. I reserve the transmusicking designation for approaches to musicking that are not possible or conceivable in their entirety within either of the previous orders of musicking. Some uses of digital media that simply make a preexisting musicking approach easier or quicker or cheaper do not qualify as transmusicking.[23] For me, the difference between third order musicking and transmusicking is that the latter inherently challenges conventional notions of artwork, artist, and audience, and it works between and not simply with different media and modalities.

Transmusicking can involve sound sources or data flows from artists musicking, ambient sounds, or archives, all blended, transformed, and transmitted over any distance, obscuring categorical distinctions between real-time and recorded or between sites of creation and sites of (re)production. Chris Salter, in "The Architecture of Listening," addresses similar themes:

> The space of the network, as both acoustic realm and transmission structure, goes a step further, completely challenging the notion of any locus of hearing. By removing the concept of source and site in general, and shattering it across a multitude of non-places, we no longer comprehend the source, locale or temporal origin of sound. Listening to sound from the Net, we have no sense of from where a sound emanates, or why it is there in the first place. Sound rests in the ultimate non-place of the networked world: the territory of the server.[24]

To return briefly to our two-by-two musicking matrix, transmusicking has the potential to blur the former distinctions between "local" and "remote" and between "synchronous" and "asynchronous." To use a language analogy, writing—normally an asynchronous communicative form—gives way in the digital realm to email, texting, and online chat, bringing us ever closer to the present moment. Add speech recognition software, and the line between oral and literate communication becomes rather fuzzy. But it is important to realize that email, texting, chat, and most recently social networking have arguably found a place in our modern communicative arsenal precisely because of their *differences* from spoken language and from more traditional correspondence. One-to-one remote and synchronous communication could already be easily facilitated via the telephone. And so-called snail mail allows remote and asynchronous communication of a more unhurried nature. These newer communicative forms differ in that they allow users to interact quickly and informally but also deliberately, leaving an inspectable trace (albeit one that is potentially more ephemeral and more easily or covertly alterable than the printed word). Email, texting, chat, and social networking differ as well in their ability to make one-to-many and many-to-many communications exponentially faster and easier. Clay Shirkey describes this as "ridiculously easy group forming."[25]

330 · TAKING IT TO THE BRIDGE

According to Hollan and Stormetta, the telecommunication tools that really succeed are those that "people prefer to use [for certain purposes] even when they have the option of interacting in physical proximity . . . tools that go *beyond being there.*"[26]

In his foreword to the edited volume *Sound Unbound*, Cory Doctorow describes a conference party he attended thrown by Linden Labs, who make the multiplayer virtual world Second Life, at which attendees were both real and virtual. The real conference-goers were treated to a live DJ but, like "geeky conference-attendees," steadfastly refused to dance. The avatars on the "jumbotron" were all dancing, but each to their own beat—presumably whatever scripts the real gamer had developed or triggered. Doctorow muses, "They tell us the Internet drives us apart. Music brings us together. It's not clear to me whether the Internet was driving those gamers apart, nor is it clear that the DJ who was drowning out our chatter was bringing us together. Somewhere in the network and the music, there's a mix that brings us together because we're apart."[27]

Reality Jockeys

Reality Jockey Ltd. first introduced "RjDj" on December 4, 2008, through Apple's iTunes Store. It is, according to the company website, a music application for the iPhone that uses sensory input to generate and control the music you are listening to: "the next generation of walkman or mp3 player."[28] The sensory input data available to the RjDj application comes from the iPhone itself and primarily includes audio input from the microphone, multi-point finger control from the device's touch screen, and orientation/motion data from the 3-axis accelerometer.

Rather than play pre-recorded songs, like a more traditional portable music player, RjDj plays "scenes" that promote active listener involvement. Unlike more traditional compositions, the website tells us, scenes have a "different musical structure" and often have "no clear beginning and end." A scene sounds different "wherever, whenever, however you listen to it. . . . It reacts on you and your environment." More precisely, scenes are patches coded in Pure Data (PD), an open-source real-time graphical programming environment developed by Miller Puckette, that are then ported to the iPhone operating system.[29] Scenes, in essence, are interactive electronic music programs that combine and transform composed materials with audio, ambient, and ambulatory input provided by the user and her iPhone.

A variety of scenes come packaged with the application. They are designed, according to the website, to suit different situations: "When you want to dance we have scenes which use accelerometer data to multiply the effect of your moves. When you walk on the street we have scenes to calm you down and we have scenes which you should listen to alone or with your friend instead of dazing you away." There are even several warnings on the website that caution users to "take care when listening to RjDj in front of other people, in the city or shaking your phone too much." The RjDJ interactive/immersive listening experience is described on the website as a "mind twisting hearing sensation" and is compared more than once to the effect of drugs. In the comments section one user writes, "RJDJ is a non-narcotic hallucinogen. Don't know much about psychology but I feel like RJDJ is enabling me to tap into something subconscious, akin to primal scream therapy or especially transcendental meditation." Another user suggested how wonderful it would be if the RjDj application could intermix snatches of music heard by others traversing the same location— presumably by uploading activity with GPS data—so they could hear "echos of the past. echos of what someone else was listening to on the very same path just earlier in the day? It would truly blow my mind." Another enamored but also frustrated user commented on the "vicious cycle" he was stuck in: "Some of the scenes produce extremely subtle effects that are overpowered by street noise and consequently best heard in closed environments, e.g., in a room or car, BUT when in a closed environment, there aren't as many sounds to generate effects."

In addition to interacting with the scenes in real time by providing gestural and audio input, RjDj users can record their experience with scenes either to hear back on their own at a later time (as old-fashioned "songs") or to share with the web-based community (referred to as the "RjDj Universe"). Users who have experience with PD programming can also create new scenes, test them in a beta phase with other invited users, and share them with the "RjDj Universe." To assist and inspire development, Reality Jockey Ltd. stages periodic events called "sprints" at various (up till now European) locales, inviting artists, composers, and developers to collaborate on creating new scenes and "to do other mad things with sound."

The number and variety of available scenes is continuing to grow as the community of developers and users establishes itself: they already range from popular to novelty, ambient to avant-garde. "Scrambler" allows users to create complex break beats with a drum sample by "scratching" their finger(s) on a virtual record player displayed on the iPhone's touch screen and/or by shaking their iPhone. "World Quantizer" samples sounds through the microphone (percussive sounds work best), quantizes them, and weaves iterations and transformations into a complex polyrhythmic mix. One user posted a self-produced video on YouTube of his "audio journey through the house," flicking light switches, tapping kitchen items and furniture, and walking about while whistling.[30] Other scenes, like "Echolon" and "Eargasm," use reverberation, transposition, and various filter effects to produce a more "trippy" sound and sensation.

Still other scenes reference contemporary compositional practices or avant-garde computer music. "Plink" and "Diving" allow users to initiate particles of sound and modify them with granular effects. With "Ghost-Wave" users can find their inner Jimi Hendrix by humming into the phone and playing with heavy distortion and feedback and triggering energetic drum rhythms. On the more sedate side, "Piano Phase" is a scene based on Steve Reich's composition of the same name in which the user can subtly shift the phasing of two piano sequences by gently tilting the iPhone.

With Pure Data as the programming backbone to RjDj scenes, users have access to the state of the art in digital signal processing and real-time computer music. Beyond the audio and accelerometer data, scene developers could also conceivably incorporate the iPhone's ambient light and proximity sensor data, information from the built-in camera(s), GPS data from the cellular network, and/or live wireless updating or peer-to-peer Bluetooth connectivity, to design additional ways to tie sound events and processes to a user's location or proximity to others. With these and other interactive alternatives it is possible to conceive of RjDj as a portable sound installation: the listening experience is influenced by, and ultimately shapes, one's activity, orientation, and location.

William J. Mitchell argues in *ME++* that "increasingly we are living our lives at the points where electronic information flows, mobile bodies, and physical places intersect."[31] Although cyberspace is often equated with the current nexus of computer and telecommunications networks, it is best understood as a virtual environment for human exchange. Cyberspace is as basic as "the place where a phone conversation appears to occur,"[32] and as complicated as the world of Second Life.[33] It should not be viewed as something that will replace physical space; rather, the two will merge into the amalgam already forming under names such as augmented reality and intelligent environments—"smart places" filled with "smart objects" and, one might hope, smart people. Novak refers to this as "newspace," the sum of local, remote, virtual, and interactivated space. Despite his futuristic bent, Novak is careful to stress that we will bring into this newspace "all our social instincts, animal and human, for better or worse."[34] Newspace will present new modes of being and engagement, but it will also be built upon our previous experiences and expectations from both the real and virtual worlds.

Before we celebrate the arrival of musical newspace too quickly, though, I offer a few words of caution. Although the "RjDj universe" is designed to nurture a sense of online community and to encourage collaboration among individual users, it is for now primarily a site for what Clay Shirkey calls "me first collaboration."[35] It remains to be seen at what level the community of RjDj users and designers will take shared responsibility for its long-term viability. And we should also remember that this particular "portable sound installation" not only is costly to individual users but also is a proprietary technology of Apple Computer, Inc. Apple was arguably slow to open its iPhone platform to independent developers, and it maintains the exclusive right to approve and sell applications through its iTunes Store (a nontransparent practice that has been criticized by many). Reality Jockey Ltd. is also not shy about its commercial pursuits. Their website suggests ways that existing corporate labels and artists can "RjDj-ify" existing tracks or release reactive scenes in tandem with traditional audio, and it provides a means to sell these either individually on their website or bundled into a co-produced stand-alone RjDj application available through the iTunes Store.

At the very least, it is clear that RjDj is part of a growing number of music applications that extend the now ubiquitous portable music player—which in its early incarnations could only play back prerecorded music—into a realm that begins to blur the distinctions between listening, sharing, and creating.[36] To argue over whether RjDj is a "legitimate" musical instrument, a bit of imaginative role playing, or some hybrid of the two may be to miss the point. While most of the "scenes" released for RjDj lack an "evaluative" dimension that might mark them clearly as games, the ludic dimensions articulated by Roger Moseley in connection with *Guitar Hero* and *Rock Band* ("Playing Games with Music," this volume) are still quite applicable. In particular, *paidia*, "a childlike delight in defying or ignoring constraints, and the pleasure taken in tumult, improvisation, and contrary behaviors," is especially pronounced in RjDj use, even as the "rules" inherent to a given scene's programming serve to significantly constrain behavior. Perhaps the biggest fear (especially among "trained" musicians) about RjDj is the extent to which, following Moseley (citing Gadamer), "people are played [by] rather than playing" the application.

While it may be true for RjDj that (following Moseley) its formations are never ideologically neutral, it is also clear that RjDj can restructure conventional notions about and perceived boundaries between artist and audience, and between artwork, ambience, and activity. For most Reality Jockeys, it seems, the experience can (at least temporarily) feel liberating rather than coercive.

Sensuous Geographies

It often takes considerable time before the possibilities inherent in new technologies become apparent. Early film, for example, was described as "photographed theater." And Thomas A. Edison (in)famously envisioned the principal uses of the phonograph in "letter writing and all kinds of dictation without the aid of a stenographer," "phonographic books, which will speak to blind people without effort on their part," and "the teaching of elocution."[37]

Marcos Novak coined the phrase "extreme intermedia" to describe a trend he discerns whereby each contemporary medium is being driven to the opposite extreme of its traditional understanding: architecture, the heaviest of the arts, becomes liquid; music, the art of fixed composition, becomes navigable; cinema, the art of narrative, becomes interactive and habitable; and dance becomes dis/embodied.[38] Navigable music, for Novak, "is not an organization of sounds in time, it is the organization of a matrix of sonic, visual, behavioral, and other possibilities"; it is a landscape. "What is experienced within this landscape," he muses, "depends entirely upon the user's individually selected, unforeseen, interest-driven trajectory."

Sensuous Geographies, a responsive sound and video environment designed by Scottish choreographer Sarah Rubidge and composer Alistair MacDonald (in collaboration with Maggie Moffat and Maria Verdicchio), offers one approach to "navigable music." It is an interactive installation-cum-performance, described by the designers as "a space of ritual, a liminal space intended to draw attention both to the intricate inter-weaving pathways of sensation in the body, and to the equally intricate pathways of subtle group behaviour."[39] The first showing was at the New Territories Festival in Glasgow in 2003, and it has been shown since in other cities in the United Kingdom and in Los Angeles.

According to its designers, Sensuous Geographies is "intended primarily to be a space for interaction, for contemplation, even for play." They conceive of the piece as simultaneously a performative space and an immersive installation environment. The installation involves an active space

(4.5 meters square) surrounded by a periphery zone, with speakers surrounding both areas. Gold, white, and bronze translucent banners hang from the ceiling, creating a fluid architecture through which visitors move and also doubling as projection screens. Visitors initially stand at the periphery awaiting their chance to enter the active space. Before entering, "guides" must prepare them by having them remove their shoes and dressing them in a brightly colored silk robe (described by one reviewer as "a cross between medieval gowns and burkas"). The participants are also given a blindfold or veil to wear, ensuring that the active space is experienced through senses other than sight.

On entering the active space—delineated by a black cloth on the floor that conceals different material textures underneath (bark, bubble wrap, sand, other fabric, and so on)—visitors are asked to stand still and listen for fifteen seconds. Then they begin by moving slowly and trying to identify the aspect of the composite sound that modulates with their motion, their "personal sound signature." Once identified, they enter into a feed-back and feed-forward cycle between their actions and the sounds that they hear.

A ceiling-mounted video camera, combined with the fact that each visitor's robe is a different color, creates a motion-tracking system that sends data to the interactive sound system. In addition to tracking the movements of individual visitors, the system responds to the proximity of other visitors, so that the movement of the whole group affects the sound environment as well. A computer operator who watches the activities unfold can make specific sonic choices depending on the behavior and energy in the space, for instance by providing certain materials to a very energetic participant, or other very different sounds to someone more concerned with delicate movements and tiny details of sound. Last, images of ethereal figures performing basic movements (walking, crouching, rising, gesturing, or fading away) are projected on the floating banners, and manipulated and processed in response to visitor movement.

As the visitors engage with the space they make a personal journey, a collective journey, and an observed journey (being watched by those awaiting their turns). Watching from the outside, visitors may feel, according to one reviewer, like "an uninitiated participant in an intricate mythological role-playing game." By participating, however, they are immersed in complex polyphonic layers of electronic sounds and voices that respond to and lead their actions. The sensuous environment of sounds, textures, and shadowy colors and images affects the way they feel in their bodies, and this modifies the quality of their movements, all of which simultaneously changes the musical dynamics and ambience of the space itself. Steve

Dixon compares this spatial engagement to an improvisation in which "individuals listen and make space for others, respond, contradict each other, and build duets and ensemble sequences together." He elaborates:

> The experience is delicate, corporeal, uplifting and distinctly liquid. You identify a sound, individual and unique only to you, and hear it modulate and transform in relation to even your slightest movements. You follow your sound, hearing and feeling its changes, and become aware of other shadowy figures moving around with you and of other alterations in the sound textures. You tentatively join in the game, traveling with other visitors, leaving them alone, standing still, listening, waiting, building the sound world, then feeling the sensations it generates, hearing the textures you are helping to create.[40]

The visitors' feedback available on the website for Sensuous Geographies attests to the novel, liberating, and, at times, confusing nature of the participation. Some commented primarily on the social dynamics at play: "Quite a fun way to let go of inhibitions," or "I even ended up dancing with a complete stranger." Others reflected on the personal journey: "I suddenly got ears and feet again . . . a good experience and new thoughts about consciousness," or "Surprisingly relaxing, therapeutic and indeed, sensuous . . . vaguely 'out of body.'" Still others struggled to engage or to understand their engagement: "A little too complex to know whether I've been actually relating with the thing or not," or "I was confused—trying to determine my sound from the underlying sound. Then when I determined the voice that was mine, wanted to control it, (not successful) and found the voice somewhat grating. Very interesting—but what does it mean?"

An interest in bodily understandings and social interactivity permeates Sensuous Geographies. According to one reviewer, "It taps into notions of wordless communication and issues of identity." Another felt the experience provides "a very particular sense not only of being in that specific space but also of 'being in the world' from moment to moment." Attempting to make sense of the piece, Dixon references Henri Bergson's notion of "deep consciousness," Anthony Demasio's idea of "core consciousness," Gerald Edelman and Giulio Tononi's idea of "primary consciousness," and Gilles Deleuze's notions of "affect" and "becoming." Dixon concludes, "Sensuous Geographies is, in a very real sense, a 'sensational' space, a space where in Deleuzian terms 'every sensation is a question,' but a question without an answer—a space of becoming, which never becomes."[41]

As the comments from participants attest, Sensuous Geographies can make one aware of one's physical and phenomenological presence—"being in a specific space but also 'being in the world'"—while simultaneously making one aware of new kinds of potential collaboration, skilled action, and intimacy. The installation seems to highlight the ways in which embodiment is essential but negotiable. Andy Clark, in his book *Natural-Born Cyborgs*, argues that our remarkably plastic brains, combined with the ways in which our embodied minds have co-evolved in tandem with a shaping environment, have primed us to seek out and incorporate non-biological resources and their supporting cultural practices into our very existence: "We are already masters at incorporating non-biological stuff and structure deep into our physical and cognitive routines."[42] Clark argues that the experiences of direct control that define "who" we are (at least in a materialist sense) can be extended via new technologies, both biomechanical and spatially disconnected.[43]

But Clark also emphasizes that "the social and personal impact of bioelectronic interpenetration is difficult to predict." "Even were the shape of the actual technologies clear," Clark muses, "the ways in which they will become most widely used and incorporated into our daily lives is elusive."[44] With regard to transmusicking, we must be careful to avoid a premature closure on our notions of interface and interaction. David Rokeby, whose *Very Nervous System* tracks intransitive body motion to control sound, writes eloquently on the profound effects that interfaces can have on our perceptual experiences and, therefore, the social responsibility we share in creating them. He worries that "the rush to stuff content into interactive media has drawn our attention away from the profound and subtle ways that the interface itself, by defining how we perceive and navigate content, shapes our experience of that content."[45]

What is crucial, according to Lydia Goehr, is to keep our eyes open to "the possibility of producing music in new ways under the regulation of new ideals" and to "the inherently critical and revisable nature of our regulative concepts." Most important, she concludes, this "helps us overcome that deep-rooted desire to hold the most dangerous of beliefs, that we have at any time got our practices absolutely right."[46]

Peter Weibel and Söke Dinkla have theorized different degrees of interactivity in digital art, and they reserve the term "floating phenomena" to describe "the most open or advanced" examples:

In the floating work of art, part of the authorship transfers from the artist to the user . . . the user becomes conscious that he is an accomplice in a fundamental sense. However, he only seemingly occupies an omnipotent position that allows him to control events, since he is always victim and perpetrator at the same time. In a web of relations he is only one of many controllers. . . . The floating work of art is no longer the expression of a single individual. Neither is it the expression of a collective, but it is the state of a "connective"—a web of influences that are continually reorganised by all participants.[47]

One of the challenges of even the most advanced examples of interactive art remains the extent to which participants can gain some level of fluency with the interface and familiarity with the work's "landscape." How much time do most participants actually spend "navigating" these new environments? If the notion of 10,000 hours to gain fluency with a given area of skill or knowledge has any currency, then a visit to the museum on a Sunday afternoon may not suffice to significantly alter our perceptions of "where" and "what" we are. It may be wonderful to envision extending one's body and mind across the network telematically via haptic, olfactory, and audiovisual connections (but how many have access to these technologies?), or extending one's body through the use of novel interfaces and instruments, but it is only when these interfaces become transparent in use so that our intentions "flow through" the tools to alter the world, Clark reminds us, that we begin to feel as if they are a part of us.[48] That being said, undoubtedly one of the reasons for the recent success of the iPhone, for example, is the simplicity of its interface: touching and shaking things is something we have all done from infancy forward (and many well-to-do cosmopolitan folk might willingly admit that their "smart phone" has become a part of them). Whether site-specific (Sensuous Geographies), mobilized (RjDj) or co-located (telematics), transmusicking practices may have the potential to alter and expand our sense of presence, body, agency, and control, as well as our conventional notions of "music" and "performance."

Beyond Performance?

"What is music if not performance," ask Nicholas Cook and Richard Pettengill in their introduction to this volume: "real-time collective practice that brings people together as players and listeners, choreographs social relationships, and expresses or constructs individual or group identities?" Transmusicking, as I have outlined it here, would seem to do all of these things as well, but it may also blur some aspects of our conventional assumptions about "performance." In particular, transmusicking can challenge our abilities to comprehend the source, locale, or temporal origin of a sound, as well as problematize our evolved and enculturated abilities to discern with whom, where, how, or even if musicking is actually taking place. It may even blur distinctions between the identity and agency of individuals and those of the group and their techno-cultural milieu.[49]

In her recent book titled *Listening Through the Noise: The Aesthetics of Experimental Electronic Music*, Joanna Demers confronts some related issues by looking for commonalities between electro-acoustic performance, electronica (a.k.a. EDM or electronic dance music), and sound art.[50] Despite their stylistic differences, Demers argues that, in addition to having something of a shared history, these three "meta-genres" of electronic music collectively work to erase the "frame" that has encased the last few centuries of (Western art) music.[51] By the "frame," she means a collection of expectations for how music should behave and what distinguishes it from nonmusical sound, as well as the customs governing (musicking) behavior.

I will not rehash here the various historical arguments for how "noise" was inserted into the twentieth-century musicking landscape, but suffice it to say that electronic sounds—and for digital instruments in particular the arbitrariness of their mappings to gestural control—all conspire against our enculturated and evolved abilities to identify instrumental timbres and action-sound relationships easily, abilities that historically "framed" musical sound and music listening/performance "apart from" the everyday world.[52] Demers argues that electronic music frequently contains mimetic sounds for which it is hard to disregard their source causes (e.g., soundscape and field recordings), and it often lacks the recurring structural features that assume a language-like role in more traditional music (e.g., dissonance and cadential consonances, motivic transfer between instruments, or call-and-response patterns) that help alert listeners to the fact that they are hearing music. In addition, Demers highlights that duration in electronic music is (mostly) arbitrary, since "musical genres in which development is no longer expected or required assail the musical frame by making it purely incidental when the piece starts and ends."[53]

Electronic music is not solely responsible for the destruction of the frame, Demers reminds us: "Schoenberg, Cage, the circulation of non-Western music, and the advent of commercial recordings have all taken their toll as well." But according to her, electronic music concentrates several anti-framing techniques: "its performance in nonconcert venues; its use of objectlike audio footage; its blurring of the divisions between 'live' and 'recorded' performance."[54] I would add that the network infrastructure that underpins both cyber- and newspace further facilitates these and other anti-framing aspects.

"Liveness" has been a perennial theoretical issue in performance studies and, to a lesser extent, in music studies (although the practice of DJs and laptop artists, for example, has recently brought the issue to the fore). Philip Auslander, in his influential book *Liveness*, debunks many of the conventional arguments in favor of the live event: it provides a fuller sensory experience; it builds community; it brings performers and audiences together; it has more cultural value. Ultimately he argues that live and mediatized forms have developed through a sort of feed-back/feed-forward cycle, wherein each influences the other, and they derive their authority in relation to one another.[55] Taking issue with Auslander's apparent conflation of the "live" and the "mediatized," Susan Fast ("*U2 3D*," this volume) argues, with Peggy Phelan, "that live and recorded performances are fundamentally different, that *both are indispensible*, and that the distinctions between them need to be preserved." Citing Jem Kelly's work, Fast argues that in "inter-medial" pop music performances the projected images actually serve to enhance the presence of a live performer. Steve Dixon, who also takes aim at Auslander's conflationary tactics but from a different vantage point, argues instead that "in digital theater it is often the media projection rather than the live performer that wields the real power, the sense of (aesthetic, semiotic) reality."[56]

It may be that we are, following Demers, at "an interstitial moment in the history of aesthetics."[57] My own position is that the (perceived) indeterminacy of events, independent of any ontological differences between "live" and various media, often matters as much or more to participants. As Steve Dixon points out, "even without recourse to raw dictionary definitions of liveness, in phenomenological terms, it must be agreed that liveness has more to do with time and 'now-ness' than with the corporeality or virtuality of subjects being observed."[58] For instance, studies have shown that people prefer watching sporting events broadcast "live" on television to viewing the same event re-broadcast (even when they have no foreknowledge of the event or its outcome), simply because in the former case the action unfolds in indeterminate ways.[59]

Applications like RjDj, sound installations like Sensuous Geographies, and telematic performances, among other transmusicking practices, all (potentially) invite and extend this sense of immediacy, indeterminacy, and improvisation, while at the same time they can blur our notions of "liveness" in both its proximal and temporal senses. It has not been my goal to downplay the intercorporeal dimensions of "being there"; rather, I wish to highlight the ways in which newer musicking practices like those discussed here may offer experiences that are qualitatively different from regular concertgoing, or that extend in some way our conventional notions of presence, agency, and interaction with regard to music performance. Even in more or less conventional performance (and teaching!) situations, audiences (both at the event and co-located elsewhere) may increasingly have available to them options for back-channel discussions or real-time emotion or sentiment analysis, among other things, that can affect or become part of the performance, if desired.

The issues surrounding "liveness" and "performance" are complex and difficult (and deserve more attention than I can offer here). At the very least, these newer forms of musicking present openings through which we can challenge the constructed binary between the live and the virtual. Even Walter Benjamin, whose "Work of Art in the Age of Mechanical Reproduction" is perhaps the most cited essay among those wishing to defend the "aura" of "liveness," acknowledged that historical circumstance and change bring about reciprocal transformations in "the mode of human sense perception . . . [and] humanity's entire mode of existence."[60] Ultimately Benjamin concludes that mechanical reproduction "emancipates the work of art from its parasitical dependence on ritual." The era of transmusicking, I would argue, has moved us well beyond "mechanical reproduction."

Some see in this potential future a means for reintegrating music and ritual. Australian composer, violinist, and instrument-maker Jon Rose, in an article extolling the Aboriginal "continuum of creative practice involving sound, stories, and image, something integrated and interchangeable with geographic location," argues,

> It is early days yet, but when the haptic feedback and kinaesthetic perspectives experienced on traditional musical instruments become possible through interactive technologies, we might be able to incorporate electronic media with an expressive physicality not yet possible. I'm talking here of a direct interconnectivity to each other and to the physical world, as was practiced by traditional societies for countless generations—the opposite of virtual reality.[61]

If history is any guide, the hardest questions for anyone to answer during and even after a revolution are those concerning the revolution itself. How did we get from there to here? As Elizabeth Eisenstein demonstrates in her book *The Printing Press as an Agent of Change*, historians are comfortable describing life prior to the era of moveable type as well as life after Guten-berg's invention had started to spread, but few engage with the really hard questions.[62] The fact that the printing press produced nearly two centuries of relative chaos as the Western world switched from the Catholic Church to the nation-state as the dominant social organizing force should remind us that revolutions both take time and can produce incredibly dramatic changes.

Nicolas Carr, in his book *The Big Switch: Rewiring the World from Edison to Google*, argues that cheap utility-supplied computing (a "World Wide Computer") will ultimately change society as profoundly as cheap electric-ity did.[63] As network speeds begin to reach the speed of internal processors, the divide between local and remote computation is already beginning to subside. The frontiers of both computation and cognition increasingly in-volve taking advantage of distributed processing, either by borrowing the surplus computational cycles from the dormant computers of millions of users or by making use of those same user's "cognitive surplus" during their "leisure" hours.

The issues surrounding this blurring of work and play and the poten-tially insidious shift toward corporate control of our recreational space are beyond the scope of this essay, but they involve, among other things, the technological preempting of "fair use" using Digital Rights Manage-ment access control techniques, and the market-based approach that sim-ply makes "fared use," the increasingly popular micro-transaction business model, the only viable or conceivable avenue for creativity. At the very least, the new "digitally empowered subject" inhabits an increasingly com-plex permissions culture. We are creating new types of content and new modes of interaction and dissemination—and new laws and conventions surrounding all of these—simultaneously.

It can be challenging to separate the hype from reality when discuss-ing the still ongoing shift from an industrial information economy to a networked information economy. The much-touted "Web 2.0" is based, we are told, on an "architecture of participation"; putting the "me" back in "media."[64] Broadcasting is shifting to "narrowcasting." "Communities of affinity" are supplanting (or at least supplementing) communities of con-sumption. Non-market, non-proprietary, and collaborative approaches to creativity are on the rise (or at the very least copyright is deeply entrenched in a war with copyleft).[65] Aggregating information is the wave of the fu-ture (or, perhaps more insidiously, getting one's customers to do it for you through "crowd sourcing"). Access capabilities and privileges are increas-ingly becoming more important than traditional forms of ownership and control of property.

Yet despite the liberatory discourse that surrounded its early days, cyberspace (and now newspace) still conceals an ability to surveil a user's every action in ways that bring to mind Big Brother or Bentham's panopticon. Novak, however, argues that this condition of surveillance and centralization characterizes an age we are leaving behind. He coined the term "pantopicon" (pan + topos), or "the condition of being in all places at one time," to signify the age we are entering:

Our time is not one of centers of power and radiating spokes of vision; it is a time of diffusion into fields of ubiquitous sensors and effectors. Everyone is everywhere, all the time, all at once. Borges saw this in the "Aleph," McLuhan saw it in the distinction between "optical" and "acoustic" space, Attali speaks about it in "Noise," and Cage made music of it in the "Roaratorio." . . . While art expanded around a fairly well defined center, the center itself is now becoming diffuse and hard to locate. This transterritoriality does not mean that centers do not exist—just that they can now only be known stochastically, like the center of mass of a swarm of bees. This is an exciting situation, since it mixes the centripetal tendencies of discourse with the centrifugal elements of art and creates strange, provocative morphings of reality.[66]

Without the previous major constraints on the supply of creative works—high costs and narrow distribution channels—the Internet provides a virtually boundless home for new cultural producers and new cultural niches. The economics of Internet distribution are also challenging previously held notions of how cultural work should be bound together and organized.[67] As the role of digital repositories continues to overtake that of physical ones, information is becoming further mobilized and decentralized. The social fabric, previously tied together by commonalities of location and schedule, no longer coheres in quite the same way.

Novak believes that

In a climate of exponentially accelerating change, slowness and hesitation are sure formulas for irrelevance. With new technological temptations arriving daily, the urge to purchase the appearance of relevance through the consumption of invention aggravates an already difficult situation. The only way out of this quandary is to approach new technologies daringly and with the intent to question the very foundations of each discipline and its role in the world that is forming around us. This must be done with the confidence that those aspects that are most important will survive any challenge, not because we are sworn to protect them, but because they are irreducible.[68]

He theorizes about "transphysical cities" and "eversion" (the opposite of "immersion"), predicting that ultimately "the phenomena we are familiar with in cyberspace will find, indeed are finding, their equivalent everted forms in ordinary space."[69] But he warns elsewhere,

> I have long argued that it makes little sense to replicate the outside world in cyberspace. It makes even less sense to take a poor replica of the familiar from cyberspace and evert it onto the real. Just as it is more challenging to explore the ways in which the virtual exceeds the real in cyberspace, it is also more interesting to evert our cyberspace discoveries from virtuality onto ordinary space.[70]

What the notions of eversion and the transphysical may mean for transmusicking practices, only time may tell. For now, it appears that the conventional frame around "music" and "performance" may continue to blur as electronic, digital, and networked practices flourish, although we must also acknowledge that new "aesthetic" frames and "social contracts" are being forged along technological, economic, and cultural lines.

Christopher Small intended his notion of musicking to encapsulate all of the activities that surround music read large (including its creation, performance, reception, and transmission). Most of our current language for discussing musicking, however, remains predicated on its first and second order logic, either as localized and linear "performance" or as a form of material inscription that provides "texts" to be "performed" later. There is little consensus at this point about what a transmusicking future might involve, but undoubtedly it will include new sounds, new practices, and new power struggles, many of which may be markedly different than what came before.

NOTES

1. See Alexander Jensenius, "Action-Sound: Developing Methods and Tools to Study Music-Related Body Movement" (PhD dissertation, University of Oslo, 2007), for more on the differences between action-sound couplings (correlations that are bound by laws of nature) and action-sound relationships (which may be inconsistent or entirely fabricated).

2. Martin Heidegger, "The Question Concerning Technology," *Martin Heidegger: Basic Writings*, ed. David Krell (New York: Harper and Row, 1977), 288.

3. For more on these ideas see Eric F. Clarke, *Ways of Listening: An Ecological Approach to the Perception of Musical Meaning* (New York: Oxford University Press, 2005).

4. Lydia Goehr, *The Imaginary Museum of Musical Works* (Oxford: Clarendon Press, 1994), 243.

5. Christopher Small first introduced the notion of musicking in *Music-Society-Education* (London: Calder, 1977), later expanding on it in *Music of the Common Tongue* (New York: Riverrun Press, 1987) and *Musicking* (Hanover: Wesleyan University Press, 1998).

6. Small, *Musicking*, 9.

7. David Borgo, "Musicking on the Shores of Multiplicity and Complexity," *Parallax 45* 13, no. 4 (2007): 92–107.

8. Marcos Novak, "Trans Terra Form: Liquid Architectures and the Loss of Inscription," *Inhalt/Impressum* (1997), all web sources accessed April 11, 2009, http:// www.krcf.org/krcfhome/PRINT/nonlocated/nlonline/nonMarcos.html.

9. Ibid., "Trans Terra Form."

10. See Steve Dixon, *Digital Performance: A History of New Media in Theater, Dance, Performance Art, and Installation* (Cambridge: MIT Press, 2007); Frances Dyson, *Sounding New Media: Immersion and Embodiment in the Arts and Culture* (Berkeley: University of California Press, 2009); William Duckworth, *Virtual Music: How the Web Got Wired For Sound* (New York: Routledge, 2005).

11. Mark Dresser, "Telematics," allaboutjazz.com electronic magazine, August 20, 2008, http://www.allaboutjazz.com/php/article.php?id=30198. All subsequent quotes by Dresser are from this essay. See also Roy Ascott, *Telematic Embrace: Visionary Theories or Art, Technology, and Consciousness* (Berkeley: University of California Press, 2003), and Pauline Oliveros, http://deeplistening.org/site/content/telematic, accessed June 21, 2012.

12. http://www.soundpainting.com/. See "Telematic Music: Six Perspectives," *Leonardo* 19 (2009), online supplement, for some discussion by participants at the event and links to related audio and video excerpts.

13. Most telematic musicking that happens outside of state-of-the-art research labs either sends MIDI control data instead of audio data to reduce latency, or implements synchronization and quantization algorithms to allow distributed musicians to perceive the co-located musical space as "in time." See http://ninjam.com/ and http://www. ejamming.com/. It is worth noting that latency is always a factor for us, both in terms of the time it takes neural signals to traverse our sensori-motor system and with regard to the speed of our conscious attention.

14. Pauline Oliveros, "From Telephone to High Speed Internet: A Brief History of My Tele-Musical Performances," *Leonardo Music Journal* 19 (2009), online supplement.

15. Jonas Braasch, "The Telematic Music System: Affordances for a New Instrument to Shape the Music of Tomorrow," *Contemporary Music Review* 28, no. 4–5 (2009): 421. A more recent telematic event coordinated by Dresser on October 25, 2008, called "Multiplicities: An Inter-Arts Telematic Performance," moved some distance in this direction.

16. Andy Clark, *Natural-Born Cyborgs: Minds, Technologies, and the Future of Human Intelligence* (New York: Oxford University Press, 2004), 108–9.

17. Jim Hollan and Scott Stormetta, "Beyond Being There," *Proceedings of the ACM* (Association for Computing Machinery), ACM 0-89791-S513-S/92/0005-0119 (1992): 119–25.

18. Clark, *Natural-Born Cyborgs*, 113. Intercorporeality, a term used by Merleau-Ponty and later Herbert Dreyfus, refers to the hard to define and articulate sense of being in the presence of other people. Despite this, Jefferson Pitcher, in an emotional essay titled "Tapes from Greece, and the Building of Community through the Telematic Medium," *Leonardo Music Journal* 19 (2009), describes how he felt closer than ever to his long-distance lover during their first experience together in a chat room.

19. Walter Ong, *Orality and Literacy: The Technologizing of the Word* (London: Routledge, 1988), 32. I do not wish to follow Ong in arguing for unique temporal and spatial characteristics of auditory phenomenology. See Jonathan Sterne, *The Audible Past: Cultural Origins of Sound Production* (Durham: Duke University Press, 2003), 16–19, for a cogent critique of Ong's theologically driven work. To be clear, different transmission media such as water can afford sonic communications over considerably longer distances, as the "song" of sperm whales attests. It may be useful to consider the Internet as its own transmission medium.

20. David Waller, "Language Literacy and Music Literacy: A Pedagogical Asymmetry," *Philosophy of Music Education Review* 18, no. 1 (2010): 30.

21. See Paul D. Miller, ed., *Sound Unbound: Sampling Digital Music and Culture* (Cambridge: MIT Press, 2008).

22. Lev Manovich, in his book *The Language of New Media* (Cambridge: MIT Press, 2002), articulates the principles of "new media" as *numerical representation* (through the process of digitization involving sampling and quantization), *modularity* (allowing larger-scale objects to be assembled from independent modules), *automation* (from low-level use of templates or algorithms to high-level automation involving aspects of artificial intelligence and semantic understanding), *variability* (objects are created and customized on a bit-by-bit basis and on the fly), and lastly *transcoding* (a type of "conceptual transfer" involving a feedback cycle from the "computer layer" of data representation and operation to the "media/culture layer" of human understanding and organization and back again).

23. For example, if a recording studio uses digital media to improve audio quality or to provide more recording tracks and storage in more cost-effective ways, that does not, in itself, make it a site of third order musicking. The same goes for a composer who uses computer notation software only to get the "same notes" down more efficiently or legibly than previously (although the computer notation interface definitely has an effect).

24. Chris Salter, "The Architecture of Listening" (2001), available at http://crossfade.walkerart.org/salter/.

25. Clay Shirkey, *Here Comes Everybody: The Power of Organizing without Organizations* (New York: Penguin Group, 2009), 54.

26. Hollan and Stormetta, "Beyond Being There," 125.

27. Miller, *Sound Unbound*, xi.

28. http://more.rjdj.me/what/.

29. http://puredata.info/.

30. http://www.youtube.com/watch?v=HnF65HBXucM.

31. William J. Mitchell, *Me++: The Cyborg Self and the Networked City* (Cambridge: MIT Press, 2004), 3–4.

32. Bruce Sterling, *The Hacker Crackdown: Law and Disorder on the Electronic Frontier* (New York: Bantam, 1993), 1.

33. http://www.secondlife.com.

34. Novak, "Trans Terra Form."

35. Clay Shirkey, *Here Comes Everybody: The Power of Organizing Without Organizations*, 49.

36. See Michael Bull, *Sounding Out the City: Personal Stereos and the Management of Everyday Life* (New York: Oxford University Press, 2000); Michael Bull, *Sound Moves: iPod Culture and Urban Experience* (New York: Routledge, 2007).

37. The reproduction of music was fourth on Edison's top-ten list supplied to *North American Review* in June 1878. http://inventors.about.com/library/inventors/bledisondiscphpgraph.htm.

38. Novak, "Transmitting Architecture," November 29, 1996, http://www.ctheory. net/articles.aspx? id=76.

39. http://www.sensuousgeographies.co.uk/. All subsequent quotes referring to the piece, unless otherwise attributed, are from this website.

40. Dixon, *Digital Performance*, 403–4.

41. Ibid., 405–6.

42. Clark, *Natural-Born Cyborgs*, 142.

43. Clark here brackets out the "narrative self," that which is identified by a story told both to ourselves and others, and also told both by ourselves and others. *Natural-Born Cyborgs*, 132.

44. Ibid., 118.

45. David Rokeby, "The Construction of Experience: Interface as Context," *Digital Illusion: Entertaining the Future with High Technology* (New York: ACM Press, 1998), 27–28.

46. Goehr, *The Imaginary Museum of Musical Works*, 284.

47. Quoted in Dixon, *Digital Performance*, 561.

48. Clark, *Natural-Born Cyborgs*, 123.

49. See David Borgo and Jeff Kaiser, "Configuring KaiBorg: Ideology, Identity and Agency in Electro-Acoustic Improvised Music," *Beyond the Centres: Musical Avant-Gardes since 1950*, conference proceedings.

50. Joanna Demers, *Listening Through the Noise: The Aesthetics of Experimental Electronic Music* (New York: Oxford University Press, 2010).

51. Demers lists the "founding fathers (and a few mothers)" as Babbitt, Messian, Oliveros, Schaeffer, Sotckhausen, and Theremin.

52. See Paul Scrutton, *The Aesthetics of Music* (Oxford: Oxford University Press, 1997), Paul Hegarty, *Noise/Music: A History* (New York: Continuum, 2008), and Eduardo Miranda and Marcelo Wanderley, *New Digital Musical Instruments: Control and Interaction Beyond the Keyboard* (Middleton, CT: A-R Editions, 2006).

53. Demers, *Listening Through the Noise*, 151.

54. Demers, *Listening Through the Noise*, 149.

55. Philip Auslander, *Liveness: Performance in a Mediatized Culture* (New York: Routledge, 1999).

56. Dixon, *Digital Performance*, 122.

57. Demers, *Listening Through the Noise*, 157.

58. Dixon, *Digital Performance*, 127.

59. Joachim Vosgerau, Klaus Wertenbroch, and Ziv Carmonty, "Indeterminacy and TV Watching," *Journal of Consumer Research* 32, no. 4 (March 2006): 487–95.

60. Benjamin quoted in Dixon, *Digital Performance*, 117.

61. Jon Rose, "Listening to History: Some Proposals for Reclaiming the Practice of Live Music," *Leonardo Music Journal* 18 (2008): 16.

62. Elizabeth Eisenstein, *The Printing Press as an Agent of Change*, 2 vols. (New York: Cambridge University Press, 1980).

63. Nicholas Carr, *The Big Switch: Rewiring the World, from Edison to Google* (New York: W. W. Norton, 2008).

64. According to *Time* magazine, "You" were the 2006 Person of the Year for "seizing the reins of the global media, for founding and framing the new digital democracy, and for working for nothing and beating the pros at their own game" (Lev Grossman, "Time's Person of the Year: You," December 13, 2006).

65. See Yochai Benkler, *The Wealth of Networks* (New Haven: Yale University Press, 2007); Rishab Aiyer Ghosh, *CODE: Collaborative Ownership and the Digital Economy* (Cambridge: MIT Press, 2005); Lawrence Lessig, *Free Culture: The Nature and Future of Creativity* (New York: Penguin, 2005).

66. Marcos Novak, interviewed by Knut Mork (1995), http://www.altx.com/int2/marcos.novak.html.

67. This "Great Unbundling" has already upended the previous logic of necessity that grouped songs into albums and individual news articles into editions. As a result, the music and publishing industries have been the hardest hit thus far, and are still struggling to find viable business models for the future. As I write these words, several major news organizations are laying off a significant portion of their workforce, cutting back on their physical circulation, and redoubling their efforts online.

68. Novak, "Transarchitecture."

69. Marcos Novak, "Eversion: Brushing Against Avatars, Aliens, and Angels," in *From Energy to Information*, ed. Bruce Clarke and Linda Dalrymple Henderson (Palo Alto: Stanford University Press, 2002), 312.

70. Ibid., 321.

PHILIP AUSLANDER

Afterword

Music as Performance:
The Disciplinary Dilemma Revisited

FIRST OF ALL, I would like to thank Nick Cook and Richard Pettengill for giving me the last word in this collection. I am flattered, but also a bit daunted at the prospect of having to follow so many excellent writers and their inspiring work.

I find it congenial that Nick and Richard have framed this collection as a discussion of the treatment of musical performance across disciplines, particularly musicology and performance studies, since disciplinary questions have been at the heart of my work in this field for over a decade. My initial disciplinary and methodological reflections were prompted by frustration at not finding a discourse within any discipline that seemed to address musical performance in a satisfactory way. As the editors suggest in their introduction, musicology traditionally is preoccupied with a textual approach to music that relegates performance to a position of little importance. In this context, "performance studies" refers to the technical and interpretive work a musician must do in order to produce a well-informed performance of a piece. It is a secondary application of musicology, which remains the privileged term.

Theater studies leaves music out of its purview because it traditionally regards musical performance as inherently non-dramatic, and performance studies has inherited this prejudice. Even opera and musical theater are relatively neglected areas of study despite their obvious relationships to other theatrical forms. Because my work focuses on popular music, I also looked to cultural studies, but its primary concern is with reception and what the music and artists mean to their audiences, rather than what the artists themselves actually *do* as musicians and performers. My purpose in

349

initiating the Working Group in Music as Performance (MAP), first under the auspices of the Association for Theater in Higher Education, then under those of Performance Studies international, was to map out a space for a discourse that focuses on what musicians do as performers (my particular interest), and on musical events as performances comprising a complexity of expressive means and social interactions.

In the essay in which I began to describe this project, "Performance Analysis and Popular Music: A Manifesto," I summarized the situation by saying, "This, then, is what I am choosing to call the disciplinary dilemma confronting the scholar who wishes to talk seriously about musicians as performers: those who take music seriously, either as art or culture, dismiss performance as irrelevant. Those who take performance seriously are reluctant to include musical forms among their objects of study."[1] More than ten years into this pursuit, I now often wonder if it is still necessary or advisable to frame MAP's mission polemically by continuing to chastise both musicologists and performance studies scholars for neglecting musical performance, as I felt was necessary at first. The mere existence of this collection is an important piece of evidence that the kind of substantive dialogue I felt was lacking at the turn of the millennium is now well under way. But I have to admit that every time I have had the opportunity to address the relationship between music and performance I have issued a fresh version of my original polemic.[2] This results, in part, from my continually encountering in the work of scholars with whom I generally sympathize an ultimate refusal to embrace the full implications of considering performance as constitutive of music. For example, some investigators enthusiastically demonstrate that performers' physical gestures are central to the audience's understanding of its musical experience on both formal and affective levels, only to insist that other kinds of imagery used in performance serve merely to distract the audience and thus fail to fulfill performance's proper role of "supporting the music."[3] They consequently reinscribe the privileging of the musical work against which the "performative turn" in the study of music positions itself.

A similar frustration echoes from the side of musicology in Alejandro Madrid's introduction to a 2009 special issue of *Trans: Revista Transcultural de Musica* on music and performance studies (full disclosure: I peer-reviewed an article for this issue). Madrid's observations about changes in the field are similar to mine: there have been steps forward, but not enough. Speaking of the special issue, Madrid writes:

> The answer to our call for papers was quite impressive, more than
> 40 abstracts were submitted for consideration, which in itself tells us

of the increasing relevance that the idea of performance has in music studies. Nevertheless, the fact that ca. 75% of those abstracts were concerned with the old performance practice paradigm also tells us that much more still needs to be done to broaden the understanding of what performance can mean in music.[4]

It is clear that there is goodwill on both sides and an active desire to develop and enhance the substantive exchanges that have begun. But the need to jump-start these exchanges may not have passed just yet.

This discursive space I seek resides "at the crossroads of performance studies and musicology,"[5] but whether it is a bridge between the two disciplines, a point at which they intersect, or a new field forged from them has been an open question. Indeed, the nature of the relationship between these two disciplines is emerging as a point of contention within the still relatively uncharted field of MAP. The nature of this contention is well expressed by Derek Miller, who argues that the performance studies approach to musical performance, at least as represented by my work, neglects the essence of music—which he considers to be sound—and instead emphasizes what he describes as the "epiphenomenal" dimensions of performance rather than its bedrock of sound-producing actions. He also accuses performance studies of demanding that musicology "abdicate entirely its formalist attention to sound."[6] Although I consider Miller's specific argument to be flawed, as I shall show, his concern that the union of performance studies with musicology may cost the latter its proper object is worth addressing, especially as it is a concern shared in some measure by the editors of this book. They write:

> Western "art" musicologists have developed sophisticated techniques of close reading and listening, but have traditionally shied away from the issues of personal, social, and cultural meaning that emerge from the act of performance. Performance theorists address the latter, but as both editors complain in their contributions to this book, the specific ways in which these meanings are conditioned by sounds and their representations within specific musical cultures sometimes seem to slip through the net.[7]

Madrid suggests a similar disciplinary dichotomy in his discussion of the different approaches each discipline takes to music.

> While music scholarship (including performance practice) asks what music is and seeks to understand musical texts and musical perfor-

352 · TAKING IT TO THE BRIDGE

mances in their own terms according to a social and cultural context, a performance studies approach to the study of music asks what music does or allows people to do; such an approach understands musics as processes within larger social and cultural practices and asks how these musics can help us understand these processes as opposed to how do these processes help us understand music.[8]

Cook and Pettengill, Madrid, and Miller all nominate musicology as the discipline that explicates *music* per se, while performance studies is the discipline that can tell us about the social meanings music generates in performance and the uses to which it can be put. Ultimately, I shall argue that a truly productive approach to music as performance must move beyond formulations that mark off disciplinary territory, even in the interest of emphasizing complementarity, in favor of an approach that sees music and its performance as inextricably imbricated with one another.

For Miller, the way to correct performance studies' ostensible neglect of sound is to emphasize technique, the technical performance skill that enables musicians to generate musical sound. I have nothing but admiration for the technical skills displayed by musicians, and there can be no principled objection to including consideration of technique when analyzing musical performances. But "technique" is a more slippery concept than Miller allows for. In order to cordon it off from the epiphenomenal, Miller distinguishes between "technical" and "ancillary" gestures in musical performance. Technical gestures are those directly involved in the production of sound, such as the pressure of a finger on a keyboard, while "ancillary gestures are a means of communicating the performer's attitude toward the music. . . ."[9] These have no direct relationship to sound production and therefore no strictly musical function from Miller's point of view. At best, they constitute a secondary iteration of what the musician communicates in sound: "Ancillary gestures enact visually what the pianist executes technically."[10]

When linked to the premise that a musician's corporeal engagement in performance is truly "musical" only when it involves actions that directly produce sound, this distinction between technical and ancillary gestures reinforces the prejudice against the body, and the concomitant valorization of interpretation as an essentially intellectual activity, that characterizes Western discourse on music.[11] As Jairo Moreno puts it, "the body is clearly seen [in this discourse] as the locus of ultimate exteriority and as a threat for contemplation of a purely musical aesthetic."[12] What Madrid calls "performatic actions," which oblige us to acknowledge the musician's corporeal presence as the material basis of the production of musical sound, are rejected as repellent.[13] For example, the normative critical reaction to musicians such as Glenn Gould and Keith Jarrett, both of them pianists famous for such eccentricities as vocalizing along with their playing and, at least in the case of Jarrett, assuming an unusually active and intimate relationship with the instrument, is to emphasize their conventional skills as pianists and to suggest not only that their other behaviors are ancillary but also that the audience should ignore them. In other words, the critical line on Gould and Jarrett is that they are brilliant musicians in spite of what they do in performance, not because of it.

But what if these things are integral to Gould's and Jarrett's respective means of producing sound, as seems to be the case? If so, why should these physical actions not come under the heading of technique? Moreno, writing on Jarrett, points to the way the limitation of *technique* to the *technical* reduces the musician's physicality to that of a machine (my image, not his): the "conventional belief in the role of the performer" mandates that "the articulations and gesticulations of the body are part of the mechanics of reproduction [of the musical composition] but not, perversely enough, of the articulation of meaning."[14] Paul Sanden, writing on Gould, argues that listening to the musician's body, rather than dismissing non-technical gestures as producing "noise," is necessary to a full appreciation of music "as a physically enacted phenomenon"—as *performance*, in short—and to grasping "the significance of Gould's *performances* and not merely that of his *interpretations*."[15]

Such positions are supported by ample empirical evidence that gestures Miller presumably would classify as ancillary in fact contribute significantly to auditors' perception of musical sound. In a review of the literature in experimental research into music perception, Michael Schutz enumerates the ways in which both technical and ancillary gestures influence how audiences hear musical sound.[16] Acknowledging that the visual aspects of musical performance contribute much to its affective experience, Schutz also summarizes the experimental evidence that perception of such formal properties of musical sound as pitch, timbre, dissonance, note duration, and the size of intervals is directly affected by gesture. The length of a tone sounded on a marimba will be heard as longer or shorter depending on the percussionist's gesture, for example, and "different facial expressions can cause the same musical events to sound more or less dissonant, the same melodic interval to sound larger or smaller."[17]

Schutz emphasizes the ways visual information can influence what we hear at both cognitive and purely perceptual levels.[18] In other words, musicians' gestures, in some cases including so-called ancillary gestures, directly influence the audience's perception of musical sound—which would be heard differently when executed with different gestures—and not just its understanding of "the performer's attitude toward the music." As Schutz points out, the implication of this research is that music—especially, I would add, in the context of performance—"is less about sound per se than it is about using sound to create a particular experience within the mind of the listener. To this end, the strategic use of visual information is no less important than manipulations of breath control, bow position, striking angle, intonation, etc."[19]

Paired analytical concepts such as technical and ancillary gestures, what music is and what it does, or, to cite another set of terms Madrid proposes, the performatics and the performativity of music, all have descriptive value. I emphasized performance analysis in my first methodological essay in MAP, mentioned earlier, and I remain committed to the value of thick description of musical performances. But thinking in dichotomies reifies conventional understandings of music and performance by reducing musical performance into components we are comfortable labeling with one term or the other, rather than facing the challenge of understanding musical performance as something other than music and performance. That is why I always intended MAP to stand for music *as* performance: I see musical performance not as an alloy that can be broken down into constituent parts but as elemental. Switching metaphors from metallurgy to linguistics, I suggest that the relationship between music and performance parallels Roman Jakobson's description of the relationship between language and speech.

Jakobson takes issue with linguists who describe emotional expression carried by speech as "nonlinguistic," arguing that "if we analyze language from the standpoint of the information it carries, we cannot restrict the notion of information to the cognitive aspect of language" and that attributing emotional expression to "'the delivery of the message and not to the message' arbitrarily reduces the informational capacity of the message."[20] I hear a similar reduction in some of the discourse around music as performance, in which music is figured implicitly as the message, which exists prior to and independent of its performance, and performance is the delivery system that brings music into the public sphere. Although music and language are not the same things, and it is always risky to compare them, they are comparable in at least one respect: music is no more independent of its expression than is language. Just as the way words are spoken determines the semantic content of the message, so the way music is performed determines its musical content. Just as speech and language are fused in the message, so music and performance are fused in musical performance. Miller argues that the specificity of music as sound, and musicologists' formalist approach to it, must be respected when looking at it from a performance studies perspective. By contrast, I argue that what must be respected is the specificity of musical performance defined not as a relationship between two autonomous practices (music and performance) or the object of a dialogue between two autonomous fields (musicology and performance studies) but as an irreducible fusion of expressive means.[21]

Moreno, too, argues for this way of thinking when he challenges the position that "music is sound, and only sound is music" in his description of Keith Jarrett's performance.

> His sounds and gestures are unquestionably part of the music, so much so that one could describe these sounds and gestures not as a translation or mechanisms in service of music, or an addition to the music, but the music itself. . . . In Jarrett's pianism, communication is aural, oral, visual, and kinetic. . . . To center music's communication in sound alone is to dehumanize it.[22]

With this in mind, I return to Madrid's distinction between what music is and what it does to suggest that these two ideas are not as easily distinguishable as they may appear. Music is not sound disengaged from the physical being of the person who makes it. Listening to Schutz's marimbist or to Keith Jarrett or Glenn Gould or any musician, the sounds I hear result directly from all aspects of the person's physical engagement with the act of music making—all of the sounds and gestures that constitute the performance—not just the limited range of actions conventionally included under the word "technique." Perhaps, then, the solution to the disciplinary dilemma is to recognize that there is no dilemma, no ontological or epistemological gap between music and performance that needs bridging. Music *is* what musicians *do*.

NOTES

1. Philip Auslander, "Performance Analysis and Popular Music: A Manifesto," *Contemporary Theatre Review* 14, no. 1 (2004): 3.

2. See Philip Auslander, "Performance Analysis and Popular Music: A Manifesto," *Contemporary Theatre Review* 14, no. 1 (2004): 1–13; Philip Auslander, "Music as Performance: Living in the Immaterial World," *Theatre Survey* 47, no. 2 (2006): 261–69; Philip Auslander, "Musical Personae," *Drama Review* 50, no. 1 (2006): 100–

119; and Philip Auslander, "Musical Persona: The Physical Performance of Popular Music," *The Ashgate Research Companion to Popular Musicology*, ed. Derek B. Scott (Farnham, UK: Ashgate, 2009), 303–15.

3. William Forde Thompson, Phil Graham, and Frank A. Russo, "Seeing Music Performance: Visual Influence on Perception and Experience," *Semiotica* 156, no. 1 (2005): 224.

4. Alejandro L. Madrid, "Why Music and Performance Studies? Why Now? An Introduction to the Special Issue," *Revista Transcultural de Música/Transcultural Music Review* 13, accessed 10 November 2009, http://www.sibetrans.com/trans/trans13/art01eng.htm.

5. Todd J. Coulter, "Music as Performance—The State of the Field," *Contemporary Theatre Review* 21, no. 3 (2011): 259.

6. Derek Miller, "On Piano Performance—Technology and Technique," *Contemporary Theatre Review* 21, no. 3 (2011): 275.

7. Nicholas Cook and Richard Pettengill, "Introduction," this volume.

8. Madrid, "Why Music and Performance Studies?"

9. Miller, "On Piano Performance," 269.

10. Ibid., 269.

11. Although Miller seems at first to challenge the mind/body distinction as it has traditionally played out in the discourse of Western music by saying "the knowledge of a musical work resides in the pianist's body," he retreats to the normative position by describing the physical process of performing as mediation "between a conceptual soundscape (the work as imagined in a pianist's 'inner ear') and a physical, perceptual soundscape (sounds produced by the piano)" (ibid., 268–69). In this schema, the function of performance is to communicate the musician's "conceptual knowledge" of the work to an audience.

12. Jairo Moreno, "Body 'n' Soul? Voice and Movement in Keith Jarrett's Pianism," *Musical Quarterly* 83, no. 1 (1999): 83.

13. Following Diana Taylor, Madrid endorses using the term "performatic" to describe the visual and physical enactments that constitute performance.

14. Moreno, "Body 'n' Soul?," 81. For another discussion of the traditional view of the musician's role in musical performance, see Philip Auslander, "Sound and Vision: The Audio-Visual Economy of Musical Performance," *The Oxford Handbook of New Audiovisual Aesthetics*, ed. Claudia Gorbman, John Richardson, and Carol Vernallis (New York: Oxford University Press, forthcoming).

15. Paul Sanden, "Hearing Glenn Gould's Body: Corporeal Liveness in Recorded Music," *Current Musicology*, no. 88 (2009): 9, 20.

16. Michael Schutz, "Seeing Music? What Musicians Need to Know About Vision," *Empirical Musicology Review* 3, no. 3 (2008): 83–108.

17. Schutz, "Seeing Music?," 88, and Thompson et al., "Seeing Music Performance," 220.

18. Schutz, "Seeing Music?," 91.

19. Ibid., 102.

20. Roman Jakobson, *Language in Literature*, ed. Krystyna Pomorska and Stephen Rudy (Cambridge: Harvard University Press, 1987), 67.

21. While I clearly take issue with Miller's positions I want to make it clear that I do not disagree with the entirety of his argument. Miller offers a persuasive analy-

sis of the relationship between musician and instrument, defining "musical performance [as] a double performance: a technological performance by an instrument
and a technical performance by a musician" (Miller, "On Piano Performance," 263).
Apart from my rejection of Miller's position that the only really relevant aspects of
the musician's performance are the technical ones, nothing I say here is inconsistent
with thinking about musical performance as a joint performance between musician
and instrument.

22. Moreno, "Body 'n' Soul?," 88–89.

Contributors

Nicholas Cook is 1684 Professor of Music at the University of Cambridge. Formerly Director of the AHRC Research Centre for the History and Analysis of Recorded Music (CHARM). His books include *A Guide to Musical Analysis* (1987); *Music, Imagination, and Culture* (1990); *Beethoven: Symphony No. 9* (1993); *Analysis Through Composition* (1996); *Analysing Musical Multimedia* (1998); and *Music: A Very Short Introduction* (1998), which has appeared in fourteen different languages. *The Schenker Project: Culture, Race, and Music Theory in Fin-de-siècle Vienna* won the Society for Music Theory's 2010 Wallace Berry Award, while his latest book—*Music as Performance: Changing the Musical Object*—is in press. A former editor of *Journal of the Royal Musical Association*, he is a Fellow of the British Academy and of Academia Europaea.

Richard Pettengill is Associate Professor and Chair of the Theater Department at Lake Forest College, where he recently directed Shakespeare's *A Midsummer Night's Dream*. Prior to his appointment at Lake Forest in 2003, he was dramaturg at the Court Theater at the University of Chicago (1982–1986), and Director of Arts in Education at the Goodman Theater (1988–2000), where he collaborated as dramaturg with such directors as Robert Falls, Frank Galati, and Peter Sellars. His essays on dramaturgy and education have appeared in the journals *Voies De La Creation Theatrale*, *Performance Research*, *Theater Research International*, *Academic Exchange Quarterly*, *English Journal*, and in the books *What Is Dramaturgy?* (1995), *Dramaturgy in American Theatre: A Sourcebook* (1997), and *The Theater of Teaching and the Lessons of Theater* (2005).

Philip Auslander's primary research interest is in performance, especially in relation to music, media, and technology. He has written on aesthetic and cultural performances as diverse as theatre, performance art, music, stand-up comedy, robotic performance, and courtroom procedures. He is the author of five books and editor or coeditor of two collections. His most recently published books are *Performing Glam Rock: Gender and Theatricality in Popular Music* (2006) and the second edition of *Liveness: Performance in a Mediatized Culture* (2008). In addition to his work on performance, Auslander contributes art criticism regularly to *ArtForum* and other publications. He is the editor of *The Art Section: An Online Journal of Art and Cultural Commentary*.

David Borgo is a Professor of Music at the University of California, San Diego, where he teaches in the Integrative Studies (IS) and Jazz and Music of the African Diaspora (JMAD) programs. In 2006 his book *Sync or Swarm: Improvising Music in a Complex Age* won the Alan Merriam Prize from the Society for Ethnomusicology. David also won first prize at the International John Coltrane Competition in 1994; as a saxophonist he has released seven CDs and one DVD and has toured widely, including performances in the United States, Europe, Asia, Mexico, Canada, and Brazil.

Daphne A. Brooks is Professor of English and African-American Studies at Princeton University, where she teaches courses on African-American literature and culture, performance studies, critical gender studies, and popular music culture. She is the author of *Bodies in Dissent: Spectacular Performances of Race and Freedom, 1850-1910* (2006), and *Jeff Buckley's Grace* (2005). Brooks is currently working on a new book entitled *Subterranean Blues: Black Women Sound Modernity* (forthcoming).

Maria M. Delgado is Professor of Theatre and Screen Arts at Queen Mary, University of London and coeditor of *Contemporary Theatre Review*. She has published widely in the area of twentieth-century Spanish theatre, performance, and film with a particular interest in the work of performers and directors and the intersections between stage and screen cultures. She has further research interests in European theatre and contemporary Argentine theatre. Her books include *Federico García Lorca* (2008), *"Other" Spanish Theatres* (2003), and eight coedited volumes, including *Contemporary European Theatre Directors* (2010) and *A History of Theatre in Spain* (2012). She is a contributing editor to *Western European Stages* and *TheatreForum* and coedits the Theatre: Theory, Practice/Performance series for Manchester University Press. Her film work includes fifteen years as a program adviser on Spanish and Spanish-American cinema to the London Film Festival and a range of curatorial and programing projects for Ciné Lumière, BFI Southbank, the London Spanish Film Festival and the London Argentine Film Festival. She is currently engaged in a project on historical memory and culture in twenty-first-century Spain.

Susan Fast is Professor in the Department of English and Cultural Studies and Director of the Graduate Program in Gender Studies and Feminist Research at McMaster University. She is a musicologist whose research focuses on popular music, performance, and subjectivity. Her publications include *In the Houses of the Holy: Led Zeppelin and the Power of Rock Music* (2001); *Music, Politics and Violence* (with Kip Pegely, 2013); and *Michael Jackson: Dangerous* (2014). She has also written on Live Aid and cultural memory; constructions of authenticity in U2; Tina Turner's gendered and racialized identity in the 1960s; feminism and rock criticism; gendered and racialized issues surrounding back-up singing; and the mass mediated benefit concerts that appeared in the wake of 9/11.

Dana Gooley, Associate Professor of Music at Brown University, is a musicologist specializing in European music of the nineteenth century, performance culture, music criticism, jazz, and improvisation. He is the author of *The Virtuoso Liszt* and co-editor of the essay collections *Franz Liszt and his World* and *Franz Liszt: Musicien Européen*. He has published in *Performance Research*, *19th Century Music*, *Musical Quarterly*, *Journal of Musicology*, *Musiktheorie*, and *Journal of the American Liszt Society*. He is on the editorial board of *19th Century Music*, and is currently writing a book on improvisation and aesthetics in nineteenth-century music.

Philip Gossett, Robert W. Reneker Distinguished Service Professor Emeritus at the University of Chicago, is a music historian with special interests in nineteenth-century Italian opera, sketch studies, aesthetics, textual criticism, and performance practice. He is author of two books on Donizetti and of *Divas and Scholars: Performing Italian Opera* (2006). One of the world's foremost experts on Italian opera, Gossett is the first musicologist to be awarded the Mellon Distingushed Achievement Award, and has worked as a lecturer and consultant at opera houses and festivals in America and Italy.

Jason King is a cultural critic and journalist; musician (performer, vocal arranger, producer, musical supervisor); manager, strategist, and consultant to artists and labels; and live event producer. He is the founding full-time faculty member of The Clive Davis Institute of Recorded Music, an innovative leadership training program for aspiring music entrepreneurs at Tisch School of the Arts, New York University. Jason is the author of *The Michael Jackson Treasures*, a 2009 Barnes and Noble exclusive biography on the King of Pop, which has been translated in more than seven languages, as well as a forthcoming book from Duke University Press called *Blue Magic*, on the role of metaphysics and energy in the music of artists like Timbaland. Jason has published numerous essays on pop culture, and his blog entry "Michael Jackson: An Appreciation of His Talent" appears in the Da Capo Press *Best Music Writing 2010* compilation, edited by Ann Powers. He is also a longtime contributing writer for magazines and newspapers such as *Vibe* and *The Village Voice*. He currently divides his time teaching between New York and the NYU campus in Abu Dhabi.

Elisabeth Le Guin has developed two careers so far, as a Baroque cellist and as a musicologist; this dual perspective has permitted her to develop a series of dialogues, in tones and words, between theory and practice. She is a founding member of the Philharmonia Baroque Orchestra and the Artaria String Quartet; appears in over forty recordings; and continues to perform and record, while aspiring ever more earnestly to the condition of an amateur. She has taught at the University of California, Los Angeles, since 1997, receiving a number of grants and awards during her tenure there. She is the author of *Boccherini's Body: An Essay in Carnal Musicology* (2006) and maintains a website with period criticism of the composer and downloadable recordings of his music, at: http://epub.library.ucla.edu/le guin/boccherini. Her current book project, tentatively titled *Indispensable Ornaments*, is on the tonadilla, a genre of comic musical theater popular in Enlightenment Madrid. She is an enthusiastic student of *son jarocho*, a traditional music of the Veracruz region of southern Mexico, and practices regularly with the community at El Centro Cultural de México in Santa Ana, California.

Aida Mbowa is a candidate for a dual PhD in Performance Studies and Humanities at Stanford University. Her current research sits at the juncture where literary and cultural studies intersect with Africana and Performance Studies, and she teaches interdisciplinary courses that draw on these disciplines. Her dissertation, "Dialogic Constructions of a New Black Aesthetic: East Africa and African America, 1952–1979," considers the aesthetics of performance and ideologies born out of a transnational traffic of ideas in these revolutionary years. The Humanities Center at Stanford has awarded her the Geballe Dissertation Prize fellowship for this work.

Aida's directorial interests include plays that challenge the constructs of racial, ethnic, national, gender and sexual identities. In 2009, she collaborated with Stanford and Makerere University (Uganda) students and practitioners to produce a multidisciplinary, multimedia performance. She co-directed and co-devised the project, which was staged at the National Theater in Uganda and at Stanford University in California. She was selected to represent Uganda at the Sundance Institute Theater Stage Directors Lab, held in Ethiopia in 2012. She has the honor of representing Uganda once again at the Sundance Institute in Utah in 2013.

Ingrid Monson is Quincy Jones Professor of African American Music at Harvard University; she also specializes in jazz and music of the African diaspora. She is author of *Saying Something: Jazz Improvisation and Interaction* (1996), winner of the Sonneck Society's Irving Lowens award for the best book published on American music in 1996. Her most recent work is on *Freedom Sounds: Jazz, Civil Rights, and Africa, 1950-1967* (2005). She is also editor of *The African Diaspora: A Musical Perspective* (2000).

Roger Moseley is an Assistant Professor in the Department of Music at Cornell University. His publications address topics including the music of Brahms, eighteenth-century keyboard improvisation, and relationships between music and visual culture in digital games. His most recent research brings together his interests in play, musical performance, and digital media under the disciplinary banner of ludomusicology, and he is currently working on a book entitled *Digital Analogies: Music, Play, and Games*.

Prior to taking up his current appointment as Sterling Professor of Theater and English at Yale University, **Joseph Roach** chaired the Department of Performing Arts at Washington University in St. Louis, the Interdisciplinary PhD in Theatre at Northwestern University, and the Department of Performance Studies at New York University. His most recent book is *It* (2007), a study of charismatic celebrity. His other books and articles include *Cities of the Dead: Circum-Atlantic Performance* (1996), which won the James Russell Lowell Prize from MLA and the Calloway Prize from NYU; *The Player's Passion: Studies in the Science of Acting* (1993), which won the Barnard Hewitt Award in Theatre History; and essays in *Theatre Journal, Theatre Survey, The Drama Review, Theatre History Studies, Discourse, Theater, Text and Performance Quarterly*, and others. He has served as Director of Graduate Studies in English and Chair of the Theater Studies Advisory Committee at Yale.

Margaret F. Savilonis is Assistant Professor of English at the University of New Haven. Her scholarship focuses on twentieth-century drama and performance, including examinations of representations of mothers and motherhood in dramatic literature and constructions of national identity in works choreographed for the Dance Units of the Federal Theatre Project from 1937–1939. Her current investigation of performance and popular music focuses on the intersections of comedy, masculinity, and ethnicity in the work of Louis Prima.

Index

Friedmann, Ignaz, 82
Fripp, Robert, 39
Frith, Simon, 4, 35, 42–44, 156, 157, 159, 164; *Sound Effects: Youth, Leisure, and the Politics of Rock ' n' Roll*, 157
Froebel, Friedrich, 294, 299; Kindergarten, 294; *Spielgabe*, 294
The Fugees, 180, 181, 191–96, 198; "I Used to Love Him," 182. *See also* Hill, Lauryn
Fulbe, 274
funew, 273
funk, 16, 17, 126, 155, 160–62, 165–67, 172–74, 176–80, 204, 211, 223, 226, 231
Funkadelic, 161, 162, 165, 177

Gaar, Gillian, 157
Gadamer, Hans-Georg, 286, 302, 303
Gallagher, Noel, 302
Gantiege, Djelika, 270
García, Emanuel, 95
Garcia, Jerry, 11, 14, 37, 39–48, 51. *See also* Grateful Dead
García, Víctor, 241
Garofalo, Reebee, 159
Gates Jr., Henry Louis, 11
Gates, Racquel, 222; "Reclaim the Freak," 222
Gaudí, Antoni, 245
Gaye, Marvin, 185, 189, 190
Geistesfreiheit, 117
Gelmetti, Gianluigi, 88
gender studies, 3, 16, 17, 50, 99, 161–64, 166, 168, 170, 175, 182–86, 188, 190, 221, 302. *See also* Butler, Judith; performativity; and sexual difference
George IV, 114
Gesellschaft der Musikfreunde, 119
Ghost-Wave, 332
Gibson Girl, 162
Gibson X-Plorer, 294
Gil Evans Orchestra, 58
Gilbert, Buxton, 5
Gilroy, Paul, 184
girl group, 11, 16, 155–61, 167, 170
Gladwell, Malcom, 212
glam, ix, 16, 50, 56, 155, 158–64, 166–69, 175, 177, 178, 300, 311
Glasgow, 334
globalization, 272
Godfather of Soul. *See* James Brown
Godlovitch, Stan, 55

Goebbels, Heiner, 255
Goehr, Lydia, 285, 321, 337
Goffman, Erving, 7, 22, 24, 55–57, 62–67; *Frame Analysis*, 55; *The Presentation of Self in Everyday Life*, 57
Goins, Glen, 174
Gollmick, Carl, 112
Gondry, Michel, 180, 194, 195; *Be Kind, Rewind*, 184; *Eternal Sunshine of the Spotless Mind*, 194. See also *Dave Chappelle's Block Party*
Gongaware, Paul, 216
Goodman, Nelson, 87
Google Docs, 323
Gooley, Dana, viii, 6, 7, 12, 15
Gordon, Kim, 182. *See also* The Kims
Gossett, Philip, viii, 5, 10, 15, 99
Gould, Carol S., 52
Gould, Glenn, 353
Goulding & D'Almaine, 95
Goya, Francisco, 248
GPS, 331, 332
Graeco-Latin, 283
Grateful Dead, ix, 6, 9, 11, 14, 37, 38, 39, 47, 48; *American Beauty*, 37; "Casey Jones," 37; "Dark Star," 14; "Drums," 47; "El Paso," "The Eleven," 38; 14; *Live/Dead*, 39, 41; "Me and My Uncle," 45; "Morning Dew," 47; "Mountains of the Moon," 41; "Sugar Magnolia," 38; "Touch of Grey," 37; "Truckin'," 37; *Workingman's Dead*, 37
The Grateful Dead in Concert: Essays on Live Improvisation, 38
Greaves, William, 217
Green, Al, 185, 188
Greenaway, Peter, 246; *The Cook, the Thief, His Wife and Her Lover*, 246
Greig, Charlotte, 156, 160, 161, 167–70
griots, 273
Grossberg, Lawrence, 300
grossen Redoutensaal, 106
Grup de Treball (Working Group), 238
Grup Instrumental Català (GIC), 238
The Guardian, 248
Guattari, Félix, 147
Guelph Jazz Festival, 323
Guinness Book of World Records, 211
Guitar Hero, ix, 12, 18, 279, 280, 282–84, 289–304, 333; "Star Power," 290. See also *Rock Band*
Gumbrecht, Hans Ulrich, 304